TAKING SIDES

Clashing Views in

Teaching and Educational Practice

THIRD EDITION

TAKING SIDES

Clashing Views in

Teaching and Educational Practice

THIRD EDITION

Selected, Edited, and with Introductions by

Dennis L. Evans
University of California-Irvine

 **Higher Education**

Boston   Burr Ridge, IL   Dubuque, IA   New York   San Francisco   St. Louis
Bangkok   Bogotá   Caracas   Kuala Lumpur   Lisbon   London   Madrid   Mexico City
Milan   Montreal   New Delhi   Santiago   Seoul   Singapore   Sydney   Taipei   Toronto

Higher Education

TAKING SIDES: CLASHING VIEWS IN TEACHING AND EDUCATIONAL PRACTICE, THIRD EDITION

Published by McGraw-Hill, a business unit of The McGraw-Hill Companies, Inc., 1221 Avenue of the Americas, New York, NY 10020. Copyright © 2008 by The McGraw-Hill Companies, Inc. All rights reserved. Previous edition(s) 2002–2005. No part of this publication may be reproduced or distributed in any form or by any means, or stored in a database or retrieval system, without the prior written consent of The McGraw-Hill Companies, Inc., including, but not limited to, in any network or other electronic storage or transmission, or broadcast for distance learning.

Some ancillaries, including electronic and print components, may not be available to customers outside the United States.

Taking Sides® is a registered trademark of the McGraw-Hill Companies, Inc.
Taking Sides is published by the **Contemporary Learning Series** group within the McGraw-Hill Higher Education division.

This book is printed on recycled, acid-free paper containing 10% postconsumer waste.

2 3 4 5 6 7 8 9 0 DOC 12 11 10
MHID: 0-07-351516-7
ISBN: 978-0-07-351516-8
ISSN: 1550-6916

Managing Editor: *Larry Loeppke*
Production Manager: *Faye Schilling*
Senior Developmental Editor: *Susan Brusch*
Editorial Assistant: *Nancy Meissner*
Production Service Assistant: *Rita Hingtgen*
Permissions Coordinator: *Lori Church*
Senior Marketing Manager: *Julie Keck*
Marketing Communications Specialist: *Mary Klein*
Marketing Coordinator: *Alice Link*
Project Manager: *Jane Mohr*
Design Specialist: *Tara McDermott*
Senior Administrative Assistant: *DeAnna Dausener*
Senior Operations Manager: *Pat Koch Krieger*
Cover Graphics: *Maggie Lytle*

Compositor: Hurix Systems Private Limited
Cover Image: Photodisc Collection/Getty Images

Library of Congress Cataloging-in-Publication Data
Main entry under title:
Taking sides: clashing views in teaching and educational practice/selected, edited, and with introductions by Brent Slife—3rd ed.

Includes bibliographical references.
1. Education, Secondary. I. Evans, Dennis L., ed. II. Series.
373

www.mhhe.com

Preface

It risks tautology to suggest that education evokes controversy. And though controversies in any field often involve conflicting values and belief systems, it is the fact that the lives of our children are so singularly impacted by the quality of the education they receive that generates the vehemence and volatility characteristic of controversy in education. The volume of voices debating what should or should not happen in classrooms and schools speaks well of our commitment and our concern regarding our most precious commodities.

Also contributing to the heritage of controversy in American public education is its democratic structure both in terms of governance and the reality that it deals with "all of the children of all of the people." Controversies created by our democratic approach to public schooling are controversies worth having. And because controversies cannot be avoided, it is important that we approach them through reasoned and respectful discourse and thus learn from them.

This book presents widely divergent beliefs and viewpoints on 18 significant educational issues. These issues and the debates they generate cut across all levels of schooling, and thus, this book can inform anyone interested in the state of education in America.

Unit 1 of the book presents nine issues that generate conflicting views regarding contemporary educational policies and/or legal/organizational issues that can be sources of dispute and even litigation. They include: national standards, home schooling, the middle school concept, a common curriculum, drug testing, charter schools, the No Child Left Behind legislation, school discipline and "zero tolerance" policies, and large versus small high schools.

Unit 2 of the book deals with classroom practices and strategies and includes: the content and teaching of American history, sex education, single-sex classrooms and schools, grade inflation, homework, sports programs, computer technology and games, accommodations for special education students, and character/moral education programs.

Considerable care has been taken to not only select issues that are of emerging or continuing interest (many of these have long histories of controversy), but also to select articles that are representative of the divergent views on each issue and that are authored by a full panoply of those who care about education: advocates, critics, jurists, philosophers, practitioners, commentators, researchers, and provocateurs. This third edition of the book presents several new topics: national standards, the middle school concept, charter schools, NCLB, large versus small high schools, history taught from a critical perspective, participation in sports, computer games, special education accommodations, and character/moral education. In addition, new perspectives from different authors are presented on topics such as school discipline, sex education, single-sex classes and schools, grade inflation, and homework. Also included are provocative pieces from commentators such as

Alfie Kohn, Chester Finn, Annie Gaylor, and AFT's Bella Rosenberg. Supreme Court Justices Ruth Bader Ginsberg and Clarence Thomas provide examples of judicial thinking as related to school policies, and researchers and educators such as Perry Zirkel, Rob Reich, Russ Skiba, historian David McCullough, and Lowell Monke contribute their expertise. Organizations and advocacy group positions are presented from the Fordham Foundation, the Cato Institute, the Center for Education Reform, the U.S. Department of Education, Public Agenda, the Bill and Melinda Gates Foundation, the Sexuality Information and Education Council of the United States, the Heritage Foundation, the National Association for Single-Sex Public Education, The American Association of University Women, The Josephson Institute of Ethics, and the Character Education Partnership.

The format for each of the 18 issues involves an introduction written by the editor that frames the controversy and sets the stage for the readings, the presentation of the two (or more) opposing articles, and a postscript by the editor that summarizes the arguments and provides related viewpoints and additional references on the issue. Additionally, at the beginning of each unit is a listing of pertinent Internet resources.

Given the format of the book, it can be used for many purposes: combined with the "Introduction" it can provide an excellent foundation for undergraduate study of American education; it can serve as a text and reference source for graduate level educational leadership and policy courses; it can be used in administrator preparation and professional development programs; it can provide the basis for school faculty professional growth and in-service activities; and it can be used by PTA, school boards, and other parent organizations in their educational programs.

A word to the instructor   An *Instructor's Resource Guide with Test Questions* (multiple choice and essay) is available through the publisher for the instructor using *Taking Sides* as a class textbook. Also available is a general guidebook, *Using Taking Sides in the Classroom,* which details methods and techniques for using the pro-con approach. An online version of *Using Taking Sides in the Classroom* and a correspondence service for those who adopt *Taking Sides* for instructional purposes are available at *http://www.mhcls.com/takingsides/*.

Taking Sides: Clashing Issues in Teaching and Educational Practice is one of several titles in the *Taking Sides* series. The table of contents for any of the other titles is also available at *http://www.mhcls.com/takingsides/*.

Acknowledgments   My sincere appreciation goes to Larry Loeppke, Managing Editor, and Susan Brusch, Sr. Developmental Editor, of McGraw-Hill Contemporary Learning Series, who shepherded me through this entire project. I am also grateful to the many individuals who provided me with contacts regarding possible references and sources.

To my love and best friend Kris and the family's best writers, Mark and Suzy

Contents In Brief

Contents

Cheri P. Yecke, chancellor of K–12 public schools for the Florida Department of Education, contends that radical advocates of the "middle school concept" turned middle schools into "havens of socialization." Sue Swaim, executive director of the National Middle School Association, suggests, "The middle school movement cannot be faulted for educational deficiencies it did not create and practices it did not recommend." In a position paper her organization also stresses that in successful middle schools, "human relationships are paramount."

Michael W. McConnell, Judge on the 10th U.S. Circuit Court of Appeals, argues that "[M]any parents have come to believe that the First Amendment is stacked against them" with respect to their desire to see more religion in the schools. Annie Laurie Gaylor, editor of the anthology *Women without Superstition: No God, No Master,* states that "Public schools exist to educate, not to proselytize."

Justice Thomas presents the legal justification for a urinalysis drug test and states, "Given the minimally intrusive nature of the sample collection and the limited uses to which the test results are put, we conclude that the invasion of students' privacy is not significant." Justice Ginsberg, in opposing the majority position, states "schools' tutelary obligations to their students require them to 'teach by example' by avoiding symbolic measures that diminish constitutional protections."

The Center for Education Reform states that results of its survey "highlight the innovation and progress that charter schools have made."

Bella Rosenberg, assistant to the president of the American Federation of Teachers, responds that results from a study conducted by the National Assessment of Educational Progress belie the claims of charter school advocates.

Margaret Spellings, U.S. Department of Education Secretary, states, "The No Child Left Behind Act is challenging our students to succeed and our schools to improve." James H. Lytle, former superintendent of the Trenton, N.J., Public Schools and a practice professor at the University of Pennsylvania's graduate school of education argues that NCLB's rigid timelines for progress and threats of sanctions are misguided and will not be successful in bringing real improvement. Ann McColl, an attorney and associate professor of education at the University of North Carolina, suggests that the courts may need to decide the constitutionality of the Act.

The *Public Agenda* in reporting on a survey of parents and teachers regarding school discipline states, "70% of teachers and 68% of parents strongly support the establishment of 'zero tolerance' policies." Russell Skiba, professor of counseling and educational psychology at Indiana University, posits that "violence is not rampant in America's schools" nor is there credible evidence to confirm the effectiveness of zero tolerance policies.

Rick Allen, a staff writer and editor for ASCD, notes that, "More than 70 percent of U.S. high school students attend schools of more than 1000 students." Tom Vander Ark, former executive director for education of the Bill and Melinda Gates Foundation and a senior fellow at the foundation, charges, "Large, comprehensive high schools shortchange too many students."

Perry A. Zirkel, university professor of education and law at Lehigh University writes that, "If a majority of students . . . are in the honor society, it is no longer an honor." Alfie Kohn, author and educational commentator, avers that there are no data to support the claims regarding the existence of grade inflation.

Robert J. Marzano, president of the Marzano and Associates educational consulting firm, and Debra J. Pickering, director of staff development in Littleton Pubic Schools, believe that homework is a "powerful instructional tool." Diane W. Dunne, a writer for *Education World,* interviews author and freelance journalist John Buell, who believes that homework places inordinate burdens on children and families, especially those who are poor.

Jordan D. Metzl, medical director of the Sport Medicine Institute for Young Athletes and Carol Shookhoff, an educational writer, propose that youth sports "offer benefits and lessons that carry over into all aspects of life." The Josephson Institute of Ethics presents results from a national survey of over 5000 high school athletes including a finding that athletes "cheat in school at a higher rate than their non-sport classmates."

Associate professor David W. Shaffer, assistant professors Kurt R. Squire and Richard Halverson, and professor James P. Gee, of the school of education at the University of Wisconsin, Madison, suggest that schools need to catch up with other sectors of society in using technology and video games as tools for improvement. Lowell W. Monke, assistant professor of education at Wittenberg University, states "nearly everything children do today involves technologies that distance them from direct contact with the living world."

MaryAnn Byrnes, associate professor in the Graduate School of Education at the University of Massachusetts and president of the Massachusetts Federation of the Council for Exceptional Children, argues that fairness and equal educational opportunities mandate that students with special needs be provided appropriate support. James M. Kauffman, professor of education at the University of Virginia, and special education teachers Kathleen McGee and Michele Brigham believe that the inappropriate use of accommodations denies special needs students the opportunity to achieve greater independence.

Thomas Lickona, professor of education at the State University of New York, Eric Schaps, president of the Developmental Studies Center, and Catherine Lewis, author and character educator, present a number of basic principles that undergird successful character education programs. The "Patriotism for All" organization states "character education is not a verifiable scientific concept."

Introduction

Sources of Controversy in Teaching and Educational Practice

Dennis L. Evans

Origins and Governance

With approximately 50 million students enrolled in nearly 100,000 K–12 public schools and right at 99 percent of children aged 7–15 involved in some form of public or private schooling (from the National Center for Education Statistics (2007), for school year 2005–2006), we have attained universal education for our citizenry beyond even that hoped for by educational visionaries such as Horace Mann (. . . if this education should be universal and complete, it would do more than all things else to obliterate factitious distinctions in society . . . from *Tenth Annual Report* and *Twelfth Annual Report, 1846* and *1848*) and Thomas Jefferson (. . . yet I believe it [the human condition] susceptible of much improvement . . . and that the diffusion of knowledge among the people is to be the instrument by which it is to be effected. [as cited in J. Pulliam and J. Van Patten, *History of Education in America*, Prentice Hall, 1995].)

It is intriguing to note that from a historical perspective this worthy attainment is a relatively recent development. The concept of extending schooling beyond rudimentary instruction in the "three R's" only gained true momentum during the Progressive Era of 1890–1920. At the beginning of that dynamic sociopolitical period, even though a majority of adults over the age of 25 had completed at least five years of elementary education, only one of ten students remained in school after age 14 and only 6 percent of the over 25 age group held a high school diploma. The number of adolescents of high school age who were in school was approximately 200,000 or slightly less than 7 percent of that age group. Thirty years later in 1920 those numbers had increased to 2 million, which represented approximately 32 percent of the high school age group. Obviously this increased enrollment resulted in more individuals completing at least a high school education with that figure for the 25 year and older age group rising to 16 percent by 1920.

Chief among the reasons for this relatively slow progress toward universal education beyond the elementary school level was the nature of society and economy during our nation's formative years. With much of the populace engaged in agrarian-related occupations and with the demands and hardships associated with the frontier and westward expansion, education and schooling were luxuries that not many could afford. Although most families desired that their children should learn to read and write, there was little utility and demand for more advanced education. Also the basic schooling that was available was in most cases directly tied to the particular religion of a given geographic area or township. One of the earliest enactments related to rudimentary schooling was the "Old Deluder Satan Act" in colonial Massachusetts in 1647. The language of the act illustrates the religious purposes of this support for elementary education:

> It being one chief object of that old deluder, Satan, to keep men from the knowledge of the scriptures, . . . It is therefore ordered, that every township . . . after the lord hath increased them to the number of fifty householders . . . shall . . . appoint one within their town to teach all children as shall resort to him to read and write. It is further ordered, that where any town shall increase to the number of one hundred families . . . they shall set up a grammar school, the master thereof being able to instruct youth so far as they may be fitted for the university.

Importantly, the "Old Deluder Satan Act" created the precedent that a colonial legislature could require local support of education and that practice continues today. However, this historical linkage of schooling with religious sectarianism made the transition to public, common schooling more difficult.

Even though many people of the colonial era saw value in at least a modicum of schooling, all did not necessarily share that viewpoint. In 1671, Sir William Berkeley, the colonial governor of Virginia, expressed his disdain for the idea of widespread and advanced education with this statement: "I thank God that there are no free schools nor printing, and I hope we shall not have them these hundred years, for learning has brought disobedience, and heresy, and sects into the world, and printing has divulged them, and libels against the best government." That type of resistance to universal education certainly did not help its advancement.

As can be seen in The Old Deluder Satan Act and later in Ben Franklin's 1749 treatise *On the Need for an Academy*, schooling that went much beyond the rudimentary subjects was considered to be only important for those "fitted for the university." From colonial days until the end of nineteenth century secondary education was fundamentally only for the wealthy elite; only for those who would benefit from such an education and who would then attend a university in order to move into the "learned professions" of law, medicine, and the clergy. Even as late as 1893, the tradition of the high school existing only for the purposes of university preparation was articulated by the National Education Association's (NEA) Committee of Ten, chaired by President Charles W. Eliot of Harvard, which prescribed that high schools offer only a college preparatory curriculum obviously aimed at the needs of the small proportion of students who could benefit from it and whose parents could afford to send them on to the university.

The historical reluctance to embrace schooling for all children beyond the basics is exemplified by the fact that although taxation for the support of elementary education had its origins and even public acceptance in colonial days and later fueled the "Common School Era" for several decades beginning in 1830; the issue of tax support for public secondary schools was not resolved until the U.S. Supreme Court decision in 1874 in the case of *Stuart v. School District No. 1 of the Village of Kalamazoo*. In the *Kalamazoo* case the Court ruled in favor of the right of state legislatures to enact legislation allowing local communities to levy taxes for the support of public secondary schools. This belated lack of resolution regarding tax support combined with general public apathy, if not antipathy, toward public secondary schooling (there were many private academies for college preparatory work) resulted in the very slow growth of the number of public high schools in existence in the United States during the early nineteenth century. The first public high school, the Boston English Classical School, was established in 1821 (renamed the English High School in 1824) to serve the needs of non-college bound boys and by 1860 only an additional 300 had appeared nationally, one-third of those in Massachusetts. The *Kalamazoo* decision along with other societal forces dramatically increased those numbers so that by 1900 nearly 6000 high schools existed (today the number of middle and high schools stands at approximately 31,000 (NCES, 2007)). (Sources for statistical information are National Center for Educational Statistics, U.S. census 2000, and infoplease.com)

In 1911, consistent with the growing sentiments to democratize secondary schooling, the National Education Association issued a new report highly critical of the Eliot group's earlier recommendations. This new report, issued by the NEA Committee of Nine, stated that high schools had responsibilities much broader than mere pre-college work, especially because so few students matriculated to the university (in 1910 only slightly more that 2 percent of the U.S. population 25 years and older had graduated from college). Such new responsibilities included preparing students for participation as citizens and as contributors to the workplace and the economy.

This clash over purposes led to a compromise document, which was to become the guidepost for secondary education in the United States. That document, which was issued by the *NEA's Commission on the Reorganization of Secondary Education* in 1918, charged high schools with the responsibility to provide a "comprehensive" curriculum that could, at once, accomplish both college preparation and preparation for life and thereby meet the needs of the entire high school age population. The document described the mission of secondary education as involving "Seven Cardinal Principles." Those principles were:

- Health
- Command of fundamental processes
- Worthy home membership
- Vocational preparation
- Citizenship
- Worthy use of leisure time
- Ethical character

Obviously these "cardinal principles" reflected the notion of educating the "whole child" and led directly to the notion of the "comprehensive secondary school," which continues to be the prevailing model of secondary education in the United States.

But in spite of this new and more democratic conception of the American high school, secondary education continued to lag far behind elementary education in terms of the public's perception of its importance and willingness to support it. Even though all of the then 48 states had enacted compulsory attendance laws by 1920 (Massachusetts pushed by Horace Mann was first in 1852; Mississippi was last in 1918), as noted above only slightly over 16 percent of the population ages 25 and older had completed high school by that year. For many years compulsory attendance requirements for secondary school-aged children were generally viewed by the public as mere "scoff laws," and it was not until well after World War II that high school graduates finally exceeded drop-outs among adults over 25. It took the combination of societal forces such as massive immigration, urbanization, industrialization and unionization, child protection laws, court decisions, and increased access to college to finally provide the momentum to bring K–12 education to the point where now more than 85 percent of the 25 and older age group possesses at least a high school diploma.

Another source of controversy regarding our public schools emanates from the type of structure by which we govern them. Reflecting our revolutionary heritage and the concomitant antipathy toward a strong, central government, the "Founding Fathers" initially designed in 1781, by way of The Articles of Confederation, a national government so bereft of power that the newly formed nation quickly teetered on the brink of chaos and collapse. It became apparent that some concession had to be made with respect to granting greater power to the central government. That realization led to the Constitutional Convention of 1787 and the eventual drafting and ratification of the U.S. Constitution.

But in spite of the crisis mentality that motivated the "Founding Fathers" to scuttle the Articles of Confederation and create a new and stronger federal system, there was still great resistance to any suggestion that the national government should have substantive power over the daily lives of the people. That fear of centralized power, which was entirely reasonable given the colonists' recently concluded struggles with Great Britain and King George III, resulted in demands that a Bill of Rights be added to the new Constitution. Indeed, for many, the only way they would agree to ratify the Constitution was with assurances that a Bill of Rights protecting the civil liberties of the people from governmental encroachment would be enacted.

That enactment, which took place in December of 1791, curtailed central government power in areas that were directly related to the daily lives of citizens. In their wisdom, the Founding Fathers not only enumerated some of these areas such as speech, religion, the press, and due process of law, but also, through the Tenth Amendment protected other unspecified areas from the power of the central government. The Tenth Amendment states, "The powers not delegated to the United States by the Constitution, nor prohibited by it to the States, are reserved to the States respectively, or to the people." With this one sentence the power to control public education, because it is not mentioned in the Constitution, devolved to the individual states and to the people. Thus, in the United States there is no national control over public education. Certainly federal government involvement in public education has increased substantially (some would suggest too much) in recent years (examples include the No Child Left Behind (NCLB) legislation and the Individuals with Disabilities Education Act (IDEA)), but the constitutional authority for public school governance remains under the purview of each of the 50 states. It is accurate to say that public education is a national interest, a state power, and a local responsibility. Obviously such a decentralized governance structure defies tight organization, consistency of operation, and agreement regarding the purposes of schooling. Advocates of our approach to governance of public schooling might say that it fits the description of democracy attributed to Winston Churchill: "It has been said that Democracy is the worst form of government except all those other forms that have been tried from time to time." Critics of the approach suggest that many of the problems facing public education are attributable to the "messiness" of the governance structure and a concomitant lack of agreement regarding standards of quality.

As noted above, constitutional authority over the public schools is vested in each individual state. Each state has created local school districts and delegated authority to the local governmental entities such as school boards to govern those districts (the only exception to this approach is Hawaii, which governs its schools as one statewide district). A fundamental feature of this governance structure is the local lay school board. The origin of citizen control over the schools predates nationhood and goes back to the colonial era when town elders would periodically check on the local school "marm/master" to make sure that the particular religious orthodoxy of the township was being duly recognized and respected.

The National School Boards Association makes the following statement regarding the role of school boards in governing American public education:

> The National School Boards Association believes local school boards are the nation's preeminent expression of grass roots democracy and that this form of governance of the public schools is fundamental to the continued success of public education.

Critics suggest that the lay local school board is an anachronism that has outlived its purposes and that its role in governing the schools undermines the professionalism of educators and thwarts reform.

The concept of "grass roots democracy" means that school board members are in close proximity to the people they represent and thus are more subject to public opinion and pressures than are other public officials who serve from more distant venues. This can be both a vice and a virtue. Local school board members know their public and their public knows them. They can be quickly responsive to local issues, but they can also be susceptible to local emotions and orthodoxies. Citizen governance of local schools means that school board members may be elected (or not) because of their stance on certain issues facing local schools. They are also likely to be subject to recall elections more than any other type of public official. Certainly the concept of local school board governance is very consistent with the American heritage of distrusting distant government.

Philosophical Differences

The myriad controversies regarding purposes, policies, and practices in education and the emotions that those controversies engender are testimony to the importance afforded to education by today's public, pundits, and politicians. That has not always been the case and thus we should view such controversies as a healthy sign that education is considered such a vital issue on the nation's agenda.

As noted above, both the history and the governance of public education make their own contributions to controversy, but beyond those contributions many of the issues dealt with in this book reflect the profound differences that good and honest people can and do have regarding fundamental questions about the nature of and the interrelationship among humankind, society, and schooling. These are philosophical and value issues and thus can be the source of conflicts and disagreements that are very difficult to resolve. Some of the major philosophical systems that impact education include the following:

Idealism (Better thought of as "idea-ism")

Essence—Ideas are the only true reality; man must search for knowledge and truth; man is capable through thought and revelation of attaining philosophic wisdom.

Educational goals and characteristics—Self-realization of each individual attained by developing reverence for ideas and the ability to think holistically. Education should focus on heritage and culture, reading and writing, intelligence and morality.

Key thinkers and works—Plato (427–347 B.C.) and Socrates (469–399 B.C.), *The Republic*; Augustine (354–430), *Confessions*; Rene Descartes (1596–1650), *Discourse on Method and Mediations on the First Philosophy*; George Berkeley (1685–1753), *Principles of Human Knowledge*; Immanuel Kant (1724–1804), *Critique of Pure Reason*; Friedrich Hegel (1770–1831), *Philosophy of Right.*

Realism

Essence—Reality, knowledge, and value exist independent of the human mind. The forms of things, the universal properties of objects, remain constant and never change.

Educational goals and characteristics—providing students with basic and essential knowledge; true understanding requires the ordering and classifying of knowledge; rigorous inquiry based upon observation and experimentation are crucial. Science and scientific principles are pre-eminent.

Key thinkers and works—Aristotle (384–322 B.C.), *Politics and Ethics;* Thomas Aquinas (1225–1274), *Summa Theologica;* Francis

Bacon (1561–1626), *Novum Organum;* John Locke (1632–1704), *Some Thoughts Concerning Education;* Alfred North Whitehead (1861–1947), *Science and the Modern World;* Bertrand Russell (1872–1970), *Principia Mathematica* (with Whitehead).

(**Perennialism/Essentialism** are later manifestations of Idealism/Realism.)

Pragmatism (Progressivism)

Essence—Seek out processes and do things that work best to achieve desirable ends. Inductive thinking, importance of human experience, humanism, and relationship between science and culture are important elements.

Educational goals and characteristics—Education is, like growth, a necessity of life. It provides people with renewal of knowledge and skills to face problems encountered through interaction with the environment. Education is not preparation for life, but life itself. Individuals are social beings and education should help people direct, control, and guide personal and social experience. Motivation, interests, and prior experiences, including knowledge of consequences, are crucial to learning. School as a "laboratory."

Key thinkers and works—Jean-Jacques Rousseau (1712–1778), *Emile;* Charles Darwin (1809–1882), *On the Origin of Species;* Charles Peirce (1839–1914), How *to Make Our Ideas Clear;* William James (1842–1910), *Talks to Teachers on Psychology;* John Dewey (1859–1952), *Experience and Education.*

Behaviorism

Essence—Behavior is caused by environmental conditions. What is real is external, factual, and observable and is thus capable of being known. A "technology" of behavior is possible through conditioning. Humans are part of, not above, nature. A "good" culture can be designed and created.

Educational goals and characteristics—Children's behavior is "programmed" long before they come to school. Primary aim of education is to change behavior and point it in more desirable directions. Change is brought about by reinforcement (aversive or positive) of specified behaviors. Immediate feedback is important. Small, incremental steps are helpful in learning a new task. Machine learning is utilized.

Key thinkers and works—Thomas Hobbes (1588–1679), *Leviathan;* Ivan Pavlov (1849–1936), *Conditioned Reflexes;* John Watson (1878–1958), *Behaviorism;* B.F. Skinner (1904–1990), *Beyond Freedom and Dignity.*

Existentialism

Essence—Man, alone, estranged and alienated, is caught up in a meaningless and absurd world. Human existence is characterized by anxiety and a lack of certainty. Individuals are confronted with life choices that only they can make and for which they must accept total responsibility. The individual's freedom to choose is daunting. Through thoughtful choice and action the individual can bring about change.

Educational goals and characteristics—Each student is an individual and must be allowed to take the major role in his/her education. Schools should be places of freedom where students do the things they want to do. Schools should provide many options and choices. Every teacher is a student and every student is a teacher. The humanities and the arts are significant in the existentialist curriculum. Individual "sense-making" is a basic goal of schooling. Differences are to be celebrated.

Key thinkers and works—Soren Kierkegaard (1813–1855), *Attack on Christendom*; Martin Buber (1878–1965), *I and Thou*; Martin Heidegger (1889–1976), *Being and Time*; Jean Paul Sartre (1905–1980), *Being and Nothingness*; Maxine Greene, *Landscapes of Learning*.

Postmodernism

Essence—Not really a belief system, but rather an iconoclastic challenge to claims of universality; a rejection of objective certainty. Traditions of knowledge (canons), scientific laws, or first principles are challenged as forms of domination. Traditional knowledge is not to be ignored but to be studied or "deconstructed" to see how it elevates some segments of society to power and affluence at the expense of others.

Educational goals and characteristics—Postmodernism in education or critical pedagogy has as its common objective the empowerment of the powerless to overcome inequities and injustices. It challenges the way schools support dominant power and maintain inequities. It envisions schools as places where self and social empowerment can be enhanced. Curriculum is successful when it empowers people and transforms society. Students should explore their own individual histories, including self-reflection on race, gender, and class issues. Teachers are both scholars and practitioners and their role is to help students see the ideological and political interests that curricular knowledge may serve.

Key thinkers and works—Michel Foucalt (1926–1984), *The Order of Things*; Jacques Derrida, *Of Grammatology*; Henry Giroux, *Border Crossings*; Peter McClaren, *Life in Schools*; Cleo Cherryholmes, *Power and Criticism*; Paolo Freire, *Pedagogy of the Oppressed*.

Other Systems

The above selections are presented to provide an overview of various ideas, influences, and competing complexities that have impacted and continue to impact schooling in our country.

The selections obviously do not represent all of the various philosophical or belief systems that deal with education. Other systems such as Marxism, empiricism, phenomenology, reconstructionism, analytic philosophy, eastern religions, etc., have also influenced educational thought. Also the views and actions of historical/political figures such as Benjamin Franklin, Thomas Jefferson, and Horace Mann, sectarian religious considerations, socioeconomic realities, and other circumstances and individuals associated with the American experience have combined to create the unique character of our educational system.

Note: The source of much of the above material is H. Ozman and S. Craver, *Philosophical Foundations of Education*, 5th ed. (Englewood Cliffs: Prentice-Hall, 1995). As those authors point out, the various labels or titles given to the philosophies are arbitrary and not universally agreed upon, thus you may find that other descriptors are used in other works.

Given the profound differences that exist between and among these different belief systems it should not be surprising that conflicts and controversies abound in education. One way that education has survived these "philosophical wars" has been through the broadening of the curriculum and creation of the "comprehensive" high school, which has allowed elements of several of the philosophies to become a part of school instruction and related programs. Manifestations of different philosophies can be seen in such features as the study of history and the literary canon, science laboratories, electives, service learning, student government, programmed learning, a focus on multiculturalism, and the provision of counseling services.

Criticism of the Schools

With so many contrasting viewpoints vying for primacy in terms of what occurs in the schools, it is inevitable that much criticism will be directed at school purposes, policies, and practices when they are perceived to run counter to a given philosophical position. Criticism is also leveled at the schools when student outcome measures such as SAT scores, international test comparisons, and readiness for college don't measure up to expectations. Schools are also criticized for what some see as a breakdown in citizenship, morality, and respect for the law.

Much of the contemporary criticism of schools can be traced from the launching of the Soviet space satellite, Sputnik I, in 1957, which led to stinging criticism from eminent Americans such as James B. Conant, former president of Harvard, and Admiral Hyman Rickover, both of whom bemoaned what they perceived as a lack of intellectual rigor and excellence in the nation's schools. The turmoil and trauma of the 1960s brought criticism to the schools from both sides of the political fence. Many suggested that the protest movements on college campuses signaled how poorly schools were doing with respect to instilling patriotism, loyalty, and traditional values in the nation's youth; whereas others such as Paul Goodman, *Growing Up Absurd* (1960), John Holt in *How Children Fail* (1964), and Neil Postman and Charles Weingartner, *Teaching as a Subversive Activity* (1969) claimed that the school curriculum was no longer relevant, failed to provide for individual needs, and thereby alienated students.

The 1970s continued that theme with a spate of searing indictments of the condition of schooling in America, especially as that schooling failed to address the realities of modern life as experienced by many students. Writer/critics of this genre included Charles Silberman, *Crisis in the Classroom* (1970), Ivan Ilich, *Deschooling Society* (1971), Holt again with *Freedom and Beyond* (1972), and Jonathan Kozol *Free Schools* (1972).

The publication of *A Nation at Risk* in 1983 by the National Commission on Excellence in Education signaled the shift of criticism of the schools from the sociological perspectives of the 1970s to concerns regarding the quality of American secondary schooling vis-à-vis the nation's ability to remain competitive on the world scene. Much of the reform literature of the 1980s and early 1990s focused on shortcomings of school curriculum and organization. Influential works from this era include Mortimer Adler's *Paideia Proposal* (1982), John Goodlad's *A Place Called School: Prospects for the Future* (1983), Ernest Boyer's *High School: A Report on Secondary Education in America* (1984), Theodore Sizer's *A Study of High Schools* (1984) and also from Sizer, *Horace's Compromise: The Dilemma of the American High School* (1984), Jeannie Oakes's *Keeping Track: How Schools Structure Inequality* (1985), a report from the Carnegie Task Force, *A Nation Prepared: Teachers for the 21st Century* (1986), E. D. Hirsch's *Cultural Literacy; What Every American Needs to Know* (1987), and Goodlad's *Teachers for Our Nation's Schools* (1990).

These insistent calls for educational change and reform combined with continuing concerns regarding the performance of American students on measures of academic performance especially with respect to international comparisons (Gerald Bracey, in his 1993 report on *The Condition of Public Education*, is one of the few voices suggesting that evaluative data regarding student performance are often misinterpreted and that American schools are not failing) created a political momentum that resulted in the 1990s becoming the decade of standards, accountability, and high-stakes testing. With presidential candidates and other political leaders stressing the importance of education, proposals such as school choice, vouchers, and the charter school movement have become part of the educational lexicon. Most recently, the No Child Left Behind legislation and its focus on standards, assessment, and accountability has driven educational reform. The future impact of these various reform initiatives remains to be seen.

The Challenge

Given the irreconcilable and irreducible differences that arise over questions regarding the fundamental purposes and processes of schooling, it becomes obvious that, even though there are many answers to such questions, there is no exclusively "right" answer. What emerges from that realization is the irony that great value can accrue from asking questions even if there is no "right" answer to them. It is important for those involved with the educational enterprise to realize that important questions need to be continually asked and that the divergent and even the diametrically opposite positions that well-meaning and thoughtful individuals will take in attempting to provide answers can become valuable stimuli for reflection and progress. Faced with questions that have many answers but no single correct one, the contemporary educator needs to possess or to develop a tremendous tolerance for ambiguity. To go beyond reactive survival and engage in proactive effectiveness, educators must be prepared to face a myriad of essentially unanswerable questions. It will be through processes such as the development and articulation of a personal/professional philosophy, self-reflection, and the analysis of the views and values of others that the thoughtful educator will best address such questions. Because we who are engaged in education cannot escape controversies, we should find ways to learn and thus benefit from them.

Some may believe that the various controversial issues that seem to characterize education are symptomatic of the contentious and litigious nature of contemporary society. But that is simply not the case. Here is one educator's response to a controversy over the relative merits of home versus public schooling: "But even if great [large enrollments] schools are to be avoided (a position to which I cannot assent, if numbers flock to a master on account of his merit), the rule is not to be carried so far that schools be avoided altogether. It is one thing to shun schools entirely, another to choose from them." That statement is from "On the Early Education of the Citizen Orator," Book I of *The Institutes of Oratory*, by Quintilian (ca 95 A.D.). Controversy and conflict regarding teaching and educational practices are not new and they will not go away because they speak to the schooling of our children.

Internet References . . .

The National Association of Secondary School Principals

This national school administrator group has policy statements on many issues including school discipline and zero tolerance policies.

www.nassp.org

The Thomas B. Fordham Foundation

The Thomas B. Fordham Foundation supports research, publications, and action projects of national significance in elementary/secondary education reform including issues such as national curriculum standards and testing.

http://www.edexcellence.net

The Home Schooling Legal Defense Association

This advocacy group for home schooling and related links present many articles promoting home schooling.

http://www.hslda.org

Office of National Drug Control Policy

This site presents the official government position regarding drug control issues.

http://www.whitehousedrugpolicy.gov

ACLU and Drug Policy Alliance

This site contains the joint antidrug testing policy statement of these two organizations.

http://www.drugpolicy.org

National Middle School Association

This site advocates for the improvement of schooling for younger adolescents.

http://www.nmsa.org/

Educational Policies and Practices

*I*n framing the classroom practices of public school teachers, there are a myriad of laws, regulations, procedures, and policies that dictate and define the parameters of teacher decision making and establish many of the dynamics operant in our schools today. With the governance of public schools being a national interest, a state power, and a local responsibility, the determinants of educational and school policies and practices come from all of those levels, but it is at the local level where most of those decisions are made. Thus, although most of the controversial issues presented in this part of the book emanate from decisions made by local school boards, school district officials, and school principals, there are other practices that flow from state and federal legislation and especially court decisions. Some of the controversies and questions regarding educational policies and practices that have generated substantive state and federal involvement include:

- Is It Time for National Standards in Education?
- Is Home Schooling a Good Idea?
- Has the Middle School Concept Failed?

School practices and their related questions that are more the purview of local community expectations, administrative judgments, collective bargaining, and school board decisions include:

- Should Religious Content and Concepts Be More Evident in Our Schools?
- Is Drug Testing of Students a Justifiable Practice?
- Have Charter Schools Fulfilled Their Promises?
- Has the "No Child Left Behind" Legislation Created Good Educational Policy?
- Should School Discipline Policies Be Stricter and Include "Zero Tolerance" Provisions?
- Can Large High Schools Provide a Quality Education?

ISSUE 1

Is It Time for National Standards in Education?

YES: Chester E. Finn Jr., Liam Julian, and Michael J. Petrilli, from "To Dream the Impossible Dream: Four Approaches to National Standards and Tests for America's Schools," Thomas B. Fordham Foundation (August 2006)

NO: Lawrence A. Uzzell, from "No Child Left Behind: The Dangers of Centralized Education Policy," Cato Institute (May 31, 2005)

ISSUE SUMMARY

Chester E. Finn, president, Liam Julian, associate writer and editor, and Michael J. Petrilli, vice president for national programs and policy, all of the Thomas B. Fordham Foundation, state, "National standards and tests may no longer be politically taboo." Lawrence A. Uzzell, an independent researcher and former staff member of the U.S. Department of Education and U.S. House and Senate committees on education, believes that "the key to rescuing our children from the bureaucratized government schools is radical decentralization."

Historically, governance of public education in the United States has aptly been described as a "national interest, a state power, and a local responsibility." With the origin of our nationhood coming through a successful revolutionary struggle against a strong central government, it is not surprising that power and control of education was not vested in a new central government. Rather, that power by way of the Tenth Amendment, devolved to the individual states that in turn delegated much responsibility for governance to local entities such as school boards. Through the years that decentralized approach has been the prevalent pattern of governance of public education. Certainly there have been notable exceptions to that pattern wherein the federal government has exercised power over public schools, but those occasions have been limited generally to constitutional issues adjudicated by the U.S. Supreme Court. Such instances include court rulings related to separation of church and state, desegregation, student rights of expression, and student privacy. On other occasions, federal legislation has tied federal funding to state adherence to provisions within that legislation. Examples include gender equity, support of special needs students, and most recently the No Child Left Behind Act (NCLB). Theoretically, states may avoid the provisions of such legislation by not taking the federal funding. Practically speaking, refusing federal funds is not generally seen as a viable option for schools and, in any event, such a decision would likely lead to court action.

It is the specificity of NCLB provisions related to traditional state-level control over issues such as teacher quality, content and strategies for reading instruction, and school accountability measures that have caused some critics to suggest that this may be the single greatest federal incursion into state power over education in our nation's history. As Lawrence Uzzell states in his response to this issue, "NCLB may end up giving us the worst possible scenario: unconstitutional consolidation of power in Washington over the schools, with that power being used to promote mediocrity rather than excellence."

Perhaps anticipating such criticism, the legislation has, thus far, left it to individual states to develop content standards and administer the assessments related to those standards in order to determine whether or not students are making adequate yearly progress. Yet some do not believe that having educational standards set by individual states is the right way to go. In their *Education Week* (March 7, 2007) article, Rudy Crew, Paul Vallas, and Michael Casserly argue that the widely disparate nature of 50 different sets of standards and related assessment systems may eventually doom any national reform effort. They state:

> In the absence of a clear and consistent set of national academic standards for what should be expected of all children, each state instead sets its own standards for what kids should know or be able to do. Sometimes these standards are high; often they are not. Either way, they drive the teaching and learning in America's classrooms and serve to perpetuate the nation's educational inequities at a time when we should be working to overcome them.

This indeed is a high-stakes debate because it has major implications for not only the children and teachers in our nation's public schools, but, more broadly for all citizens, with respect to how we will govern our public schools in the future.

YES

Chester E. Finn Jr., Liam Julian, and Michael J. Petrilli

To Dream the Impossible Dream: Four Approaches to National Standards and Tests for America's Schools

For the first time in almost a decade, people are seriously weighing the value of instituting national standards and tests in American K-12 education. Yet despite many pervasive and commonsense reasons (explained below) to support such a reform, two large obstacles loom. The first is political: a winning coalition must be assembled, probably by a presidential contender—no small challenge, considering that the failed attempts of the 1990s to create national standards and tests left a bad taste in many politicians' mouths. The second obstacle is substantive: until policymakers can envision what a system of national standards and tests might look like, how it would work, and how its various logistical challenges might be addressed, this idea will remain just that. This report addresses the second obstacle and, in so doing, also helps with the political challenge. Once the key design issues are hammered out, it will be easier to tackle ideology and votes.

To gather input on how a system of national standards and tests might be designed, we queried a bipartisan selection of prominent experts. We knew that we would not agree with all of their views, nor would they agree with all of ours. But we certainly benefited from their varied and informed opinions and we're profoundly grateful for their cooperation—and their willingness to tackle this topic in public view. We asked them to answer a series of questions (see Appendix B) ranging from the macro—should the federal government design the tests—to the micro (e.g., ought the tests be given annually?). As we pondered their responses, certain patterns became clear. Within their excellent advice and good ideas are four distinct approaches to national standards and tests that we describe and appraise in the following pages:

1. **The Whole Enchilada.** This is the most direct and aggressive approach. The federal government would create and enforce national standards and assessments, replacing the fifty state-level sets of standards and tests we have now. The United States would move to a national accountability system for K-12 education.

2. **If You Build It, They Will Come.** This is a voluntary version of the first model. Uncle Sam would develop national standards, tests and accountability metrics, and provide incentives to states (such as additional money or fewer regulations) to opt into such a system. A variant would have a private group frame the standards. Either way, participation would be optional for states.
3. **Let's All Hold Hands.** Under this approach, states would be encouraged to join together to develop common standards and tests or, at the least, common test items. Uncle Sam might provide incentives for such collaboration, but that's it.
4. **Sunshine and Shame.** This model, the least ambitious, would make state standards and tests more transparent by making them easier to compare to one another and to the National Assessment of Educational Progress (NAEP).

In this paper, we outline how each model might work in practice, and we evaluate the likelihood that each would:

- End the "race to the bottom"
- Result in rigorous standards rather than merely politically acceptable ones
- Expand Washington's role in education
- Prove politically feasible.

It's no secret that we, at the Thomas B. Fordham Foundation, favor national standards and tests—provided they are done right. We believe they are needed now more than ever. But as policy analysts have begun seriously to debate the idea in recent months and a few politicians have begun (at least privately) to flirt with it, a sure conversation stopper kept getting in the way. Someone would ask, "So how exactly would this work in practice?" Tumbling from their lips would be five, ten, a dozen legitimate and important questions about the implementation of this basic idea. Who would write the standards? The federal government? Congress or the Department of Education? What would happen to state standards and tests? Which subjects would you test? How often? Who would deliver the results? How would this intersect with No Child Left Behind? And on and on. We quickly realized that for this idea to advance beyond the domain of wishful thinking and knee jerk reacting, someone would have to take a stab at answering such questions. This is our attempt.

Recent history illustrates the need to address these design problems. Mistakes can be costly. President George H.W. Bush watched his ambitious plan for national standards sink after his administration outsourced the job to professional organizations of educators such as the National Council of Teachers of English. President Bill Clinton found his "voluntary national tests" proposal lampooned by concerns over student privacy, overweening government involvement, and "fuzzy" math. If tomorrow's political leaders are to tackle this topic, they will need a plan that's fully baked.

We knew we could not flesh out these design issues alone, so we called upon a dozen eminent colleagues from left, right, and center. Some are scholars, others policymakers. Some support national standards and tests while others abhor the notion. All, however, are thoughtful, creative, and experienced policy entrepreneurs. And they did not disappoint—their lucid and insightful comments are found throughout this report. . . .

We started by posing twelve important questions that one would have to answer if he or she were serious about actually implementing national standards and tests. . . . We sent these stumpers to our esteemed experts and solicited their responses. What we received surprised us. First, many of our colleagues showed themselves to be more skeptical about the project of national standards and tests than we—or even they—assumed they would be. Second, as we sifted through their answers, we noticed some patterns. Four distinct approaches to national standards and tests, rose to the surface, each with its own pluses and minuses. Fleshing out and evaluating this quartet of models became the purpose of this report:

1. **The Whole Enchilada.** This is the most direct and aggressive approach. The federal government would create and enforce national standards and assessments, replacing the fifty state-level sets of standards and tests we have now. The United States would move to a national accountability system for K-12 education.
2. **If You Build It, They Will Come.** This is a voluntary version of the first model. Uncle Sam would develop national standards, tests and accountability metrics, and provide incentives to states (such as additional money or fewer regulations) to opt into such a system. A variant would have a private group frame the standards. Either way, participation would be optional for states.
3. **Let's All Hold Hands.** Under this approach, states would be encouraged to join together to develop common standards and tests or, at the least, common test items. Uncle Sam might provide incentives for such collaboration, but that's it.
4. **Sunshine and Shame.** This model, the least ambitious, would make state standards and tests more transparent by making them easier to compare to one another and to the National Assessment of Educational Progress (NAEP).

Drawing heavily on our expert contributors, we describe what each of these models might look like in practice, with particular reference to these three design elements:

- **Politics & Process.** Who sets the standards? What is their relationship to the federal government? How are they developed? How do educators and the public weigh in?
- **Scope.** How many subjects get tested? How frequently?
- **Consequences.** How do these standards interact with state accountability systems? Is anyone held accountable for the standards' rigor?

Why National Standards and Tests?

Once this four-entree menu of options for policymakers took shape, we felt an obligation to provide an evaluation of each—a Zagat's review, if you will. What are their relative pros and cons?

Of course, this is a matter of values and judgment. Just as a food critic has her own biases (simple versus complex, classic versus cutting edge), so do we have our own policy preferences. We can cite plenty of reasons why one might support national standards and tests, but which do we find most compelling? In other words, which pressing problems do we think standards-based reform, and specifically national standards and tests, are needed to solve?

Let's start with standards-based reform. At a time when much of the No Child Left Behind debate centers around "teaching to the test," it's worth remembering why policymakers embarked on this reform agenda in the first place.

The first reason was educational: to create a more coherent and consistent educational experience for American children. Back in the day when teachers could simply close their doors and teach whatever they wanted, students faced a real risk of learning about dinosaurs every year and never encountering the solar system. Standards provided the opportunity for the system to map out a coherent curricular plan grade-by-grade, ideally culminating in the knowledge and skills needed for success in higher education, the workplace, and our democratic polity. As E.D. Hirsch, Jr., has masterfully explained, this curricular coherence in the schools is especially critical for poor children, who are least likely to develop the "cultural literacy" at home that will allow them to compete in a meritocracy. Standards also allow educators to work collaboratively on curriculum, professional development and so forth, though, importantly, standards are not themselves the curriculum. Done right, they focus on the results to be achieved and leave room for individual schools and educators to figure out the best way to reach them.

The second reason was moral and political: where standards existed, they tended to be higher for affluent children and lower for those living in poverty and for children of color. Schools (and parents) in leafy suburbs pushed their students (at least their affluent students) to tackle rigorous Advanced Placement courses; meanwhile, poor urban districts made excuses for their pupils and seemed content with basic literacy (or just school completion). Statewide standards, measured by standardized tests and linked to meaningful accountability, were seen as the antidote to inequitable expectations.

The final reason was organizational: it was hoped that, by focusing on results, states could scrap myriad input-and-process regulations that sought to improve the schools through the force of coercion. One of the earliest advocates of this approach was the National Governors Association (NGA). Led by Tennessee's Lamar Alexander, it embarked in 1985 on a multi-year education reform initiative—most unusual for an outfit that traditionally changed priorities as often as it changed chairs, i.e. annually. The keystone event was the governors' release and endorsement, during their annual summer meeting in 1986, of an Alexander-inspired report called *Time for Results*.

The governors accepted the post-Coleman reasoning that, if stronger achievement is what's needed, policymakers should focus on the results they seek and how to extract these from the education system, willing or not. They introduced a conceptual quid-pro-quo that foreshadowed charter schools and other potent structural innovations. Experts call it "tight-loose" management: being demanding with regard to outcomes but relaxed about how those outcomes are produced. In Alexander's more homespun phrasing, the governors declared themselves ready for "some old-fashioned horse-trading. We'll regulate less, if schools and school districts will produce better results."

We believe that although these arguments are still valid today, ultimately state standards and tests are inadequate to address four of America's greatest challenges:

1. Global competition.
2. A fragmented education marketplace.
3. The unwillingness of states to set and police their own rigorous standards.
4. An overweening federal government.

Global Competition

The United States faces unprecedented competition from nations around the planet. If all of our young people are to succeed in the "flat" global economy of the 21st century, they will need to achieve to world-class standards.

Globalization, outsourcing, and the Internet have created a worldwide marketplace. Fifty years ago, students graduating from our public school system faced competition from peers in their own town or region. Today, American students must compete with children from India, China, and Brazil.

Virtually all of the world's advanced nations recognize this challenge and have aligned their educational systems with a uniform set of nationwide academic expectations or requirements. Yet, in the United States, we continue to pretend that math in Birmingham is different than math in Boston, much less Bangalore. We cannot afford the parochialism of our current system if we want to maintain our economic position in the world. Plus, the United States is no longer a country in which people are born, live their lives, and die in the same town or even the same state. Americans move frequently, and that means children move frequently, too. National standards and tests could ensure high expectations from sea to shining sea.

A Fragmented Education Marketplace

One of the promises of standards-based reform was that it would allow for, even demand, the development and alignment of powerful educational resources: stronger teacher preparation, content-rich professional development, multimedia curricular materials, etc. Yet the variability and mediocrity of state-by-state standards have made the fruition of this promise much more challenging. Take teacher training. While science teacher candidates in Ohio could conceivably be prepared to teach to Ohio's science standards, many of them will leave Ohio after graduation. The result? Teacher training stays at 30,000 feet rather than drilling down to specific content and concepts.

Or take curricular materials. While it's easy to imagine teachers using well-developed digital content in their classrooms instead of the shoddy text-books available today, companies that could provide this content are hampered by the fractured educational marketplace that (understandably) demands alignment with state standards. Moving to national standards, and thus creating a national market, would create strong incentives for companies to invest in developing the successors to today's lackluster materials. Across all aspects of our educational system, common expectations would allow for a common conversation among educators and collaborative problem-solving.

Of course, the problem of varying standards is not faced by our education system alone. Take the technology sector: at key moments the industry has coalesced around common standards in order to improve efficiency and facilitate innovation. For instance, people around the world enjoy wireless Internet access when they travel because the industry agreed on a common wireless technology protocol. Rather than bickering over standards, technology companies and other providers can compete over the services and content they offer customers. This could happen in education, too.

The Unwillingness of States to Set and Police Their Own Rigorous Standards

The state standards movement has been in place for almost fifteen years. For almost ten of those years, we at the Thomas B. Fordham Foundation have reviewed the quality of state standards. Most were mediocre-to-bad ten years ago, and most are mediocre-to-bad today. They are generally vague, politicized, and awash in wrongheaded fads and nostrums. With a few exceptions, states have been incapable (or unwilling) to set clear, coherent standards, and develop tests with a rigorous definition of proficiency. By our lights, you can count on one hand the number of states with clear proficiency standards in reading and math and expectations even approaching those of the National Assessment of Educational Progress.

No Child Left Behind was supposed to improve on the situation, by taking the example of leading standards-based reform states such as Texas and North Carolina and applying their successful policies to the entire nation. But its designers made a critical mistake. Rather than settling on a common standard for school performance and allowing states and schools to meet that standard as they judged best, it developed a common timeline for achieving "universal proficiency" but allowed states to define "proficiency" in reading and math as they saw fit. The result: there is now heavy pressure on states to define "proficiency" downward and to make Swiss cheese out of NCLB's accountability provisions. Already many states, in order to explain the discrepancy between their passing rates on state tests and their students' performance on NAEP, are claiming that journalists and others should equate state "proficiency" with NAEP's "basic" level. In other words, they are satisfied to get their students to "basic"—"proficiency" be damned. A system that allows such quibbling puts the entire standards-based-reform enterprise in peril.

An Overweening Federal Government

Finally, and counter-intuitively, we see national standards and tests as an opportunity to rein in the federal government. For forty years, Washington has sought to improve the nation's schools by regulating what they do. To date, scant evidence exists that this strategy works.

Common standards and tests could allow Washington to back away from its top-down, regulatory approach and settle instead for clarifying the objectives to be achieved and measuring (and publicizing) whether states, schools, and students are in fact meeting them. Many think that national standards entail an increased federal role. We see it in precisely the opposite way—that a good set of national standards will lead to a reduced and focused federal role that is also better suited to Uncle Sam's particular skill set.

Judging Each Approach

With those biases and objectives in mind, we evaluate each model against the following criteria:

- Is it likely to end the "race to the bottom"? As noted above, because NCLB requires states to adopt standards and tests, get all students to proficiency by 2014, and hold schools accountable for the results, states face great pressure to lower their standards and ease the rigor of their tests. A few states have done this in plain view; we worry that many more are doing so behind closed doors via the many, many ways that expectations can surreptitiously be softened. So a critical question to ask of the four approaches to national standards and testing is whether they will halt any backsliding and lead to world-class standards suited to the demands of the 21st century.
- Is it likely to result in rigorous standards rather than merely politically acceptable ones? As explained above, the ugly truth about standards-based reform is that most of the academic standards in use today are slipshod. A reasonable concern, then, is whether any of these approaches to national standards and tests will be able to get it right when it comes to the content and rigor of the standards themselves.
- Is it likely to lead to an expanded federal role in education? In other words, can we set national standards and tests without federalizing the U.S. education system and thereby doing it a disservice? To what degree do these four approaches require a stronger role for Uncle Sam? Do they make it more or less likely that Congress will intervene in a larger swath of issues or that federal courts will mandate spending levels supposedly needed to achieve the standards?
- Is it likely to prove politically feasible? We offer our best judgment about the odds that any of these four approaches could survive the political minefield. Of course, some will argue that any version of national standards and tests are infeasible, even that this is a "third

rail" type of political problem. We disagree and think this is the wrong reading of history. The evolution of bipartisan support for standards-based reform in American K-12 education can be traced from Charlottesville (1989) through the setting of national education goals (1990) to the National Assessment Governing Board's establishing of "achievement levels" (early 1990s). And further to the composition of the National Council on Education Standards and Testing (1991) and the National Education Goals Panel (1990) through the Goals 2000 and Improving America's Schools Acts (1994) and through any number of education "summits" to the enactment in 2001 of NCLB itself. What went wrong in the early 1990s wasn't the principle of national education standards; it was a misjudgment as to where and by whom these should be set. While one of us once said that "national testing is doomed because the right hates 'national' and the left hates 'testing,'" we believe that times are a changing. Business leaders' concerns about economic competitiveness and civil rights leaders' (belated) embrace of testing as a tool to close the achievement gap indicate that national standards and tests may not longer be politically taboo.

Lawrence A. Uzzell

NO

No Child Left Behind: The Dangers of Centralized Education Policy

The No Child Left Behind Act (NCLB), which the Bush administration claims as its proudest achievement in domestic policy, directly contradicts the principles of an "ownership society," which the administration is promoting in areas such as Social Security reform. The administration recognizes that the educational policies of the last four decades, a period of almost uninterrupted centralization, have failed, but its remedy is yet more centralization.

The NCLB statute is a reform strategy at war with itself. It virtually guarantees massive evasion of its own intent, ordering state education agencies to do things that they mostly don't want to do. Washington will be forced either to allow the states great leeway in how they implement NCLB or to make NCLB more detailed, prescriptive, and top-heavy. If Washington chooses the former, the statute might as well not exist; if the latter, federal policymakers will increasingly resemble Soviet central planners trying to improve economic performance by micromanaging decisions from Moscow. NCLB may end up giving us the worst possible scenario: unconstitutional consolidation of power in Washington over the schools, with that power being used to promote mediocrity rather than excellence.

It is too early to know for certain which scenario will prevail, but it is already clear that state and local education officials are skillfully protecting their interests in ways that undermine the intent of NCLB. Especially telling has been their widespread dishonest reporting in at least four areas: graduation rates, school violence, qualified teachers, and proficiency tests. As it becomes increasingly clear that the states can satisfy the requirements of NCLB by lowering their standards, there will likely be a "race to the bottom."

Instead of using centralized decrees to turn mediocre institutions into excellent ones, as they have been trying but failing to do for the last several decades, the state and federal governments should be empowering individual families to "vote with their feet" by transferring to the schools of their own choice.

The key locus for such revolutionary reforms is the states. The best contribution the national government can make to educational improvement is to avoid educational policymaking and allow states to experiment with school choice programs.

From *Policy Analysis* no. 544, May 31, 2005, pp. 1-6, 16-18. Copyright © 2005 by Cato Institute. Reprinted by permission.

Introduction

In domestic policy, the No Child Left Behind (NCLB) education act is the Bush administration's top claim to visionary leadership. The president and his aides have compared NCLB to landmark programs such as the Social Security Act or the Homestead Act. In his acceptance speech at the 2004 Republican convention, President Bush stated that NCLB is "the most important federal education reform in history." Both during and since the 2004 election campaign, President Bush's speeches have depicted the 2002 act as an unqualified success; even before his second inauguration, the president proposed to extend its provisions from elementary schools to high schools.

Especially striking is the boast that Bush has increased federal spending on education faster than any president since Lyndon Johnson. That is a reversal as profound as the Clinton administration's embrace of sweeping welfare reform in 1996; in both cases the party in power accepted ideas long associated with its opponents. The Republican reversal is the more stunning of the two because most members of the president's party on Capitol Hill changed course with him. During the Republican Party's rise to majority status from the 1960s to the 1990s, by contrast, it usually opposed centralized federal programs in education as in other areas of governance. As recently as 1996, the party's platform pledged to abolish the U.S. Department of Education.

What ultimately matters is NCLB's success not as a one-shot campaign tactic but as a long-term strategy for bringing genuine reform to the country's dysfunctional public schools. With party loyalty keeping most congressional Republicans from criticizing the statute, its skeptics currently find themselves marginalized in Washington. But in the long run NCLB should and will be judged by its actual results.

Dangers of Centralization

No Child Left Behind was enacted in the form of a reauthorization of the 1965 Elementary and Secondary Education Act, one of the centerpieces of President Lyndon Johnson's Great Society. Once it takes full effect, the statute will require states that receive ESEA subsidies annually to test third to eighth grade students in reading and mathematics. By 2014 the states must bring all of their students up to the "proficient" level on those tests. In the meantime the states must demonstrate "adequate yearly progress" (AYP) toward the goal of 100 percent proficiency—including progress toward eliminating achievement disparities between ethnic subgroups. Schools that receive subsidies under the ESEA Title I program for disadvantaged children and that repeatedly fall short of their AYP targets are subject to an escalating series of corrective measures: allowing their students to transfer to other public schools after two years, providing supplementary services such as private tutoring after three years, and possibly becoming subject to mandatory restructuring thereafter.

NCLB's success will depend on whether it is possible to produce excellent educational performance through centralization. Its advocates are in a self-contradictory position. They recognize that the educational policies of the last four decades, a period of almost uninterrupted centralization, have failed, but their remedy for that failure is yet more centralization. While invoking the principles of an "ownership society" on issues such as Social Security reform, they are pursuing almost the exact opposite model in schools. In a period of growing social mobility and individual autonomy, they are promoting a top-down, Great Society model of reform—transferring power from individual parents, teachers, and principals to distant bureaucracies such as state education agencies.

Ironically, the Bush administration has made a key exception to its "ownership society" precisely in the area of social policy that by its very nature is *least* susceptible to centralization. Education is inherently personal and inherently value laden. The key relationships in schools are those between individual teachers and individual students: If the teachers are not committed and highly motivated, no centralized rule books or formulas are going to inspire peak performance from their students. To use social science jargon, schools are "loosely coupled systems"; therefore, decrees from centralized administrators have little power to boost school performance but enormous power to impede progress. Indeed, before the mid-20th century such administrators were either nonexistent or mostly irrelevant; key decisions were made at the level of the individual school by principals and teachers.

Moreover, schooling inescapably involves judgments about truth and virtue, about what kind of person a youngster should aspire to be. In an increasingly pluralistic society, Americans are inevitably going to disagree with each other about those judgments. Which historical figures should children be encouraged to revere as heroes? What should they be taught about ancient belief systems such as Christianity and Islam—and about modern ideologies such as feminism and environmentalism? Should "traditional values" such as piety, chastity, and asceticism be celebrated, ridiculed, or simply ignored? Americans in the 21st century have no more chance of reaching consensus on those questions than of agreeing on what church (if any) we should all attend. That is why we keep the state out of controlling churches, just as we keep it out of other value-forming institutions such as publishing and journalism. The more we entrust such decisions to centralized state agencies, the more conflicts we foment—conflicts that in a truly free society would be unnecessary. As legal scholar Stephen Arons observed in 1997: "One civic group after another attempts to impose its vision of good education, and all join in a struggle over the one true morality to be adopted by the public schools. The outcomes of the conflicts over curriculum, texts, tests, and teachers seem less and less like constructive compromises that knit communities together; more and more they resemble blood feuds, ideological wars, episodes of selfishness wrapped in the rhetoric of rectitude."

Zero-sum "culture wars" for control of coercive state monopolies thus make enemies of people who could otherwise be friends. Perhaps in some bygone era each local public school reflected a local consensus. But in today's ultra-mobile society, in which communities are less and less defined by geography, the only way to keep the culture wars from engulfing the schools is a comprehensive strategy of parental choice. The key to rescuing our children from the bureaucratized government schools is radical decentralization: tuition tax credits, tax deductions, and vouchers. Unfortunately, NCLB is taking us in precisely the opposite direction.

Granted, NCLB does not explicitly call for national curricula. The statute mandates standards for testing, not for curricula, and it leaves the specific content and design of the tests up to the states. But in the long run the tests will, at least to some degree, drive the curricula, and that will loom even larger if NCLB is extended to high school programs as well as to elementary-level reading and math. The statute is already promoting centralization within each state, to the detriment of pluralism and local control. It could become a force for national centralization as well if future administrations should exercise to its full potential their power to deny federal funding to states whose testing programs are deemed inadequate.

So far, the Bush administration has been cautious in exercising that power. During last year's presidential election campaign, the administration wanted to avoid headlines about conflicts with state education agencies; it tried to perpetuate as best it could the congenial atmosphere of the bipartisan signing ceremony when NCLB became law in January 2002. Nevertheless, the states are restive. Many are complaining that NCLB is excessively intrusive; dozens of state legislatures have passed resolutions criticizing the statute. Such complaints are not necessarily unjustified. Any statute as long and complicated as NCLB inevitably requires that state and local school officials spend thousands of manhours filling out federal forms and complying with procedural requirements from Washington—even if that red tape produces little or nothing in the way of genuine academic improvement. It would be not at all surprising if NCLB turned out to be both meddlesome and impotent, as have many previous federal programs.

The Bush administration, and future administrations, will now face a dilemma. The NCLB statute virtually guarantees massive evasion of its own intent: It orders the state education agencies to do things that many of them don't want to do, such as institute detailed, rigorous testing programs that enable the public to distinguish successful from unsuccessful schools, and it gives those agencies broad discretion about just how to do those things. The U.S. Department of Education has little role in creating content standards and assessments under NCLB; it only decides whether to approve those created by the states. But as the states devise various tactics for evading both the letter and the spirit of the law, lawmakers will be forced either to let them get away with those tactics or to continuously amend NCLB's statutory text (already about 1,100 pages long) and associated regulations in order to keep up with the states' ever more inventive evasions.

If policymakers choose the former course, NCLB might as well not exist; it will just be one more drain on taxpayers, like scores of previous education programs, and one more source of special-interest group subsidy—in this case to the testing companies. But if Washington policymakers instead choose to amend the statute, they will end up making it steadily more detailed, prescriptive, and topheavy. Washington's education officials will more and more resemble Soviet central planners trying to improve economic performance by micromanaging decisions from Moscow. Unlike Soviet bureaucrats, however, the federal government lacks a captive labor force; the more centralized the system becomes, the more likely those teachers and potential teachers with the greatest creativity and leadership ability will be to seek careers elsewhere rather than accept being mere pawns of the federal government. As a strategy for promoting "excellence," centralization will be inherently self-defeating.

Thus, NCLB is a reform strategy at war with itself: It can work only if federal officials ride tight herd on their state counterparts, overriding them whenever they sacrifice reform to special-interest pressures. The authors of NCLB have already said that they will do no such thing, rightly invoking principles such as states' rights and the absence of a constitutional warrant for federal control of local schools. But if they were serious about those principles, they would never have enacted NCLB to begin with. On the other hand, if they decide to use NCLB as a tool to muscle through fundamental reforms against the will of the entrenched special interests, they will find that they have to discard whatever remains of their constitutional scruples. They or their successors may even conclude that that is the best possible outcome: If the Constitution and the principles it embodies stand in the way of urgently needed reforms, then the devil take the Constitution. Many previous would-be reformers have made that judgment, from the advocates of centralized economic planning who created the short-lived National Recovery Administration in the 1930s to the Supreme Court in its 1972 ban (also shortlived) on all forms of capital punishment.

Future historians, then, may look back on NCLB as simply one more phase in the gradual building of a national ministry of education—a ministry explicitly responsible not only for testing but for curriculum content and even for the administration of schools. Parents with complaints about their children's textbooks or teachers would have to take those complaints, not to their local school board, but to Washington. That scenario may seem far-fetched: There is no clear evidence that the proponents of NCLB consciously intend to create a national curriculum or a national, European-style ministry of education. But few members of Congress who voted for the 1965 Elementary and Secondary Education Act, which was only a few dozen pages long, consciously intended to start down a path leading to ever more detailed federal controls and culminating in the 1,100-page NCLB. Once Washington sets up such regulatory and spending machines, they tend to acquire a life and logic of their own. Moreover, one should consider that it took only seven years from the congressional elections of 1994 for many of that year's "Republican revolutionaries" to reverse course and vote for the most centralizing education bill in American history. It seems not at all implausible that Congress may be willing to enact even more sweeping centralization within the next decade—especially if an increasingly comfortable Republican majority grows ever more accustomed to bloating the Department of Education's budget with "pork-barrel" earmarks for its political allies.

Setting aside its difficulties from the standpoint of constitutionalism and the rule of law, would such hypercentralization actually bring genuine reform? Optimists might suggest that it could bring us back to the educational standards of 1901, when the College Entrance Examination Board published a list of specific literary classics that it recommended that every would-be college freshman should have read before matriculating. The firm, exacting standards of those educators stand in striking contrast to the curricular relativism of the late 20th century, with its faddish lessons in popular culture. If education means requiring a youngster to learn things that he is unlikely to learn if left unsupervised, then perhaps centralized coercion is a good thing.

What that argument ignores is the crucial fact that in America, unlike much of Europe and Asia, curricular relativism and fragmentation have grown hand in hand with the growth of centralized power over education policy in both Washington and the state capitals. The people who control the key institutions in this country's government school establishment—the teachers' unions, the teacher-training institutions, the state education agencies, the career staff of the federal education colossus—are not Victorian-style elitists seeking to mold the masses according to lofty standards of classical learning. Quite the opposite. In today's America, the masses are more elitist (in the desirable sense of demanding serious academic standards) than is the educational establishment with its focus on "self-esteem." When given a free hand, American working-class parents make sounder educational choices than the establishment tries to dictate to them. Consider, for example, the nearly total absence of destructive fads such as bilingual education in private schools, even when those schools have large minority enrollments.

Judging from the experience of the last four decades, NCLB may end up giving us the worst possible scenario: unconstitutional consolidation in Washington of power over the schools, with that power being used to further mediocrity rather than excellence. Experience shows that centralized government agencies are especially prone to capture by ideological factions that want to shield children from unwelcome facts and opinions. In a 2001 study for the Cato Institute, Sheldon Richman cited the case of the proposed national history standards developed in the early 1990s by the National Center for History in the Schools at the University of California at Los Angeles under a grant from the U.S. Department of Education and the National Endowment for the Humanities. According to Richman, those draft standards "set off a firestorm of controversy led by Lynne V. Cheney, who had chaired the NEH when the National Center was commissioned to write the standards. . . . Cheney condemned the standards as an exercise that put Western-bashing political correctness ahead of good history. She feared that an 'official knowledge' would be adopted, 'with the result that much that is significant in our past will begin to disappear from our schools.' The irony is that, until the standards were released, she favored in principle the government's adoption of an 'official knowledge.'"

Richman rightly concluded that "we do not face a choice between government standards for education and no standards at all, no more than we face a choice between government standards for computers and no standards at all." Those who call for educational statism in the name of "standards" seem blind to the vital distinction between standards set by private institutions and standards set by government. . . .

Some observers hope that the statute can be fixed by further amendments, but experience with most other large federal programs, from health care subsidies to the tax code, suggests the opposite. With the passage of time, such programs tend to become even more complicated, internally contradictory, and captive to various lobbies with their own inconsistent objectives.

Before NCLB, several states imposed accountability systems on schools with statewide testing, reporting, and (supposedly) clear consequences for failure. Frederick Hess found that over time those state systems have tended to drift from "tough" to "soft," with standards and penalties being relaxed as interest groups mobilize against them. As summarized by Martin West and Paul Peterson of Harvard University's Program on Education Policy and Governance, the findings of Hess and other researchers suggest that

> keeping intact the necessary political will over the long run is likely to be highly problematic. . . . If authentic accountability is to be established, presidents, governors, and mayors, backed by a well-organized business community, need to remain committed to the effort. Yet such leaders, with their numerous responsibilities, are easily distracted. Fighting wars, preventing terrorism, maintaining economic growth, balancing budgets, and many other issues, too unpredictable to anticipate, can easily shift educational accountability to the back burner. When that happens, well-organized, narrow interests gain the upper hand. All in all, there is every reason to believe that tough, coercive accountability will gradually evolve into something softer, nicer, more acceptable to those directly affected.

Conclusion and Recommendations

NCLB reflects an ideological strain that is novel for Republican presidents: utopianism. As did the older, left-wing forms of utopianism, the Bush administration emphasizes collective action rather than individual responsibility: NCLB implicitly treats students not as individuals but as passive commodities mass-produced by state programs. In its plans for extending NCLB to the high school level, the Bush administration has yet to signal that it will even try to revive the parental choice provisions that were part of its original proposal in early 2001—and that it utterly failed to defend against the implacable statists among Capitol Hill Democrats. As individuals who respond to incentives, both parents and students are for the most part curiously absent from NCLB; its focus, like that of nearly all federal education programs for the last four decades, is on administrative units such as schools and school districts.

Utopianism usually ends up transforming rhetoric more than reality. In the real world, the chance that not one child in America will fall short of academic "proficiency" within a decade is the same as the chance that not one child will be a juvenile delinquent: zero. By 2014, if not before, NCLB will be seen to have failed, just as the centralized education programs enacted from the 1960s through the 1990s have failed. But like those programs, NCLB may be so deeply entrenched by then that it will be difficult to repeal. In any case, it will have absorbed time, money, and energy that could otherwise have been spent on more promising measures. Like the so-called reform measures of the 1980s and 1990s, NCLB has not destroyed the chances of genuine, radical reforms in America's profoundly dysfunctional school system, but it has almost certainly postponed them.

It will always be true that some of America's tens of thousands of schools are excellent and some mediocre (or worse). Rather than continue to use centralized government decrees (both state and federal) to turn mediocre institutions into excellent ones, as they have been trying but failing to do for the last several decades, the state and federal governments should empower individual families to "vote with their feet" by transferring to the schools of their own choice. That strategy would bring three advantages that are absent from the monopolistic command-and-control model embodied in NCLB. First, it would allow parents to rescue their children from dysfunctional schools immediately rather than continue to wait for the public school establishment's endless tinkerings with the status quo to produce the glorious results that have long been promised but never arrive. Second, it would allow families to pick schools that are compatible with their own philosophical and religious beliefs instead of locking them into poisonous, zero-sum conflicts to determine which groups will win the power to impose their beliefs on other groups within the coercive, one-size-fits-all government schools.

Third, a reform model based on free markets rather than state monopolies would unleash the dynamic force of competition. When schools know that they cannot take their customers for granted, they face a whole new incentive structure: They have to concentrate on producing solid results rather than on paper compliance with top-down regulations. Nothing concentrates the mind as effectively as the threat of having to go out of business. Real, ongoing accountability to customers who are free at any moment to take their children (and dollars) elsewhere is qualitatively different from imitation accountability to centralized government structures that can almost always be coaxed or pressured into keeping the money flowing to schools that are manifestly failing. The latter model, as practiced by so-called reform strategies such as NCLB, simply adds one more layer of bureaucracy to a system that is far too bureaucratized already. As education researchers John Chubb and Terry Moe observed 15 years ago in a now-classic study for the Brookings Institution, parental choice is a "revolutionary reform" rather than a "system-preserving" one: "The whole point of a thoroughgoing system of choice is to free the schools from these disabling constraints by sweeping away the old institutions and replacing them with new ones."

The key locus for such revolutionary reforms is the states. Under the Constitution it is the states that have legal responsibility for education. Even after decades of unconstitutional federal education programs, more than 90 percent of government financing for elementary and secondary schools still comes from state and local taxes. Education is thus one of the most promising areas for taking advantage of the flexibility and diversity that the nation's Founders gave us: Let some states try tuition tax credits or tax deductions, let others try vouchers, and let all learn from each other's experience.

This process has of course begun with the parental choice programs already enacted in Wisconsin, Ohio, Florida, and elsewhere. In education as in other areas, the 18th-century principles built into the country's federalist design are better adapted to the challenges of the fast-moving, down-sizing, open-ended 21st century than are the static, top-heavy, homogeneous structures left over from the mid-20th century.

POSTSCRIPT

Is It Time for National Standards in Education?

Born out of our revolutionary heritage of mistrusting distant centralized government, many important elements of governance were either reserved for state and local governments or, as contained in the Bill of Rights, explicitly denied to the central government (those proscriptions were eventually extended to include all government levels and entities with the addition of the Fourteenth Amendment to the Constitution). The historical primacy of state and local governments in matters related to education was underscored by the U.S. Supreme Court in its 1954 decision in *Brown v. Board of Education* with the following statement: "Education is perhaps the most important function of state and local governments." That strong tradition of state and local rights to control education creates a political challenge for those who believe that children and their schooling would be better served by a more centralized approach. The following statement by Margaret Spellings, U.S. Secretary of Education, exemplifies the caution that politicians manifest when they approach this issue:

> Education is primarily a State and local responsibility in the United States. It is States and communities, as well as public and private organizations of all kinds, that establish schools and colleges, develop curricula, and determine requirements for enrollment and graduation. The structure of education finance in America reflects this predominant State and local role. Of an estimated $909 billion being spent nationwide on education at all levels for school year 2004–2005, about 90 percent comes from State, local, and private sources. That means the Federal contribution to national education expenditures is about 10 percent. . . . (2006)

(It is interesting to note that federal expenditures for education were in the 7 percent range only a couple of decades back.) It is through the allocation and administration of those federal dollars that the federal government gains the ability to become involved with education. If States wish to receive federal funding, they must agree with the provisions attached to the allocations. In effect it is a contractual arrangement.

When discussing national curricular and assessment standards for education, most proponents are astute enough to emphasize that national standards do not necessarily need to be federal government standards. They suggest that national curricular standards could emerge from national groups representing certain content areas such as the National Council for Social Studies, the National Council of Teachers of English, the National Science

Teachers Association, etc. National assessment standards could be based on national tests and evaluations such as the National Assessment of Educational Progress (NAEP) or approaches developed by testing organizations or textbook publishers. Although such nonfederal government approaches are possible, it is difficult to imagine that states would voluntarily give up their rights to determine curricular and assessment standards. Including "voluntary" national standards in federal funding legislation such as NCLB would be very complex in terms of political overtones and might even be viewed by the courts as a coercive act by the federal government.

Detailed information regarding national standards can be found in publications from various national education organizations including the groups noted above, as well as the National Council of Teachers of Mathematics, the Center for Civic Education, and the International Society for Technology in Education.

ISSUE 2

Is Home Schooling a Good Idea?

YES: Thomas W. Washburne, from "The Boundaries of Parental Authority: A Response to Rob Reich of Stanford University," Paper of the National Center for Home Education (April 22, 2002)

NO: Rob Reich, from "The Civic Perils of Homeschooling," *Educational Leadership* (April 2002)

ISSUE SUMMARY

YES: Thomas W. Washburne, director of the National Center for Home Education, suggests that as the home-schooling movement continues to grow, the educational establishment will become increasingly troubled.

NO: Rob Reich, assistant professor at Stanford University, states that students should encounter materials, ideas, and people that they or their parents have not chosen or selected in advance.

With estimates of one to two million children involved in home schooling there is little question that the once seemingly radical idea of "unschooling" proposed by John Holt in his 1981 book *Teach Your Own* has gained mainstream acceptance and thus media and political interest. Parents who choose to home-school their children often point to issues such as school violence, drugs and teen pregnancies, overcrowded classrooms, and a lack of quality teachers as some of the reasons that have caused them to turn to this approach. Others believe that the special needs of their children can be better served through home schooling. And even though home schooling has outgrown its radical genesis, there remain those who, like Holt, find their advocacy in their desire to liberate their children from what they see as monolithic control by "government schools." Home schooling is legal in every state, but regulations related to it vary from almost none to formal processes involving approval and periodic inspections by educational agencies such as school districts.

Even with home schooling gaining legal and public acceptance, the next controversy regarding the practice will likely be regulatory. Freelance writer Brett Schaeffer in "Grace Under Pressure" (*Teacher Magazine,* March 2004) states, "In the era of *No Child Left Behind*—the federal education law that ratchets up testing requirements, teacher certification guidelines and a host of other regulations—policymakers are looking to apply similar accountability measures to homeschoolers." In the same article, Dennis Evans of the University of California, Irvine, argues that, "At minimum all students, regardless of the school venue—public, private, or home—should be required to take mandated state tests. If public schools are to be held accountable for student performance on legally required standardized tests, then shouldn't it follow that any form of 'schooling' with legal status should also be held accountable?" For their part, home-schooling advocacy groups promise to resist any government regulations that would attempt to restrict the rights of parents to educate their children as they believe appropriate.

Critics of home schooling see it as an extension of the notion that "anyone can teach." They argue that good teaching is a complex act that involves more than simply loving children and suggest that even though there may be some parents who have the competencies and training to teach very young children, those competencies may not be enough in more advanced grades and specific subjects. Home-schooling advocates counter with references to the wide range of instructional resources and support systems available in their communities and on the Internet. They stress the advantages of home schooling such as flexibility of time utilization, the ability to capitalize on "teachable moments," and the natural capacity and responsibility of parents to teach their children.

With respect to how home-schooled children do academically when compared to children who attend school, there is little empirical evidence. Although home-schooling advocates do present self-reported and anecdotal data regarding the superiority of home-schooled students on certain academic measures such as the SAT, there is no definitive study proving or disproving that assertion.

Debate also exists regarding the values of schooling beyond academic learning. Proponents of attending a school argue that it is an important element in the development of the "whole child" and that virtues and values such as respect for others, the ability to communicate and collaborate, and an openness to diversity and new ideas are best developed in a school setting. Home-schooling supporters reject that contention and, like Holt, claim that schools are actually counterproductive to such development. They assert that all sorts of antisocial and negative attitudes and behaviors characterize schools and classrooms.

In their respective articles, Thomas Washburne suggests that the educational establishment is critical of home schooling because of the predominant worldview of relativism and secular humanism, whereas Rob Reich expresses concern that highly customized home schooling may deprive students of exposure to the diversity of a democratic society and narrow their experiences, which can curtail their freedom.

YES ⤶

Thomas W. Washburne

The Boundaries of Parental Authority: A Response to Rob Reich of Stanford University

From August 30 to September 2, 2001, the American Political Science Association held its annual meeting in San Francisco, California. Rob Reich, of the Department of Political Science at Stanford University, presented a paper at this meeting which has captured the attention of many home schooling families, including members of the Home School Legal Defense Association (HSLDA). Several members of HSLDA have asked for our opinion of this paper. This report has been prepared to satisfy these inquiries. It is not intended to be a point by point refutation of the paper, but is rather a brief examination of the major themes explored, and some of HSLDA's major criticisms and concerns. Reich's position should not be taken lightly. It is illustrative of many of the challenges home educators are facing as their numbers increase. Moreover, if Reich's views were adopted by the courts, home education as we know it today would simply cease to legally exist.

Mr. Reich's paper was entitled *Testing the Boundaries of Parental Authority Over Education: The Case of Homeschooling.* The paper is a precursor to a book by Reich to be entitled *Bridging Liberalism and Multiculturalism in Education,* which the University of Chicago Press is anticipated to publish in 2002. In his paper, Reich traces the rise of home education, the interests in education held by the government, the parent, and the child, and sets forth his suggestions for balancing these interests. These suggestions lead Reich to conclude that "while the state should not ban homeschooling it must nevertheless regulate its practice with vigilance." He then briefly offers a few suggestions for how a state should regulate home education, and some of the difficulties the state may encounter.

Reich's proposed regulations include "periodic assessments that would measure their success in examining and reflecting upon diverse worldviews." These regulations are in furtherance of Reich's view that:

> Children are owed as a matter of justice the capacity to choose to lead lives—adopt values and beliefs, pursue an occupation, endorse new traditions—that are different from those of their parents. Because the child cannot him or herself ensure the acquisition of such capacities and the parents may be opposed to

such acquisition, the state must ensure it for them. The state must guarantee that children are educated for minimal autonomy.

A brief review of the constitutional basis for home education will lead one to quickly understand the serious implications of Reich's theories. It has long been recognized by Americans, legal scholars, and the Supreme Court that the original intent of the drafters of the Constitution of the United States was to protect many rights which are not expressly set forth in the founding documents. It has also long been held by Americans and the Supreme Court, and rightfully so, that the right of parents to direct the upbringing of their children is a fundamental right. In fact, this basic understanding of the role of parents long predates the founding of the United States.

Nevertheless, no right is absolute. In that regard, the American legal system has created a method by which the limits of fundamental rights are tested. It is said by the Courts examining constitutional challenges to government law and regulation that the fundamental right at issue may not be infringed upon unless the government can show a compelling interest in doing so, and, if there is such an interest, it then infringes in the least restrictive manner. In such cases, the court must balance the "interests" of the state against the "interests" of the individual asserting a right. For example, in the case of the First Amendment right to free speech, the government has a compelling interest to maintain public safety and order and can therefore prohibit the wrongful shouting of "fire" in a crowded theatre, even though this infringes a person's right to free speech.

As noted before, the regulation of home education by the government is limited by the fact that parents have a fundamental right to direct the upbringing of their children which is protected by the Constitution. Accordingly, unless the state can show some compelling interest in regulating the parent's involvement in education, the parent's views are heeded. So, it becomes critical to understand what the state's interest in education is.

Fortunately for home schoolers, this issue was addressed decades ago, and reaffirmed on occasion since. It is well understood from a legal perspective that the government's *compelling* interest in education is limited. It has been held numerous times that the government's interest in education is basically only of two varieties: civic and economic. The first involves the government's interest in seeing that a child is prepared for citizenship. In other words, will he have capability to vote? The economic interest addresses the state's desire to see that citizens will be able to provide for themselves and not become a burden. So, for example, when a state attempts to impose a requirement that all home educators have teaching degrees, the state must show that this requirement is essential in achieving its interest in education—that is, good citizenship, economic success, etc. To rebut the government, the home educator merely needs to show that home educators without teaching degrees are raising children who are competent, functional. Such a showing renders the government's proposed regulation as unnecessary to achieve the government's compelling interest.

There has been considerable debate about whether the government's interest in education should be extended. So far, thankfully, the courts have been reluctant to do so. Not even the most liberal of judges have taken the initiative to override centuries of respect for the institution of the family and the parental interest in raising children.

It is at this point that we can begin to see the implications, indeed danger, of Reich's ideas for home education. For Reich, while recognizing that there can be debate on the topic, essentially concedes that the state's interest in education does not lend itself to regulating home education. It is not Reich's contention that parental rights should be overridden because the state's compelling interest in education is not being fulfilled. Reich rather sets forth the argument that children have their own interests in education, which are different from both the parent's and the state's. It is this interest, the child's, which in Reich's view justifies limiting parental rights.

Reich sees the interest of the child as being twofold. First, "a child has an interest in education because education is necessary to developing into an adult capable of independent functioning." While setting forth this interest, it appears that Reich sees it as largely duplicating what are already addressed by the state and parental interests in education. Reich does "not mean to imply anything potentially controversial about independent functioning." It is in the second interest of children in education, as seen by Reich, that the controversy is made clear.

For Reich, children have a fundamental interest in "becoming autonomous." This refers "to the capacity of the child to develop into an independent adult who can seek and promote his or her own interests, as he or she understands them, and who can participate, if he or she chooses, in political dialog with others." This interest comes from his perception that children should be shielded from "an unquestioning subordination of one's own will to the ethical ideals of another person or persons." In Reich's view, "Neither parents nor the state can justly attempt to imprint indelibly upon a child a set of values and beliefs, as if it were an inheritance one should never be able to question, as if the child must always defer and be obedient. To do so would in effect render the child servile."

The insertion of the supposed interest of children to be autonomous into the balancing of parental and state interests leads to interesting conclusions. Reich provides the following:

> I submit that even in a minimal construal of autonomy, it must be the function of the school setting to expose children to and engage children with values and beliefs other than those of their parents. [citation omitted] To achieve minimal autonomy requires that a child know that there are ways of life other than that into which he or she has been born. Minimal autonomy requires, especially for its civic importance, that a child be able to examine his or her own political values and beliefs, and those of others, with a critical eye. It requires that the child be able to think independently. If this is all true, then, at a bare minimum, the structure of schooling cannot simply replicate in every particularity the values and beliefs of a child's home.

To ensure the children's interest, "[t]he state must therefore ensure that all children, regardless of the environment in which they are schooled, receive an education that exposes them to and engages them with values and beliefs other than those they find at home." Moreover, "[b]ecause children are a politically inert group, regulations in their interest must be defended by other organizations, such as the Children's Defense Fund, which typically have less at stake in home schooling, or by state officials, who are of course responsible for a much broader children's agenda than guarding against home schooling abuses."

At first glance, Reich's arguments appear persuasive. We cannot deny that children have significant rights which the state protects. For instance, children may not be abused, neglected, or abandoned. In fact, the entire juvenile justice system is predicated on the fact that children have unique interests, that children have special concerns. All of this begs the question, "why don't children have an interest in education?" And if they do, could Reich be right? As Reich points out, children are not the property of their parents to do with whatever they desire.

But the subject is more complex than what Reich is setting forth. First and foremost, children are not adults. Children are people, yet children, by their very nature, are in a class of their own. When children are involved, society, and the law, duly note their special status. Accordingly, some human rights are afforded children, and some are not. Generally, this reflects the fact that children cannot fend for themselves and lack the capacity to form certain judgments. In examining what rights children enjoy, and what rights they do not, a helpful distinction may be drawn between rights of children to protection and rights of children to choice.

Rights of protection involve the right to life, freedom from bodily harm, etc. All people, by being people, are entitled to some liberty in their person. Children are no exception. In children, rights of protection take the form of protection from abuse, abandonment, etc.

Rights of choice are legal rights that permit persons to make "affirmative choices of binding consequence. Rights of choice includes such rights as voting, marrying, exercising religious preference, and choosing whether to seek education." These rights, however, are not extended to all. Our law has always recognized that to exercise these rights, a person must have capacity. This is why contracts with children are unenforceable. This is why children may not vote, or marry without permission. These are adult rights and children are not adults. It is in the consideration of rights of choice that Reich's arguments begin to lose their persuasion.

Consider a child's right to autonomy as posited by Reich. Can it really be said that children are owed, "as a matter of justice," the capacity to lead lives different than their parents? Most parents would quickly concur that children do not have, nor should they have, the right to dictate when they go to bed, what they watch on television, what magazines they read, whether they do their chores, or whether they obey their parents. To recognize a child's right to choice would lead to the child's doom. Yes, the law protects children. But the law cannot change children into adults simply by giving them the choices of adults. The law cannot give them something which, being children, they do not have by nature the ability to exercise.

The right to autonomy, to view the world as you want to, is only properly enjoyed by adults. While prudent parenting includes efforts to inform and help children understand the world about them, responsible parenting also demands that children be taught right from wrong, in a word—truth.

A major problem Reich's theory does not directly address is that all teaching has at its base a worldview, a philosophy of life. Even so-called neutrality betrays an underlying worldview of relativism. Accordingly, by definition, reality, or whatever label one puts on it, every child is being taught a worldview by someone. There really is no such thing as neutrality in education. Putting it in Reich's language, even if a child had a right to autonomy in education, it could never be exercised. The state, in enforcing the child's interest, will by necessity become an advocate of some worldview. While there might be some danger in allowing parents to convey worldviews to children, history will attest that having the state indoctrinate children has much larger consequences.

Granting choice rights to children, and having the state enforce them, is especially problematic for worldviews arising out of religion. Many religions, and especially Christianity, necessitate the teaching of truth. Not, "This is my truth," but "True truth." There is no room for relativism. There is no way that the child can be merely exposed to all worldviews. While Christian parenting can involve exposure to other worldviews, Christian parenting cannot allow for a neutral presentation. Christian parents cannot say to the child: "This is true for me, it may not be true for you." The best Christian parents can do is say, "This is true, and you must come to terms with your response to this truth."

In at least one way, Reich anticipates this objection. He notes that:

> [T]he problem arises when the secular state authority is exercised over the rearing of children. Conflict between the state and religious parents on this score may be endemic and inevitable. On my view, even given the deep importance of religious freedom, the state cannot relinquish its regulatory role in education in cases where parents invoke their religious beliefs as a bulwark against secular authority.

One of the reasons why home education has exploded as a movement is that the public schools no longer teach truth as truth. The court has so hemmed in the role of public education that secular humanism and relativism have become the only underlying philosophies that survive constitutional scrutiny. To a certain degree, Reich's ideas have met with success, as evidenced by the number of children in public education. While this is acceptable to many Americans, and in particular the so-called intellectual elite, it is simply unacceptable to many others.

We must ask ourselves at this point, "why is Reich so afraid of home education?" We are a small segment of society. If we are really afraid that children are suffering from a lack of autonomy in education, why not focus upon the much larger populations of children who really will suffer a lack of autonomy, even as adults. By any definition, children who grow up illiterate, unable to do basic math, and lack even the capacity as adults to exercise choice rights are far less autonomous than home educated children who have received an education based on the worldview of their parents. Home schoolers represent little more than 2% of school aged students. Why focus on them? If it is children we care about, we should focus on those kids who are not being given even the most rudimentary of education in America's failing public schools. If Reich really cares, perhaps he should initially focus on those children trapped in educational failure.

The real root of the problem home education presents to Reich is that home educators have removed themselves from America's educational system and its underlying values. Their children are beyond the reach of the elite and the predominate worldview of relativism or secular humanism. As home schooling continues to grow and prosper, this will become increasingly troublesome to the educational establishment. But more than being beyond the intellectual elite, the children of home educators are largely beyond the reach of the state. It will take novel legal theories to break this constitutional protection. And it is here that Reich's theories are most concerning, indeed dangerous.

What Reich is doing, intentional or not, is setting an academic framework by which an activist judge might rule in favor of heavy restrictions on home education, while at the same time avoiding the obvious assault on precedent and the Constitution. By extending what are in essence adult rights of choice to children, and declaring children to have an interest in education separate from the state's and separate from their parent's, Reich provides the opportunity to take away freedoms which Americans, indeed humans in general, have deemed fundamental for thousands of years.

Rob Reich

→ **NO**

The Civic Perils of Homeschooling

Just 10 years ago, educating a child at home was illegal in several states. Today, not only is homeschooling legal everywhere, it's booming. Homeschooling is probably the fastest-growing segment of the education market, expanding at a rate of 15 to 20 percent a year (Lines, 2000a). More children are homeschooled than attend charter schools. More children are homeschooled than attend conservative Christian academies.

And it's not just left-wing unschoolers and right-wing religious fundamentalists who are keeping their children at home. Taking advantage of the Internet and other new technologies, more middle-of-the-road suburbanites are homeschooling, too. *Time* and *Newsweek* have featured homeschooling on their covers. The U.S. Congress passed a resolution in 1999 declaring the week of September 19 to be National Home Education Week. Homeschooling has gone mainstream.

In response to the rise of homeschooling, policymakers and public school administrators and teachers need to consider what makes homeschooling so popular. Chief among the many reasons to homeschool is the ability to customize a child's education at home.

Customizing Education at Home

The ability to custom-tailor an education for their children is often the motivation for parents to homeschool. No other education arrangement offers the same freedom to arrange an education designed for an individual student; in homeschools, parents are responsible not only for selecting what their children will learn, but when, how, and with whom they will learn. In this sense, homeschooling represents the apex of customization in education.

But is this customization always a good thing? From the standpoint of the parents who choose to homeschool, it surely is; they wouldn't be doing it otherwise, especially in light of the considerable energy and time it requires of them. But considered from the standpoint of democratic citizenship, the opportunity to customize education through homeschooling isn't an unadulterated good. Customizing education may permit schooling to be tailored for each individual student, but total customization also threatens to insulate students from exposure to diverse ideas and people and thereby to shield them from the vibrancy of a pluralistic democracy. These risks are perhaps greatest for homeschoolers. To understand why, we need first to understand more about the current practice of homeschooling.

Homeschooling Today

Homeschooling is more than an education alternative. It is also a social movement (Stevens, 2001; Talbot, 2001). In 1985, approximately 50,000 children were being educated at home. In 2002, at least 1 million children are being homeschooled, with some estimates pegging the number at 2 million, an increase of 20- or 40-fold. (It's symptomatic of the unregulated environment of homeschooling that precise figures on the number of homeschoolers are impossible to establish.) Depending on the estimate you choose (Bielick, Chandler, & Broughman, 2001; Lines, 2000a), homeschoolers account for 2–4 percent of the school-going population.

Homeschooling parents are politically active. Former Pennsylvania Representative Bill Goodling, the former chair of the House Committee on Education and the Workforce, has called homeschoolers "the most effective education lobby on Capitol Hill" (as cited in Golden, 2000). Homeschoolers have established both local and national networks for lobbying purposes and for offering curricular support to one another. Several national organizations, led by the Home School Legal Defense Association, promote homeschooling. Even the former Secretary of Education, William Bennett, is a fan—he has created a for-profit company called K12, the purpose of which is to supply curricular and testing materials to homeschoolers.

But who homeschools, and why? Two main groups of homeschoolers have emerged, both of which raise difficult questions about customization.

The larger of the groups is the Christian right. Although homeschooling has become a much more diverse enterprise in the past 10 years, its strength as a social movement and the majority of its practitioners are conservative Christians. Precise data are scarce, but researchers tend to agree that whereas homeschools of the 1970s "reflected a liberal, humanistic, pedagogical orientation," the majority of homeschools in the 1980s and 1990s "became grounds of and for ideological, conservative, religious expressions of educational matters" (Carper, 2000, p. 16). Today, most parents choose to educate their children at home because they believe that their children's moral and spiritual needs will not be met in campus-based schools.

Those who educate their children at home for religious reasons often object to the secular bias of public schools. By keeping their children at home, they seek to provide a proper religious education free from the damning influences of secularism and pop culture. These homeschoolers wish to avoid the public school at all costs.

The second group practices a different kind of homeschooling. They seek partnerships with public schools to avail themselves of resources, support, guidance, and extracurricular activities that they could not otherwise obtain or provide at home. For these parents, some participation in public schools is desirable.

Various mechanisms have emerged to allow homeschooled students to connect on a partial basis with the public school system. In California, for example, approximately 10 percent of the charter schools serve students whose primary learning is at home (Lines, 2000b). Other districts have set up "virtual" academies online to aid in the enrollment of homeschoolers. Still other school districts permit students to attend some classes but not others and to participate in extracurricular activities (Rothstein, 2002). Finally, a few public school districts have set up homeschooling resource centers, staffed by public school teachers and professional curriculum developers, that homeschooling parents can use at their convenience.

Democratic Citizenship and Customization

Each kind of homeschooler—the family who teaches the child solely at home and the family who seeks some interaction with the public school system—is practicing customization in education. For the first, parents can tailor the education environment to their own convictions and to their beliefs about what their child's needs and interests are. For the second, parents can select the aspects of the public system they and their child want, creating an overall program designed for their child.

What's to worry about either kind of customization? Let me put the matter quite simply. Customizing a child's education through homeschooling represents the victory of a consumer mentality within education, suggesting that the only purpose that education should serve is to please and satisfy the preferences of the consumer. Education, in my view, is not a consumption item in the same sense as the food we select from the grocery store.

Many homeschoolers would surely protest here that their energetic efforts to overcome numerous obstacles to educate their children at home are motivated by a desire to shield their children from rampant consumerism and to offer their children a moral environment in which they learn deeper and more important values. No doubt this is true.

But my point is not that homeschooling parents are inculcating in their children a consumer mentality. My point is that many homeschooling parents view the education of their children as a matter properly under their control and no one else's. They feel entitled to "purchase" the education environment of their children from the marketplace of learning materials, with no intermediary between them and their child. The first kind of homeschooler actually does purchase learning materials for the home. The second kind of homeschooler treats the public school system as a provider of services and activities from which parents choose what they want, as if it were a restaurant with an extensive menu.

And this attitude is the crucial point. Homeschooling is the apogee of parental control over a child's education, where no other institution has a claim to influence the schooling of the child. Parents serve as the only filter for a child's education, the final arbiters of what gets included and what gets excluded.

This potentially compromises citizenship in the following ways:

- In a diverse, democratic society, part of able citizenship is to come to respect the fact that other people will have beliefs and convictions, religious and otherwise, that conflict with one's own. Yet from the standpoint of citizenship, these other people are equals. And students must learn not only that such people exist, but how to engage and deliberate with them in the public arena. Thus, students should encounter materials, ideas, and people that they or their parents have not chosen or selected in advance.
- Citizenship is the social glue that binds a diverse people together. To be a citizen is to share something in common with one's fellow citizens. As the legal scholar Sunstein (2001) has argued, a heterogeneous society without some shared experiences and common values has a difficult time addressing common problems and risks social fragmentation. Schooling is one of the few remaining social institutions—or civic intermediaries—in which people from all walks of life have a common interest and in which children might come to learn such common values as decency, civility, and respect.
- Part of being a citizen is exercising one's freedom. Indeed, the freedoms that U.S. citizens enjoy are a democratic inheritance that we too often take for granted. But to be free is not simply to be free from coercion or constraint. Democratic freedom requires the free construction and possible revision of beliefs and preferences. To become free, students must be exposed to the vibrant diversity of a democratic society so that they possess the liberty to live a life of their own design.

Because homeschooled students receive highly customized educations, designed usually to accord with the preferences of parents, they are least likely in principle to be exposed to materials, ideas, and people that have not been chosen in advance; they are least likely to share common education experiences with other children; and they are most likely to have a narrow horizon of experiences, which can curtail their freedom. Although highly customized education for students may produce satisfied parents as consumers, and even offer excellent academic training to the student, it is a loss from a civic perspective.

Civic Perils

I do not argue that homeschooling undermines citizenship in all cases. On the contrary, I have elsewhere defended the practice of homeschooling, when properly regulated (Reich, 2002). Many homeschooling parents are deeply committed to providing their children with an education that introduces them to a great diversity of ideas and people. And for those homeschoolers who seek partnerships with public schools, their children do participate in common institutions with other children. I do not intend to condemn homeschooling wholesale, for I have met many homeschooled students who are better prepared for democratic citizenship than the average public school student.

My claim is about the potential civic perils of a homeschooled education, where schooling is customizable down to the tiniest degree. Customization, and, therefore, homeschooling, seem wonderful if we think about education as a consumption item. But schooling, from the time that public schools were founded until today, has served to cultivate democratic citizenship. And though this may be a largely forgotten aim, as many have argued, we should not allow a new consumer mentality to become the driving metaphor for the education of children.

References

Bielick, S., Chandler, K., & Broughman, S. (2001, July 31). *Home schooling in the United States: 1999* (NCES 2001-033). Washington, DC: U.S. Department of Education.

Carper, J. C. (2000, April). Pluralism to establishment to dissent: The religious and educational context of home schooling. *Peabody Journal of Education, 75*(1, 2), 8–19.

Golden, D. (2000, April 24). Homeschoolers learn how to gain clout inside the beltway. *Wall Street Journal,* p. A1.

Lines, P. (2000a, Summer). Home schooling comes of age. *Public Interest, 140,* 74–85.

Lines, P. (2000b, April). When homeschoolers go to school: A partnership between families and schools. *Peabody Journal of Education, 75*(1, 2), 159–186.

Reich, R. (2002). *Bridging liberalism and multiculturalism in American education.* Chicago: University of Chicago Press.

Rothstein, R. (2002, January 2). Augmenting a home-school education. *New York Times,* p. B11.

Stevens, M. (2001). *Kingdom of children: Culture and controversy in the homeschooling movement.* Princeton, NJ: Princeton University Press.

Sunstein, C. (2001). *Republic.com.* Princeton, NJ: Princeton University Press.

Talbot, M. (2001, November). The new counterculture. *Atlantic Monthly, 288*(4), 136–143.

POSTSCRIPT

Is Home Schooling a Good Idea?

Much of the philosophical basis for the home-schooling movement can be found in a deep-seeded antipathy toward compulsory "government [public] schooling." Admittedly the historical development of free public education in America does not reflect a purely altruistic commitment to the virtues of learning or to the betterment of the individual child. Rather it was the sense of early advocates such as Benjamin Franklin, Thomas Jefferson, and later Horace Mann that it was in the best interest of a stable society, and most certainly a stable democratic society to have an educated citizenry. Much of the motivation for the common school movement of the of the mid-nineteenth century came from conservative Whigs and persons of wealth who were fearful that the forces of immigration, urbanization, and industrialization, if coupled with rigid class distinctions based on restricted access to education, could lead to discontent and eventual disruption of society. The vision of demagoguery and an ignorant and angry "mob" rising against established order was not considered far-fetched. Public education was seen as working at several different levels to ensure stability. A common education for all would include citizenship training and thus promote national unity; by reducing ignorance, it would reduce the appeal of demagogues; and by allowing the common man to improve his station in life, it would give everyone a stake in maintaining a stable society.

With universal education emerging as a compelling interest of society, it was only logical that such an education would eventually be made mandatory. Beginning with Massachusetts in 1852, the notion of state-mandated compulsory education for all children spread across the nation and by 1918 all states had enacted such legislation. Although these compulsory education laws have been consistently upheld by the courts because of the compelling interest that society has in an educated citizenry, the United States Supreme Court in 1925 (*Pierce v. Society of Sisters*) did turn back an attempt in Oregon that would have compelled attendance at public schools. Thus, even though all school-age children must attend some form of schooling, it does not necessarily need to be in a public school. Approximately 12 percent of school-age children attend nonpublic schools (NCES, 2001).

Since the 1950s the concept of compulsory education has come under increasing attack, especially with respect to concerns regarding the quality of public schools. Movements to give parents greater control over the nature and the location of their child's education are manifested in school choice initiatives, vouchers, charter schools, and home schooling. Expressing a caveat regarding the privatization of education, Deborah Meier states in *The Power of Their Ideas* (Boston Beacon Press, 1995), "If we abandon a system of private schools through apathy or privatization, we deprive everyone, not just the least advantaged, of the kind of clash of ideas that will make us all more powerful. . . . Schools embody the dreams we have for our children. All of them. These dreams must remain public property."

At its core this issue is one of conflicting philosophies and values. Holt in *Escape from Childhood* (E.P. Dutton, 1974), and other home-schooling advocates such as Grace Llewellyn, *The Teenage Liberation Handbook: How to Quit School and Get a Real Education* (Lowry House, 1991), John Taylor Gatto, *Dumbing Us Down: The Hidden Curriculum of Compulsory Education* (New Society Publishers, 1992), Lillian Jones, *An Introduction to Homeschooling* (NLD on the Web, 1998), and Home School Legal Defense Association, *Parental Rights: Why Now Is the Time to Act* (March/April 2006), speak to the violation of the rights of children and parents brought about by compulsory education and especially public education. Others, though recognizing the importance of education for the individual, expand that into an exposition regarding the compelling interest to society in having an educated populace and thus present the rationale for mandatory schooling. The seminal works expressing that sentiment include Mann's writings in the *Tenth and Twelfth Annual Report* (1846, 1848), Robert M. Hutchins in *The Conflict in Education in a Democratic Society* (Harper and Row, 1953), and John Goodlad in "Education and Democracy: Advancing the Agenda" (*Phi Delta Kappan,* September 2000).

ISSUE 3

Has the Middle School Concept Failed?

YES: Cheri Pierson Yecke, from "Mayhem in the Middle: Why We Should Shift to K–8," *Educational Leadership* (April 2006)

NO: Sue Swaim, from "Strength in the Middle," *Education Week* (April 21, 2004) and National Middle School Association, from "This We Believe: Successful Schools for Young Adolescents" Position Paper (2003)

ISSUE SUMMARY

Cheri P. Yecke, chancellor of K–12 public schools for the Florida Department of Education, contends that radical advocates of the "middle school concept" turned middle schools into "havens of socialization." Sue Swaim, executive director of the National Middle School Association, suggests, "The middle school movement cannot be faulted for educational deficiencies it did not create and practices it did not recommend." In a position paper, her organization also stresses that in successful middle schools, "human relationships are paramount."

The "middle school" movement or concept developed out of the realization that the middle grade levels are crucial to the academic and social development of young adolescents. The importance of those years was underscored in a reform document developed in California in 1987. That document, entitled *Caught in the Middle* (updated in 2001 as *Taking Center Stage*), opened with the following statement:

> Middle grade students are unique. No other grade span encompasses such a wide range of intellectual, physical, psychological, and social development, and educators must be sensitive to the entire spectrum of these young people's capabilities. For many students the middle grades represent the last chance to develop a sense of academic purpose and personal commitment to educational goals. Those who fail at the middle grade level often drop out of school and may never again have the opportunity to develop to their fullest potential.

In that same document the essence of the middle school concept was articulated as, "[t]he most effective instruction at the middle school level emphasizes academic integrity while making an emotional connection with students." Those subscribing to the middle school philosophy believe that the traditional "junior high school" was just that: a "mini high school" in which many teachers, frustrated by not being at a high school, taught as if they were. Middle school advocates argued that students coming out of the nurturing environment of elementary school often found themselves without a support system in the "mini high school" environment of junior high.

The middle school concept/movement is founded on what advocates see as the dual mission of middle schools: maintaining a nurturing and supportive environment for middle grade students, while preparing them for the academic rigors of high school. That dual mission is articulated by the National Middle School Association (NMSA) in *This We Believe: Successful Schools for Young Adolescents*, in which one of the characteristics of a successful middle school is described as, "[a] successful school is an inviting, supportive, and safe place, a joyful community that promotes in-depth learning and enhances students' physical and emotional well-being. In such a school, human relationships are paramount."

It is exactly that type of statement about the mission of middle schools that rankles critics such as Cheri Yecke. She and other opponents of what they dub as "middle schoolism," assert that middle school advocacy groups such as the NMSA have, in the words of Chester E. Finn Jr., decided "that the middle grades are not a time for academic learning so much as social adjustment, individual growth, coping with early adolescence and looking out for the needs of the 'whole child.'" In his foreword to the Yecke article, Finn quotes Hayes Mizell, another critic of "middle schoolism," who states:

Too many middle school teachers continue to buy into the myth that young adolescents are so distracted by their social, emotional, physical, and psychological development that they have no interest in learning, and that there is no point in challenging them.

Obviously this dispute evokes strong feelings and strong words.

YES

Cheri Pierson Yecke

Mayhem in the Middle: Why We Should Shift to K–8

In early 2005, the National Governors Association convened an education summit to address the dismal state of U.S. high schools. Nearly one-third of students eventually drop out, which annually costs the U.S. economy an estimated $16 billion in lost productivity. Although well intended, the solutions that many governors offered at the summit misidentified the cause of "high school" problems. Abundant evidence indicates that the seeds that produce high school failure are sown in grades 5–8 (National Center for Education Statistics, 2000). In far too many cases, U.S. middle schools are where student academic achievement goes to die.

As measured by international comparisons, such as the Trends in International Mathematics and Science Study (TIMSS), the achievement of U.S. students begins to plummet in middle school. And, as countless teachers and parents will attest, contemporary middle schools have become places where discipline is often lax and intermittent. Too many educators view middle school as an environment in which little is expected of students, either academically or behaviorally, on the assumption that students must place self-discipline and high academic expectations on hold until the hormone-driven storms of early adolescence have passed.

But if surging hormones truly drive middle school students' supposed lack of capacity to focus on academics, why does this phenomenon strike only in the United States? Other countries don't experience a similar decline in achievement at these grades. Something else is driving this precipitous drop in achievement. I propose that it is the anti-intellectualism inherent to the middle school concept.

To understand, we need to differentiate between *middle schools* and the *middle school concept*. Middle schools are simply organizational groupings, generally containing grades 6, 7, and 8. The middle school concept, on the other hand, is the belief that the purpose of these schools is to create students who are imbued with egalitarian principles; who are in touch with their political, social, and psychological selves; and who eschew competition and individual achievement to focus on identity development and perceived societal needs (Gallagher, 1991; Sicola, 1990; Toepfer, 1992). Although many U.S. middle schools are flourishing with strong and rigorous academic programs, the middle

From *Educational Leadership*, April 2006, pp. 20–25. Copyright © 2006 by ASCD. Reprinted by permission. The Association for Supervision and Curriculum Development is a worldwide community of educators advocating sound policies and sharing best practices to achieve the success of each learner. To learn more, visit ASCD at www.ascd.org

school concept—the notion that middle schools should be havens of socialization and not academies of knowledge—has wrought havoc on the intellectual development of many middle school students.

As any reform-minded superintendent or courageous middle school principal may tell you, reclaiming middle-grades schools from the clutches of the middle school concept has not been an easy task. In fact, this goal has been so elusive in some districts that the only alternative has been to eliminate the middle school grade configuration altogether, returning instead to the K–8 model.

Several urban school districts, such as Baltimore, Maryland, and Philadelphia, Pennsylvania, are now abandoning both the middle school concept and middle schools. By 2008, the number of K–8 schools in Philadelphia will have increased from 61 to 130. Baltimore has opened 30 K–8 schools in the last few years. Districts like Brookline, Massachusetts, and Cincinnati, Ohio, are now exclusively K–8. The goal for these districts is the same: to increase academic achievement and create an atmosphere more conducive to learning (Chaker, 2005).

Why K–8?

Although many U.S. educators embraced the middle school concept during the 1970s, 1980s, and 1990s, some educators refused to jump on the bandwagon. As a result, parents, teachers, and administrators at many schools that remained K–8 discovered anecdotally that their students demonstrated fewer behavioral problems and higher academic achievement than many students enrolled in middle schools.

School district leaders in Milwaukee, Wisconsin, Baltimore, and Philadelphia wanted to determine whether they could verify these anecdotal observations through research. The studies they undertook convinced them to accelerate a shift to the K–8 model in their districts.

The Milwaukee Study

Researchers in Milwaukee conducted a longitudinal analysis of 924 Milwaukee students who either attended K–8 schools or attended K–6 elementary schools and then proceeded to a middle school for 7th and 8th grade (Simmons & Blyth, 1987). The study controlled for race, ethnicity, teacher-student ratios, and levels of teacher education.

The researchers found that the students in the K–8 schools had higher academic achievement as measured by both grade point averages and standardized test scores, especially in math. These students also participated more in extracurricular activities, demonstrated greater leadership skills, and were less likely to be bullied than those following the elementary/middle school track. The authors concluded that the intimacy of the K–8 environment and the delay of the transition to a new school until students were more mature may have accounted for the discrepancy.

The Baltimore Study

In Baltimore, researchers undertook a longitudinal study of two cohorts of students: 2,464 students who attended K–5 schools and then went on to middle schools, and 407 students who attended K–8 schools (Baltimore City Schools, 2001). After controlling for baseline achievement, the researchers found that the students in the K–8 schools scored much higher than their middle school counterparts on standardized achievement measures in reading, language arts, and math. The students in the K–8 schools were also more likely to pass the required state tests in math. Further, more than 70 percent of the K–8 students were admitted into Baltimore's most competitive high schools, compared with only 54 percent of students from the middle schools (Baltimore City Schools, 2001).

The Philadelphia Study

Philadelphia carried its examination of the achievement of students progressing through either K–8 or middle schools into high school to determine whether academic gains or losses from either model were sustained over time. After controlling for student background, researchers analyzed achievement data from approximately 40 K–8 schools and 40 middle schools.

The analysis showed that the students in the K–8 schools had higher academic achievement than those in the middle schools and that their academic gains surpassed those of the middle school students in reading and science, with statistically higher gains in math (Offenberg, 2001).

Eleven percent more students from the K–8 schools were accepted into the most challenging high schools. Moreover, once in high school, the grade point averages of students who had attended K–8 schools were higher than those of former middle school students. Offenberg concluded, "As a group, K–8 schools are more effective than middle-grades schools serving similar communities" (2001, p. 28).

The study noted that one factor possibly contributing to these differences is the number of students at a specific grade level. Although a K–8 school and a middle school might have the same total number of students, they are spread over more grades in the K–8 school, reducing the number of students in each grade. Offenberg's report suggests that as the number of students in a given grade increases, performance gains decrease.

Ten Strategies for Transition

I conducted site visits in all three school districts—Milwaukee, Baltimore, and Philadelphia—to see how the K–8 model was working and to gather advice for those interested in making the transition to the K–8 model. I selected one school in each district to visit on the basis of the school's ethnic diversity. The schools serve low-income urban students; each school faces its own demographic challenges. All three schools came to the K–8 model by a different route.

Humboldt Park K–8 School in Milwaukee shifted from K–5 to K–8 a few years ago. Its student population is notably diverse: Approximately 35 percent of students are Hmong, 30 percent are white, 15 percent are Hispanic, and 15 percent are black. Hamilton Elementary/Middle School in Baltimore has been a K–8 school for more than 20 years; its student body is 75 percent black. The Julia de Burgos School in Philadelphia, originally a 6–8 middle school, expanded downward to add grades K–5; its student body is 89 percent Hispanic.

In all three schools, staff and administrators were committed to meeting the needs of underprivileged students and believed that they could best accomplish this in a K–8 setting. Their advice, along with feedback from students and parents, suggests 10 strategies that can ease the transition to a K–8 model.

Strategy 1: Include parents in the process.   To ensure the success of the K–8 model, parents should participate in all aspects of the planning process. Policy decisions concerning such varied issues as curriculum, dress code, and behavioral expectations call for parental input. The most academically successful school that I visited, Humboldt Park K–8 School in Milwaukee, also has the most active and organized parents. Parents initiated the move to transition Humboldt Park into a charter school because they were concerned that district policies might undermine the school's academic program. This high level of engagement was not a reflection of higher socioeconomic status: 70 percent of students at Humboldt Park come from low-income homes.

Strategy 2: Add higher rather than lower grades.   Incrementally adding higher grades to shift an elementary school to a K–8 school appears to be a smoother process than adding lower grades to a middle school. This approach seems to minimize grade-level imbalances and necessitate fewer building modifications. Faculty members at Humboldt Park unanimously agreed that when adding grades 6, 7, and 8, schools should add only one grade each year. This gives time for students, faculty, support staff, and administration to adjust.

Strategy 3: Ensure grade-level balance.   Attaining demographic balance among the various grade levels should be a priority. Having too many older or younger students means that the needs of the dominant group can drive school policies and set the school tone. For example, one schoolwide policy limited bathroom passes because some of the middle-grades students used them to roam the halls. However, because younger students tend to use the bathroom more frequently than older students do, lower-grades teachers challenged this policy.

If transition logistics require a temporary imbalance, schools should ensure that staff members are aware of the undue weight that the overrepresented grades might bring to a school and remind them that the imbalance is only temporary.

Strategy 4: Make 6th grade a transition year.   Moving from the elementary to the upper-grades section of the school requires students to become familiar with a different location and learn rules that often give them greater freedom.

Because this change usually occurs in 6th grade, it would be helpful to provide flexibility as students make the transition.

Retaining some elements of the elementary school—such as recess, classroom learning centers, or walking in lines during classroom changes—may help 6th grade function as a bridge between the elementary and middle grades.

Strategy 5: Establish a strict transfer policy.   District officials need to acknowledge the challenges that transfer students bring to schools. Involuntary transfers are harder for schools to deal with and typically occur when the district administration decides to relocate students who have had difficulties elsewhere. Philadelphia wisely handles this issue through an alternative program that accommodates students with the most serious discipline problems. Baltimore has no such program in place, leaving staff members and faculty frustrated as they struggle to balance teaching students who do not have serious behavior problems with rehabilitating those who do.

Voluntary transfers present other challenges. Students who arrive from schools that have less structure and lower academic standards might find the transition to a challenging K–8 setting difficult. Humboldt Park addresses this issue by requiring mandatory after-school lessons to help transfer students catch up. Schools can also provide an opportunity for students to receive remediation in the summer before the school year starts. Either way, schools should establish a policy that helps transfer students adjust to the level of work required.

Strategy 6: Modify facilities.   A school transitioning into a K–8 structure may need to make certain physical modifications to adapt its facility to students of various ages. For example, elementary schools adding middle grades will need to add computers in the library and include books appropriate for middle-grades students. If the library has limited space, the school may need to create a separate computer lab. The school might also consider adding lockers for older students or building a more advanced science lab. For any newly K–8 school, the cafeteria will most likely require scheduling changes and menu revisions to adapt to an influx of older or younger students. Moreover, making the transition from a middle school to a K–8 school entails creating centers and "nooks" in primary classrooms and modifying restrooms by lowering toilets and sinks.

In addition, designating a separate building wing for the upper grades provides older students with some time on their own and reduces unsupervised interactions with younger students. Humboldt Park in Milwaukee does a good job of this. In contrast, Philadelphia's Julia de Burgos School, which of the three schools observed had the least separation among its students, reported the most challenges with interactions between older and younger students.

Strategy 7: Have high expectations for both academics and behavior.   High academic achievement rarely happens in an undisciplined environment. Of the schools I visited, Baltimore's Hamilton had the most behavior problems. This was also the only school in which student achievement declined in the upper grades. In contrast, Milwaukee's Humboldt Park had the strictest discipline policy. There, 75 percent of students leave kindergarten reading at the 2nd grade level.

Policies establishing academic and behavioral norms—such as consistent expectations regarding homework or dress code—will set the K–8 school's tone for years to come, and parents should be involved in drafting them. Behavioral expectations don't need to be uniform throughout the school. Schools should provide some flexibility for upper-grades students, giving them greater freedom and responsibility as they prepare to transition to high school. For example, most K–8 schools allow upper-grades students to change classes independently as opposed to walking in lines.

Strategy 8: Decide on the academic approach.   The schools that I visited in Baltimore and Milwaukee organize their upper-grades teachers by academic department. The teachers at Julia de Burgos School in Philadelphia initially sought that structure but now prefer the self-contained approach.

The self-contained model, in which students stay with the same teacher for the core subjects of reading, math, science, and social studies, appears to foster better teacher-student relationships and a more nurturing environment. But it also means that teachers must prepare for four subjects instead of one, and it may force them into unfamiliar fields in which they have received no specialized training. The departmentalized setting, in which each teacher is a specialist in one or more areas, is more likely to produce higher academic achievement but provides fewer opportunities to counsel and mentor students.

It is fairly well established that strong subject-area knowledge in teachers correlates with higher student achievement (Whitehurst, 2002). It is therefore unfortunate that in 2004, half of Philadelphia's middle-level teachers failed exams assessing their content knowledge (Snyder & Mezzacappa, 2004). Although colleges of education might bear some of the blame, these gaps might also reflect a shift away from academics that has characterized much of the middle school movement's troubled history.

U.S. middle-level teachers with subject-specific certificates appear to be a dying breed. In 1980, 80 percent of middle-level teachers held subject-specific certificates, but that number had dropped to 52 percent by 2000 (Clark, Petzko, Lucas, & Valentine, 2001). One study shows that during the 1999–2000 school year, alarming percentages of middle-grades teachers lacked a college major or certification in the areas in which they taught: 58 percent lacked a major or certification in English, 57 percent in science, 69 percent in math, 71 percent in history, and 93 percent in physical science (National Center for Education Statistics, 2002). Another recent study found that only 22 percent of middle school math teachers surveyed indicated that they had majored in math, and fewer than half had a teaching certificate in that subject (Loveless, 2004).

K–8 planners need to find the right balance. A truly compassionate education cannot allow the desire for a nurturing environment to trump access to a rigorous, well-taught curriculum.

Strategy 9: Provide greater access to advanced courses and electives.   Because the upper grades have fewer students, K–8 schools have difficulty offering advanced subjects—such as foreign language classes or advanced math—that can enrich a curriculum. However, schools should not deny challenging academic opportunities to their students because of their particular grade configuration. One solution is to work collaboratively with other K–8 schools in the district, or even with the local high school, to have itinerant teachers come to the school to offer such classes. This may require some flexibility in scheduling. Another option might involve distance learning.

Above all, students need access to higher levels of math. A study from the U.S. Department of Education found that the academic intensity and quality of a students high school curriculum were the most important factors in determining whether students completed a bachelor's degree (Adelman, 1999). Students cannot take rigorous courses in high school—especially advanced math courses—if they have not prepared themselves for this challenging work in their middle grades.

Strategy 10: Provide greater access to extracurricular opportunities. With a larger student body in a given age group, middle schools can offer band, choir, and sports activities to a degree that K–8 schools cannot. However, several K–8 schools working together might field a team or create a band or choir. Schools could also coordinate extracurricular activities after school for all students in grades 6, 7, and 8, regardless of whether they attend a K–8 school or a middle school.

A number of districts—even those on the cutting edge of the K–8 movement—are guilty of lumping K–8 schools with elementary schools in various administrative funding classifications. This practice often rules out funding for extracurricular activities.

Moving Forward

The K–8 model is no silver bullet for middle school reform, but it deserves consideration. In this era of flexible education options, K–8 schools and middle schools can coexist—provided that middle schools embrace standards and accountability.

C. S. Lewis once wrote,

> If you are on the wrong road, progress means doing an about-turn and walking back to the right road; and in that case, the man who turns back soonest is the most progressive man. Going back is the quickest way on. (1943)

This summarizes the key strategy for undoing the damage that the middle school concept has done to U.S. education: We must *go back* to find scientifically based research that reveals the strengths or weaknesses of specific education practices, *go back* to proven methodologies, and *go back* to parents and empathetically listen to their concerns.

The key to renewing middle-grades education in the United States is to treat it as education rather than as personal adjustment. That means having high academic standards, a coherent curriculum, effective instruction, strong leadership, results-based accountability, and sound discipline. That formula has begun to pay off in the primary grades. It can pay off in the middle grades as well.

References

Adelman, C. (1999). *Answers in the toolbox: Academic intensity, attendance patterns, and bachelor's degree attainment.* Washington, DC: U.S. Department of Education.

Baltimore City Schools, Division of Research, Evaluation, and Accountability. (2001). *An examination of K-5, 6-8 versus K-8 grade configurations.* Baltimore: Author.

Chaker, A. M. (2005, April 6). Middle school goes out of fashion. *The Wall Street Journal.*

Clark, D., Petzko, V., Lucas, S., & Valentine, J. (2001, Nov. 1). *Research findings from the 2000 National Study of Leadership in Middle Level Schools.* Paper presented at the National Middle School Association annual conference, Washington, DC.

Gallagher, J. J. (1991). Education reform, values, and gifted students. *Gifted Child Quarterly, 35*(1).

Lewis, C. S. (2001). *Mere Christianity* (Book One, Chapter Five) (Rev. ed.). New York: HarperCollins.

Loveless, T. (2004, November). *The 2004 Brown Center Report on American Education: How well are American students learning?* Washington, DC: The Brookings Institution.

National Center for Education Statistics. (2000). *Mathematics and science education in the eighth grade: Findings from the Third International Mathematics and Science Study.* Washington, DC: Author.

National Center for Education Statistics. (2002). *Qualifications of the public school teacher workforce: Prevalence of out-of-field teaching 1987-88 to 1999-2000.* Washington, DC: Author.

Offenberg, R. M. (2001). The efficacy of Philadelphia's K-to-8 schools compared to middle grades schools. *Middle School Journal, 32*(4), 23-29.

Sicola, P. K. (1990). Where do gifted students fit? *Journal for the Education of the Gifted, 14*(1).

Simmons, R., & Blyth, D. (1987). *Moving into adolescence: The impact of pubertal change and school context.* New York: Aldine de Gruyter.

Snyder, S., & Mezzacappa, D. (2004, March 23). Teachers come up short in testing. *Philadelphia Inquirer.*

Toepfer, C. F. (1992). Middle level school curriculum: Defining the elusive. In J. L. Irvin (Ed.), *Transforming middle-level education; Perspectives and possibilities.* Needham Heights, MA: Allyn and Bacon.

Whitehurst, G. J. (2002, March 5). *Research on teacher preparation and professional development.* Speech presented at the White House Conference on Preparing Tomorrow's Teachers. . . .

Sue Swaim

NO

Strength in the Middle

Advocating for middle-grades education makes me sometimes feel like the young adolescents we serve: excited by the possibilities of growth and maturity, yet perplexed by other people's frequent criticisms and cautions.

A few recent examples:

In her book *The War Against Excellence: The Rising Tide of Mediocrity in America's Middle Schools,* Cheri Pierson Yecke asserts that middle-level educators, through "forced" implementation of cooperative learning, peer tutoring, and heterogeneous grouping, are endangering the education of all middle school students, especially those who are gifted. Responding to a book of this nature, which relies on inflammatory language and distorted evidence to make its case, is difficult, to say the least. That Ms. Yecke's book was released while she serves as Minnesota's commissioner of education is even more disturbing. (A full response to the book is available at. . . .)

The RAND Corp., in early March, released "Focus on the Wonder Years: Challenges Facing the American Middle School," a much more balanced report, but one that also relies on limited research and logical fallacies to suggest, among other things, that middle schools be replaced by K–8 schools to eliminate the transitions young adolescents experience as they advance through grade levels.

Ensuring smooth transitions for students is an important responsibility, and effective middle-level educators pay careful attention to the tensions young adolescents may experience in the midst of change. But school structure is not, in and of itself, the answer. Students face unsettling transitions in any school environment, whether moving to a new wing of a K–12 school building or leaving an elementary school classroom where they learned all of their core subjects from one teacher. The key is taking proactive steps to nurture and guide young adolescents as they mature, which is one of the fundamental principles of the middle school movement.

Yet, rather than address the conditions that can cause problems in middle schools—large class sizes, an overcrowded curriculum, inconsistent professional development for teachers, and more—districts have adopted a strange amalgam of grade configurations for students ages 10 to 15. For example, New York City, the nation's largest school system, has announced plans to eliminate up to two-thirds of its middle schools and replace them with both K–8 grade schools and high schools serving students in grades 6–12. In the Kansas City area, overcrowding and tight budgets have caused districts to try a wide range of grade-level structures, such as 6th grade centers, 9th grade centers, and combined middle school/junior high centers.

Many of these efforts may be guided by good intentions, but their emphasis is misdirected. Why do education leaders look at grade configuration as the first step to school improvement? There is no definitive research available that says one grade configuration is preferable to another. Corporate America understands that reorganization without regard to processes, personnel, and resource allocation simply shuffles problems into new patterns. The same is true for education. Focusing our inquiry solely on grade configuration ignores the more important issues in middle-level schools: the need for challenging and relevant curriculum, instruction, and assessment in every classroom; ongoing, job-embedded professional development for all teachers; positive relationships with adult advocates for all students; and strong, two-way communication between families and educators.

Even though we have made great strides in improving the conditions for learning in middle schools, I know that much work remains. But let's be clear about what the scope of that work should include.

The reality is that bearing the title "middle school" and enrolling students in grades 5–8 or 6–8 has never meant that an education community is implementing all the recommended middle school practices. In fact, nationwide, many middle schools took the name while only adopting selected middle school practices, rather than focusing on their full integration. Despite our best efforts, most have not embraced the entire range of recommendations that research has shown to be effective in raising academic achievement.

The middle school movement cannot be faulted for educational deficiencies it did not create and practices it did not recommend. Critics should instead be helping us ensure that all middle-level schools use proven methods of addressing the intellectual, emotional, and social needs of young adolescents. The framework for effective middle schools is delineated in "This We Believe: Successful Schools for Young Adolescents," the 2003 edition of the NMSA's position paper, and "Turning Points 2000: Educating Adolescents in the 21st Century," Anthony W. Jackson and Gayle A. Davis' update of the Carnegie Corporation's landmark report on middle-grades education.

Middle-level schools also must have highly skilled teachers and administrators who understand the characteristics unique to young adolescents. As the RAND study correctly notes, many middle school teachers and principals do not have sufficient knowledge of the developmental stages of young adolescents. Some lack strong backgrounds in the subjects they are expected to teach and the collaborative practices they are supposed to use, a deficiency not surprising, given that most have little time in their daily schedules to plan interdisciplinary lessons, sharpen their skills, or work with team members. In a recent study of 8,300 middle-grades teachers in four states, University of Illinois researchers Nancy Flowers and Steven Mertens found that the frequency and depth of most professional development falls "well short of meeting [these teachers'] needs."

And as the NMSA has pointed out, most teachers who work with young adolescents do not have specific middle-level certification or licensure.

While the RAND report calls for extensive professional development for current educators, it misses a major opportunity by not calling for middle-level licensure in every state and the aggressive expansion of middle-level preservice teacher education programs. Specific-to-the-field preservice education, licensure, and ongoing professional development is the combination needed to address both the short-term and long-term needs of middle-level educators.

Why do critics blame the middle school movement for these gaps? Middle school advocates have worked for more than 30 years to improve the professional development of teachers and principals who work with young adolescents. Two of the 14 characteristics of a successful middle school are: "high expectations for every member of the learning community" and "educators who value working with this age group and are prepared to do so." The truth is that policies from federal, state, and local government create the conditions that impair teachers' effectiveness. Some of these include cutting funds and restricting opportunities for ongoing professional development, cramming 1,000-plus students into middle schools without supporting the implementation of personalized small learning communities, and hiring teachers based on the flexibility of their state certifications instead of their knowledge of young adolescents.

We need to persuade voters, elected officials, and other policymakers that helping teachers refine their skills throughout the year should be a valued—and fully funded—part of each school's improvement plan. No other expenditure will do more to raise student achievement. And we should be championing the need for specific, middle-level credentialing for new teachers in the field. Since we expect it for every other level of education, why not for this critical phase?

We also must insist that professional development not be restricted to the one or two designated days during the year many districts offer. The National Staff Development Council recommends that school districts dedicate at least 10 percent of their budgets—excluding salaries and benefits—to professional development, and that they devote at least 25 percent of a teacher's work time to learning and collaborating with colleagues. We concur.

Moreover, we think that all middle-grades teachers, both new and experienced, must have access to professional development with a balanced approach that includes both deep understanding of their content areas and sound instructional methods for young adolescent students. They also need a wide range of professional-development options: attending workshops, observing master teachers in their classrooms, receiving on-the-job coaching from specialists, participating in online tutorials and other technology-based study sessions, and more.

Education in the middle grades will improve only when everyone involved is held accountable. This means not letting politicians off the hook when they champion education in their campaigns but fail to fully fund school programs once they get into office. It means not forgetting the important contributions parents must make by sending their children to school ready to learn. And it means not becoming distracted by those whose primary objective is to divide, not unite, the efforts under way to strengthen this crucial level of schooling and make middle schools the pride of American education.

~⊙~

This We Believe: Successful Schools for Young Adolescents

National Middle School Association

Every day, twenty million diverse, rapidly changing 10- to 15-year-olds enrolled in our nation's middle level schools are making critical and complex life choices. They are forming the attitudes, values, and habits of mind that will largely direct their behavior as adults. They deserve schools that support them fully during this key phase of life. Therefore, National Middle School Association seeks to conceptualize and promote successful middle level schools that enhance the healthy growth of young adolescents as lifelong learners, ethical and democratic citizens, and increasingly competent, self-sufficient young people who are optimistic about the future.

For middle schools to be successful, their students must be successful; for students to be successful, the school's organization, curriculum, pedagogy, and programs must be based upon the developmental readiness, needs, and interests of young adolescents. This concept is at the heart of middle level education.

The association's vision for a successful middle school is primarily delineated in 14 characteristics. Eight are facets of the culture of such schools, while six are programmatic characteristics that can evolve in such a culture. While presented as a list, the most profound and enduring lesson learned in 30 years of active middle school advocacy is that the characteristics are interdependent and must be implemented in concert. Research and cumulative, empirical evidence have confirmed that these characteristics when present over time lead to higher levels of student achievement and overall development.

National Middle School Association believes successful schools for young adolescents are characterized by a culture that includes

- **Educators who value working with this age group and are prepared to do so.** Effective middle level educators understand the developmental uniqueness of the age group, the curriculum they teach, and effective learning and assessment strategies. They need specific teacher preparation before entering the classroom and continuous professional development as they pursue their careers.

- **Courageous, collaborative leadership.** Middle level leaders understand adolescents, the society, and the theory and practice of middle level education. As the prime determiner of the school culture, the principal influences student achievement and teacher effectiveness by advocating, nurturing, and sustaining an effective instructional program.
- **A shared vision that guides decisions.** All decisions made about the school should be guided by a shared vision and the mission statement derived from it.
- **An inviting, supportive, and safe environment.** A successful school is an inviting, supportive, and safe place, a joyful community that promotes in-depth learning and enhances students' physical and emotional well-being. In such a school, human relationships are paramount.
- **High expectations for every member of the learning community.** Educators and students hold themselves and each other to high expectations. Such confidence promotes positive attitudes and behaviors and motivates students to tackle challenging learning activities. Successful schools recognize that young adolescents are capable of far more than adults often assume.
- **Students and teachers engaged in active learning.** The most successful learning strategies are ones that involve each student personally. When students routinely assume the role of teacher, and teachers demonstrate that they are still learners, a genuine learning community is present.
- **An adult advocate for every student.** Academic success and personal growth increase markedly when young adolescents' affective needs are met. All adults in successful middle level schools are advocates, advisors, and mentors.
- **School-initiated family and community partnerships.** Successful middle schools promote family involvement and take the initiative to develop needed home-school bonds. The involvement of family is linked to higher levels of student achievement and improved student behavior.

Therefore, successful schools for young adolescents provide

- **Curriculum that is relevant, challenging, integrative, and exploratory.** An effective curriculum is based on criteria of high quality and includes learning activities that create opportunities for students to pose and answer questions that are important to them. Such a curriculum provides direction for what young adolescents should know and be able to do and helps them achieve the attitudes and behaviors needed for a full, productive, and satisfying life.
- **Multiple learning and teaching approaches that respond to their diversity.** Since young adolescents learn best through engagement and interaction, learning strategies involve students in dialogue

with teachers and with one another. Teaching approaches should enhance and accommodate the diverse skills, abilities, and prior knowledge of young adolescents, and draw upon students' individual learning styles.

- **Assessment and evaluation programs that promote quality learning.** Continuous, authentic, and appropriate assessment and evaluation measures provide evidence about every student's learning progress. Grades alone are inadequate expressions for assessing the many goals of middle level education.
- **Organizational structures that support meaningful relationships and learning.** The interdisciplinary team of two to four teachers working with a common group of students is the building block for a strong learning community with its sense of family, where students and teachers know one another well, feel safe and supported, and are encouraged to take intellectual risks.
- **School-wide efforts and policies that foster health, wellness, and safety.** A school that fosters physical and psychological safety strives to build resiliency in young people by maintaining an environment in which peaceful and safe interactions are expected and supported by written policies, scheduled professional development, and student-focused activities.
- **Multifaceted guidance and support services.** Developmentally responsive middle level schools provide both teachers and specialized professionals who are readily available to offer the assistance many students need in negotiating their lives both in and out of school.

We urge every reader of this summary to secure, read, and act on the full position paper, *This We Believe: Successful Schools for Young Adolescents*, and the supporting publication *Research and Resources in Support of This We Believe*. To implement National Middle School Association's strong statement about exemplary middle level schools, actions on the part of many individuals and agencies are needed. The position paper's **Call to Action** offers specific steps people in various roles should take to revitalize middle level schools. Finally, since middle level education is grounded in the nature of young people ages 10 to 15, the position paper includes an authoritative listing of the characteristics of young adolescents. All those who interact with young adolescents, and ultimately young adolescents themselves, will benefit from these recommendations.

POSTSCRIPT

Has the Middle School Concept Failed?

The April 2006 issue of *Educational Leadership* is focused on "teaching the tweens." In the introduction to the topic, the following description of this age group was drawn from *Breaking Ranks in the Middle* (2006), a report of the National Association of Secondary School Principals (NASSP): "They [early adolescents] are five years away from their teddy bears and five years away from college." Thus, the appellation "tweens" is fitting. The NASSP report went on to describe the controversy regarding approaches to middle school education:

> A great tug-of-war has existed for 40 years about how best to address the needs of students "in the middle"—the sixth, seventh, and eighth grades. Keep them with the elementary students? Create 6–12 schools? . . . Only one right answer can be universally applied: Regardless of grade configuration, policymakers, school boards, and superintendents must stop making decisions primarily based on budgets and the transportation schedules and instead create schools based on what is best for young adolescents—schools that address the intellectual and developmental needs of each student.

It is the balance between intellectual and developmental needs that has and continues to be at the crux of this debate. As mentioned in the introductory summary to this issue, the California reform document *Caught in the Middle* (1987) endorsed the middle school philosophy and placed an emphasis on the developmental needs of young adolescents. Note the emphasis and primacy given to those developmental needs in this statement in the foreword of the document authored by then-superintendent of public education, Bill Honig:

> The first challenge for schools which enroll middle grade students is to make sure that they are "connected" to the goals and purposes of their schools in positive ways, and have an opportunity to increase their self-esteem. Young adolescents become intensively self-conscious and self-evaluative. Middle grade schools must provide students with a caring transition as they move from elementary to high school. The second challenge is to prepare students for academic success in high school.

Critics of the middle school philosophy claim that developmental needs and "self-esteem" of students were overemphasized to the detriment of academic rigor and standards. In some ways, responses to these charges can be seen in a second-generation reform document in California, *Taking Center Stage* (2001), which, though not eschewing the middle school philosophy, nevertheless placed greater emphasis on academic standards and excellence than seen in *Caught in the Middle*. Note the change in emphasis and tone in this introductory statement from the second document as compared to the first:

> Standards-based education in the middle grades is the dominant theme around which this document is organized. Many observers of the middle school movement believe that it is now possible to implement a powerful model for schooling young adolescents in the middle grades and to make the educational experience even more dynamic and effective. A passion on the part of teachers, principals, and parents for academic excellence as well as a deep commitment to opportunities for engaging young adolescents during their formative stages of development will count most in preparing them for successful productive citizenship in the new millennium.

One of the more valuable things to emerge from this debate is the recognition of not only the uniqueness of early adolescence but also an awareness of its pivotal role in the future of these young people. Other resources dealing with this topic include journals such as *Middle School Journal, Middle Ground,* and materials from the Center for Collaborative Education and the Fordham Foundation.

ISSUE 4

Should Religious Content and Concepts Be More Evident in Our Schools?

YES: Michael W. McConnell, from "Testimony before the Subcommittee on the Constitution, Committee on the Judiciary" (June 8, 1995)

NO: Annie Laurie Gaylor, from "The Case against School Prayer," *A Brochure of the Freedom from Religion Foundation* (1995)

ISSUE SUMMARY

YES: Michael W. McConnell, Judge on the 10th U.S. Circuit Court of Appeals, argues that "[M]any parents have come to believe that the First Amendment is stacked against them" with respect to their desire to see more religion in the schools.

NO: Annie Laurie Gaylor, editor of the anthology *Women without Superstition: No God, No Master,* states that "Public schools exist to educate, not to proselytize."

There is perhaps no educational issue that generates as much emotion and disagreement as allowing religious practices and beliefs into our public schools. Public school authorities often find themselves in the middle of highly contentious and volatile arguments with one side asserting the absolute imperative of bringing religious perspectives and practices such as prayer into the schools in order to imbue our young people with a sense of morality; the other side is equally adamant about the fundamental need to maintain a strict separation between church and state-controlled public schools.

Each side claims that our history supports their views. Advocates of increasing the role of religion in our schools can point to the origins of schooling in America, which were directly tied to the purposes and promulgations of church and religion. Indeed, the 1647 enactment in colonial Massachusetts of the Old Deluder Satan Act, which is generally accepted as the first legislative mandate for the creation and public support of schools and schooling, found its fundamental purpose in *"It being one chief object of*

that Old Deluder, Satan, to keep men from the knowledge of the scriptures, . . .
it is therefore ordered, . . . that every township, . . . shall appoint one within their
town to teach all children as shall resort to him to read and write."

Opponents of religious involvement in public schools find their mantra
in the First Amendment of the U.S. Constitution (made applicable to the
States by the Fourteenth Amendment), which establishes that the *Congress*
shall make no law respecting an establishment of religion, or prohibiting the free
exercise thereof. . . . Thomas Jefferson is credited with creating the phrase most
often invoked in discussions of that part of the amendment when he wrote of
"building a wall of separation between Church and State."

These arguments go beyond school prayer and include issues such as
the teaching of evolution versus creationism, the posting of the Ten Commandments in classrooms, and Christmas decorations and displays in the
schools. Also the school choice and voucher movements are impacted by this
controversy. Advocates of choice and vouchers argue that by supporting
those concepts, we will enable more students to benefit from religious
instruction and values and thus improve society. Opponents assert that
choice and vouchers are merely not-so-subtle attempts to circumvent the
strictures against state support of religion and religious schooling.

A recent development that broadens the range of this controversial
issue to include the public university level is the U.S. Supreme Court's decision (April 2004) to not review a 4th Circuit Court of Appeals decision in
Bunting v. Mellen (2003) that declared that the traditional recitation of grace
before the evening meal at the Virginia Military Institute (a public institution) violated the First Amendment's ban on an "establishment of religion"
and thus was unconstitutional. The arguments in this case are summarized by
statements issued from two opposing advocacy groups: the Americans United
for Separation of Church and State and the American Center for Law and Justice. The Americans United for Separation of Church and State applauded the
decision thusly, "The Constitution does not allow public schools to pressure
students to pray, and this action is reaffirmation of that important principle."
The American Center for Law and Justice countered with, "It is disappointing
to see the court let stand a decision that bars voluntary prayer at dinner—
a respected and time-honored tradition at a military institution that has
played a vital role in training military leaders for more than 160 years."

The articles that follow summarize many of the arguments pro and
con regarding this issue. The Michael McConnell material stresses that bans
on religion in the schools go far beyond what true government neutrality on
religious issues mandates, while the article by Annie Laurie Gaylor takes the
position that mixing public schools and church issues is counterproductive
to preserving and promoting freedom of religion and invariably will lead to
persecution of some children.

YES ⤶

Testimony of Michael W. McConnell

Causes of the Present Discontent

By any realist standard of comparison, religious liberty in the United States is in excellent shape. There is no official state religion, Americans are free to practice their faith, for the most part, without fear or hindrance, with a diversity and freedom that does not exist anywhere else in the world.

But for many Americans, especially those in public schools and other parts of the government-controlled sector, religious liberty is not all it should be, or all that our Constitution promises. All too often, religious Americans, young and old, are finding that their viewpoints and speech are curtailed because of its religious character. In the past few decades, there has been an extraordinary secularization of American public life, especially in the schools. Religious and traditionalist parents are finding that their viewpoints and concerns are ruled out-of-order, while at the same time the schools can be used to promote ideas and values that are sometimes offensive and hostile to their own.

Tolerance and diversity, it often seems, are one-way streets. There is scrupulous concern lest any child (and increasingly, any adult) be exposed to unwanted religious influence, but little or no concern for the religious or traditionalist child (or adult) who objects to the far-more-prevalent proselytizing that is carried on under the banner of various progressive causes. To object to foul language, relativistic values education, or inappropriate sex education is to risk being branded as a censor. To object to a moment of silence at the beginning of the classroom day, or to the singing of the Hallelujah Chorus, makes one a champion of civil liberty. Students who circulate scurrilous underground newspapers or who interrupt the school day with political causes receive the full protection of the First Amendment; but students who circulate Bible verses or try to meet with their friends for prayer or Bible study are often silenced. In reported cases in state and federal court . . ., valedictory speeches have been censored, student research topics have been selectively curtailed, distribution of leaflets has been limited on the basis of religious content, and public employees have been forced to hide their Bibles. All too often, the freedom of religion protected by the First Amendment has been twisted into a one-sided freedom religion. . . .

In the decades preceding World War II, the dominant Protestant majority in this country not infrequently ran roughshod over the rights of

U.S. House of Representatives. Committee on the Judiciary, Subcommittee on the Constitution. Religious Liberty and the Bill of Rights. Testimony, June 8, 1995. Washington, DC: U.S. Government Printing Office, 1995.

others: Catholics, Jews, and other non-Christians alike. Public schools were the vehicle for transmission of majority values, which were heavily imbued with a Protestant orientation. Aid to non-public schools was opposed because such schools were generally Roman Catholic. Prayer, Bible reading, and the celebration of holidays was often conducted without regard to the coercive impact on children of other faiths. Much of the Religion Clause jurisprudence of the past 40 years has been a response to this. And properly so. I cannot read accounts by those who grew up in the era of Protestant hegemony without a keen appreciation for the injustice and casual cruelty of the system.

But—largely under the prodding of courts with little understanding or appreciation for the place of religion in the lives of ordinary Americans—we adopted the wrong solution to this very real problem. We should have opened up the government sector to a wider range of voices, promoted diversity and choice in education, sought pluralistic approaches to public activities with a cultural and religious aspect, and reduced the ability of those with power over public institutions to monopolize channels of education and influence. Instead, we preserved the structures by which Protestant Christians had dominated the public culture, and only changed the content. Secular ideologies came into a position of cultural dominance. The tables were turned. The winners and losers changed places. But the basic injustice—the use of government authority, over education and elsewhere, to favor and promote the values and ideals of one segment of the community—continued unabated.

Some have responded with a call to cultural warfare: if one worldview or another is to be in the ascendancy, let it be ours. Hence the persistent calls for return to a "Christian America." I think there is a better way. The solution is to insist, in a rigorous and principled way, on the rights of all Americans, without regard to faith and ideology, to participate in public life on an equal basis. No more double standard. When speech reflecting a secular viewpoint is permitted, then speech reflecting a religious viewpoint should be permitted, on the same basis. And vice versa. When the government provides benefits to private activities—be it charitable endeavor, health care, education, or art—there should be no discrimination or exclusion on the basis of religious expression, character, or motivation. Religious citizens should not be required to engage in self-censorship as a precondition to participation in public programs. Public programs should be open to all who satisfy the objective purposes of the program. This is already the rule for controversial secular ideas and viewpoints; it should be the rule for religious ideas and viewpoints as well.

The beginning of wisdom in this contentious area of law is to recognize that neutrality and secularism are not the same thing. In the marketplace of ideas, secular viewpoints and ideologies are in competition with religious viewpoints and ideologies. It is no more neutral to favor the secular over the religious than it is to favor the religious over the secular. It is time for a reorientation of constitutional law [and move] from the false neutrality of the secular state, toward a genuine equality of rights.

This will require a great deal of forebearance, for toleration of the expression of others does not come easily. But toleration must be even-handed. I am hard pressed to understand why traditionalist citizens should be expected to tolerate the use of their tax dollars for lewd and sacreligious art, while others go to court to ban nativity scenes from public property at Christmas. The proper task of the Establishment Clause of the First Amendment is to ensure that no religion is given a privileged status in American public life—indeed, that religion in general is not given a privileged status. There is no basis in the history or purpose of the Establishment Clause for the secularization of society, or for discriminating against religious voices in the public sphere. As Justice William J. Brennan, Jr., wrote in *McDaniel v. Paty,* 435 U.S. 618, 641 (1978), "Religionists no less than member of any other group enjoy the full measure of protection afforded speech, association, and political activity generally. The Establishment Clause . . . may not be used as a sword to justify repression of religion or its adherents from any aspect of public life." . . .

Why Not School Prayer?

. . . The great problem is not that public officials are failing to sponsor prayers, but that—in a well-meaning but mistaken commitment to what they think is a constitutional ideal of a secular public sphere—teachers, principals, school boards, and other public officials often engage in discrimination against religious expression. . . .

Some of this anti-religious discrimination is blatantly unconstitutional; some of it has been upheld under current constitutional doctrine; all of it thrives on the uncertainty and confusion of Supreme Court decisions over the past 40 years. And however problematic Supreme Court decisions have been, the effect "in the trenches" has been much, much worse. Among lower courts and governmental administrators, the nuance and confusion of Supreme Court rulings tends to be resolved by a wooden application of the three part test of *Lemon v. Kurtzman,* 403 U.S. 602, 612–13 (1971), and a reflexive invalidation of anything that might be thought to "advance" religion or "entangle" religion and government—no matter how neutral, voluntary, or fair that religious participation might be.

Interpretation of the Establishment Clause of the First Amendment during the past 40 years has wavered between two fundamentally inconsistent visions of the relation between religion and government. Under one vision, which has gone under the rubric of the "no aid" view or the "strict separation" view, there is a high and impregnable wall of separation between government and religion. Religion is permitted—indeed it is constitutionally protected—as long as it is confined to the private sphere of home, family, church, and synagogue. But the public sphere must be strictly secular. Laws must be based on strictly secular premises, public education must be strictly secular, public programs must be administered in a strictly secular manner, and public monies must be channeled only to strictly secular activities. This vision is reflected in the lemon test, which states that all law must have a "secular purpose"; that governmental action may not "advance" religion; and that religion and government must not become excessively entangled." . . .

Under the separationist view, the various parts of the First Amendment are at war with one another. The Free Exercise Clause forbids the government from inflicting penalties for the practice of religion. As the Court stated in *Sherbert v. Verner*, 374 U.S. 398, 404 (1963), "the liberties of religion and expression may be infringed by the denial of or placing of conditions upon a benefit or privilege," just as they may by the imposition of a "fine" for the exercise of religion. But the Establishment Clause (under the separationist interpretation) requires the government to withhold otherwise available benefits if the beneficiaries would use it for a religious activity. . . .

When different parts of the same constitutional amendment are in conflict, the results inevitably will be confusing, inconsistent, and unpredictable. . . . Worse yet, in the hands of school administrators, local officials, and lower courts, the effect is all too often to deny religious citizens benefits to which they would otherwise be entitled. In the public schools in particular, this means that religious references in the curriculum have been comprehensively eliminated and religious students forced to shed their constitutional rights at the schoolhouse gate—all the while advocates of various "progressive" ideologies are free to use the schools to advance their ideas of public morality, even when it means running roughshod over the desires and convictions of religious and traditionalist parents. It is no wonder that many parents have come to believe that the First Amendment is stacked against them. . . .

Denial of Benefits on Account of Religion

. . . [N]o discussion of problems in this area would be complete without reference to the Supreme Court's disgraceful record with regard to educational choice. Much of the problematic precedent in this area arose in the context of state efforts to provide some assistance to parents who choose to educate their children under religious auspices. The Supreme Court, in a series of decisions beginning with *Lemon v. Kurtzman,* has made these efforts virtually impossible. The most egregious decision, in my opinion, was *Aquilar v. Felton,* 473 U.S. 402 (1985), in which the Court struck down those portions of the Elementary and Secondary Education Act that provided remedial English and math training by public school teachers to educationally and economically disadvantaged students on the premises of their schools, both public and private. The effect has been to deny less affluent parents the practical ability to exercise choice in education, as is their constitutional right, and to deny to urban school districts the more practicable way to provide remedial services to some of their neediest children. This makes no sense, either pedagogically or constitutionally. In a pluralistic nation, the parents—not the voting majority—should determine the content of their children's education, and they should not be penalized for it. Diversity and choice are far more consistent with the purposes of the First Amendment than the present system.

Even today, when most expert observers believe the Supreme Court would uphold a well-drafted, genuinely neutral educational choice plan, the lower courts continue to rule to the contrary. A recent example is *Miller v. Benson,* 878 F. Supp. 1209 (E.D.Wis.), in which the federal district court ruled that the

State of Wisconsin may not extend its private school choice plan to so-called sectarian schools. In Milwaukee, a student qualifying for the program can attend the private school of his choice, including progressive schools, Afrocentric schools, or other schools reflecting the philosophical orientation of the parents, teachers, and administration. But he cannot attend a school where the philosophical orientation is religious. This obviously excludes a large number of the schools parents would like to choose in Milwaukee, and which deliver an excellent education where the public schools have failed. . . .

Is Congressional Action Appropriate?

. . . I agree with those who say that the First Amendment does not require improvement. But it is plain that the interpretation of the First Amendment by the courts does require improvement. This could come about in one of three ways. First, we could hope that the courts will correct their ways. This is always possible, but the record of inconsistent interpretations of the Establishment Clause for the past 40 years does not give much ground for optimism that the Court will adopt a clear position and stick to it. Second, Congress could pass a statute, modelled after the Equal Access Act or the Religious Freedom Restoration Act. This could well be an effective strategy. But since much of the problem here is caused by an exaggerated and distorted interpretation of the Establishment Clause, it is far from obvious that such a statute would be enforceable. Where the problem is constitutional in nature, a constitutional solution may be required. Third, Congress could propose a constitutional amendment, embodying the fundamental principle of religious equality. Although it is to be expected that some separationist groups would fight such an effort with great vigor, the principle of religious equality will no doubt strike a chord with the American public as reflecting a fair and workable approach to church-state problems. If adopted, it would guarantee that religious expression is given equal treatment in public forums and that religious activities are given equal access to public benefits, without giving religion in general (or any specific religion) an advantage. It would thus contribute to religious liberty while guaranteeing to all Americans, secular as well as religious, an equal liberty. Unlike separationist and secularist interpretations of the First Amendment, it would stand for neutrality.

Even if not ultimately adopted, public deliberation over such a proposal would bring these important questions to the forefront, and—like the proposed Child Labor Amendment and Equal Rights Amendments in the past—might well be a stimulus for reform that would make ultimate ratification unnecessary. Because of a lack of interest among the press and the often arcane language of legal decisions, the public has not been made aware of the extent to which our constitutional freedom of religion has been transformed into a freedom from religion. Public discussion of these issues would in itself be a positive development. Much of the problem has occurred because religious discrimination has been cloaked in language of "the separation between church and state" and other legal formulas that disguise what really is going on. It is time to bring these issues out into the open.

Annie Laurie Gaylor

 **NO**

The Case against School Prayer

"I pledge allegiance to the flag of the United States of America, and to the republic for which it stands, one nation indivisible, with liberty and justice for all."

—The "godless" Pledge of Allegiance, as it was recited by generations of school children, before Congress inserted a religious phrase, "under God," in 1954.

Keep the Church and State Forever Separate

Should Students Pray in Public Schools?

Public schools exist to educate, not to proselytize. Children in public schools are a captive audience. Making prayer an official part of the school day is coercive and invasive. What 5, 8, or 10-year-old could view prayers recited as part of class routine as "voluntary"? Religion is private, and schools are public, so it is appropriate that the two should not mix. To introduce religion in our public schools builds walls between children who may not have been aware of religious differences before.

Why Should Schools Be Neutral?

Our public schools are for *all* children, whether Catholic, Baptist, Quaker, atheist, Buddhist, Jewish, agnostic. The schools are supported by *all* taxpayers, and therefore should be free of religious observances and coercion. It is the sacred duty of parents and churches to instill religious beliefs, free from government dictation. Institutionalizing prayers in public schools usurps the rights of parents.

School prayer proponents mistake government *neutrality* toward religion as *hostility*. The record shows that religious beliefs have flourished in this country not in spite of but because of the constitutional separation of church and state.

What Happens When Worship Enters Public Schools?

When religion has invaded our public school system, it has singled out the lone Jewish student, the class Unitarian or agnostic, the children in the minority. Families who protest state/church violations in our public schools invariably experience persecution. It was commonplace prior to the court decision against school prayer to put non-religious or nonorthodox children in places of detention during bible-reading or prayer recitation. The children of Supreme Court plaintiffs against religion in schools, such as Vashti McCollum, Ed Schempp and Ishmael Jaffree, were beaten up on the way to and from school, their families subjected to community harassment and death threats for speaking out in defense of a constitutional principle. We know from history how harmful and destructive religion is in our public schools. In those school districts that do not abide by the law, school children continue to be persecuted today.

Can't Students Pray in Public Schools Now?

Individual, silent, personal prayer never has and never could be outlawed in public schools. The courts have declared *government-fostered* prayers unconstitutional—those led, required, sanctioned, scheduled or suggested by officials.

It is dishonest to call any prayer "voluntary" that is encouraged or required by a public official or legislature. By definition, if the government suggests that students pray, whether by penning the prayer, asking them to vote whether to pray or setting aside time to pray, it is endorsing and promoting that prayer. It is coercive for schools to schedule worship as an official part of the school day, school sports or activities, or to use prayer to formalize graduation ceremonies. Such prayers are more "mandatory" than "voluntary."

What's Wrong with a "Voluntary" Prayer Amendment?

Proponents of so-called "voluntary" school prayer amendment (such as the one proposed in 1995) are admitting that our secular Constitution prohibits organized prayers in public schools. Otherwise, why would an amendment to our U.S. Constitution be required? The nation must ask whether politically motivated Newt Gingrich & Co. are wiser than James Madison, principal author of the Constitution, and the other founders who engineered the world's oldest and most successful constitution!

The radical school prayer amendment would negate the First Amendment's guarantee against government establishment of religion. Most distressing, it would be at the expense of the civil rights of children, America's most vulnerable class. It would attack the heart of the Bill of Rights, which safeguards the rights of the individual from the tyranny of the majority.

What Would the Prayer Amendment Permit?

The text of the proposed federal amendment (as of January, 1995) reads:

> "Nothing in this Constitution shall be construed to prohibit individual or group prayer in public schools or other public institutions. No person shall be required by the United States or by any State to participate in prayer. Neither the United States or any State shall compose the words of any prayer to be said in public schools."

Since the right to "individual prayer" already exists, the real motive is to instill "group prayer."

No wording in this amendment would prevent the government from *selecting* the prayer, or the particular version of the bible it should be taken from. Nothing restricts prayers to "nondenominational" or "nonsectarian" (not that such a restriction would make it acceptable). Nothing would prevent a school from selecting the Lord's Prayer or other prayers to Jesus, and blasting it over the intercom. For that matter, nothing would prevent the school from sponsoring prayers to Allah or Zoroaster. Nothing would prevent principals, teachers or clergy from leading the students. Nothing would prevent nonparticipating students from being singled out. The proposal also seeks to institutionalize group prayer in other public settings, presumably public-supported senior centers, courthouses, etc.

School prayer supporters envision organized, vocal, group recitations of prayer, daily classroom displays of belief in a deity or religion, dictated by the majority. Those in the minority would be compelled to conform to a religion or ritual in which they disbelieve, to suffer the humiliation and imposition of submitting to a daily religious exercise against their will, or be singled out by orthodox classmates and teachers as "heretics" or "sinners" for not participating.

Haven't Public Schools Always Had Prayer?

At the time the U.S. Supreme Court issued its 1962 and 1963 decrees against school-sponsored prayers and bible-reading, it is estimated religious observances were unknown in about half of the nation's public schools.

Horace Mann, the father of our public school system, championed the elimination of sectarianism from American schools, largely accomplished by the 1840's. Bible reading, prayers or hymns in public schools were absent from most public schools by the end of the 19th century, after Catholic or minority-religion immigrants objected to Protestant bias in public schools.

Until the 20th century, only Massachusetts required bible-reading in the schools, in a statute passed by the virulently anti-Catholic Know Nothing Party in the 1850's. Only after 1913 did eleven other states make prayers or bible-reading compulsory. A number of other states outlawed such practices by judicial or administrative decree, and half a dozen state supreme courts overruled devotionals in public schools.

As early as the 1850's, the Superintendent of Schools of New York State ordered that prayers could no longer be required as part of public school activities. The Cincinnati Board of Education resolved in 1869 that "religious instruction and the reading of religious books, including the Holy Bible, was prohibited in the common schools of Cincinnati."

Presidents Ulysses S. Grant and Theodore Roosevelt spoke up for what Roosevelt called "absolutely nonsectarian public schools." Roosevelt added that it is "not our business to have the Protestant Bible or the Catholic Vulgate or the Talmud read in these schools."

For nearly half a century, the United States Supreme Court, consistent with this nation's history of secular schools, has ruled against religious indoctrination through schools (*McCollum v. Board of Education,* 1948), prayers and devotionals in public schools (*Engel v. Vitale,* 1962) and prayers and bible-reading (*Abington School District v. Schempp,* 1963), right up through the 1992 *Weisman* decision against prayers at public school commencements.

How Can Prayer Be Harmful?

Contrary to right-wing claims, piety is not synonymous with virtue. People should be judged by their actions, not by what religion they believe in or how publicly or loudly they pray.

Some Americans believe in the power of prayer; others believe nothing fails like prayer. Some citizens say prayer makes them feel better, but others contend that prayer is counterproductive to personal responsibility. Such a diversity of views is constitutionally protected; our secular government simply is not permitted to pick a side in religious debates.

"The hands that help are better far than lips that pray," wrote Robert G. Ingersoll. Who could disagree?

Should Government Become "Prayer Police"?

How ironic that those campaigning on an anti-Big Government theme, who contend that government should get out of our private lives, would seek to tell our children who to pray to in our public schools! As many editorials across the country have pointed out, the school prayer debate seems calculated to deflect attention away from the more pressing economic questions facing our nation. As one conservative governor put it: "If we don't deal with the economic issues, we'll need more than prayer to solve our problems."

Can't Moral Decline Be Traced to the Prayer Decisions?

Some politicans like to blame everything bad in America upon the absence of school prayer. Get real! Entire generations of Americans have grown up to be law-abiding citizens without ever once reciting a prayer in school! If prayer is the answer, why are our jails and prisons bulging with born-agains! Japan, where no one prays at school, has the lowest crime rate of any developed nation.

Institutionalizing school prayer cannot raise the SAT scores (only more studying and less praying can do that). It is irrational to charge that the complicated sociological problems facing our everchanging population stem from a lack of prayer in schools.

One might just as well credit the lack of prayer with the great advances that have taken place since the 1962 and 1963 decisions on prayer. Look at the leap in civil liberties, equality, environmental awareness, women's rights, science, technology and medicine! The polio scare is over. Fountains, buses, schools are no longer segregated by law. We've made great strides in medical treatment. We have VCRs and the computer chip. The Cold War has ended! Who would turn the clock back?

What about the Rights of the Majority?

Our political system is a democratic republic in which we use majority vote to elect certain officials or pass referenda. But we do not use majority vote to decide what religion, if any, our neighbors must observe! The "majority" is free to worship at home, at tax-exempt churches, on the way to and from school, or privately in school. There are 16 school-less hours a day when children can pray, not to mention weekends.

Many in the "majority" do not support school prayers. And if the majority religion gets to choose which prayers are said in schools, that would mean a lot of Protestant kids will be reciting Catholic prayers! The Roman Catholic Church is the single largest denomination in our country. Should Protestant minorities be excused so the classroom can pray in unison to the Virgin Mary? In a few school districts, Muslims outnumber other religions. Should Christian minorities march into the hall with their ears covered while the principal prays to Allah over the intercom?

What's Wrong with a Moment of Silence?

Given the regimentation of school children, it would make more sense to have a "moment of bedlam" than a "moment of silence"! Obviously, the impetus for "moments of silence or meditation" is to circumvent the rulings against religion in schools. The legislative history of such state laws reveals the religious motives behind the legislation, as in the Alabama law struck down by the U.S. Supreme Court in 1985 calling for a "moment of silence for meditation or prayer."

When a "moment of silence" law was enacted in Arkansas at the suggestion of then-Gov. Bill Clinton, the law mandating this meaningless ritual was later repealed following popular indifference. We know from experience that many teachers and principals would regard a "moment of silence" mandate as a green light to introduce prayers, causing more legal challenges at the expense of taxpayers.

Should Commencements Start with Prayers?

In 1992, the Court ruled in *Lee v. Weisman* that prayers at public school commencements are an impermissible establishment of religion: "The lessons of the First Amendment are as urgent in the modern world as the 18th Century when it was written. One timeless lesson is that if citizens are subjected to state-sponsored religious exercises, the State disavows its own duty to guard and respect that sphere of inviolable conscience and belief which is the mark of a free people," wrote Justice Kennedy for the majority. He dismissed as unacceptable the cruel idea that a student should forfeit her own graduation in order to be free from such an establishment of religion.

What about "Student-Initiated" Prayer?

This is a ruse proposed by extremist Christian legal groups such as the Rutherford Institute, and the American Center for Law and Justice run by televangelist

Pat Robertson. Religious coercion is even worse at the hands of another student, subjecting students to peer pressure, pitting students in the majority against students in the minority, treating them as outsiders with school complicity.

Imposing prayer-by-majority-vote is flagrant and insensitive abuse of school authority. Such schools should be teaching students about the purpose of the Bill of Rights, instead of teaching them to be religious bullies. Some principals or school boards have even made seniors hold open class votes on whether to pray at graduation, leading to hostility and reprisal against those students brave enough to stand up for the First Amendment.

"The notion that a person's constitutional rights may be subject to a majority vote is itself anathema,' wrote Judge Albert V. Bryan, Jr. in a 1993 ruling in Virginia, one of several similar district court rulings around the nation banning any prayer, whether student- or clergy-led.

We cannot put liberties protected by our Bill of Rights up to a vote of school children! Should kindergartners be forced about whether to pray before their milk and cookies? Under such reasoning, what would make it wrong for students to vote to segregate schools or otherwise violate the civil liberties of minorities?

Keep the State and Church Forever Separate

Our founders wisely adopted a secular, godless constitution, the first to derive its powers from "We, the People" and the consent of the governed, rather than claiming divine authority. They knew from the experience of religious persecution, witchhunts and religious discrimination in the Thirteen Colonies, and from the bloody history left behind in Europe, that the surest path to tyranny was to entangle church and state. That is why they adopted a secular constitution whose only references to religion are exclusionary, such as that there shall be no religious test for public office (Art. VI). There were no prayers offered at the Constitutional Convention, which shows their intent to separate religion from secular affairs.

Prayers in schools and religion in government are no panacea for social ills—they are an invitation to divisiveness. More people have been killed in the name of religion than for any other cause. As Thomas Paine pointed out, "Persecution is not an original feature in any religion; but it is always the strongly marked feature of all religions established by law."

Even Jesus Was against School Prayer

"Thou shalt not be as the hypocrites are: for they love to pray standing in the synagogues and in the corners of the streets, that they may be seen of men . . .

"But thou, when thou prayest, enter into thy closet, and when thou hast shut thy door, pray to thy Father which is in secret."

—Matt. 6:5–6

"There is no such source and cause of strife, quarrel, fights, malignant opposition, persecution, and war, and all evil in the state, as religion. Let it once enter our civil affairs, our government would soon be destroyed. Let it once enter our common schools, they would be destroyed."

—Supreme Court of Wisconsin, Weiss v. District Board
March 18, 1890

"Leave the matter of religion to the family altar, the church, and the private school, supported entirely by private contributions. Keep the church and state forever separate."

—Ulysses S. Grant
"The President's Speech at Des Moines" (1875)

"Congress shall make no law respecting an establishment of religion, or prohibiting the free exercise thereof."

—First Amendment, Bill of Rights, U.S. Constitution

Thomas Jefferson, author of the sweeping Virginia Statute of Religious Freedom, stating that no citizen "shall be compelled to frequent or support any religious worship, place, or ministry whatsoever . . ." and that to "compel a man to furnish contributions of money for the propagation of [religious] opinions which he disbelieves is sinful and tyrannical."

"I contemplate with sovereign reverence that act of the whole American people which declared that their legislature should make no law 'respecting an establishment of religion, or prohibiting the free exercise thereof,' thus building a wall of separation between church and state."

—President Thomas Jefferson
1802 letter to the Baptists of Danbury, Connecticut

Supreme Court Cases Opposing Religious Worship in Schools

- *McCollum v. Board of Education,* 333 U.S. 203, 212 (1948). Struck down religious instruction in public schools. The case involved school-sponsored religious instruction in which the sole nonreligious student, Jim McCollum, was placed in detention and persecuted by schoolmates in Champaign, Illinois.
- *Tudor v. Board of Education of Rutherford,* 14 J.N. 31 (1953), cert. denied 348 U.S. 816 (1954). Let stand a lower court ruling that the practice of allowing volunteers to distribute Gideon Bibles at public school was unconstitutional.
- *Engel v. Vitale,* 370 U.S. 421 (1962). Declared prayers in public school unconstitutional.

- *Abington Township School District v. Schempp,* 374. U.S. 203 (1963). Declared unconstitutional devotional Bible reading and recitation of the Lord's Prayer in public schools.
- *Epperson v. Arkansas,* 393 U.S., 97, 104 (1968). Struck down state law forbidding schools to teach the science of evolution.
- *Stone v. Graham,* 449 U.S. 39 (1980). Declared unconstitutional the posting of the Ten Commandments in classrooms.
- *Wallace v. Jaffree,* 472 U.S. 38, 72 (1985). Overturned law requiring daily "period of silence not to exceed one minute . . . for meditation or daily prayer."
- *Jager v. Douglas County School District,* 862 F.2d 824 (11th Cir.), Cert. den. 490 U.S. 1090 (1989). Let stand a lower court ruling in Georgia that pre-game invocations at high school football games are unconstitutional.
- *Lee v. Weisman,* 120 L.E. 2d 467/ 112 S.C.T. 2649 (1992). Ruled prayers at public school graduations an impermissible establishment of religion.
- *Berger v. Rensselaer,* 982 F.2d, 1160 (7th Cir.) Cert. denied. 124 L.E. 2d 254 (1993). Let stand ruling barring access to Gideons to pass out bibles in Indiana schools.

POSTSCRIPT

Should Religious Content and Concepts Be More Evident in Public Schools?

It is understandable that where there is a coming together of competing or conflicting core values there is a potential for conflict. Thus it should come as no surprise that when our historic and constitutional commitment to the right of free exercise of religious belief and the equally fundamental tradition of separating government from establishing or supporting religious practices meet at the public schoolhouse door, we do indeed have controversy.

Many parents want their children to be educated in public school, but they also want such education to include values and ideas drawn from religious beliefs and practices. Other parents, equally adamant about public education for their children, see real dangers to the diversity of religious beliefs (or the lack thereof), if religion is brought into public schools.

It is a well-established point of constitutional law that state-sponsored public schools and public school teachers, administrators, and school board members are considered extensions of state government and as such are subject to the provisions of the Constitution. (The proscriptions and limitations of governmental power contained in the Bill of Rights originally applied only to the national government, but with the adoption of the Fourteenth Amendment in 1868 and subsequent court decisions, those proscriptions and limitations have been extended to include state and local government entities such as school boards as well.) Over the past 60 years, the Supreme Court has made numerous rulings on the relationship between religion and state-sponsored public schools. A cursory review of a few such cases shows the wide-ranging topics involved in this on-going controversy (see end of Gaylor article).

Obviously this church state issue and the controversies surrounding it will continue to be of great interest and importance and will necessitate future decisions by the High Court. Given the sometimes competing/conflicting decisions of lower courts regarding the constitutionality of using public monies by way of vouchers and/or tax credits to assist parents in sending their children to parochial schools, it can be anticipated that the Supreme Court will provide some clarifications in the future. Other looming sources of litigation are the still pending "under God" phrase in the Pledge of Allegiance, abstinence-only sexuality education programs with religious connections, and the growing practice in public schools of offering courses on the Bible as literature.

ISSUE 5

Is Drug Testing of Students a Justifiable Practice?

YES: Clarence Thomas, from the Majority Opinion, *Board of Education of Independent School District No. 92 of Pottawatomie County, et al., Petitioners v. Lindsay Earls et al.,* Supreme Court of the United States (June 27, 2002)

NO: Ruth Bader Ginsberg, from the Dissenting Opinion, *Board of Education of Independent School District No. 92 of Pottawatomie County, et al., Petitioners v. Lindsay Earls et al.,* Supreme Court of the United States (June 1, 2002)

ISSUE SUMMARY

YES: Justice Thomas presents the legal justification for a urinalysis drug test and states, "Given the minimally intrusive nature of the sample collection and the limited uses to which the test results are put, we conclude that the invasion of students' privacy is not significant."

NO: Justice Ginsberg, in opposing the majority position, states "schools' tutelary obligations to their students require them to 'teach by example' by avoiding symbolic measures that diminish constitutional protections."

The role of the courts in school discipline policies is best understood by placing it in some sort of historical perspective. In the early years of public education, school teachers and school administrators enforced school discipline from the very comfortable legal status of "in loco parentis." Corporal punishment, public humiliation, and other forms of draconian control in the schoolhouse went unchallenged. However, as state control over the public schools became more established and as state certification of public school educators became more commonplace, it also became clear that school officials functioned more as representatives of the state than they did as surrogate parents. This trend away from "in loco parentis" was solidified in 1969 when the United States Supreme Court issued its famous *Tinker v. Des Moines* decision establishing that students do not lose their constitutional rights at "the schoolhouse gate."

Although the *Tinker* case signaled the passing of the "in loco parentis" era, it also ushered in a decade or so of legislation and school policymaking aimed at protecting student rights and limiting the discretion of school administrators in the handling of disciplinary cases. Due process considerations became part of suspension and expulsion hearings and generally the overall approach to student discipline issues became more legalistic. The *Tinker* decision expanding student rights coincided with increased student activism and protests related to the Vietnam War and with what many in the public felt was a deterioration of discipline in the schools. Also contributing to this growing concern about students and the quality of our schools was the release of the 1983 report *A Nation at Risk* by the National Commission on Excellence in Education, which detailed a steady pattern of decline in achievement levels of American school children.

Whether motivated by such concerns or not, the United States Supreme Court in 1985 made the first of three decisions that reversed the trend toward increased student rights, and although falling short of reestablishing "in loco parentis" for school officials, these decisions did reassert administrative authority to deal with school disciplinary matters in a "reasonable" manner without being encumbered by legal standards imposed on law enforcement officials. The three cases were *New Jersey v. TLO* (1985), *Bethel School District v. Fraser* (1986), and *Hazelwood School District v. Kuhlmeier* (1988). The *TLO* case dealt with the Fourth Amendment and searches of students by school officials whereas the other two involved First Amendment issues regarding student speech (*Fraser*) and the student press (*Hazelwood*). In each case the Court held that schools are special places and student rights in school are not coextensive with their rights elsewhere. Common themes in these cases were the Court's expressed concerns regarding the school's responsibility to protect students and the maintenance of an environment in which learning can take place.

With the above decisions firmly establishing that the protection of student safety is a fundamental responsibility of schools, it is not surprising that schools would take proactive steps to reduce or eliminate substance abuse among students and that such steps would invoke controversy. Thus, it was in 1995, that a case involving a school district's drug-testing policy reached the U.S. Supreme Court. That case, *Vernonia School District v. Wayne Acton*, involved a drug-testing program using urinalysis that was required for participation in the district's athletic programs. By a 5 to 4 decision the Court upheld the district's right to administer the program.

The 2002 case described by the following two opinions involves an extension of required drug testing to students who wish to participate in any school-sponsored extracurricular activity. Justice Thomas in delivering the Court's 5 to 4 majority opinion supporting the constitutionality of this drug-testing program stated that testing students is a reasonably effective means of addressing the school district's legitimate concerns in preventing, deterring, and detecting drug use. In her dissenting opinion, Justice Ginsberg argues that this particular testing program is not reasonable and that the *Vernonia* decision did not support this type of expanded drug testing.

YES

Clarence Thomas

Board of Education of Independent School District No. 92 of Pottawatomie County, et al., Petitioners v. Lindsay Earls et al.

SUPREME COURT OF THE UNITED STATES
122 S. Ct. 2559
June 27, 2002, Decided

Justice Thomas Delivered the Opinion of the Court

The Student Activities Drug Testing Policy implemented by the Board of Education of Independent School District No. 92 of Pottawatomie County (School District) requires all students who participate in competitive extracurricular activities to submit to drug testing. Because this Policy reasonably serves the School District's important interest in detecting and preventing drug use among its students, we hold that it is constitutional.

❧

The city of Tecumseh, Oklahoma, is a rural community located approximately 40 miles southeast of Oklahoma City. The School District administers all Tecumseh public schools. In the fall of 1998, the School District adopted the Student Activities Drug Testing Policy (Policy), which requires all middle and high school students to consent to drug testing in order to participate in any extracurricular activity. In practice, the Policy has been applied only to competitive extracurricular activities sanctioned by the Oklahoma Secondary Schools Activities Association, such as the Academic Team, Future Farmers of America, Future Homemakers of America, band, choir, pom pon, cheerleading, and athletics. Under the Policy, students are required to take a drug test before participating in an extracurricular activity, must submit to random drug testing while participating in that activity, and must agree to be tested at any time upon reasonable suspicion. The urinalysis tests are designed to detect only the use of illegal drugs, including amphetamines, marijuana, cocaine, opiates, and barbituates, not medical conditions or the presence of authorized prescription medications.

Supreme Court of the United States, 122 S. Ct. 2559, June 27, 2002.

At the time of their suit, both respondents attended Tecumseh High School. Respondent Lindsay Earls was a member of the show choir, the marching band, the Academic Team, and the National Honor Society. Respondent Daniel James sought to participate in the Academic Team, Together with their parents, Earls and James brought a 42 U.S.C. § 1983 action against the School District, challenging the Policy both on its face and as applied to their participation in extracurricular activities. They alleged that the Policy violates the Fourth Amendment as incorporated by the Fourteenth Amendment and requested injunctive and declarative relief. They also argued that the School District failed to identify a special need for testing students who participate in extra-curricular activities, and that the "Drug Testing Policy neither addresses a proven problem nor promises to bring any benefit to students or the school. . . ."

Given that the School District's Policy is not in any way related to the conduct of criminal investigations, respondents do not contend that the School District requires probable cause before testing students for drug use. Respondents instead argue that drug testing must be based at least on some level of individualized suspicion. It is true that we generally determine the reasonableness of a search by balancing the nature of the intrusion on the individual's privacy against the promotion of legitimate governmental interests. But we have long held that "the Fourth Amendment imposes no irreducible requirement of [individualized] suspicion." "In certain limited circumstances, the Government's need to discover such latent or hidden conditions, or to prevent their development, is sufficiently compelling to justify the intrusion on privacy entailed by conducting such searches without any measure of indi-vidualized suspicion." Therefore, in the context of safety and administrative regulations, a search unsupported by probable cause may be reasonable "when 'special needs, beyond the normal need for law enforcement, make the warrant and probable-cause requirement impracticable.'"

Significantly, this Court has previously held that "special needs" inhere in the public school context. While schoolchildren do not shed their constitu-tional rights when they enter the schoolhouse, "Fourth Amendment rights . . . are different in public schools than elsewhere; the 'reasonableness' inquiry cannot disregard the schools' custodial and tutelary responsibility for children." In particular, a finding of individualized suspicion may not be necessary when a school conducts drug testing.

In *Vernonia*, this Court held that the suspicionless drug testing of athletes was constitutional. The Court, however, did not simply authorize all school drug testing, but rather conducted a fact-specific balancing of the intrusion on the children's Fourth Amendment rights against the promotion of legit-imate governmental interests. Applying the principles of *Vernonia* to the some-what different facts of this case, we conclude that Tecumseh's Policy is also constitutional.

We first consider the nature of the privacy interest allegedly compromised by the drug testing. . . . *A student's privacy interest is limited in a public school environment where the State is responsible for maintaining discipline, health, and safety. Schoolchildren are routinely required to submit to physical examinations and vaccinations against disease.*

Respondents argue that because children participating in nonathletic extracurricular activities are not subject to regular physicals and communal undress, they have a stronger expectation of privacy than the athletes tested in *Vernonia.* This distinction, however, was not essential to our decision in *Vernonia,* which depended primarily upon the school's custodial responsibility and authority.

In any event, students who participate in competitive extracurricular activities voluntarily subject themselves to many of the same intrusions on their privacy as do athletes. Some of these clubs and activities require occasional off-campus travel and communal undress. All of them have their own rules and requirements for participating students that do not apply to the student body as a whole. . . . We therefore conclude that the students affected by this Policy have a limited expectation of privacy.

Next, we consider the character of the intrusion imposed by the Policy. Urination is "an excretory function traditionally shielded by great privacy." But the "degree of intrusion" on one's privacy caused by collecting a urine sample "depends upon the manner in which production of the urine sample is monitored." Under the Policy, a faculty monitor waits outside the closed restroom stall for the student to produce a sample and must "listen for the normal sounds of urination in order to guard against tampered specimens and to insure an accurate chain of custody." The monitor then pours the sample into two bottles that are sealed and placed into a mailing pouch along with a consent form signed by the student. This procedure is virtually identical to that reviewed in *Vernonia,* except that it additionally protects privacy by allowing male students to produce their samples behind a closed stall. Given that we considered the method of collection in *Vernonia* a "negligible" intrusion, the method here is even less problematic.

In addition, the Policy clearly requires that the test results be kept in confidential files separate from a student's other educational records and released to school personnel only on a "need to know" basis. Respondents nonetheless contend that the intrusion on students' privacy is significant because the Policy fails to protect effectively against the disclosure of confidential information and, specifically, that the school "has been careless in protecting that information: for example, the Choir teacher looked at students' prescription drug lists and left them where other students could see them." But the choir teacher is someone with a "need to know," because during off-campus trips she needs to know what medications are taken by her students. Even before the Policy was enacted the choir teacher had access to this information. In any event, there is no allegation that any other student did see such information. This one example of alleged carelessness hardly increases the character of the intrusion.

Moreover, the test results are not turned over to any law enforcement authority. Nor do the test results here lead to the imposition of discipline or have any academic consequences. . . . Given the minimally intrusive nature of the sample collection and the limited uses to which the test results are put, we conclude that the invasion of students' privacy is not significant.

Finally, this Court must consider the nature and immediacy of the government's concerns and the efficacy of the Policy in meeting them. This Court has already articulated in detail the importance of the governmental concern in preventing drug use by schoolchildren. The drug abuse problem among our Nation's youth has hardly abated since *Vernonia* was decided in 1995. In fact, evidence suggests that it has only grown worse. . . . Additionally, the School District in this case has presented specific evidence of drug use at Tecumseh schools. Teachers testified that they had seen students who appeared to be under the influence of drugs and that they had heard students speaking openly about using drugs. A drug dog found marijuana cigarettes near the school parking lot. Police officers once found drugs or drug paraphernalia in a car driven by a Future Farmers of America member. . . . We decline to second-guess the finding of the District Court that "viewing the evidence as a whole, it cannot be reasonably disputed that the [School District] was faced with a 'drug problem' when it adopted the Policy."

Furthermore, this Court has not required a particularized or pervasive drug problem before allowing the government to conduct suspicionless drug testing. . . . Indeed, it would make little sense to require a school district to wait for a substantial portion of its students to begin using drugs before it was allowed to institute a drug testing program designed to deter drug use.

Given the nationwide epidemic of drug use, and the evidence of increased drug use in Tecumseh schools, it was entirely reasonable for the School District to enact this particular drug testing policy. . . .

Respondents also argue that the testing of nonathletes does not implicate any safety concerns, and that safety is a "crucial factor" in applying the special needs framework. They contend that there must be "surpassing safety interests" or "extraordinary safety and national security hazards" in order to override the usual protections of the Fourth Amendment. Respondents are correct that safety factors into the special needs analysis, but the safety interest furthered by drug testing is undoubtedly substantial for all children, athletes and nonathletes alike. We know all too well that drug use carries a variety of health risks for children, including death from overdose. . . .

Finally, we find that testing students who participate in extracurricular activities is a reasonably effective means of addressing the School District's legitimate concerns in preventing, deterring, and detecting drug use. While in *Vernonia* there might have been a closer fit between the testing of athletes and the trial court's finding that the drug problem was "fueled by the 'role model' effect of athletes' drug use," such a finding was not essential to the holding. *Vernonia* did not require the school to test the group of students most likely to use drugs, but rather considered the constitutionality of the program in the context of the public school's custodial responsibilities. Evaluating the Policy in this context, we conclude that the drug testing of Tecumseh students who participate in extracurricular activities effectively serves the School District's interest in protecting the safety and health of its students.

Justice Breyer, Concurring

I agree with the Court that *Vernonia School Dist. 47J v. Acton,* 515 U.S. 646 (1995), governs this case and requires reversal of the Tenth Circuit's decision. . . .

In respect to the privacy-related burden that the drug testing program imposes upon students, I would emphasize the following: First, not everyone would agree with this Court's characterization of the privacy-related significance of urine sampling as "negligible."

Second, the testing program avoids subjecting the entire school to testing. And it preserves an option for a conscientious objector. He can refuse testing while paying a price (nonparticipation) that is serious, but less severe than expulsion from the school.

Third, a contrary reading of the Constitution, as requiring "individualized suspicion" in this public school context, could well lead schools to push the boundaries of "individualized suspicion" to its outer limits, using subjective criteria that may "unfairly target members of unpopular groups," or leave those whose behavior is slightly abnormal stigmatized in the minds of others. . . .

Emphasizing the considerations I have mentioned, along with others to which the Court refers, I conclude that the school's drug testing program, constitutionally speaking, is not "unreasonable." And I join the Court's opinion.

Ruth Bader Ginsberg

 NO

Board of Education of Independent School District No. 92 of Pottawatomie County, et al., Petitioners v. Lindsay Earls et al.

Justice Ginsburg, with Whom Justice Stevens, Justice O'Connor, and Justice Souter Join, Dissenting

Seven years ago, in *Vernonia School Dist.* v. *Acton* (1995), this Court determined that a school district's policy of randomly testing the urine of its student athletes for illicit drugs did not violate the Fourth Amendment. In so ruling, the Court emphasized that drug use "increased the risk of sports-related injury" and that Vernonia's athletes were the "leaders" of an aggressive local "drug culture" that had reached "epidemic proportions." Today, the Court relies upon *Vernonia* to permit a school district with a drug problem its superintendent repeatedly described as "not . . . major" to test the urine of an academic team member solely by reason of her participation in a nonathletic, competitive extracurricular activity–participation associated with neither special dangers from, nor particular predilections for, drug use.

"The legality of a search of a student," this Court has instructed, "should depend simply on the reasonableness, under all the circumstances, of the search." Although "'special needs' inhere in the public school context," those needs are not so expansive or malleable as to render reasonable any program of student drug testing a school district elects to install. The particular testing program upheld today is not reasonable, it is capricious, even perverse: Petitioners' policy targets for testing a student population least likely to be at risk from illicit drugs and their damaging effects. I therefore dissent. . . .

This case presents circumstances dispositively different from those of *Vernonia*. True, as the Court stresses, Tecumseh students participating in competitive extracurricular activities other than athletics share two relevant characteristics with the athletes of *Vernonia*. First, both groups attend public schools. Concern for student health and safety is basic to the school's caretaking, and it is undeniable that "drug use carries a variety of health risks for children, including death from overdose."

Supreme Court of the United States, 122 S. Ct. 2559, June 1, 2002.

Those risks, however, are present for *all* schoolchildren. *Vernonia* cannot be read to endorse invasive and suspicionless drug testing of all students upon any evidence of drug use, solely because drugs jeopardize the life and health of those who use them. Many children, like many adults, engage in dangerous activities on their own time; that the children are enrolled in school scarcely allows government to monitor all such activities. If a student has a reasonable subjective expectation of privacy in the personal items she brings to school, surely she has a similar expectation regarding the chemical composition of her urine. Had the *Vernonia* Court agreed that public school attendance, in and of itself, permitted the State to test each student's blood or urine for drugs, the opinion in *Vernonia* could have saved many words.

The second commonality to which the Court points is the voluntary character of both interscholastic athletics and other competitive extracurricular activities. "By choosing to 'go out for the team,' [school athletes] voluntarily subject themselves to a degree of regulation even higher than that imposed on students generally." Comparably, the Court today observes, "students who participate in competitive extracurricular activities voluntarily subject themselves to" additional rules not applicable to other students.

Students "volunteer" for extracurricular pursuits in the same way they might volunteer for honors classes: They subject themselves to additional requirements, but they do so in order to take full advantage of the education offered them.

Voluntary participation in athletics has a distinctly different dimension: Schools regulate student athletes discretely because competitive school sports by their nature require communal undress and, more important, expose students to physical risks that schools have a duty to mitigate. For the very reason that schools cannot offer a program of competitive athletics without intimately affecting the privacy of students, *Vernonia* reasonably analogized school athletes to "adults who choose to participate in a closely regulated industry." Interscholastic athletics similarly require close safety and health regulation; a school's choir, band, and academic team do not.

In short, *Vernonia* applied, it did not repudiate, the principle that "the legality of a search of a student should depend simply on the reasonableness, *under all the circumstances*, of the search." Balancing of that order, applied to the facts now before the Court, should yield a result other than the one the Court announces today.

Vernonia initially considered "the nature of the privacy interest upon which the search [there] at issue intruded." The Court emphasized that student athletes' expectations of privacy are necessarily attenuated: "Legitimate privacy expectations are even less with regard to student athletes. School sports are not for the bashful. They require 'suiting up' before each practice or event, and showering and changing afterwards. Public school locker rooms, the usual sites for these activities, are not notable for the privacy they afford. The locker rooms in Vernonia are typical: No individual dressing rooms are provided; shower heads are lined up along a wall, unseparated by any sort of partition or curtain; not even all the toilet stalls have doors. . . . There is an element of communal undress inherent in athletic participation."

Competitive extracurricular activities other than athletics, however, serve students of all manner: the modest and shy along with the bold and uninhibited. Activities of the kind plaintiff-respondent Lindsay Earls pursued—choir, show choir, marching band, and academic team—afford opportunities to gain self-assurance, to "come to know faculty members in a less formal setting than the typical classroom," and to acquire "positive social supports and networks [that] play a critical role in periods of heightened stress."

On "occasional out-of-town trips," students like Lindsay Earls "must sleep together in communal settings and use communal bathrooms." But those situations are hardly equivalent to the routine communal undress associated with athletics; the School District itself admits that when such trips occur, "public-like restroom facilities," which presumably include enclosed stalls, are ordinarily available for changing, and that "more modest students" find other ways to maintain their privacy. According to Tecumseh's choir teacher, choir participants who chose not to wear their choir uniforms to school on the days of competitions could change either in "a rest room in a building" or on the bus, where "many of them have figured out how to [change] without having [anyone] . . . see anything. . . ."

Finally, the "nature and immediacy of the governmental concern" faced by the Vernonia School District dwarfed that confronting Tecumseh administrators. Vernonia initiated its drug testing policy in response to an alarming situation: "[A] large segment of the student body, particularly those involved in interscholastic athletics, was in a state of rebellion . . . fueled by alcohol and drug abuse as well as the student[s'] misperceptions about the drug culture." Tecumseh, by contrast, repeatedly reported to the Federal Government during the period leading up to the adoption of the policy that "types of drugs [other than alcohol and tobacco] including controlled dangerous substances, are present [in the schools] but have not identified themselves as major problems at this time." As the Tenth Circuit observed, "without a demonstrated drug abuse problem among the group being tested, the efficacy of the District's solution to its perceived problem is . . . greatly diminished. . . ."

Not only did the Vernonia and Tecumseh districts confront drug problems of distinctly different magnitudes, they also chose different solutions: Vernonia limited its policy to athletes; Tecumseh indiscriminately subjected to testing all participants in competitive extracurricular activities. . . .

The Vernonia district, in sum, had two good reasons for testing athletes: Sports team members faced special health risks and they "were the leaders of the drug culture." No similar reason, and no other tenable justification, explains Tecumseh's decision to target for testing all participants in every competitive extracurricular activity. . . .

In *Chandler*, this Court inspected "Georgia's requirement that candidates for state office pass a drug test"; we held that the requirement "did not fit within the closely guarded category of constitutionally permissible suspicionless searches." Georgia's testing prescription, the record showed, responded to no "concrete danger," was supported by no evidence of a particular problem, and targeted a group not involved in "high-risk, safety-sensitive tasks." We concluded: "What is left, after close review of Georgia's scheme, is the image the State seeks to project. By requiring candidates for public office to submit to drug testing, Georgia displays its commitment to the struggle against drug abuse. . . . The need revealed, in short, is symbolic, not 'special,' as that term draws meaning from our case law."

Close review of Tecumseh's policy compels a similar conclusion. . . .

In *Chandler,* the Court referred to a pathmarking dissenting opinion in which "Justice Brandeis recognized the importance of teaching by example: 'Our Government is the potent, the omnipresent teacher. For good or for ill, it teaches the whole people by its example.'" That wisdom should guide decisionmakers in the instant case: The government is nowhere more a teacher than when it runs a public school.

It is a sad irony that the petitioning School District seeks to justify its edict here by trumpeting "the schools' custodial and tutelary responsibility for children." In regulating an athletic program or endeavoring to combat an exploding drug epidemic, a school's custodial obligations may permit searches that would otherwise unacceptably abridge students' rights. When custodial duties are not ascendant, however, schools' tutelary obligations to their students require them to "teach by example" by avoiding symbolic measures that diminish constitutional protections. "That [schools] are educating the young for citizenship is reason for scrupulous protection of Constitutional freedoms of the individual, if we are not to strangle the free mind at its source and teach youth to discount important principles of our government as mere platitudes."

For the reasons stated, I would affirm the judgment of the Tenth Circuit declaring the testing policy at issue unconstitutional.

POSTSCRIPT

Is Drug Testing of Students a Justifiable Practice?

The mere fact that the U.S. Supreme Court has come down on the side of the constitutionality of certain types of student drug testing does not mean that the controversy over the practice has lessened. To the contrary, it appears that the decisions have galvanized both advocates and opponents to increase their persuasive efforts. John Walters, the director of the National Drug Control Policy group in his introduction to a recently released publication entitled *What You Need to Know About Drug Testing in School*, states, "Parents, educators, indeed anyone concerned about the welfare of our young people should welcome the High Court's action. It's a big step in the right direction, for it gives every school in every city and every town a powerful new tool for controlling one of the worst threats facing kids today."

Walters offers statistics from *Monitoring the Future*, a national survey tracking drug use among teenagers showing that in 2001 more than half of all students had used illicit drugs by the time they finished high school. He further reports that of the 4.5 million people age 12 or older who need drug treatment, 23 percent are teenagers.

The American Civil Liberties Union (ACLU) and the Drug Policy Alliance (DPA) have countered with their joint publication, *Making Sense of Student Drug Testing: Why Educators Are Saying No* (2004). With this booklet the ACLU/DPA are trying to persuade school boards, administrators, and parents that in spite of its constitutionality drug testing is an ill-conceived and ineffective means of combating drug abuse among students. The deputy director of the DPA, Judy Appel states, "Drug testing is humiliating, costly, and ineffective, but it's an easy anti-drug soundbite for the White House. [Our booklet] is for the people and educators across the country who've got to make serious decisions about young people's safety. They need actual research, not slogans and junk science." The ACLU/DPA booklet also refers to a study funded by the National Institute of Drug Abuse in which Lloyd D. Johnston states, "that there isn't an impact from drug testing as practiced." The study revealed that the strongest predictors of student drug use are attitudes toward drug use and perceptions of peer use. According to Johnston drug testing doesn't bring about any "constructive changes" in students' attitudes about the dangers of drug use.

Student safety at school is a primary concern of parents, teachers, school administrators, and policymakers. The ACLU/DPA attempt to persuade such individuals to oppose drug testing reflects their understanding that the courts are generally very supportive of school efforts to maintain a safe and orderly environment and thus will not likely force schools to stop the practice of drug testing. The courts have consistently held that student constitutional rights in the school setting are not coextensive with their rights elsewhere and must be balanced against a school's responsibility to maintain safety and orderliness. The importance of that responsibility can be seen in development of school "zero tolerance" policies that are aimed at deterring and punishing acts that might endanger students. The National Association of Secondary School Principals policy statement regarding "zero tolerance" speaks to that group's awareness of the obligation its members have with respect to student safety:

> Students have the right to expect that their lives will not be endangered in a school building and that the climate is free of threats and violence. Zero tolerance policies, clearly stated and fairly administered, meet parental and societal expectations and protect the physical well-being of students and staff. It is our hope that parents, communities, and governments all support school leaders as they make difficult decisions and exert leadership in maintaining a school climate that is safe, orderly, drug-free, and conducive to teaching and learning. (February 2000)

Other references on this issue include: ACLU, "Drug Testing Cases Across the Nation," *ACLU Fact Sheet* (March 2002); Drug Policy Alliance, *Student Drug Testing: An Investment in Fear* (July 2003); R. Dupont, T. Campbell, and J. Marza, *Report of a Preliminary Study: Elements of a Successful School Based Drug Testing Program* (USDE, July 2002); R. Yamaguchi, L. Johnston, and P. O. Malley, "Relationship Between Student Illicit Drug Use and School Drug Testing Policies" (*Journal of School Health*, 2003); and National Center on Addiction and Substance Abuse at Columbia University (CASA), Eleventh Annual: *National Survey of American Attitudes on Substance Abuse* (2006).

ISSUE 6

Have Charter Schools Fulfilled Their Promises?

YES: The Center for Education Reform, from "2007 Annual Survey of America's Charter Schools" (2007)

NO: Bella Rosenberg, from "America's Charter Schools: Results from the NAEP 2003 Pilot Study," American Federation of Teachers (December 15, 2004)

ISSUE SUMMARY

YES: The Center for Education Reform states that results of its survey "highlight the innovation and progress that charter schools have made. . . ".

NO: Bella Rosenberg, assistant to the president of the American Federation of Teachers, responds that results from a study conducted by the National Assessment of Educational Progress belie the claims of charter school advocates.

Originally conceived as providing a middle ground between traditional public education and vouchers to allow parental choice of private/parochial schools, the charter school movement, dubbed by some as private/public schools, began with one school in Minnesota in 1992 and now numbers more than 4000 schools in 40 states and the District of Columbia, with nearly a million students enrolled. The charter concept entails public funding of schools that are empowered to operate unfettered by school district policies/regulations and teacher union contracts. The following is a description of the charter school concept from the Center for Education Reform, a charter school advocacy group:

Charter schools operate on three basic principles:

- *Choice*: Charter schools give families an opportunity to pick the school most suitable for their child's educational well-being. Teachers choose to create and work at schools where they directly shape the best working and learning environment for their students and themselves. Likewise, charter sponsors choose to authorize schools that are likely to best serve the needs of the students in a particular community.

- *Accountability*: Charter schools are judged on how well they meet the student achievement goals established by their charter contract. Charter schools must also show that they can perform according to rigorous fiscal and managerial standards. If a charter school cannot perform up to the established standards, it will be closed.
- *Freedom*: While charter schools must adhere to the same major laws and regulations as all other public schools, they are freed from the red tape that often diverts a school's energy and resources away from educational excellence. Instead of constantly jumping through procedural hoops, charter school leaders can focus on setting and reaching high academic standards for their students.

Critics of charter schools, including the two largest teacher unions, the National Education Association (NEA) and the American Federation of Teachers (AFT), claim that charter schools do not deliver what they promise. These critics cite various statistics and research studies to show that charter school students do not outperform public school students and in some cases do not do as well academically; that charter schools are often poorly managed and fiscally irresponsible; that charter schools do not accept minority students in the numbers promised; that charter schools employ a significant number of noncredentialed, ill-prepared teachers; and that charter schools hurt public schools. AFT's Rosenberg makes her opposition clear with her statement:

> the evidence indicates that most charter schools are doing worse than our much-maligned public schools. If charter schools are supposed to "rescue" children trapped in so-called failing public schools, who will rescue the children trapped in demonstrably more failing charter schools?

YES

Annual Survey of America's Charter Schools

The first charter school opened in Minnesota in 1992, and heated policy debate over choice, charter schools, and efforts to offer alternatives to public schools have not waned.

While education reformers have enjoyed remarkable success against education bureaucracies, the overwhelming political and economic power continues to lie in the hands of those who argue on behalf of the status quo in public education. The Center for Education Reform (CER) believes that offering parents a range of educational choices for their children is the only way to help improve conventional public schools.

School choice and competition force schools to continually examine their curricula and improve their education services and overall educational delivery to give children a chance for improved academic achievement. Choice re-asserts the rights of the parent and the best interests of the child over the convenience of the system, infuses accountability and quality into the system, and provides educational opportunity where none existed before.

The story of charter schools, which is arguably in its early phase, is still unfolding. They survive, and succeed, because they operate on the principles of choice, accountability and autonomy not readily found in traditional public schools. Yet, charter schools continue to struggle to overcome obstacles conventional public schools do not have to face, such as lack of funding. The results of this survey highlight the innovation and progress charter schools have made, but also show the continuing obstacles and vocal opposition school choice and charter school supporters must overcome.

For the last few years, federal data issues have sparked debate about charter schools under-performing because they are not serving disadvantaged students. We knew that this false assumption was based on charter school participation in the free-and-reduced lunch program, and we wanted to set the record straight. For the first time in our annual survey, we asked charter schools about their participation in the program and the results confirm what we already knew; that charter schools do educate poor, at-risk populations, and these students are achieving.

CER has surveyed charter schools since 1997 to provide the public with unprecedented, first-hand information on the growing charter school movement. The results from the survey are then compiled and published in *The Annual Survey of Charter Schools*, ensuring that the true story of charter schools is told.

Summary of Key Findings

This report emphasizes the clear message of charter schools:

- Charter schools are public schools that use innovative practices to help students meet high standards.
- Even though they are public and are open and free to all students, charter schools still receive fewer public dollars than other public schools.
- There are more charter schools in states that allow various state-approved entities to sponsor them, and do not limit their existence to the single power of a school board.
- Charter schools provide parents an opportunity to choose from among a number of public school options.
- Charter schools remain smaller than conventional public schools and use innovative practices to help students meet high standards.
- Charter schools continue to serve a disproportionate share of at-risk and minority children, who are most adversely affected by the status quo.

Size and Scope

Growing Interest

In the 2006-07 school year, there are 3,940 charter schools serving over 1.16 million students in 40 states and Washington, D.C.

Charter schools have experienced double-digit annual growth since the mid-1990's. This year was no exception with an 11 percent increase in the number of schools across the country.

Meeting Parent Demands for Smaller Schools

Charter schools enroll on average 328 students, nearly 40 percent less than conventional public schools. According to the National Center for Education Statistics, in 2003-04, the average number of students per public school was 521. Research has shown that smaller schools can be advantageous for learning, creating an intimate environment to better serve the individual needs of students within the school.

While the number of charter schools across the country continues to grow at a rapid rate, the interest in these innovative schools also continues to rise. Sixty-one percent of schools that responded said that they have significant waiting lists, averaging 150 students in length.

Expanding the Number of Chartering Authorities

In 2006, 12 states had authorizers other than local school boards that approved and managed charter schools. An additional 8 states had strong binding appeals processes that allowed applicants an open and objective avenue to seek a charter if it is initially denied by the local school board. In 2007, there will be 14 states with multiple authorizers, increasing the total number from 20 to 22 states with multiple authorizers and/or a strong binding appeals process. States with multiple chartering authorities have almost 4 times more charter schools than states requiring only local school board approval. Local boards, however, are more likely to grant charters when state laws permit multiple authorizers. Seventy-nine percent of the nation's charter schools are in states with multiple authorizers or a strong appeals process. These states are also home to the highest quality charter schools. . . .

Education Opportunities for the Under Served

Contrary to the flawed data that has been released over the years, charter schools do not "cherry pick" the best students from conventional public schools. Half of charter school students fall into categories defined as "at-risk". Charter schools serve students who are largely under served in the conventional public school environment: minority students, at-risk students, and low-income students. Conventional public schools do not provide the individualized attention and tailored curricula that charter schools can offer these students.

Charters continue to target services to students at both ends of the instructional spectrum who are being failed by a "one-size-fits-all" education system: teen parents, special education students, adjudicated youth, English language learners, and gifted and talented students.

Operations

Ensuring Accountability

All charter schools must test to the requirements of their state or district. Ninety-four percent of survey respondents report administering a specific standardized test, and most schools require more than one test. The 6 percent of schools that do not require a standardized test likely provide alternative learning programs with non-traditional assessments for students that have dropped out of school or serve only pre-school age children.

Providing Innovative, Quality Choices

Charter schools provide multiple curricula options, responding to the demand for better and more focused curricula that meet the needs of each school's student population. Of the survey respondents, 82 percent said that they have a particular theme or curriculum focus to their school, ranging from focusing on specific disciplines (math, science or the arts), or built around students' futures (college preparation or school-to-work).

One of the most innovative, yet simple values provided by charter schools is increased instructional time. Few conventional public schools have gone beyond the traditions of school 180 days a year for 6.5 hours a day. Among survey respondents, 32 percent have increased instructional time.

Management

Doing More With Less

Charter schools spend less and receive fewer dollars than conventional schools. Among reporting charter schools, the average per-pupil cost was $7,155, and the average revenue per-pupil was $6,585. According to the National Center for Education Statistics, the total per-student expenditure for public schools in fiscal year 2004 was $8,310, with revenue of $9,518. On average, charter schools spend more money than they receive and are forced to find creative ways to increase their revenues and raise money.

Maximizing Resources

Unlike conventional district schools, most charter schools do not receive funding to cover the cost of securing a facility. Of charter schools that responded, only 25 percent receive some funding specifically targeted towards facilities. Charter schools improvise by converting spaces such as retail facilities, former churches, lofts and warehouses, into classroom, cafeteria, assembly and gym space. Sixty-three percent of survey respondents rent their school facility.

An effective balance between teachers and administrators is key to ensuring schools meet their primary responsibility, to educate children. Charter schools generally maintain high ratios of teachers to administrative personnel, averaging 19 full-time teachers to 4 full-time administrative staff.

Size and Scope

Charter Schools Generate Increasing Interest and Growth

Charter schools are one of the fastest and most successful growing reforms in the country. The first charter school opened its doors in St. Paul, Minnesota in 1992 and now, 15 years later there are 3,940 charter schools serving over 1.16 million children across 40 states and Washington, D.C.

The number of charter schools grew modestly until the mid-to-late 1990s, as more state legislatures passed charter laws. Since then, charter schools have experienced enormous annual growth, and this year the number of charter schools grew by 11 percent from the previous school

Figure 1

Growth in Operational Charter Schools 1992–2006

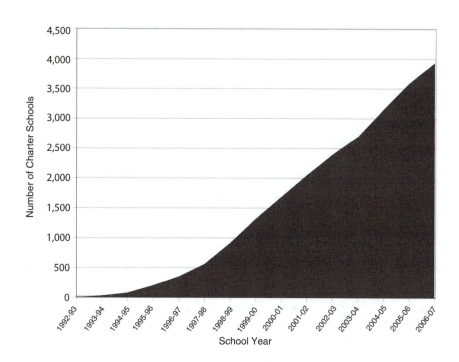

year (Figure 1). States with strong charter school laws, such as California, Minnesota, Ohio, Arizona, and Michigan have experienced some of the largest growth (Figure 2).

Unlike conventional schools, charter schools face enormous challenges to open and survive, and of the over 4,000 charter schools that have ever opened, 11 percent have been closed for various reasons. Closure may be due to academic, financial or management problems, or in some cases consolidation or district interference. Charter schools are and should be held accountable for their academic and managerial performance.

Meeting Parent Demands for Smaller Schools

On average, charter schools enroll 328 students, nearly 40 percent less than conventional public schools. According to the National Center for Education Statistics (NCES), the average number of students in a conventional school in 2003-04 was 521. Research has shown that smaller schools may lead to higher achievement and can be more advantageous for learning, depending on the programs being used and what is expected.

Figure 2

Charter School Enrollment and Closures, by State

State	Total Schools Operating	Enrollment	Average Enrollment	Closures Since 1992
Alaska	24	4,814	201	5
Arizona	462	105,422	228	83
Arkansas	15	3,998	267	4
California	637	219,460	345	83
Colorado	132	47,443	359	6
Connecticut	19	3,577	188	4
Delaware	19	7,826	412	2
Washington, D.C.	68	19,143	282	13
Florida	347	96,007	277	53
Georgia	59	25,882	439	4
Hawaii	27	5,538	205	0
Idaho	28	9,384	335	1
Illinois	55	21,343	388	8
Indiana	38	8,274	218	2
Iowa	8	1,249	156	0
Kansas	26	2,588	100	8
Louisiana	46	17,315	376	8
Maryland	23	4,870	342	0
Massachusetts	60	21,987	366	6
Michigan	241	96,200	399	22
Minnesota	137	23,455	171	24
Mississippi	1	367	367	0
Missouri	27	11,134	412	4
Nevada	22	5,979	271	5
New Hampshire	8	388	49	1
New Jersey	53	15,381	290	17
New Mexico	62	10,034	162	2
New York	95	23,972	252	7
North Carolina	99	29,070	294	27
Ohio	301	87,288	289	20
Oklahoma	15	4,606	307	1
Oregon	71	10,105	142	8
Pennsylvania	120	55,760	465	9
Rhode Island	11	2,723	248	0
South Carolina	31	5,844	189	8
Tennessee	12	1,891	158	0
Texas	283	94,429	334	27
Utah	54	18,985	352	1
Virginia	3	241	80	3
Wisconsin	198	32,667	165	18
Wyoming	3	235	78	0
TOTAL	**3,940**	**1,156,874**	**267**	**494**

*Data current as of March 2007

Figure 3

Charter School Enrollment and Waiting List

	2006	2005
Average Enrollment	328	297
Percentage of Schools with Waiting Lists	61	56
Average Number of Students on Waiting List	149	166
Number of Students on a Typical Waiting List	40	50

Over 1.16 million students are enrolled in charter schools across the country, and 61 percent of survey respondents said that their school currently has a waiting list for one or more grades. The typical charter school waiting list has 40 students. Last year, the typical waiting list was 50 students, and this change can be attributed to an increased number of charter schools and spaces available for students (Figure 3).

Multiple Chartering Authorities

In 2006, 12 states had authorizers other than local school boards that approved and managed charter schools. An additional 8 states had strong binding appeals processes that allowed applicants an open and objective avenue to seek a charter if it is initially denied by the local school board. States with multiple chartering authorities have almost 4 times more charter schools than states requiring only local school board approval. Seventy-nine percent of the nation's charter schools are in states with multiple authorizers or a strong appeals process. These states are also home to the highest quality charter schools. The goal is to give parents the most options and having multiple sponsors helps reach this goal (Figure 4).

Some states with non-school board authorizers have reached their cap on the number of schools that can be authorized, hence the reason some of the various authorizers' numbers have gone down since last year.

Figure 4

Percentage of Charters Approved by Various Authorizers

	2006	2005
Local School Boards	48 percent	42 percent
State Boards of Education	28 percent	30 percent
State Chartering Boards	10 percent	14 percent
Universities/Colleges	9 percent	9 percent
Mayor or City	2 percent	1 percent
Other (or did not specify)	3 percent	4 percent

Demographics

Charters Serve Students Most in Need

For the last few years, federal data issues have sparked debate about charter school achievement. The National Center for Education Statistics (NCES) issued a report in which researchers argued that charter schools are under-performing because they are not serving disadvantaged students. Using the free and reduced lunch program to guide their poverty conclusions, researchers and critics have issued reports and statements that suggest charter school achievement is actually lower than other public schools because their scores, when adjusted for a lower poverty rate, are less than what they would expect from children with more advantages. Thus the prime indicator used by statisticians to determine poverty and thus compare achievement of like students is deeply flawed. For the first time, CER offers evidence that should put to rest the notion that charter students are less poor—and achieving less—than other public schools.

According to the survey, 54 percent of all charter school students qualify for free and reduced lunch, so charter schools definitely educate and change the lives of disadvantaged children. However, 37 percent of all responding charter schools said they do not participate in the federal free and reduced lunch program for a variety of reasons. Of that 37 percent, 23 percent choose not to apply to participate because of the paperwork, bureaucratic red tape and other difficulties involved (Figure 5). This is consistent with what CER has found in over ten years of outreach to charter schools. In many cases, charter schools do not fail to qualify for such programs—they instead choose not to participate. . . .

Methodology and Data Notes

In November 2006, CER distributed survey instruments to 3,900 operating charter schools. The survey posed general questions about educational programs and operations, standardized testing, and demographics. Through January 2007, 920 charter schools returned their surveys, representing a 24 percent return rate.

Figure 5

Why Charter Schools Do Not Participate in Free/Reduced Lunch

School does not have the facilities	42 percent
Chose not to apply because of bureaucratic difficulties	23 percent
School feeds students with own resources	10 percent
Not enough eligible students	6 percent
Other reason (cyber school, half day schedule, etc.)	26 percent

CER compiled and tabulated the data presented in this report. CER maintains and regularly updates a database of information on charter schools. Figures 1 and 2 represent a snapshot of charter school information taken in March 2007. Figures 3–15 are drawn from the most recent survey data.

Addendum: Charter School Achievement Data

All across the country charter schools are continuing to provide parents with an exceptional choice, and kids a chance for improved academic achievement. While parental satisfaction is important, local and state measures offer the depth and validity in studying charter school success. The following is a sampling of key findings from around the states:

From the States

- In 2006, 56 percent of New Mexico's charter schools made AYP compared to 45 percent of the conventional public schools statewide. Charter schools improved 9 points from the 2004–2005 academic year. With New Mexico's tradition of poor academic performance, these results illustrate the promise, over time, that charter schools are improving public education.
- In Massachusetts, almost 75 percent of charter schools outperformed their host districts in English and math on the 2006 state assessment test, with average proficiency rates that were almost 8 percentage points higher than neighboring district schools.
- During the 2005–2006 school year, 2 out of 3 New York City charter school students in grades 3–8 met or exceeded grade level standards on the state math exam. Charter school students scored 13 percent higher than public school students within the same districts. Fifty-six percent of students at 35 New York City public charter schools were proficient in reading and 66 percent were proficient in math, compared with 48 percent proficiency in reading, and 53 percent proficiency on the state math exam, achieved by students in grades 3–8 attending traditional public schools located in the same districts as the city's charter schools.
- Charter students in the District of Columbia now account for 26 percent of all public school students, the highest in the nation. The 65 charter schools are also scoring higher in reading and math. Fifty-four percent of D.C. charter students are proficient in math, a full 10 percent higher than conventional schools. In reading, 45 percent of charter students are proficient compared to 39 percent of students in conventional public schools.
- The percentage of charter school students in Florida who tested proficient in the state's reading assessment has grown faster than the gains posted by conventional public school students—charter school students rose from 55 percent to 58 percent, compared with an increase of 54 percent to 56 percent among conventional public school students.

- In 2006, Georgia charter schools made AYP at an unprecedented rate. As in 2004 and 2005, Georgia charter schools made AYP at a higher rate than traditional public schools, but in 2006 the gap between charter schools and traditional schools increased substantially. In 2006, 87.8 percent of Georgia charter schools made AYP compared to 78.7 percent of traditional public schools.
- Michigan's charter public schools exceed the average scores of their host districts on 23 of 27 state assessment tests in 2006, once again improving on their performance from the previous year. In addition, the number of schools "beating the odds" climbed from 25 last year to 40 this year. These primarily urban schools meet a state formula requiring at least 60% proficiency in math and English language arts, with at least half of the students qualifying for free-and-reduced lunch.

Bella Rosenberg

→ **NO**

America's Charter Schools: Results from the NAEP 2003 Pilot Study

On behalf of the American Federation of Teachers (AFT) and F. Howard Nelson and Nancy Van Meter, who, along with me, co-authored the AFT's August 2004 report in which the 2003 National Assessment of Educational Progress (NAEP) results for charter schools were unofficially released, I appreciate the National Assessment Governing Board's (NAGB) graciousness in inviting me to speak on the occasion of its official release of those results. I am particularly moved because it was the AFT, under its late president, Albert Shanker, that gave charter schools their first public face—a kinder, gentler and more honest face than the ideological one now most in evidence.

Let me also thank NAGB for taking the public information concerns we raised in our report seriously and moving up the release date for the official report. We are especially pleased that today also marks the public release of the results of the NAEP Charter School Survey Questionnaire, which were not available on the NAEP Data Tool when we prepared our August report. As you can see from the items that were included in the official NAEP report, and as I will highlight shortly, the Questionnaire results we pressed for turned out to be every bit as important as we had surmised.

We also applaud the decision to release the Questionnaire data before the National Center for Education Statistics (NCES) releases its special explanatory analysis, which would have further delayed public access to the Questionnaire results. Now, independent researchers and other interested parties, along with the government, can also analyze these data—a move that furthers the prospects for sound and open public discourse on charter schools.

So, after all the dustup about a report that straightforwardly, accurately, and fairly presented unofficial NAEP charter school results, how is the official NAEP report different from ours? In terms of the substantive results, not at all (with the one exception I'll soon discuss). Nonetheless, the official report deserves even closer attention because the new information it provides from the full sample and from the results of the Questionnaire—again, neither of which was publicly available when we prepared our report—indicates that there is even more reason to be disappointed and troubled by charter school performance than the unofficial NAEP results indicated.

When the AFT published its report last August, prominent charter school advocates responded to the typically poorer NAEP results for charter schools

Statement on the Official Release of the 2003 NAEP Charter School Results, 2007, pp. 1–4. Copyright © 2004 by Bella Rosenberg. Reprinted by permission.

relative to other public schools mainly by arguing that charter schools educate the most disadvantaged of disadvantaged youngsters. The fact that AFT's report included breakdowns by poverty, race and ethnicity, and central-city location—every fair comparison that the NAEP Data Tool allowed—either was ignored by the critics or dismissed as being insufficient for capturing this most-disadvantaged-of-the-disadvantaged phenomenon.

Indeed, like everything else, the NAEP Data Tool and NAEP itself have limitations. Curiously, however, our critics utterly dismissed the statistically significant underperformance of low-income charter school students relative to their peers in regular public schools but were virtually ebullient over our finding that there was no significant difference between the poor performance of minority students in charter and other public schools. Whether this jubilation was caused by the "soft bigotry of low expectations," the unseemly assumption that racial and ethnic minorities are all poor or, ipso facto, hard to educate, or by forgetfulness that charter schools were built on the promise of doing better than other public schools with these students, I leave to others to decide. What is clear, however, is that the allegation that charter schools educate the most disadvantaged of the disadvantaged, let alone do a better job of it, gets even less support from the official NAEP report than it did in the preliminary NAEP results.

First, the new NAEP data reveal that charter schools do *not* educate a disproportionate percentage of low-income (free/reduced-price lunch eligible) students after all. Indeed, the percent of low-income students in charter schools fell from 54 percent in the NAEP sample reported on by the AFT to 42 percent in the fuller sample—two percentage points *lower* than the percentage in other public schools. Yet even though charter and regular public schools turn out to have about the same percentage of low-income students, the results from the preliminary NAEP sample are echoed in the official report: Low-income charter school students perform significantly worse than their peers in other public schools in both math and reading; moreover, the *average* performance of charter schools is significantly worse than other public schools in math and, as we shall soon see, in reading, as well. If educating the most disadvantaged of the disadvantaged is a legitimate explanation for poor relative performance, it is not an explanation that charter schools are in much of a position to make.

Second, it also turns out that charter schools enroll a statistically significant lower proportion of special education students than regular public schools do (and almost certainly students with milder disabilities). Because special education students, on average, are the lowest-scoring students, their low representation in charter schools further undercuts the claim that these schools are educating the most disadvantaged of the disadvantaged.

Indeed, as Table A-1, which is buried in the appendix of the official NAEP report, indicates, when you break down the average reading comparison—the only one of our significantly lower NAEP charter school results that was not replicated in the official report—by excluding special education students, the statistical significance of the lower reading score of charter school students relative to other public school students is restored.

Third, it also turns out that charter school enrollment is not quite as concentrated in central-city schools after all. In the fuller sample, the proportion of charter school students in urban charter schools fell from our sample's average of 62 percent to 50 percent. While this is still significantly higher than the proportion of other public school students attending urban public schools, it also indicates that charter schools are today just as likely to locate in areas without disproportionately high concentrations of "hard-to-educate" students as they are to locate in central cities.

If anything, then, the new data provide even clearer evidence that, far from educating the most disadvantaged of the disadvantaged, charter schools are doing a poorer job with a student body that is slightly less poor and has a significantly lower percentage of special education students than the student body found in other public schools. As for the statistically insignificant achievement differences both reports found between racial and ethnic minorities in charter and other public schools, when charter schools are disproportionately located in central cities and yet do *not* have disproportionately more low-income students than other public schools do on *average*—but do have a disproportionately *lower* percentage of special education students—there is good reason to suspect that the racial and ethnic minority students in charter schools are, if not less disadvantaged than their peers in other public schools, then at least no more disadvantaged. We look forward to the opportunities that the release of the full NAEP data set will allow for performing cross-tabulations to shed light on this important question.

Another major line of argument we heard about the "meaninglessness" of the unofficial NAEP results was that they revealed nothing about how long charter schools had been in operation, which was true enough since the Questionnaire results that could address this were not publicly available. According to this argument, most charter schools are new schools, which need a few years to get up to speed, so it is understandable that charter school students would do worse on NAEP. It is therefore worth examining what the Questionnaire results reveal.

As the tables in the Appendix demonstrate, the argument does not hold water. Students in charter schools that were open for a longer time did no better than students in newer charter schools. Nor does it turn out that the majority of charter school students are in newer schools; two out of three charter school students in the sample were in charter schools that had been providing instruction for at least four years.

The Questionnaire results also deliver a blow to the theoretical underpinnings of the prevailing charter school movement. Charter schools pledged to produce superior achievement results in return for greater autonomy, the theory being that freedom from rules and regulations and the creation of a competitive environment would unleash the creativity and productivity now presumably absent in regular public schools. Our report could only shed preliminary light on this subject, by looking at performance in states with "strong" or "weak" charter school laws, according to the criteria of the Center for Education Reform (CER). The official report casts a more comprehensive shadow.

Consistent with our results, the new NAEP data show that the more autonomy a charter school has, the worse it does. Students in charter schools that were authorized by and part of a school district posted average results that were indistinguishable from those of their peers in regular public schools. In contrast, students in charter schools that were not chartered by a school district and that operated as their own school district had the worst performance among charter school students and also achieved at a significantly lower level than students in other public schools. Students in charter schools run by educational management organizations (EMOs), which enrolled about one-third of charter school students in the NAEP sample, performed no better than other charter schools.

Last but not least is the information on teachers this report provides, which, previously, also could not be accessed. In charter and other public schools, regular certification is associated with higher achievement. Not surprisingly, students in charter schools were less likely to be taught by regularly certified teachers than students in other public schools (66–69 percent vs. 90 percent). Although charter school students taught by either type of teacher scored lower than other public school students with either type of teacher, the difference was not statistically significant. The abysmal results for charter school students taught by teachers with no teaching credentials (9–12 percent)—there were no such students in the regular public school sample—speak for themselves.

Charter school students were also twice as likely as other public school students to have teachers with 0–4 years of experience (43 and 42 percent vs. 23 percent). Both for charter and other public school students, having more-experienced teachers was associated with higher achievement. Yet the negative impact of inexperienced teachers was significantly worse for charter school students than it was for other public school students.

If the official 2003 NAEP charter school report and Questionnaire results, along with the corroborating evidence that has been amassed over the years, does not cause policymakers to re-examine the misleading claims and specious theories of the charter school movement, it is hard to imagine what will. True, NAEP does not measure growth, which, according to the U.S. Secretary of Education and CER, for example, renders NAEP scientifically suspect when it reports on charter schools but not apparently when it reports on other public schools, which it has been doing since 1969. But if charter schools produced higher achievement growth, we would expect that students in charter schools that were in operation the longest to perform better than their peers in newer charter schools, and they did not on NAEP. Moreover, Helen Ladd and Robert Bifulco's comprehensive study of charter schools in North Carolina did directly measure growth by tracking the same children over time, and, if anything, its results deal a bigger blow to charter school claims than NAEP does.

When Chester Finn learned the unofficial NAEP charter school results from the *New York Times* prior to their publication in the newspaper, he reacted to the findings by commenting that charter schools needed a dose of tough love. That is still sound advice.

According to CER, there are about a million youngsters in charter schools. The evidence is strong that far too many of them are paying a heavy price for policymakers having dropped the ball on charter school oversight. While no doubt there are some outstanding charter schools, the evidence indicates that most charter schools are doing worse than our much-maligned regular public schools. If charter schools are supposed to "rescue" children trapped in so-called failing public schools, who will rescue the children trapped in demonstrably more failing charter schools?

POSTSCRIPT

Have Charter Schools Fulfilled Their Promises?

Although the preceding articles on this issue focus primarily on the characteristics and academic achievement of students being served by public charter schools as compared to students attending non-charter public schools, there are a number of other points of contention and conflict between supporters and critics of the charter school movement. Much of the following description of those different controversies comes from a June 2007 report on charter schools from EdSource, a California-based policy analysis group. The report, beyond its analysis of student academic performance, described three other issues: facilities, financial impacts, and governance that "provide ongoing sources of friction and have provoked intermittent calls for policy solutions." With respect to facilities, EdSource points out that the original legislation did not provide for facility costs, but that has changed not only with legislation but also because of a state proposition passed by voters in 2000 that was quite favorable to charter schools. That proposition required school districts to provide facilities for charter schools if there were at least 80 charter students. EdSource reports that

> Many charter schools and their districts have butted heads over the interpretation and implementation of the law. Many charters say that their districts have not fulfilled their duties under the proposition. However, some districts are struggling to build, modernize, or equip the facilities needed to house "their own" students and have difficulty adapting their facilities plans to the wishes of charter schools.

Another major issue is how schools are funded. With "average daily attendance" providing the basis for school funding, any significant loss of student enrollment will have a negative impact on a school district's budget. When a student opts for enrollment in a charter school, the money generated by that student will follow the student to the charter school. This appeals to charter school advocates who believe that competition is healthy and that the financial incentive to attract and/or retain students will improve school quality. But districts respond that the loss of students to charter schools is harmful because the decrease in costs to the district is not commensurate with the income lost because of departing students. The example provided by EdSource is that "if ten students of a district-run school transfer to a charter school, the district loses funding for ten students but must still keep its teachers, maintain its facilities, and so forth."

The third area of controversy involves governance issues. If a school district denies a request to approve a charter school, the petitioner can seek redress and approval at the county office of education. This obviously may put the county office of education into a difficult position with the school district in that the school district would certainly be displeased if the county office of education overruled the district's denial of the charter. Another governance issue arises over the school district's oversight responsibilities vis-à-vis charter schools. In large school districts this can be very complex if the district must maintain oversight of multiple charter schools "that are not affiliated with each other and have very different procedures and policies."

Additional coverage and perspectives regarding this issue can be found in the November 2005 and February 2006 issues of *Phi Delta Kappan*, position papers from the *National Education Association* and the *American Federation of Teachers,* and publications from the charter school advocacy group, *Center for Education Reform.*

ISSUE 7

Has the "No Child Left Behind" Legislation Created Good Educational Policy?

YES: Margaret Spellings, from "Building on Results: A Blueprint for Strengthening the No Child Left Behind Act," U.S. Department of Education (January 2007)

NO: James H. Lytle, from "The Snake in the 'No Child Left Behind' Woodpile," *Education Week* (February 7, 2007) and **Ann McColl,** from "Tough Call: Is No Child Left Behind Constitutional?" *Phi Delta Kappan* (April 2005)

ISSUE SUMMARY

YES: Margaret Spellings, U.S. Department of Education Secretary, states, "The No Child Left Behind Act is challenging our students to succeed and our schools to improve."

NO: James H. Lytle, former superintendent of the Trenton, N.J., Public Schools and a practice professor at the University of Pennsylvania's graduate school of education argues that NCLB's rigid timelines for progress and threats of sanctions are misguided and will not be successful in bringing real improvement. Ann McColl, an attorney and associate professor of education at the University of North Carolina, suggests that the courts may need to decide the constitutionality of the Act.

The No Child Left Behind Act (NCLB) has provoked controversy not only with respect to the substance of its mandates and its sanctions, but also with respect to its intrusion into educational issues traditionally reserved for individual states. In spite of such controversies, it is difficult to argue with the fundamental goals of the legislation, that is, a commitment to closing the significant academic achievement gaps that exist between white students and African American and Hispanic students, while at the same time improving the achievement of all students. Disquieting statistics coming from the *National Assessment of Educational Progress* (NAEP) show that African American

17-year-olds read at the level of white 13-year-olds. Equally troubling is the NAEP data showing that at the fourth grade level 13 percent of African American children and 19 percent of Hispanic children performed at or above the proficient level on mathematics tests, compared to 47 percent of white students. Proponents of educational reform also point to the fact that only 70 percent of ninth-graders graduate from high school in four years (NCES, 2004).

A report from the Center on Education Policy (2006) included the following specific effects of NCLB:

> Teaching and learning are changing as a result of NCLB. Administrators and teachers have made a concerted effort to align curriculum and instruction with state academic standards and assessment. Principals and teachers are also making better use of test data to adjust their teaching to address students' individual and group needs. Many districts have become more prescriptive about what and how teachers are supposed to teach. Some districts encourage teachers to follow pacing guides that outline the material to be covered by different points in the school year, while others have hired instructional coaches to . . . give teachers feedback on ways to improve.

Critics of the NCLB point out that federal funding has not been adequate to cover the costs of its various mandates especially in the areas of increased testing and data collection. They also point out the pressure on teachers and administrators "to teach to the test," while at the same time reducing the time spent on other valuable subjects if those subjects are not tested. Others point out that some states in order to meet the NCLB's requirements for "Annual Yearly Progress" (AYP) have "dumbed-down" their curricular standards so that students will appear to be doing better on the state standardized tests used to assess AYP. Support for this latter assertion can be found in the comparison of student scores on state-developed assessments and national testing samples from the NAEP (2005). Examples include Tennessee where 87 percent of eighth-graders were deemed proficient in mathematics by state tests, but only 21 percent on the NAEP; in Georgia, 83 percent of eighth-graders were deemed proficient by state testing, but only 24 percent by NAEP standards.

YES ↰

Margaret Spellings

Building on Results: A Blueprint for Strengthening the No Child Left Behind Act

Introduction

Five years ago, Americans united behind a revolutionary idea: Every child can learn.

With these words, on Jan. 8, 2002, President Bush signed the landmark *No Child Left Behind Act* (*NCLB*) into law. Passed by an overwhelming bipartisan majority in Congress, it was designed to end the "soft bigotry of low expectations" so that, as the president said, "all students will have a better chance to learn, to excel, and to live out their dreams."

The law, which reauthorized the 1965 *Elementary and Secondary Education Act*, signaled a fundamental and common-sense change in American education. Academic standards would be set by states, schools would be held accountable for results, and the federal government would support both with increased resources and flexibility. And it's working, with test scores rising and achievement gaps narrowing.

All of these results point to the law's ultimate goal: steady academic gains until all students can read and do math at or above grade level, closing for good the nation's achievement gap between disadvantaged and minority students and their peers. "This law finally puts muscle behind the attempt to close that gap," said New York City Schools Chancellor Joel Klein. "We can no longer mask the deficiencies of some students with outsized gains by others."

The *No Child Left Behind Act* recognizes what truly makes a difference in providing a quality education. It calls for a highly qualified teacher in the core subjects in every classroom; the use of proven, research-based instructional methods; and timely information and options for parents. Schools that under-perform are held accountable, providing their students with free tutoring or transfer to a better-performing public school. In other words, children's education needs are placed first—where they belong.

The law has helped revitalize the states' constitutional leadership role in education. Before *NCLB* was passed, less than half the states fully measured their students against clear academic standards. Today, every state and the

From U.S. Department of Education, January 2007.

District of Columbia hold schools accountable for improving academic achievement. Every state also participates in the National Assessment of Educational Progress (NAEP)—the Nation's Report Card—allowing policymakers and parents alike to compare progress. "The premise of *NCLB* is clear and essential," said former Colorado Gov. Bill Owens. "All children can learn. Not just children from homes of privilege, children from suburbia or children from a certain ethnic background."

Federal resources have been increased to match this enhanced role. Total federal funding for *No Child Left Behind* rose 34 percent between 2001 and 2006. Funding for Title I schools serving low-income students rose 45 percent. States and school districts also have unprecedented flexibility in how they use federal funds in exchange for greater accountability for results.

"*NCLB* has helped by setting very clear, very high achievement targets for all students," said Washington, D.C., public schoolteacher Jason Kamras, the 2005 National Teacher of the Year. "I think that's an incredibly positive step in American public education."

No Child Left Behind Is Working

The *No Child Left Behind Act* is challenging our students to succeed and our schools to improve. Early data comparisons suggest that they are responding.

In the 1990s, reading remained stagnant for fourth-graders nationwide, according to NAEP, while achievement gaps in math grew larger for African-American and Hispanic nine- and 13-year-olds. By contrast, according to several recent NAEP assessments:

- More reading progress has been made by nine-year-olds in five years (1999–2004) than in the previous 28 years combined;
- Math scores for fourth- and eighth-graders and nine- and 13-year-olds have reached new heights; and
- Achievement gaps in reading and math between African-American and Hispanic nine-year-olds and their white peers have fallen to all-time lows.

This progress has occurred as the academic bar has been raised and our schools have become more diverse. In fact, some of the largest gains are being made by children once left behind, including many in big-city public schools. Under *NCLB*, fourth-graders in a majority of sampled urban school districts made greater gains in reading and math than students nationwide on average, according to the NAEP Trial Urban District Assessments. The Council of the Great City Schools also reported double-digit gains in large urban districts for fourth-graders in both subjects between 2002 and 2005.

These positive national results are reflected in state proficiency scores in individual schools:

- **North Glen Elementary (Glen Burnie, Md.)**—In 2003, just 57 percent of students in this high-poverty school rated proficient in reading, while 46 percent were proficient in math. By 2005, those numbers had risen to 82 and 84 percent, respectively. African-American students improved their math proficiency by an astounding 47 percentage points. "They've taken advantage of all the aspects of the *No Child Left Behind* law and they've been able to raise their scores and make sure that no child is left behind in their school," said Mrs. Laura Bush.

They are also reflected in school districts:

- **Garden Grove School District (Garden Grove, Calif.)**—All but two of the district's schools met or exceeded their adequate yearly progress (AYP) goals in the 2004–05 school year. Three-fourths of the district's students spoke English as a second language, and nearly six in 10 were from low-income families. "We use the data behind *No Child Left Behind* to set the targets we want to hit. We align all our actions and resources to hit those targets. And our teachers believe the kids can do it," said Garden Grove Superintendent Laura Schwalm.

And the results are reflected throughout states:

- **New York**—Fourth-grade math achievement rose 11 points between 2002 and 2004, while the achievement gap for both African-American and Hispanic students narrowed by 10 points. A record 70 percent of New York's fourth-graders met all state Learning Standards in English in 2005, 22 points better than in 1999—including, for the first time, a majority of African-American and Hispanic students.
- **Georgia**—More than 70 percent of third-grade English language learners scored proficient or better in reading in 2004–05, up 23 percentage points from 2002. Among third-graders with disabilities, 81 percent scored proficient or better in reading, up 26 percentage points.

Of course, test scores do not tell the whole story. Ninety percent of teachers have met *NCLB*'s highly qualified teacher requirements—a bachelor's degree, state certification and demonstrated expertise in the subject matter taught. At-risk students are getting help earlier, while children with disabilities are receiving more classroom time and attention, according to the independent Center on Education Policy. And students in the groundbreaking Reading First program receive on average 100 extra minutes per week of proven, research-based instruction from teachers, tutors and reading coaches.

With the help of *No Child Left Behind*, and working together as legislators, policymakers and educators, we've been able to turn the tide. "*NCLB* called on educators to embrace a new challenge—not just access for all, but achievement for all. Thousands upon thousands are answering that call," said Kati Haycock, director of the non-partisan Education Trust. . . .

Building on Results: A Blueprint for Strengthening the *No Child Left Behind Act*

In five short years, the *No Child Left Behind Act* has evolved from an idea to a law to a way of life. Today, educators, public officials and the media are engaged in a nationwide conversation, debating whether academic standards are high enough, assessments are fair enough, and enforcement is tough enough. This conversation would not be occurring without *No Child Left Behind*.

As we approach the law's reauthorization, the conversation must focus on how to turn around struggling schools and improve the academic performance of older students. *No Child Left Behind* has given us the data to see what is working—and what is not. One of the biggest challenges is the performance of late middle and high school students. Between 1999 and 2004, reading scores for 17-year-olds fell three points, and math scores fell one point, according to NAEP. Achievement gaps between Hispanic and white 17-year-olds actually grew wider in both subjects.

Achievement by students requires action by schools. In 1983, the *A Nation at Risk* report called on high school students to take a minimum of three years each of math and science to graduate. A generation later, less than half the states have met this goal. A recent survey found that only one in five high school graduates in the workforce say they were challenged by their coursework while in school.

We also must reward teachers and principals who make the greatest progress in improving student performance and closing the achievement gap. This is especially important in high-poverty schools, where students are less likely to be taught by a credentialed teacher. To speed up our progress, we must work to match the very best teachers with our most challenging schools.

This is critical for America's competitiveness. Our 15-year-olds ranked 24th out of 29 developed nations in math literacy and problem-solving, according to the 2003 Programme for International Student Assessment (PISA). The U.S. has fallen to ninth place in the world in high school graduation rates among young adults, according to the Organization for Economic Cooperation and Development.

Compounding the problem, about 1 million students drop out every year, making the "million-dollar mistake"—the difference in lifetime earnings between the average high school dropout and bachelor's degree recipient. Less than half of the students who *do* graduate are ready for college-level math and science coursework, according to ACT, Inc.

Since the passage of *NCLB*, research has shown a convergence in the skills and knowledge needed to succeed in both college and the global workforce. According to the U.S. Department of Labor, about 90 percent of the fastest-growing jobs require postsecondary education or training. Math and science have become the new currencies of the global economy. Our students must have the knowledge and skills needed to succeed in this changed world.

Building on Results: The Policy

To ensure our students' success, we will build on *NCLB*'s results in the following ways:

- A stronger effort must be made to close the achievement gap through high state standards and accountability.
- Middle and high schools must offer more rigorous coursework that better prepares students for postsecondary education or the workforce.
- States must be given flexibilities and new tools to restructure chronically underperforming schools, and families must be given more options.

The Bush administration will continue to work with Congress to give educators, policymakers and parents the tools to get the job done, without straying from *NCLB*'s core principles, including:

- All students reading and doing math at or above grade level by 2014;
- Annual assessments and disaggregation of data to close the achievement gap;
- Qualified teachers in core academic subjects in every classroom; and
- Timely information and options for all parents.

No Child Left Behind is a work in progress: every day, we learn what works so students can make greater progress. Five years after the law's passage, we have collected more data than ever before about the academic performance of our students and schools. This information enables us to take action—and act we must. . . .

Building on Results: Policy Proposals

1. Every Child Performing at or above Grade Level by 2014

Overview
We remain committed to ensuring that all students can read and do math at grade level or better by 2014. This is the basic purpose and mission of the *No Child Left Behind Act.* . . .

Summary of Proposals

  a. **Maintain Annual Academic Assessments and Accountability**
     Information is at the core of *NCLB*. Over the past five years, states have developed the ability to provide regular and reliable reporting about student achievement. Through annual assessments, parents now receive information about how well their child is doing in school and about how well a school is educating all children. . . .

     Two critical components of *NCLB*—measuring achievement and holding schools accountable for results—must continue. First, states will continue to assess students in reading/language arts and math in each of grades 3–8. To help states ensure they are reaching towards high standards and to provide a comparative benchmark, the National Assessment of Educational Progress (NAEP) will continue to be administered in the fourth and eighth grades in reading and math, with all states participating. Second, in keeping with current law, states will report student assessment results to parents and hold schools accountable for improving the performance of all students. The disaggregation of achievement results and the required 95 percent participation rate, hallmarks of *NCLB*, will continue to ensure that students in critical subgroups (race, ethnicity, English language proficiency, disability, and socio-economic status) remain the focus of attention.

b. **Promote High State Academic Standards**

The administration will maintain its commitment to local control as states continue to establish the required academic standards and assessments for students. To support greater transparency, states must report the proficiency rates for state and NAEP assessments on the same public report card. . . .

2. Flexibility for Innovation and Improvement

Overview
The real work of educating America's students does not happen at the federal level. It happens in the states and schools. States and localities have the primary responsibility to direct and manage education. They should have the opportunity to innovate and show creativity as they work to meet the fundamental goals of *No Child Left Behind.* . . .

Summary of Proposals

a. **Greater Use of Growth Models**

One clear benefit from *NCLB*'s focus on transparency of information—and from increased federal resources for that purpose—is improved data systems in the states. Many states can now implement more sophisticated accountability systems to measure and follow the progress of individual students. A growth-based accountability model is one of those systems.

For those states with well-established assessments and robust data systems, growth models will be permitted in their overall accountability systems. Growth models allow states to measure individual students' progress over time, giving schools credit for improvement from year to year and providing another way to show whether achievement gaps are closing. They may be particularly useful in charting the progress of students whose achievement may follow a different path from that of their peers, such as students with disabilities or LEP students. . . .

For a growth model to work under **Building on Results**, it must follow these core principles:

• **Growth toward Standards**—The growth model must ensure that all students are proficient by 2014 in reading/language arts and math while setting individual student progress measures to ensure that achievement gaps are closing for all student groups. The annual goals must be based on grade-level proficiency, not on student background or school characteristics.

- **Assessments and Data**—Schools and districts must be held accountable for the performance of each student subgroup in reading/language arts and mathematics in grades 3–8. Student participation rates and one other academic indicator must be included as separate academic indicators in the state accountability system. . . .

b. **Flexibility through Prioritized Support for Schools**

Another result of improved data systems and rigorous accountability mechanisms is the opportunity to treat schools appropriately based on their record in meeting accountability targets. Capitalizing on improved state data systems, states will be able to prioritize their school improvement activities based on the specific needs of the school.

To make the accountability provisions of *NCLB* more meaningful, states will have more flexibility to precisely focus their technical assistance, interventions and direct resources to schools identified for improvement, corrective action or restructuring. This flexibility will help states do what is necessary to enable all students to read and do math at grade level or better by 2014 in a more effective and efficient manner.

For example, schools will be able to focus their choice options and SES resources on students not yet proficient, so long as the "all-students" group meets the state's proficiency target and the school meets the 95 percent participation requirement for assessments. . . .

c. **Provide More Flexibility in Use of Federal Funds**

Current state and local flexibility provisions are too limited to provide significant, meaningful flexibility to states and districts. Under **Building on Results**, states' ability to efficiently and effectively direct federal resources will be expanded. We will streamline the application process for federal support and afford states greater flexibility in allocating federal funds throughout the state. . . .

d. **Improved Assessments and Accountability for Students with Disabilities**

NCLB is committed to the academic achievement of students with disabilities. Therefore, students with disabilities must participate fully and meaningfully in state assessments. To ensure districts receive credit for their work in helping these students make academic progress, states will have the option of assessing a small group of students with disabilities based on alternate and modified achievement standards. These standards must meet high quality standards and promote challenging instruction so students with disabilities can reach the highest possible levels of achievement.

e. **Accelerate English Language Acquisition for LEP Students**

By disaggregating achievement data by student subgroups, *NCLB* has focused attention on the academic achievement of our nation's more than 5 million-strong and growing population of LEP students. **Building on Results** will maintain a strong commitment to assessment and accountability for all LEP students in the content areas as a driving force for improving instruction and outcomes. More attention will be focused on English language acquisition as the foundation for academic achievement. . . .

f. **Support Innovation in the Safe and Drug-Free Schools Program**

Many schools and education agencies have made great strides toward creating safe and drug-free learning environments. The 2006 Indicators of School Crime and Safety found declining crime rates in our nation's schools. But we must do more. The Safe and Drug-Free Schools (SDFS) grant program was designed to support the creation of positive and safe learning environments through education and prevention activities. . . .

3. Challenging Our Students and Preparing Them to Succeed

Overview

When 90 percent of the fastest-growing jobs require postsecondary education or training, it is unacceptable that almost a third of incoming high school students—and about half of African-American and Hispanic students—do not make it to graduation day on time. Many are not challenged by their coursework; others fall behind in earlier years and do not catch up in the more fast-paced high school environment.

Since the National Governors Association held its National Education High School Summit in 2005, many states have worked to increase the rigor of high schools. The reauthorization of *NCLB* must set a national expectation of real high school reform. **Building on Results** establishes the expectation that every high school student graduate on time with a diploma that indicates readiness for success in postsecondary education and the 21st-century workforce.

Summary of Proposals

a. **Improve Graduation Rates**

There can be no debate about the need to increase the number of high school students who graduate with a meaningful diploma and relevant skills. All 50 governors have agreed to use a more accurate graduation rate calculation in the National Governors Association's Graduation Rate Compact. . . .

b. **Ensure That Students Graduate Ready to Succeed**

In this global economy, it is critical that the K–12 and higher education communities work together to build common expectations for high school students so they are fully prepared to enter college or the workforce with the skills they need to succeed. Under **Building on Results**, states must develop by 2010–11 course-level academic standards for two years of English and math that will prepare high school graduates to succeed in college or the workplace. . . .

c. **Promote Rigor in High School Coursework**

Rigorous coursework in high schools is critical to ensuring that students are learning the skills they need to compete in the global economy. . . . To promote student participation in courses required for success in college, states will report completion rates of these college readiness courses by relevant subgroups.

d. **Increase Funding for High Schools That Serve Low-Income Students**

To ensure that high schools have the resources to help low-income students, there will be a substantial increase in funds for Title I high school students. . . .

e. **Provide Specific Expertise through a New Adjunct Teacher Corps**

Many schools, particularly in low-income areas, suffer from a lack of qualified or expert instructors. The Adjunct Teacher Corps will offer an opportunity for talented and dedicated professionals from outside the teaching profession to share their expertise in core academic subjects, especially math and science, in middle and high school classrooms. . . .

4. Helping Teachers Close the Achievement Gap

Overview

The academic progress made by states and students in the last five years is testament to the fact that the achievement gap is not intractable. However, while we have narrowed the gap, we are a long way from closing it. Teachers are instrumental to this effort. They must be equipped with the most current, research-based instructional tools to help them do their jobs. We need to find ways to get our best teachers into our neediest schools. And we must offer more intensive instruction and tutoring to help children catch up and keep pace.

Summary of Proposals

a. **Reward Exceptional Teaching**

Bringing every student up to grade level demands high-quality teachers. The Teacher Incentive Fund will provide resources to help states and school districts develop compensation systems that reward teachers and principals who make progress in raising student achievement and closing achievement gaps. Teachers and principals who choose to work in the neediest schools can also be rewarded.

b. **Focus On Mathematics Achievement**

According to a 2004 Department study, only a small fraction of mathematics coursework in our nation's middle schools has scientific evidence of effectiveness. To strengthen the teaching of math in elementary and middle schools, President Bush has proposed the Math Now program, which will provide resources to help teachers use scientifically proven practices, including those soon to be recommended by the National Math Panel, so that students enter high school ready to take challenging and advanced coursework. . . .

c. **Focus On Science Achievement**

In introducing the American Competitiveness Initiative in 2006, President Bush announced his commitment to improving student achievement in math and science in order to maintain our nation's competitive advantage. Including science in *NCLB* accountability determinations will encourage a greater focus on this critical subject and ultimately lead to greater science achievement. . . .

d. **Build Expertise in Reading Instruction through Reading First**

The administration is committed to ensuring that every child can read by the third grade. To meet this goal, the administration will continue to invest in and expand Reading First, the largest, most focused and most successful early reading initiative ever undertaken in this country. The program applies scientifically based reading research and instructional tools and assessments to help teachers improve student achievement. . . .

5. Strengthening Public Schools and Empowering Parents

Overview

Before the *No Child Left Behind Act* was passed, parents—especially those of modest means—were often relegated to the education sidelines. When their child's school did not improve, they were given few alternatives. *NCLB* has empowered families with new options, including the choice to attend a better-performing public school or a public charter school. The law also provides free tutoring and after-school help, called Supplemental Educational Services (SES), to qualified low-income students. . . .

We remain committed to restructuring and fixing troubled public schools. But we must also provide more parents the opportunity to make appropriate choices for their children. To that end, we support the spread of charter schools. . . .

Summary of Proposals

a. **Invest in the School Improvement Fund**

Funds will be targeted to ensure improvement in some of the nation's most challenging schools. School Improvement Grants will support implementation of the schools' improvement plans and will assist states' efforts to closely monitor and review those plans for each school while providing technical assistance to turn around low-performing schools.

b. **Strengthen School Restructuring**

Some schools that are subject to restructuring for chronic underperformance are simply not pursuing the quality and depth of reform that will lead to adequate yearly progress. Current law permits these schools to implement only minor reforms as corrective actions even when they are in the fifth year of program improvement. Under **Building on Results**, the menu of actions authorized under restructuring will commit these schools either to make substantial changes in staff or to reconstitute the schools' governance structure, except in special circumstances (e.g., when a school is in restructuring status only because of the performance of one subgroup). . . .

c. **Enhance Choice through Public and Private School Scholarships**

The administration strongly believes in public education. We also believe that private schools are an important and effective alternative for many parents, especially those whose children attend chronically underperforming schools. Parents deserve the opportunity to have their child attend a quality school. Public schools that go into restructuring status will offer Promise Scholarships, which would allow low-income students in grades 3–12 to attend a private school or an out-of-district public school, or receive intensive tutoring. Federal funds will follow the child to his or her new school. . . .

The need to offer low-income parents the option of private schools for their children is intensified by a lack of real public school choices in some districts. Nationally, only around 1 percent of eligible students have exercised *NCLB*'s public school choice option and transferred to a higher-performing public school. This low participation rate is often due to districts' inability to accommodate parents' transfer requests because high-quality local public school options are lacking. . . .

d. **Provide Additional Staffing Freedom at the Most Troubled Schools**

Schools that are required to be restructured will be authorized by Title I law to remove limitations on teacher transfers from their collective bargaining agreements. . . . Removal of these provisions will provide these schools with greater freedom to pursue aggressive reform by ensuring that the school leadership has the right staff in place. This provision will apply only to schools in restructuring, not to all schools in the district.

e. **Augment Charter School Options**

In order to enhance charter school availability and performance, the federal charter school program will now support all viable charter applications that can improve outcomes for students. . . .

The development of new charter schools would help states and school districts address the primary challenge many districts face in implementing public school choice: insufficient seats at schools where students could transfer. . . .

f. **Enhanced Supplemental Educational Services (SES)**

The SES provisions of *NCLB* are designed to help students achieve or exceed grade-level standards by providing extra support such as tutoring. Larger SES per-child amounts for students who live in rural areas or who have disabilities or limited English proficiency will be permitted. As the cost of tutoring these students is on average higher than for other students, SES funding will increase by an appropriate amount or proportion. This change should also increase the pool of SES providers with the capacity to serve these students. . . .

g. **Provide Equitable Services to Private School Students and Teachers**

"At-risk" students should have access to academic services regardless of where they attend school. We propose extending the longstanding requirements for equitable participation by private school students and teachers to new programs and initiatives where appropriate. . . . Service providers affiliated with a religious organization should not be restricted from providing services so long as those services are secular, neutral and non-ideological, as required under *NCLB*. Additionally, we support greater private school flexibility in the use of federal funds and improved communication between private and public schools.

James H. Lytle  **NO**

The Snake in the "No Child Left Behind" Woodpile

In the first five years of the federal No Child Left Behind Act, much attention has been focused on implementation issues—from how to manage the increasing number of schools and districts "in need of improvement" or in "corrective action," to problems with testing programs, adequate-yearly-progress reporting, and the law's highly-qualified-teacher requirements. But looming in the background is an element that will soon raise the stakes for implementation, one that has received much less public discussion: the requirement that states intervene in schools and districts not meeting AYP requirements.

As Congress takes up the law's reauthorization this year, it's important to keep in mind the legislation's time frame: Public schools and districts receiving federal funds must have *all* their students (less those with severely handicapping conditions) at proficient levels of performance in reading, mathematics, and science by 2014. The trick is that the performance standard increases every two years to ensure attainment of the required 100 percent proficiency. Thus, schools that have apparently been making progress are continually held to higher standards; those that have not been making adequate progress (even if they have shown improvement) have an even more difficult challenge; and those that have consistently met the standard may suddenly find their levels of performance no longer sufficient. As a result, the number of schools identified as needing intervention is likely to accelerate.

The emergent No Child Left Behind issue is the mandate that state departments of education intervene in schools (or districts) that have not made adequate progress for four or more years, and that the intervention follow the prescriptions in the federal legislation. These include the following (with the date they became applicable in parentheses):

- Offer students public school choice (spring 2003).
- Offer "supplemental educational services," or after-school tutoring (2003–04).
- Implement "corrective action" (2004–05).
- Replace school staff members (2005–06).
- Institute a new curriculum (2005–06).
- Decrease school management authority (2005–06).
- Extend the school year or day (2005–06).

From *Education Week*, February 7, 2007, pp. 1–2. Copyright © 2007 by James Lytle. Reprinted by permission.

- Bring in outside experts (2005–06).
- Restructure (2005–06).

If these actions do not produce the intended results, then the following additional prescriptions are available in 2007:

- Continue to offer choice and supplemental programs.
- Convert to charter schools.
- Make significant staff changes.
- Turn the school (or the district) over to a state agency or private firm.

There is no existing knowledge base in research or practice, however, that demonstrates whether universal proficiency is even possible. Nor is there accumulated research demonstrating that *any* of the sanctions mandated in the law, either singly or in combination, will lead to sustained improvement in student achievement or school performance. There are no explicit incentives offered—other than to avoid intervention, corrective action, reconstitution, or takeover. The presumption in the No Child Left Behind law is that the threat of sanctions will force schools and districts to implement research-tested best practices, yet the evidence on school change indicates that trust and willingness to risk are the precursors to sustained improvement.

The evidence to date for the efficacy of interventions already tried is limited. The choice sanction has been notably unsuccessful (fewer than 1 percent of eligible children participate), and the supplemental-services intervention has been the subject of heated controversy over who will provide the services and who will evaluate their effects. None of the other sanctions has yet been broadly enough implemented to yield a sufficient record for evaluation. But as the list of interventions indicates, spring 2007 is "showtime." State departments of education and/or local school boards will have the authority and responsibility then to make drastic changes at schools that have not made progress.

Yet many states have not been able to manage relatively simple components of the No Child Left Behind Act, including timely AYP reporting, accounting for dropouts, and identifying highly qualified teachers. Nor have they been inclined to use the interventions available in 2005–06. Soon they will be responsible for leading improvement at a scale and depth they have so far been unable to demonstrate they can manage (see New Jersey's 15-year record of urban-district takeovers as an example).

At this point, the typical state response to poor school performance is to organize "corrective-action teams" of experts (read state department employees and retired school administrators and teachers) and send them to schools to conduct inspections, typically for three to five days. A team writes a critique based on its review of school programs, staffing, and performance data; this is forwarded to the school, to be transformed into a plan for implementation in the coming months, all culminating with the next spring state-testing cycle. Other common solutions include sending in an "intervention specialist," a "distinguished educator," or a magician of a similar sort, who is expected single-handedly to turn around the failing school.

Behind these strategies is the assumption that a school which has been unable to make adequate progress will seize upon a critique, defer to the experts, address all deficiencies, and make dramatic strides. The question of how the school suddenly develops the capacity or the inclination to do what it previously has been unable to is left unattended. (In my own experience, these corrective-action plans may have from 90 to 100 recommendations, but no discussion of funding or strategy.) The team walks away; the school is left to its own accord. The No Child Left Behind mandates have been served, and the state education department is in compliance.

My sense is that, so far, both states and districts have responded to low performance by creating the facade of intervention through assessment teams, intervention specialists, administrative and curriculum changes, and tight school improvement plans. But they have rarely used the responsibility implicit in the law to do the deep work, the re-imagining, the research and development that high levels of proficiency will require.

For its part, the U.S. Department of Education has embarked on an ambitious program of basic research in such areas as cognitive sciences, and has charged its What Works Clearinghouse to identify effective interventions that practitioners and policymakers could access to deal with inadequate performance. By its own acknowledgment, though, the Institute of Education Sciences cannot currently provide the knowledge base that schools in corrective action would in theory need, if they were realistically expected to make the dramatic improvements in student achievement the No Child Left Behind law requires.

The modifications to the law under consideration by key members of Congress and Secretary of Education Margaret Spellings include permitting "growth models" for assessing adequate yearly progress, providing financial aid and staffing incentives for schools not meeting proficiency goals, and improved assessment techniques for special-needs students and English-language learners. (**"Bush to Start NCLB Push in Congress,"** Jan. 10, 2007.) Each of these modifications might be welcomed by the practitioner community, but they are technical solutions, not innovations, and not likely to have more than an incremental effect on student performance.

Moreover, the education private sector (in contrast to the health-care and pharmaceutical industries) has been unwilling to provide the venture capital and investment that might lead to dramatic improvement. If *Education Week*'s advertisements are any indication, the private-sector solution seems to be to take existing test-item banks that various corporations already own, assign the items to designated state curriculum objectives, peddle "formative" assessments that use the items, feed the results into the great student database in the sky, and then claim that instruction should be designed to address the indicated deficits. Again, there is no evidence that this strategy will ensure that schools meet the law's standards.

Thus the conundrum: How can schools and districts (and states, for that matter) be held to account for improvement that no one currently knows how to accomplish? Are the imminent sanctions really solutions? Shouldn't the intervention timelines be postponed, modified, or extended until the knowledge base catches up with the policy?

The prospect of a rapid increase in the number of schools and districts in "corrective action" status and the inability of state departments of education to provide support and oversight are likely to open the door wide for private-sector management, choice, and consulting interventions. Leading-edge versions of this have already emerged in Philadelphia, Chicago, Washington, and Cleveland, cities whose central offices are becoming management corporations for diverse sets of schools and services: charters, private and nonprofit corporately managed schools, special-needs student outplacements, tutoring services, packaged curricula, and voucher programs for private and parochial schools. An increasing number of urban districts are complying with No Child Left Behind mandates by outsourcing low-performing schools, then changing vendors in the instances when a school doesn't make adequate progress. Yet none of the vendors has been able to demonstrate that it can intervene in low-performing schools, whether elementary or high schools, and consistently help those schools meet AYP-mandated levels of achievement. In effect, the districts move the walnut shells each time the Education Department can't find the pea.

This spring, the growing number of schools and districts in corrective action will provide the prospect of expanded corporate entrée. Shareholders, CEOs, and state bureaucrats may prosper, but nothing would suggest that kids will be better served.

The right thing to do is to slow down the sanctions timetable until the reauthorization debate is completed, funding for necessary supports is in place, and a research base has been developed that undergirds the proposed interventions. Otherwise, we are conducting another grand experiment with those least able to control their fates.

༄༅

Tough Call: Is No Child Left Behind Constitutional?

Ann McColl

The No Child Left Behind (NCLB) Act, the 2001 reauthorization of the Elementary and Secondary Education Act, has become a symbol of all things good and bad in education. While the basic concepts of the legislation—accountability for results, research-based education programs, increased parental options, and expanded local control and flexibility—have wide support, some critics

From *Phi Delta Kappan*, by Ann McColl, April 2005, pp. 604–610. Copyright © 2005 by Phi Delta Kappan. Reprinted by permission of the publisher and Ann McColl.

have argued that NCLB has failed to deliver.[1] Others have focused on how best to implement its provisions.[2] Although this scrutiny of the requirements and outcomes of NCLB is crucial to the policy debate, the law has largely escaped a more fundamental review, and answers to the following questions are needed: Has Congress overstepped its legal authority with No Child Left Behind? Is NCLB a constitutional exercise of congressional power, or does it infringe on states' rights? What is the role of the U.S. Department of Education (ED) in addressing ambiguities in the law? Answering these questions requires a close examination of federalism as it is expressed in the U.S. Constitution and interpreted by the U.S. Supreme Court.

The call to examine the law in this light comes with a warning: reaching conclusions about whether Congress acted within the limits of its constitutional authority may cause some discomfort. "Liberals" may find their customary inclination to favor a more expanded role for the federal government to be in conflict with their concern about the substance of NCLB. "Conservatives" may similarly find their general bias in favor of states' rights to be in conflict with their support for the accountability and school-choice elements of NCLB. And if the courts ignore, as they should, both the politics surrounding NCLB and its education reform goals, the results of a legal challenge could be interesting, indeed. A conservative Supreme Court may ultimately conclude that President George W. Bush's education agenda exceeds constitutional bounds.

Is There Constitutional Authority for NCLB?

There is little dispute over whether NCLB represents an unprecedented level of federal involvement in the affairs of our public schools. However, there is disagreement between the law's supporters, who hail this federal intrusion into state and local education as effective national reform, and its detractors, who argue that the intrusion consists of a set of politically motivated mandates that are detrimental to our schools. The language of NCLB speaks to the sweeping authority intended by its passage: "The purpose of the title is to ensure that all children have a fair, equal, and significant opportunity to obtain a high-quality education and reach, at a minimum, proficiency on challenging state academic achievement standards and state academic assessments." To accomplish this, NCLB sets extensive requirements for states, including establishing an accountability system and staffing schools with high-quality professionals.

This level of federal intrusion into a domain typically under state control raises legal questions because Congress must act within the limits of federal authority established by the U.S. Constitution. The Constitution reflects a careful balance between the powers of the federal government and those of the states. James Madison argued, "The powers delegated by the proposed Constitution to the federal government are few and defined. Those which are to remain in the State governments are numerous and indefinite."[3] The Constitution defines this balance in the 10th Amendment: "The powers not delegated to the United States by the Constitution, nor prohibited by it to the States, are reserved to the States respectively, or to the people."

Past court decisions, most notably *San Antonio* v. *Rodriguez* (1973), have declared that the Constitution does not establish, either explicitly or implicitly, education as a right or delegate the authority over schools to the federal government. Instead, education is within the domain of state and local governments. As the U.S. Supreme Court said in the celebrated 1954 *Brown* v. *Board of Education* opinion, "Education is perhaps the most important function of state and local governments."

If the federal government is not specifically authorized by the Constitution to delve into matters of education, what other grounds could there be that would satisfy the 10th Amendment's conditions for the assignment of powers? For the authority to legislate as broadly as it has in NCLB, Congress relied on a provision in the Constitution that provides power unlike any other defined in that document: the spending clause. In archaic-sounding language, the spending clause (Art. I, sec. 8, cl. 1) states: "The Congress shall have Power To lay and collect Taxes, Duties, Imposts and Excises, to pay the Debts and provide for the common Defence and general Welfare of the United States. . . ." The spending clause is the basis not only for NCLB but also for most federal education policies, including those that prohibit discrimination—Title VI (race, ethnicity, and national origin), Title IX (gender), and the Individuals with Disabilities Education (IDEA) Act and Section 504 of the Rehabilitation Act (disability)—and those, like the Family Education Rights and Privacy Act, that protect student privacy. Any future federal education reforms, including a national curriculum, national tests, or national licensure standards, will almost certainly have to be crafted as spending clause legislation.

Spending Clause Legislation as a Contract

The spending clause is unique in that it allows Congress to enact legislation in areas over which it otherwise has no authority, *if* the legislation is in the form of an offer of a contract—i.e., if federal funds are offered to states as an inducement to meet certain conditions. In constitutional parlance, this arrangement, also known as a conditional grant, does not "offend" the 10th Amendment reservation of certain powers to states since states can simply refuse the contract.

Because spending clause legislation operates as a contract, its provisions must be clear enough for states to be able to decide whether to accept the terms of the contract. As the Supreme Court stated in *Pennhurst State School* v. *Halderman* (1981), "The legitimacy of Congress' power to legislate under the spending power thus rests on whether the State *voluntarily* and *knowingly* accepts the terms of the 'contract'" (emphasis added). The Court further identifies the parameters of this authority, stating that, "by insisting that Congress speak with a clear voice, we enable the States to exercise their choice knowingly, cognizant of the consequences of their participation." This conforms to the understanding that most people have of what makes a contract valid.

But the requirement for clarity in spending clause legislation stems from broader concerns having to do with democratic principles and the 10th Amendment. Because such legislation is probably addressing an issue normally reserved for the states—such as education—it is crucial that the citizenry of the states understand the terms of the contract and have the choice to accept or reject it. As the Supreme Court explained in *New York* v. *United States* (1992), "The residents of the State retain the ultimate decision as to whether or not the State will comply. If a State's citizens view federal policy as sufficiently contrary to local interests; they may elect to decline a federal grant." While this may sound unrealistic to those who are familiar with how policy decisions are typically made, the debates in Utah, Arizona, Wyoming, and other states over accepting the NCLB contract are consistent with the process envisioned by the Supreme Court.

In *South Dakota* v. *Dole* (1987), the Supreme Court has provided further guidance for determining whether Congress has met spending clause requirements. To be constitutionally valid, legislation that relies on the spending clause must be in pursuit of the "general welfare," related to the federal interest in particular national projects or programs, not prohibited by other constitutional provisions, unambiguous in describing the conditions for the States' receipt of federal funds, and cast as a financial inducement, not a coercion.

Based on prior court analysis of other federal legislation, it seems quite likely that NCLB will easily pass legal muster on the first three criteria. The fourth and fifth criteria raise more issues. The requirement for the legislation to be unambiguous in describing its conditions goes to the heart of the contract issue. Using the Supreme Court's language, the issue is whether a state "knowingly and voluntarily accepts the terms of the [NCLB] 'contract.'" In other words, were the critical provisions of NCLB clear and unambiguous when it was enacted? It is tempting to be flippant in answering this. If the law were clear, why would we need all of these conferences, regulations, and instances of informal guidance? Why would members of Congress be in such disagreement over the law's intent? Why would commentators still be unraveling the implications of the legislation? But a serious issue deserves a serious answer.

Are the Terms of NCLB Unambiguous?

Achieving the requisite level of clarity is extremely difficult to do with such a vast reform as NCLB, which leads to the policy question of whether Congress should be able to use a backdoor approach to pass any legislation that is so far-reaching on an issue reserved for the states. While only a court of law can make the ultimate decision, it is easy enough to conclude from the sheer extent of ED's efforts to clarify NCLB and provide guidance to the states on its implementation that the law was not clear. By the end of February 2004, ED reported that it had issued 29 guidance documents, 20 letters to chief state school officers and state officials, and over 500 letters to various state and local offices. In addition, ED has issued formal regulations on at least three occasions in order to clarify key issues, including public school choice requirements, standards and assessments, the definition of a highly qualified teacher, the inclusion of students with significant cognitive disabilities, and several aspects of the accountability model.

These efforts to clarify various provisions of NCLB are not addressing issues around the fringes. How the law defines "highly qualified" has a dramatic impact on whether states can meet the requirement for staffing their schools in a time of teacher shortages and retention problems. How NCLB determines which students are counted toward a school's AYP (adequate yearly progress) and what tests can be used has a direct bearing on how many schools and school districts will be identified as needing improvement. The ED regulation mandating that neither capacity issues nor desegregation orders can be a barrier to school choice means that many more schools and school districts must offer this option to their students. These are not small issues, and they do not have insignificant financial implications for school districts.

From a constitutional perspective, this means that there were many important issues that were not clear in the legislation. And there simply is no role for ED in resolving these ambiguities. In another spending clause case, *Virginia Dept. of Educ.* v. *Riley* (1997), ED asserted that it could withhold funds from Virginia on the basis that it had clarified ambiguities in IDEA through an interpretive rule and that Virginia had failed to comply. The Fourth Circuit rejected this argument, responding that "it is axiomatic that statutory ambiguity defeats altogether a claim by the Federal Government that Congress has unambiguously conditioned the States' receipt of federal monies in the manner asserted."

Shifting Positions

The lack of clarity in NCLB is also evident in ED's review of state accountability plans, which are intended to outline the states' efforts to comply with the conditions of the legislation. These plans are the clearest measure of how the states are responding to the law. If NCLB were clear, then the approval process for the plans would be fairly straightforward—states would either meet the conditions or they would not. Instead, the approval process has been characterized by confusion, the application of inconsistent standards, and even reversals in ED's positions. On numerous occasions, the department has allowed some states to proceed with their accountability programs after having rejected similar plans from other states.[4]

The process of approving accountability plans has state boards of education and state school officers scrambling to change their state's accountability system based on ED's latest interpretation of the law. If one state is successful in securing approval for a dual accountability system, then other states seek to amend their plan so that they can do it too. Or once statistical tests in safe harbor become acceptable—after having been rejected in earlier plans—states seek to add them to their plans. NCLB has been a moving target and has forced state education leaders to continually revise their strategies for compliance.

Two of the most controversial areas have been the testing of both students with severe cognitive disabilities and those who are not proficient in English. These students pose a challenge to test-based accountability systems because, while there are strong policy arguments for including them in the assessment system, it is difficult to test them in the same way as other students. NCLB made the stakes higher with the requirement that these students be included in AYP calculations, which means that failure to get them to attain grade-level proficiency could ultimately cause a school or school district to miss its AYP target. Without clear guidance in the law itself, states chose to address the testing of these students in different ways, and ED's position on the issue changed over time in the process of approving accountability plans. . . .

It is perhaps easy to say from a policy perspective that some issues will have to be worked out and that the implications of the legislation are better understood after they are implemented. But to the extent that the shifts in ED's interpretation of NCLB prevented a state from knowingly accepting the terms of the contract, the law is unconstitutionally ambiguous and is an invalid exercise of spending clause power.

Shifting Resources

In addition to being confused over exactly what was expected of them, the states did not know how much money they would receive in exchange for meeting all of the conditions in the law. In funding NCLB, Congress took the unusual step of setting authorization levels for the next five years. The authorization level for Title I-A increases each year in roughly a stepwise progression, beginning at $13.5 billion in FY 2002 and climbing to $25 billion in FY 2007. The FY 2007 authorization level represents full funding of the Title I basic formula, based on the cost of serving all counted children and the law's expenditure factors. The substantial increase in funding over the five-year period is also consistent with the increased requirements placed on states and the schools. The House-Senate conference report (H. Rept. 107-334) accompanying NCLB reflects this, stating that the conferees "recognize that to implement fully the reforms incorporated in the conference agreement, the local educational agencies will require increased Title I resources, for which reason the Conferees have agreed to significant and annual increases in Title I authorizations."

If authorization levels guaranteed states particular funding amounts, then states would clearly understand the terms of the NCLB contract. And presumably, this matters to states. As is true with most contracts, participants want to know what they will get in return for meeting the conditions. But the only thing that is clear with regard to NCLB is that authorization levels *do not* guarantee any particular amount of funding. . . .

In the political arena, the difference between authorization levels and actual funding has caused some members of Congress, especially Democrats, to criticize the President and the process for failing to fully fund NCLB and to keep the promises made to schools. Supporters of the legislation counter that it is a mistake to use authorization levels as the benchmark for comparison and that the emphasis should be on the actual increases in funding. The disparity between authorized and actual funding also raises a constitutional question: If the funding level has nose-dived so much from the time the contract was offered (i.e., when the legislation was enacted), was it possible for states to have "knowingly" accepted the terms of the contract? Probably not.

Having big decreases from authorized to appropriated levels means that states cannot know how much funding they will receive to implement the law until the federal budget is approved, which can occur even after the fiscal year has begun. What courts will say about this issue is less clear, as Supreme Court opinions have tended to focus on the clarity of a law's provisions rather than the clarity of its funding.

Is NCLB an Inducement?

The question of whether states feel pressured to accept the additional requirements in NCLB in order to continue receiving federal funds or whether they feel the law merely offers an inducement to act also requires more scrutiny. Before jumping into this analysis, it is worth explaining the concepts of inducement and coercion as the courts use them in reviewing spending clause legislation. First, some courts are reluctant to pursue this analysis at all because of a belief that it simply does not make sense to think of a state being coerced. In other words, coercion would seem to be more applicable to individuals, who might cave in to psychological pressure, than to the decision-making process of a governmental entity. . . .

To examine the issue of coercion as it relates to NCLB, it is useful to know that for most states federal funds account for approximately 7% to 10% of total funds for public education. The largest source of federal funds is Title I. States have been receiving these funds since 1965, when the ESEA was passed. Currently about 94% of all local education agencies receive Title I funds. Most of the funding provided under NCLB continues to be through Title I. While these funds historically have been targeted to the neediest children, Title I—as reauthorized in NCLB—establishes many conditions that affect all students and all schools. For example, NCLB sets the date by which all teachers of core academic subjects must be highly qualified. And all schools in a state—including high schools, which receive little Title I funding—must participate in the accountability program (although some sanctions apply only to Title I schools). NCLB also alters Title funding formulas in order to shift more resources to high-poverty states.

The constitutional question is whether NCLB coerces rather than induces states to accept the extensive new requirements in order to continue to receive Title I funds. There are several factors that are particularly important in this analysis: 1) states have relied on Title I since 1965 and have developed ongoing programs and positions with their Title I funds; 2) NCLB dictates state policy choices pertaining to a core function of state government—education—that go well beyond the scope of Title I funding; and 3) high-poverty states will find it even more difficult to reject the offer because of both the increased funding they would receive under the new Title I funding formula and the greater challenge they would face in replacing the federal funds with state resources.

As a realistic matter, the answer to the coercion question seems quite simple. Most, if not all, states faced with the combination of state budget crises that have loomed since NCLB was enacted and the prospect of losing significant federal funds would indeed conclude that they had no choice but to accept the law's additional requirements. So, while states may resent that the source of only 7% to 10% of total education funding can dictate policy in such an intrusive manner, they recognize that every source of funds for schools is critical, especially if they lack other resources with which to replace the loss of federal dollars. And so the states are forced to accept the new requirements in NCLB.

As a matter of law, some courts still may be reluctant to characterize the states' reliance on funds or the federal intrusion into state programs as "coercion," but it is certainly possible that NCLB will be vulnerable to this challenge. Indeed, states that have relied on Title I funds as part of a piecemeal strategy for serving at-risk children certainly have no realistic choice but to accept the conditions of the law.

NCLB could also be considered coercive because of the rules governing its implementation. Congress has authorized ED to withhold funds from states for failure to comply with various NCLB provisions. Depending on how ED wields this authority, it could be considered coercion if all or a large proportion of a state's funding is withheld for minor violations. So far, the department has withheld administrative funds from Georgia and Minnesota in the amounts of $700,000 and $113,000 respectively, which should not be large enough sums to raise constitutional issues.

What about the Supremacy Clause?

In examining the constitutional issues related to NCLB, it is worth considering one more repercussion of this expansive federal legislation. Not only have states had to accept many more conditions for only slightly more money, but any state law that contradicts NCLB in any way will have to be adjusted or dismantled. This is required by the supremacy clause (Art. VI, cl. 2) of the U.S. Constitution: "This Constitution, and the Laws of the United States which shall be made in Pursuance thereof . . . shall be the supreme Law of the Land; and the Judges in every State shall be bound thereby, any Thing in the Constitution or Laws of any State to the Contrary notwithstanding." In *Lawrence Co.* v. *Lead-Deadwood School District* (1985), the court determined that the supremacy clause applies not only to state laws that may be in direct conflict with federal law but to any state law that "stands as an obstacle to the accomplishment of the full purposes and objectives of Congress." Because spending clause legislation is so different from other types of legislation, some have challenged whether the supremacy clause should apply when state laws conflict with federal laws in this category. Appellate courts, however, have repeatedly held that it does.[5]

To comply with NCLB, many states have had to change laws related to their accountability systems, high school exit exams, licensure requirements, and class-size requirements. As broad as these changes may be, imagine the possible impact on states that have been through litigation regarding their responsibility to provide a constitutionally adequate education. Even state constitutions and court orders requiring certain actions can be displaced if they present an "obstacle to the accomplishment of the full purposes and objectives of Congress." While state constitutional provisions may, in many respects, be aligned with the goals of NCLB, it is certainly possible that specific court orders may require different approaches to raising student achievement, such as reducing class size, providing prekindergarten, or increasing teacher salaries. If such efforts conflict with those necessary to fulfill NCLB mandates, such as the "highly qualified teachers" requirement, then they must be stopped. With this kind of implication for state education programs, it is particularly egregious that Congress did not speak with a clear voice on the requirements and funding for NCLB.

Conclusion

So what conclusion can we reach about whether NCLB is constitutional? Issues of governance tend to be highly controversial, and many of the major decisions of the past have come from a deeply split Supreme Court. In the 1990s, the Supreme Court acted to severely curtail congressional power under two major sources of broad legislative authority found in the Constitution—the commerce clause (*U.S.* v. *Lopez*, 1995) and the enforcement of equal protection of the laws under the 14th Amendment (*City of Boerne* v. *Flores*, 1997). These decisions show a clear willingness on the part of some of the justices to narrow Congress' authority. Will the current Court do the same with the spending clause?

The Supreme Court opinion that gives the most guidance on the spending clause is the aforementioned *South Dakota* v. *Dole*. While Justice O'Connor provided a compelling dissent, most justices upheld the condition for federal highway funds. But, as already discussed, there are notable differences between the highway funds law and NCLB. Will the Supreme Court scrutinize Congress' authority more closely when the subject is education—a core responsibility of the states? Will the complexity and ambiguity of the legislation affect the Court's analysis? Will it matter that the legislation was not clear about the amount of funding states would receive? Will the Court consider the states' historical reliance on Title I funds in determining whether coercion applies? . . . It is a tough call.

So what happens if NCLB is challenged, and the Supreme Court determines that it was an unconstitutional use of the spending clause? Congress would have some options. If it wants to proceed with the reform goals of the law, it must draft a contract that clearly describes its conditions and that induces, but does not coerce, states to choose to participate. This is the absolute minimum required for a constitutional exercise of Congress' spending clause power. Of course, Congress can go beyond this minimum and offer a great contract that no state would want to refuse. This is the policy choice before our federal legislators, and there are many experts who could assist Congress in crafting better legislation. But if Congress is unwilling to meet spending clause requirements, then it will have to take a very hard look at how it justifies its intrusion into the state domain of education.

Notes

1. Perry Bacon, "No Child Left Behind Leaving States Cold," *Time*, 23 February 2004, p. 14; Anne C. Lewis, "A Horse Called NCLB," *Phi Delta Kappan*, November 2002, pp. 179–80; idem, "Where Is the NCLBA Taking Us?," *Phi Delta Kappan*, September 2002, pp. 4–5; David Marshak, "No Child Left Behind: A Foolish Race into the Past," *Phi Delta Kappan*, November 2003, pp. 229–31; William J. Mathis, "No Child Left Behind: Costs and Benefits," *Phi Delta Kappan*, May 2003, pp. 679–86; Monty Neill, "Leaving Children Behind: How No Child Left Behind Will Fail Our Children," *Phi Delta Kappan*, November 2003, pp. 225–28; Lowell C. Rose, "No Child Left Behind: Promise or Rhetoric?," *Phi Delta Kappan*, January 2003, p. 338; Alan Sturrock, "Left Behind," *Phi Delta Kappan*, March 2003, p. 560; and M. Donald Thomas and William L. Bainbridge, "No Child Left Behind: Facts and Fallacies," *Phi Delta Kappan*, June 2002, pp. 781–82.

2. Marc S. Tucker and Thomas Toch, "The Secret to Making NCLB Work? More Bureaucrats," *Phi Delta Kappan*, September 2004, pp. 28–33; and Frederick M. Hess and Chester E. Finn, Jr., "Inflating the Life Rafts of NCLB: Making Public School Choice and Supplemental Services Work," *Phi Delta Kappan*, September 2004, pp. 34–40, 57–58.

3. James Madison, "The Alleged Danger from the Power of the Union to the State Governments Considered for the Independent Journal," *The Federalist Papers: No. 45*, 26 January 1788.

4. For a thorough review of this issue, see William Erpenbach, Ellen ForteFast, and Abigail Potts, *Statewide Educational Accountability Under NCLB: Central Issues Arising from an Examination of State Accountability Workbooks* (Washington, D.C.: Council of Chief State School Officers, July 2003). U.S. Department of Education Decision Letters for State Accountability Plans are available at. . . .

5. See, for example, *Fraser* v. *Gilbert*, 300 F.3d 530 (5th Cir. 2002); *Westside Mothers* v. *Haveman*, 289 F.3d 852 (6th Cir. 2002); and *Blum* v. *Bacon*, 457 U.S. 132 (1982).

POSTSCRIPT

Has the "No Child Left Behind" Legislation Created Good Educational Policy?

It is difficult to argue with the perception that the No Child Left Behind Legislation (NCLB), first enacted in 2002, has pulled education onto the national stage. Certainly the publicity and politics generated by both the support and the criticism of the legislation means that education has "arrived" as a front-page item. From this point forward any presidential aspirant will need to have a well-developed educational plan as part of his/her overall campaign platform. Political debates will henceforth always include questions regarding the various candidates' stances on educational issues. In terms of bringing about greater public awareness regarding the quality of our schools, NCLB has to be given high marks. Also at the school level NCLB has caused a much greater emphasis on reading and mathematics because those are the two curricular areas currently assessed to determine if schools are making the required Annual Yearly Progress (AYP). Critics assert that this greater emphasis on reading and math comes at the expense of less time being spent on subjects such as history, art, music, and civics.

Another feature of the assessment and accountability focus of NCLB is the reporting of student scores on a disaggregated basis within a single school. This means that scores for different subgroups of students such as English language learners, racial minorities, and students with special needs are reported separately. Proponents of this disaggregation of test scores point out that this approach "ensures that schools don't bury these students' test scores in schoolwide and gradewide averages or gloss over the achievement gaps that these scores reveal" (C. Guilfoyle, *Educational Leadership,* November 2006). Opponents of disaggregation assert that this practice can cause scapegoating of certain groups of children and/or encourage schools to give certain students more resources and attention than others.

Another feature of NCLB that has initiated policy reviews and changes at the state level is its requirement that all students have a "highly qualified" teacher. In support of this federal mandate Linda Darling-Hammond and Barnett Berry wrote in *Educational Leadership* (November 2006):

> Studies show that well-prepared and well-supported teachers are important for all students, but especially for students who come to school with greater needs. That is why one of the most important aspects of NCLB is its demand that states ensure a "high qualified teacher" for every student. . . . This first-of-a-kind federal intervention is intended to correct one of the

most egregious injustices in the U.S. public school system: Poor students and those of color are the ones most likely to be taught by inexperienced and underqualified teachers.

Critics of this feature of NCLB will point to the phrase "first-of-a-kind federal intervention" as evidence of this legislation's major incursion into and violation of state and local constitutional rights as related to educational matters.

Additional sources of information and commentary on this important piece of educational policy can be found in the aforementioned volume of *Educational Leadership,* and in June 2006, December 2005, and October 2004 issues of *Phi Delta Kappan.* For the public's views on NCLB see the poll in the September 2006 issue of *Phi Delta Kappan.*

ISSUE 8

Should School Discipline Policies Be Stricter and Include "Zero Tolerance" Provisions?

YES: *Public Agenda,* from "Teaching Interrupted: Do Discipline Policies in Today's Public Schools Foster the Common Good?" *Public Agenda* (May 2004)

NO: Russell Skiba, from "Zero Tolerance: The Assumptions and the Facts," Center for Evaluation and Education Policy (Summer 2004)

ISSUE SUMMARY

YES: The *Public Agenda* in reporting on a survey of parents and teachers regarding school discipline states, "70% of teachers and 68% of parents strongly support the establishment of 'zero tolerance' policies."

NO: Russell Skiba, professor of counseling and educational psychology at Indiana University, posits that "violence is not rampant in America's schools" nor is there credible evidence to confirm the effectiveness of zero tolerance policies.

Effective discipline, whether at the classroom or schoolwide level, is an obvious and fundamental need if an environment conducive to student learning is to be created and maintained. It risks tautology to state that not much can occur educationally unless students and staff feel safe and secure at school. That commonsense truism has been recognized consistently by federal and state legislation as well as in a number of U.S. Supreme Court decisions on issues such as student expression, drug testing, and searches of students by school officials. Much of the related legislation and many of the court decisions are founded on concerns regarding student and staff safety. Indeed, the most recent iteration of the No Child Left Behind Act includes the authorization for a Safe and Drug-Free Schools Advisory Committee to provide advice to the Secretary of Education regarding safe schools and crisis planning. Certainly the horrific events at Columbine and Virginia Tech have underscored the need for school officials to make issues related to student safety among their top priorities.

In dealing with school and classroom discipline educators have a broad range of practices and procedures available to them. For serious violations, especially those involving student safety, all states have authorized the use of suspension and/or expulsion from school. In many states, state legislation or local school board policy mandate that these serious violations be responded to with "zero tolerance" punishment. Although "zero tolerance" means different things in different school locales, at its core is a commitment to strict and consistent administration of strong discipline upon a first offense, if that offense involves behavior inimical to the safety and security of students and school personnel. Even though supported by most teachers and school administrators, this type of stern discipline has come under scrutiny and criticism by some observers, who question not only its efficacy but also the equity of its application with respect to different racial and ethnic groups. In some ways the phrase itself is an unfortunate one, because critics of zero tolerance policies can stress the draconian ring of the phrase and point to instances of overzealousness in its administration.

Fortunately, for most teachers and school administrators, their daily dealings with school discipline do not involve serious student safety issues, but rather the maintenance of a classroom and school environment in which teachers can teach and students can learn. What approaches to school and classroom discipline seem to be the most effective? Although that question may invoke many different and often conflicting answers among educators, there is a consensus that characteristics such as consistency, fairness, and logical consequences for student misbehavior are at the core of effective disciplinary practices. In an article entitled "Principles of Discipline in the Secondary School: A System That Works" (*Issues in Teacher Education*, 1994), author Dennis L. Evans states, "In all matters related to discipline, teachers and school administrators must, through word and deed, continually manifest their commitment to consistency and fairness."

Indeed, one of the rationales for a "zero tolerance" policy is that punishment for an act covered by the policy will be the same, regardless of the perpetrator.

In the article from *Public Agenda*, high percentages of teachers and parents support the "broken windows" approach, that is, "strictly enforcing the little rules so the right tone is created and bigger problems are avoided." In his article Russ Skiba asserts that despite public support of strict discipline, research does not support its efficacy.

YES ⮌

Teaching Interrupted: Do Discipline Policies in Today's Public Schools Foster the Common Good?

Too many students are losing critical opportunities for learning—and too many teachers are leaving the profession—because of the behavior of a few persistent troublemakers. What's more, say teachers, today's misbehaving students are quick to remind them that students have rights and their parents can sue.

These are some key findings in *Teaching Interrupted: Do Discipline Policies in Today's Public Schools Foster the Common Good?* based on national random sample surveys of 725 middle and high school teachers and 600 parents of middle and high school students. The surveys offer a detailed look at the discipline issue, exploring its causes, the effectiveness of current policies, the impact on school climate and receptivity to various solutions. *Teaching Interrupted* was underwritten by Common Good, a nonpartisan policy group focusing on legal issues in the United States today.

A Culture of Second-Guessing

According to the study, teachers operate in a culture of challenge and second-guessing—one that has an impact on their ability to teach and maintain order. Nearly half of teachers (49%) complain that they have been accused of unfairly disciplining a student. More than half (55%) say that districts backing down from assertive parents causes discipline problems. Nearly 8 in 10 teachers (78%) say that there are persistent troublemakers in their school who should have been removed from regular classrooms. Both teachers and parents support a variety of remedies, ranging from more special schools for misbehaving students to removing monetary awards for parents who sue.

Discipline: An Old Story

Discipline has been a recurring theme in public opinion research on public schools for years, and *Teaching Interrupted* suggests that educators have made only limited progress addressing it. The issue continues to bedevil teachers, concern parents and derail learning in schools across the country.

It's almost unanimously accepted among teachers (97%) that a school needs good discipline and behavior in order to flourish, and 78% of parents agree. It's also widely accepted among both groups that part of a school's mission—in addition to teaching the three R's—is to teach kids to follow the rules so they can become productive citizens (93% and 88%).

Yet, the observations of both teachers and parents collected in this study suggest that today's school discipline policies may not be working in the interest of the common good. For example:

- *The vast majority of both teachers (85%) and parents (73%) say the school experience of most students suffers at the expense of a few chronic offenders.* Most teachers (78%) report that students who are persistent behavior problems and should be removed from school grounds are not removed.
- *Students pay a heavy price academically when schools tolerate the chronic bad behavior of the few.* Most teachers (77%) admit their teaching would be a lot more effective if they didn't have to spend so much time dealing with disruptive students. Similarly, many parents (43%) believe their child would accomplish more in school if teachers weren't distracted by discipline issues.
- *Lack of parental support and fear of lawsuits are ever-present concerns for many teachers.* Nearly 8 in 10 teachers (78%) say students are quick to remind them that they have rights or that their parents can sue. Nearly half (49%) say they have been accused of unfairly disciplining a child. More than half (52%) say behavior problems often stem from teachers who are soft on discipline "because they can't count on parents or schools to support them." Nevertheless, approximately 7 in 10 teachers (69%) and parents (72%) say it's just a handful of parents in their own school who challenge or threaten to sue when their child is disciplined.
- *Many teachers say documentation requirements go beyond common sense.* Although relatively few teachers (14%) reject the need to document incidents of misbehavior as too cumbersome, more than 4 in 10 (44%) say the requirements in their own school "go beyond common sense" and are used primarily to protect the schools from potential lawsuits. The overwhelming majority of teachers (79%) would reserve the use of special hearings—where witnesses are called and lawyers are present—for only the most egregious discipline cases.
- *Student discipline and behavior problems are pervasive.* More than half of the teachers surveyed (52%)—and 43% of the parents—report having an armed police officer stationed on their school grounds, and large numbers indicate that discipline is a concern in their own school. On the whole, the findings suggest that the schools are doing a good job responding to the most serious behavior problems, like drugs and guns, but that they should be doing a lot better when it comes to minor violations of the rules, such as talking out, horseplay, disrespect and the like.
- *Student discipline takes a toll on teachers.* More than 1 in 3 teachers say they have seriously considered quitting the profession—or know a colleague who has left—because student discipline and behavior became

so intolerable. And 85% believe new teachers are particularly unprepared for dealing with behavior problems.

- *Problems with student behavior appear to be more acute in urban schools and in schools with high concentrations of student poverty.* Compared with their counterparts, teachers in these schools are more likely to cite student discipline as a top problem, more likely to say it is driving teachers out of the profession and more likely to indicate it has a serious negative impact on student learning.

The Main Culprits

Topping the list of causes of behavior problems in the nation's schools is parents' failure to teach their children discipline (82% of teachers and 74% of parents). Second on the list is: "There's disrespect everywhere in our culture—students absorb it and bring it to school" (73% and 68%). Other Public Agenda research shows that only about a third of parents say they have succeeded in teaching their child to have self-control and discipline, while half say they have succeeded in teaching their child to do their best in school.

Along with inattentive parents and an overall culture of disrespect, teachers and parents also attribute behavior problems to: overcrowded schools and classrooms (62% of teachers and 54% of parents); parents who are too hasty in challenging school decisions on discipline (58% of teachers and 42% of parents); districts that back down from assertive parents (55% of teachers and 48% of parents); and teachers who ease up on discipline because they worry they may not get support (52% of teachers).

Open to Many Solutions—from Alternative Schools to Limits on Litigation

Despite multiple and complicated causes, the discipline problem is not insurmountable, according to the teachers and parents who participated in this study. In fact, majorities of both teachers and parents voice support for all of the ideas tested in the surveys, although some garner much more intense backing than others. The number of respondents who show "very" strong support (as opposed to "somewhat" strong) indicates the intensity of support. The proposals fell into the following categories:

Dealing with "persistent troublemakers"

- Seventy percent of teachers and 68% of parents strongly support the establishment of "zero-tolerance" policies so students know they will be kicked out of school for serious violations, with another 23% of teachers and 20% of parents indicating they support this idea somewhat (Total support: 93% teachers; 89% parents).
- In addition, 46% of teachers and 33% of parents strongly support giving principals a lot more authority to handle discipline issues as they see fit, with another 38% of teachers and 37% of parents supporting this idea somewhat (Total support: 84% teachers; 70% parents).

- More than half of teachers (57%) and 43% of parents also especially liked proposals for establishing alternative schools for chronic offenders, with another 30% of teachers and 32% of parents liking this idea somewhat (Total support: 87% teachers; 74% parents).

Putting more responsibility on parents

- A strong majority of teachers (69%) say finding ways to hold parents more accountable for kids' behavior would be a very effective solution to the schools' discipline problems, with another 25% saying they think it would be somewhat effective (Total support: 94% teachers).

Limiting lawsuits on discipline

- Forty-two percent of teachers and 46% of parents strongly support limiting lawsuits to serious situations like expulsion, with another 40% of teachers and 32% of parents liking this idea somewhat (Total support: 82% teachers; 78% parents).
- Fifty percent of teachers and 43% of parents also strongly approve of removing the possibility of monetary awards for parents who sue over discipline issues, with another 32% of teachers and 27% of parents approving somewhat (Total support: 82% teachers; 69% parents).

Consistently enforcing the little rules

- Both groups show high levels of support for the "broken windows" approach— strictly enforcing the little rules so the right tone is created and bigger problems are avoided: 61% of teachers and 63% of parents strongly support this, with another 30% of teachers and 25% of parents supporting this idea somewhat (Total support: 91% teachers; 88% parents).
- Parents, in particular, think dress codes are a very (59%) or somewhat (25%) good idea (Total support: 75% teachers; 84% parents).
- Most teachers believe putting more of an emphasis on classroom management skills in teacher education programs would go a long way toward improving student discipline and behavior: 54% say this would be a very effective solution and another 37% somewhat effective (Total support: 91% teachers).
- Teachers also believe that treating special education students just like other students, unless their misbehavior is related to their disability, is a good approach: 65% of teachers say this would be a very effective solution, while another 29% consider it somewhat effective (Total support: 94% teachers). . . .

Finding 1: An Old Problem with Real Costs

For teachers and parents, student discipline and behavior is a major concern, one that affects both teacher morale and student learning.

Probably few people will be surprised that this study shows student discipline and behavior to be an important concern for teachers and parents. Past surveys, including some conducted by Public Agenda, have shown this to be a persistent issue. But it is eye-opening to consider the very real costs the problem exacts of education in terms of teacher morale, teacher attrition and student learning.

In *Teaching Interrupted*, we tally the damaging impact student misbehavior is having on today's schools. . . .

Teachers and parents agree in overwhelming numbers that good student behavior is a must-have for schools and kids to thrive—an essential condition before teaching and learning can take place. Virtually all teachers (97%) and an overwhelming majority of parents (78%) say good discipline and behavior is a prerequisite for a successful school. Vast majorities go further, saying the job of the public schools is not simply to ensure that kids achieve academically but also to "teach kids to follow the rules so they are ready to join society" (93% of teachers and 88% of parents).

According to these data, however, there is much room for improvement in terms of student discipline and behavior. Speaking of their own school, pluralities of teachers (49%) and parents (45%) say student discipline ranks "somewhere in the middle" in the range of problems. And some teachers (30%) and parents (15%) say it is one of the top problems.

Cops with Guns

Perhaps the harshest testimonial to the seriousness of the problem is this simple data point: 52% of America's teachers report their school has an armed police officer stationed on school grounds. . . .

Instruction Is the Minimal Piece

In the context of the national push to raise standards and academic expectations, the discipline problem gains even greater relevance. In one of the most profound findings in this study, most teachers—and many parents—say discipline is such a distraction that student learning is suffering. More than 3 in 4 teachers (77%) acknowledge that "if it weren't for discipline problems, I could be teaching a lot more effectively," with 40% saying that they *strongly* agree. . . .

"I'm Not Doing It Anymore"

Lack of discipline in the schools engenders other serious costs as well. The findings in *Teaching Interrupted* reveal that problems with student discipline and behavior are driving substantial numbers of teachers out of the profession. More than 1 in 3 teachers (34%) have seriously considered quitting because of student discipline and behavior. "I haven't [quit] yet. I have wanted to many times. I have cried and been very upset. I have actually had students lie to the point where I could have been written up," said a Florida middle school teacher.

And it appears that teachers are actually leaving their jobs—not just thinking about it. More than 1 in 3 teachers (34%) responding to this survey say colleagues in their school have quit or were asked to leave because student discipline and behavior were too challenging. . . .

Teachers are not the only ones who leave: 1 in 5 parents (20%) have considered moving their child to another school or have already done so because discipline and behavior were such problems. . . .

Sink or Swim

Teachers in the focus groups said that newer teachers are particularly vulnerable to the negative consequences of discipline problems. They pointed out that newcomers typically lack the experience or training to deal with behavior issues, that students are more likely to test them and that they are often assigned the harder-to-manage classes.

The survey indicates this is more than anecdotal. For example, 85% of teachers who took part in *Teaching Interrupted* believe that "new teachers are particularly unprepared for dealing with behavior problems in their classroom," a sentiment Public Agenda has uncovered in previous surveys. One second-year teacher was feeling the pressure: "It has been tough . . . it is kind of a sink-or-swim program right now. You are just thrown in there [to] see if you can handle it."

Is Anybody Listening?

The education field bemoans the rate at which teachers drop out of their profession, yet few focus on student discipline as a serious cause of the problem. These findings provide fresh evidence that the losses and costs in terms of attrition of personnel are very real and deserve attention. Who knows just how much motivated talent the public schools lose every year when teachers are overwhelmed by problems with discipline? And these findings suggest an even more important rationale for taking a serious look at the urgency of the problem: the large number of teachers reporting significant consequences for the academic achievement of students—especially when they are in the nation's cities and highest poverty schools. Even as the pressure to raise standards and improve student performance mounts, it is apparent that much time and opportunity to learn is being lost. Finally, the fact that so many of the nation's middle and high schools feel they need an armed police officer on their grounds is a sobering reality whose cost may be more than can be measured in dollars.

Finding 2: The Tyranny of the Few

Teachers and parents are convinced that the school experience of most students suffers because of the unruly, disruptive behavior of just a handful of students.

America's public schools were founded on the belief that all members of society benefit from an educated citizenry, that a basic education for all citizens is essential for a democracy. But today, teachers and parents believe that the good of the many is in jeopardy because of the misbehavior of the few. . . .

The Same Names Over and Over Again

Both teachers and parents clearly believe that most discipline problems in schools are caused by just a few kids but that all students end up paying the price. Large majorities of teachers (78%) and parents (74%) say it's just a handful of students who cause most of the problems in their school. . . .

The source of the problem may be limited, but the consequences and costs are widely felt. An overwhelming 85% of teachers agree that "in the end, most students suffer because of a few persistent troublemakers" (43% *strongly* agree). Most parents (73%) are of the same mind on this point. "It's a low number [of students], but the effect is disproportionate. You can have one kid blow up a whole class," said a Florida teacher. "There are kids that are trying to learn. They definitely feel like they are losing out," added a colleague. . . .

Treading Lightly on Special Education

Public schools also appear to be failing when it comes to disciplining special needs students. Focus group participants didn't say that special needs kids were especially prone to misbehave. But there was a definite sense—especially among teachers—that the authority of the public schools to effectively discipline special needs students who do break the rules is constrained both by the law and by anticipatory fears of parental challenge. More than 3 in 4 (76%) teachers believe that "students with I.E.P.'s who misbehave are often treated too lightly, even when their misbehavior has nothing to do with their disability.". . .

Better on the Most Serious Offenses

Disturbingly high numbers of the teachers and parents surveyed in *Teaching Interrupted* report serious problems in their school with issues like illegal drugs (41% and 46%) and physical fighting (36% and 30%). But it is at least somewhat reassuring that most teachers and parents believe their school responds swiftly and forcefully to these serious offenses. Overwhelming majorities (83% and 88%) say their school has a quick, no-nonsense response to weapons or drugs, with 63% of teachers and 76% of parents saying they *strongly* agree. In New Jersey, a teacher said, "There are some no-brainers, like no guns, no weapons, no drugs, none of that kind of stuff going on. There are certain things that are certainly zero tolerance.". . .

Yawning Aloud, Putting Their Feet up on the Desk

If the schools respond quickly to transgressions that compromise the safety of their students and teachers, they appear to be far less effective in dealing with the low-intensity violations of school order. Nearly 6 in 10 teachers (and 43%

of parents) believe that their school should be doing a lot better in dealing with routine misbehavior.

When asked about nine specific student misbehaviors, majorities of teachers say their school has serious problems with six of them. . . . Topping the list is students who disrupt class by talking out of turn and horsing around (69%). Almost 6 in 10 teachers also point to cheating, lateness, disrespect and bullying as serious problems; more than half say rowdiness is a serious concern. . . .

Kids Will Be Kids?

Taken individually, these more typical problems might draw a "what else is new, kids will be kids" response. But teachers having to deal with a series of such low-level interruptions, day in and day out, complain that they are in the business of crowd control, not education—and many in our focus groups talked about exactly that. What's more, when it comes to student learning and teacher morale, the cumulative impact of such disruptions may be as costly as the most dramatic incidents—although they garner less press coverage and op-ed outrage. . . .

Finding 3: Getting the Support They Need

Most teachers say their principals support them on discipline, but many say formal documentation requirements sometimes go beyond common sense.

Teachers overwhelmingly accept responsibility for handling behavior problems in their own classroom. To them, it's part of the job. At the same time, they believe the principal sets the tone for the building—and in one of the good news stories to come out of this study, a large number say they can count on their own principal for help when it comes to backing them on discipline decisions. . . .

It's Part of the Job

Teachers still see managing student discipline and behavior as primarily a teacher's job and are hardly anxious to hand off responsibility for classroom discipline to administrators. In the focus groups, teachers sometimes criticized colleagues who they thought were shirking their responsibility by being too quick to send students to the principal's office. Almost 9 in 10 (89%) believe that an integral part of being a teacher is knowing how to handle the inevitable misconduct that will crop up in the classroom. Just 9% of teachers believe instead that "the profession would be better off if discipline were the responsibility of the supervisors in the building."

Lean on Me

Nevertheless, teachers believe that the overall atmosphere of a school and enforcement of policies concerning student behavior are determined by a school's leadership. Almost 9 in 10 (89%) agree it's the principal who sets the tone when it comes to discipline and order, with more than half (53%) saying they *strongly* agree. What's more, experience tells teachers that sooner or later someone will challenge their decisions on discipline, and that's when they need their principal's support. In fact, nearly 1 in 2 teachers (49%) say they have been accused of unfairly disciplining or reprimanding a child. . . .

Too Many Rights?

There are more telling indications that many teachers feel the schools have gone too far in expanding the power of students and parents to challenge educators over discipline decisions. For one thing, teachers feel their authority is undermined when students are overly empowered. Nearly 8 in 10 teachers (78%) agree that "today's students are all too quick to remind you that they have rights or that their parents can sue." . . .

Finding 4: Who's to Blame?

Topping the list of causes of behavior problems in the schools is parents' failure to teach children discipline, followed by a general disrespect in society and a growing willingness on the part of parents and students to challenge schools' authority.

The conviction that parents play the central role in the way children learn and behave in school is one of the most unambiguous and recurring trends in Public Agenda's extensive body of opinion data on the public schools. A recent Public Agenda survey showed the degree to which parents themselves accept responsibility for their own shortcomings on this front: almost 6 in 10 agreed that when a child doesn't know how to behave, it usually means parents are not doing their job. . . .

"I'm Lucky If I Get a Response"

Parents' failure to teach their children discipline tops the list of the underlying causes of behavior problems in today's public schools. . . . On a scale of 1 to 5, 82% of teachers and 74% of parents rate this as either a "4" or a "5." Moreover, more than half of teachers (52%) believe that the schools' problems with student behavior result from teachers being soft on discipline "because they can't count on parents or schools to support them." Other Public Agenda research shows that only 34% of parents say they have succeeded in teaching their child to have self-control and discipline and only half say they have succeeded in teaching their child to do their best in school. . . .

Teachers Get a Pass?

Although conventional wisdom puts much of the onus on teachers, most teachers and parents surveyed for *Teaching Interrupted* reject the notion that teachers are a main cause of student discipline problems. Only about 1 in 4 teachers (26%) and 1 in 3 parents (32%) agree with the statement, "When students misbehave, it usually means the teacher has failed to make lessons engaging," with barely handfuls saying they *strongly* agree (2% and 12%). Similarly small proportions say that the discipline problem resides mainly in teachers who "try to be friends to students rather than authority figures" (34% and 19%). And despite concerns reported earlier about inadequate classroom management skills among new teachers, the charge that too many don't know how to run a classroom is toward the bottom of the list of possible causes (30% and 25%).

Power to the Teachers

A close look at the data also shows that many teachers and parents are in fact confident in the power of teachers to positively influence student behavior, even in those children who come to school lacking family support or basic values. Majorities of teachers (58%) and parents (60%) believe most students, regardless of the neighborhood, will behave properly as long as expectations are clear and rules are enforced. In contrast, smaller numbers say discipline problems are inevitable in the toughest schools (35% and 33%). . . .

Finding 5: Solving the Problem

Teachers and parents gravitate toward solutions that address the problem of persistent troublemakers, that hold parents more accountable and limit their capacity for legal challenges, and that contribute to an orderly school environment.

Seasoned observers of public opinion know there are countless social policy issues where Americans overwhelmingly agree there's a problem but where there is no consensus about action. But on the issue of discipline in the schools, there are high levels of agreement on both the sources of the problem and solutions. The most popular approaches for solving the discipline problem fall into the following general categories: The first looks at diminishing the impact of those "few persistent troublemakers." The second focuses on ways to hold parents more responsible for their own child's behavior. Another aims to limit parents' capacity for frivolous challenges or lawsuits. The last category revolves around ideas for creating an orderly school environment. . . .

Strong Medicine, A Dose of Common Sense

Given that so many teachers and parents trace most discipline problems to a few chronic offenders—many of whom should already have been removed from the building, according to most teachers—it is not surprising that solutions addressing this issue resonate strongly.

Approximately 7 in 10 teachers (70%) and parents (68%) strongly support establishing and enforcing "zero-tolerance" policies so students know they will be kicked out of school for serious violations. But focus group participants were quick to caution that they did not want to see a blind application of the rules. Instead, they expected the strong medicine to include a dose of common sense. A New Jersey teacher said, "The point is zero tolerance, it's good. It kind of scared some of the kids, but it's with common sense. Every case is different." The appeal of zero-tolerance proposals no doubt stems from people's desire to recapture the sense of accountability they feel has been lost.

Moving the Onus from the Schools to the Parents

As we saw in Finding 4, large majorities of teachers and parents believe that inadequate parenting is a primary cause of student behavior problems. Thus, it makes sense that so many also point to solutions that deal directly with parents' behavior. Both groups seem to rally around approaches that have the potential to either pull in parents who've checked out in terms of taking responsibility for their kids' behavior or rein in those who are relentless about defending their children, right or wrong.

Almost 7 in 10 teachers (69%), for instance, feel strongly about a solution that would "find ways to hold parents more accountable for their kids when they misbehave in school." "We have to find some way of engaging the parents," a Missouri teacher said. "We're putting the onus on the schools. We're nagging at the child. That's a *child*. Something has to happen with these parents that are neglecting their children."

Russell Skiba

 **NO**

Zero Tolerance: The Assumptions and the Facts

In the face of serious incidents of violence in our schools in the last decade, the prevention of school disruption and violence has become a central and pressing concern. Beyond the prevention of deadly violence, we know that teachers cannot teach and students cannot learn in a school climate characterized by disruption. A recently released national survey of middle and high school teachers and parents found almost universal support for the proposition that schools need good discipline and student behavior in order to flourish; a large majority felt that the school experience of most students suffers at the expense of a few disruptive students.[1] Clearly, schools have the right and responsibility to use all effective means at their disposal to maintain the integrity, productivity, and safety of the learning climate. About this, there can be no dispute.

Great controversy has arisen, however, about *how* to keep schools safe and productive. In the last ten to fifteen years, many schools and school districts have applied a disciplinary policy that has come to be known as zero tolerance. The philosophy of zero tolerance, adapted from the war on drugs in the late 1980's . . . encourages a no-nonsense approach to school discipline, increasing both the length and numbers of suspensions and expulsions for a broader range of behavior. By punishing both serious and less serious disruptions more severely, the goal of zero tolerance is to send a message to potential troublemakers that certain behaviors will not be tolerated.

Zero tolerance discipline relies upon a certain set of assumptions about schools, violence, and the outcomes of discipline. In the period of heightened fear about school-based violence during the 1990's, it was not always easy to dispassionately examine the evidence for different strategies of violence prevention. It seemed imperative to put an end to school shootings immediately, and those strategies promising the shortest route to that goal were often the most appealing.

In the last few years, however, there has been an enormous amount of study concerning the most promising methods for preventing school violence and promoting effective school learning climates. Unfortunately, much of this evidence has not supported the assumptions that guided the acceptance of zero tolerance discipline in the 1990's. The purpose of this briefing paper is to examine that evidence. To what extent are the promises and assumptions of

From *Education Policy Briefs*, vol. 2, no. 1, Summer 2004, pp. 1–7. Copyright © 2004 by Center for Evaluation & Education Policy. Reprinted by permission.

zero tolerance borne out by our rapidly increasing knowledge about school violence prevention? . . .

Zero Tolerance School Discipline: What Have We Assumed? What Do We Know?

Federal educational policy under *No Child Left Behind* has begun to stress the importance of using only those educational interventions that are supported by research-based evidence. Thus, it makes sense to examine the empirical support for a disciplinary practice that has been widely implemented in our schools. Below, we list each assumption commonly associated with zero tolerance, briefly review the evidence concerning that assumption, and close with the facts reflecting the match between the assumption and the research-based evidence.

What Is Zero Tolerance?

Zero tolerance first received national attention as the title of a program developed in 1986 by U.S. Attorney Peter Nunez in San Diego, impounding seagoing vessels carrying any amount of drugs. U.S. Attorney General Edwin Meese highlighted the program as a national model in 1988, and ordered customs officials to seize the vehicles and property of anyone crossing the border with even trace amounts of drugs, and charge those individuals in federal court.

Beginning in 1989, school districts in California, New York, and Kentucky picked up on the term zero tolerance and mandated expulsion for drugs, fighting, and gang-related activity. By 1993, zero tolerance policies had been adopted across the country, often broadened to include not only drugs and weapons, but also smoking and school disruption.

This tide swept zero tolerance into national policy when the Clinton Administration signed the Gun-Free Schools Act of 1994 into law. The law mandates a one-year calendar expulsion for possession of a firearm, referral of law-violating students to the criminal or juvenile justice systems, and the provision that state law must authorize the chief administrative officer of each local school district to modify such expulsions on a case-by-case basis.

State legislatures and local school districts have broadened the mandate of zero tolerance beyond the federal mandates of weapons, to drugs and alcohol, fighting, threats, or swearing.[2] Many school boards continue to toughen their disciplinary policies; some have begun to experiment with permanent expulsion from the system for certain offenses. Others have begun to apply school suspensions, expulsions, or transfers to behaviors that occur outside of school.

(From Skiba & Knesting, 2001)

Assumption

School violence is nearing an epidemic stage, necessitating forceful, no-nonsense strategies for violence prevention.

It is true that there was a substantial increase in youth violence in the early 1990's, an increase that leveled off in the latter part of the decade.[3] Advocates of zero tolerance pointed to the presumed increase in violence in schools as a rationale for a newer, tougher approach to school safety.

Over time, however, we have come to understand that violence is not rampant in America's schools, nor does it appear to be increasing. Data consistently support the assertion of the U.S. Department of Education's Annual Report on School Safety that "The vast majority of America's schools are safe places."[4] Serious crimes involving gangs, weapons, or drugs constitute less than 10% of the problems cited by principals in their schools; where crimes against students occur, the majority of incidents appear to be theft or vandalism, rather than physical attacks or threats with a weapon. With a school homicide rate of less than one in a million, the chances of violent death among juveniles are almost 40 times as great out of school as in school. Nor does there appear to be any evidence that violence is becoming more prevalent in schools. While shocking and senseless shootings give the impression of dramatic increases in school-related violence, national surveys consistently find that school violence has stayed essentially stable or even decreased slightly over time. As noted school violence researcher Irwin Hyman concludes from an examination of these data, "Despite public perceptions to the contrary, the current data do not support the claim that there has been a dramatic, overall increase in school-based violence in recent years."[5]

Fact

Violence and disruption are extremely important concerns that must be addressed in our schools, but national reports have consistently found no evidence that violence is out of control in America's schools, nor that school violence is worsening.

Assumption

Zero tolerance increases the consistency of school discipline and thereby sends an important message to students.

Unless an intervention can be implemented with some degree of consistency, it is unlikely that intervention can have a positive effect. In particular, behavioral psychologists have argued that punishment, applied inconsistently, will be ineffective and probably lead to a host of side-effects, such as counter-aggression. Federal policy in the Gun-Free Schools Act of 1994 mandating a one-year expulsion for firearms appears to have increased statewide consistency in response to students bringing weapons to school. But zero tolerance has also been extended to a host of other infractions from fighting to drugs and alcohol to threats to disruption, and these other applications of zero tolerance have resulted in a high degree of inconsistency and controversy.[6]

In general, there is wide variation across states, school districts, and schools in how suspension and expulsion are used. Although student behavior does contribute to the probability of discipline, idiosyncratic classroom and school characteristics may be more important than student behavior in determining who will be suspended or expelled. In one study, one-quarter of classroom teachers were found to be responsible for two-thirds of the referrals to the office. . . . School-to-school variability in suspension and expulsion are so great that one set of investigators concluded that students who wish to change their chances of being suspended or expelled "will be better off by transferring to a school with a lower suspension rate than by improving their attitudes or reducing their misbehavior."[7]

Fact

Beyond federal policy on weapons possession, the consistency of implementation of zero tolerance is so low as to make it unlikely that it could function effectively to improve school climate or school safety.

Assumption

The no-nonsense approach of zero tolerance leads to improved school climate.

Advocates of zero tolerance argue that it makes sense that removing the most troublesome students from a school would lead to an overall improvement in the quality of the learning climate for those students that remain. Once again however, the facts don't support the intuition. Rather than making a contribution to school safety, the increased use of suspension and expulsion seems to be associated with student and teacher perceptions of a less effective and inviting school climate. Schools with higher rates of suspension have been reported to have higher student-teacher ratios and a lower level of academic quality, spend more time on discipline-related matters, pay significantly less attention to issues of school climate, and have less satisfactory school governance.[8] In the long-term, there is a moderate correlation between the use of exclusionary discipline and school dropout. Even more troubling are emerging data suggesting that higher rates of school suspension are associated with lower average test scores on tests of achievement.[9]

Fact

It is difficult to argue that disciplinary exclusion is an essential tool in promoting a productive learning climate when schools that use suspension more frequently appear to have poorer school climates, higher dropout rates, and lower achievement.

Assumption

Zero tolerance has made a difference in school safety and improved student behavior.

There are currently no controlled and comprehensive studies that could be used as an evaluation of the effectiveness of zero tolerance at the national level. The most comprehensive data, released by the U.S. Department of Education in its progress report on the Gun-Free Schools Act,[10] showed a change in weapons reports on school campuses over a two-year period after the implementation of the Act, but there was also a concurrent change in reporting requirements during that period, making the data all but uninterpretable.

More generally, data on the effectiveness of suspension and expulsion for changing student behavior are not promising. Descriptive studies of school suspension have typically found that 30% to 50% of those suspended are repeat offenders. Such a high rate of recidivism suggests that school suspension is not a particularly effective deterrent to future disruptive behavior. Indeed, in one study, students who were suspended at the sixth-grade level were more likely to be referred to the office or suspended in eighth grade, leading the researchers to conclude that "for some students, suspension functions more as a reinforcer than a punisher."[11]

Fact

Fifteen years after the rise of zero tolerance, and almost ten years since it became national policy for weapons, there is still no credible evidence that zero tolerance suspensions and expulsions are an effective method for changing student behavior.

Assumption

Students learn important lessons from the application of zero tolerance, and ultimately feel safer.

The purpose of the application of punishment is to teach students a lesson about behavior. Yet published interviews of students regarding suspension and expulsion have found them less likely than adults to believe that discipline keeps them safe and more likely to perceive that school suspension and expulsion are ineffective and unfair. Even students who are most successful within current school structures are likely to criticize school disciplinary policies as meaningless and stultifying. Those students whose behavior does put them at risk for contact with school discipline believe that enforcement is based more on reputation than behavior. Regardless of their own background, most high school students appear to share the perception that school discipline, especially school suspension, unfairly targets poor students and students of color.[12]

Fact

Students resent arbitrary enforcement of rules and tend to believe that suspension and expulsion are used unfairly against certain groups.

Assumption

Zero tolerance is more equitable for minorities, since it treats everyone the same.

Federal education policy prohibits discrimination in the application or outcomes of educational interventions. Yet disciplinary exclusion in general and zero tolerance in particular have consistently led to the disproportionate punishment of students of color. Students of color have consistently been found to be suspended at rates two to three times that of other students, and similarly overrepresented in office referrals, corporal punishment, and school expulsion. If anything, those disparities appear to have increased since the passage of the Gun Free Schools Act. Statistical analyses have shown that racial disparities in school discipline cannot be accounted for by the economic status of minority students; nor is there evidence that minority students misbehave to a degree that would warrant higher rates of punishment.[13] Rather, available data make a case that the use, and especially the overuse, of disciplinary removal carries with it an inherent risk of racial bias.

Fact

Increased use of zero tolerance only seems to increase the disproportionality of African American students in school discipline.

Assumption

Regardless of the negative effects of suspension and expulsion, there are simply no alternatives to zero tolerance, suspension, and expulsion.

It is probably true that there is a connection between the use of zero tolerance and the belief that there is no alternative. It is most likely the case that schools who believe they must resort to zero tolerance probably do so simply because they believe they have no other choice.

Yet as we learn more about school violence prevention, we have discovered that there are numerous effective alternatives for preserving the safety and integrity of the school learning climate. Educators, researchers, and policymakers have increasingly coalesced around a three-tiered prevention model for improving school safety.[14] . . . That is, at the first level, the school implements programs such as Life Skills or Conflict Resolution on a schoolwide basis to promote a positive climate that teaches all students alternatives to disruption and violence. At the second level, programs such as Anger Management are targeted for students who may be at risk for disruption or aggression. Finally, a variety of effective and planned responses are in place to address the issues raised by students who are already engaged in disruptive behavior.

Consistently, programs that effectively cut violence are proactive rather than reactive; involve families, students, and the community; and include multiple components that can effectively address the complexity of school disruption. . . . Effective schools assess their own needs and choose those strategies and interventions that can best meet those local needs.

Fact

A wide range of alternatives to zero tolerance has emerged and are available to promote a productive learning climate and address issues of disruptive behaviors in the schools.

Assumption

Prevention sounds good, but we lack data on its effectiveness and it takes too long to work.

In the last ten years, there have been numerous studies, including some sponsored by Congress, the U.S. Surgeon General, the Centers for Disease Control, and the Departments of Education,[15] on the most effective methods for preventing youth violence. None of those reports has identified zero tolerance as an effective method for reducing youth violence. Rather, programs that are identified as effective or promising include elements such as bullying prevention, conflict resolution, improved teacher training in classroom management, parent involvement, anger management, and multi-agency collaboration.

Using highly rigorous experimental criteria, these programs have in fact been shown to be far more effective than disciplinary removal in addressing violence and disruption. Further, these types of comprehensive and preventive programs appear to be able to work in a surprisingly short period of time. One program in an inner-city school with high minority dropout rates was able to reduce suspension by 35% in one year by implementing more positive classroom management practices.[16] Here in Indiana, the Safe and Responsive Schools Project worked with schools in urban, suburban, and rural school districts to develop comprehensive school safety programs. Within one year, the majority of schools showed substantial improvements in both the number and type of school suspensions. . . .

Fact

Our best data on school violence support preventive strategies as being most likely to ensure school safety. Further, it appears that such programs can have an effect on student behavior and school climate in a surprisingly short period of time.

Summary

Preserving Both School Safety *and* Educational Opportunity

As noted at the outset, educators have the responsibility to use all effective tools at their disposal to maintain the safety and integrity of the school learning climate. There are clearly student behaviors and situations in which the safety of students and teachers demands that certain students be removed from school for a given period of time through suspension or expulsion. Both state law and common sense demand that administrators have the latitude to make those difficult decisions.

Yet at the same time, . . . educators are acutely concerned that we maximize educational opportunities for all children, especially in light of findings that among the strongest predictors of academic achievement is the amount of time spent in learning. It is reasonable then to evaluate any educational intervention or policy that might threaten student educational opportunity to ensure that the risks of that procedure are outweighed by its benefits.

Unfortunately, despite almost 15 years of implementation in some of America's schools, there are virtually no data supporting the effectiveness of zero tolerance. Federal zero tolerance policy on weapons seems to have improved consistency of definition in that area. Beyond that, however, there are no data showing that zero tolerance can ensure school safety and improve student behavior. Indeed, the weight of the evidence suggests that zero tolerance suspensions and expulsions are applied too inconsistently to have a positive effect, that they create racial disparities, and that they are associated with negative outcomes in student behavior, school dropout, and academic achievement. Simply put, school suspension and expulsion cannot be viewed as risk-free procedures.

Knowing that a procedure carries certain risks does not mean it should not be used. In the field of medicine, procedures like heart surgery or radiation therapy carry fairly high levels of risk, but are clearly indicated for certain patients. It is also true however, that such procedures are clearly the last medical resort, to be used only after all other alternatives have been exhausted. The problem with the zero tolerance philosophy may not be simply that it increases the use of school suspension and expulsion, but that it may encourage the use of those procedures as a first line of treatment, before other alternatives have been tried. In a recent survey of secondary teachers on school discipline issues, most supported zero tolerance policies for serious behaviors such as drugs and weapons, and thought their schools were adequately responding to these threats. But teachers also believed that if zero tolerance is used as a "blind application of the rules" and without "common sense," the learning climate and their students will suffer.[17]. . .

There are effective programs and interventions to maintain a safe and productive school climate. . . . In recent years, rigorous analyses of experimental evidence have identified a number of strategies that have proven to be effective in reducing the likelihood of violence and disruption, without removing students from the opportunity to learn.

The safety of our children, as well as the ability of teachers to teach them in a climate free of disruption, is of utmost importance. Thus, school discipline, school safety, and school violence are all topics that have generated controversy and will doubtless continue to do so. Yet the increasing reliance in federal law upon the principle of evidence-based educational practice suggests that our best hope in addressing even the most difficult of our quandaries is in the examination of what has been shown to work best in promoting safe schools and improved achievement. . . .

End Notes

1. Public Agenda. (2004). Teaching interrupted: Do discipline policies in today's public schools foster the common good? [online] . . .

2. Although the term is widely used, there is no single widely accepted definition of "zero tolerance." The National Center on Education Statistics [Heaviside, S., Rowand, C., Williams, C., & Farris E. (1998). *Violence and discipline problems in U.S. Public Schools: 1996-97.* (NCES 98-030). Washington, DC : U.S. Department of Education, National Center for Education Statistics.] defined zero tolerance as a policy that mandates predetermined consequences or punishments for specified offenses. That definition of zero tolerance may be overly broad, however; one would expect that there are few schools in America that do not mandate some predetermined consequences for specific behaviors. A more limited definition of zero tolerance is a disciplinary policy "intended primarily as a method of sending a message that certain behaviors will not be tolerated, by punishing all offenses severely, no matter how minor." [Skiba, R.J., & Peterson, R.L. (1999). The dark side of zero tolerance: Can punishment lead to safe schools? *Phi Delta Kappan, 80,* 372-376, 381-382.]

3. Elliott, D.S., Hamburg, B.A., & Williams, K.R. (1998). *Violence in American schools: A new perspective.* New York: Cambridge University Press; Gottfredson, D. (1997). *School-based crime prevention.* Washington, DC: U.S. Department of Justice, National Institute of Justice. [online] . . .

4. U.S. Department of Education (1998). *Annual report on school safety.* Washington, DC: Author.

5. Hyman, I.A., & Perone, D.C. (1998). The other side of school violence: Educator policies and practices that may contribute to student misbehavior. *Journal of School Psychology, 30,* 7-27.

6. Skiba, R.J., & Knesting, K. (2001). Zero tolerance, zero evidence: An analysis of school disciplinary practice. In R.J. Skiba & G.G. Noam (Eds.), *New directions for youth development (no. 92: Zero tolerance: Can suspension and expulsion keep schools safe?)* (pp. 17-43). San Francisco: Jossey-Bass.

7. Wu, S.C., Pink, W.T., Crain, R.L., & Moles, O. (1982). Student suspension: A critical reappraisal. *The Urban Review, 14,* 245-303.

8. Hellman, D.A., & Beaton, S. (1986). The pattern of violence in urban public schools: The influence of school and community. *Journal of Research in Crime and Delinquency, 23,* 102-127; Davis, J.E., & Jordan, W.J. (1994). The effects of school context, structure, and experiences on African American males in middle and high schools. *Journal of Negro Education, 63,* 570-587;

Bickel, F., & Qualls, R. (1980). The impact of school climate on suspension rates in the Jefferson County Public Schools. *The Urban Review, 12,* 79–86.

9. Raffaele-Mendez, L.M. (2003). Predictors of suspension and negative school outcomes: A longitudinal investigation. In J. Wald & D.J. Losen (Eds.), *New directions for youth development: Deconstructing the school-to-prison pipeline. (no. 99)* (pp. 17–34). San Francisco: Jossey-Bass.

10. Sinclair, B. (1999). *Report on state implementation of the Gun-Free Schools Act: School year 1997-98.* Rockville, MD: Westat.

11. Costenbader, V.K., & Markson, S. (1994). School suspension: A survey of current policies and practices. *NASSP Bulletin, 78,* 103–107; Tobin, T., Sugai, G. & Colvin, G. (1996). Patterns in middle school discipline records. *Journal of Emotional and Behavioral Disorders, 4*(2), 82–94 (quote, p. 91).

12. Brantlinger, E. (1991). Social class distinctions in adolescents' reports of problems and punishment in school. *Behavioral Disorders, 17,* 36–46; Sheets, R. H. (1996). Urban classroom conflict : Student-teacher perception: Ethnic integrity, solidarity, and resistance. *The Urban Review, 28,* 165–183.

13. Costenbader & Markson (1994); Shaw, S.R., & Braden, J.P. (1990). Race and gender bias in the administration of corporal punishment. *School Psychology Review, 19,* 378–383; Skiba, R.J., Michael, R.S., Nardo, A.C., & Peterson, R. (2002). The color of discipline: Sources of racial and gender disproportionality in school punishment. *Urban Review, 34,* 317–342.

14. American Psychological Association. (1993). *Violence and youth: Psychology's response.* Washington, DC: Author; Dwyer, K., Osher, D., & Warger, C. (1998). *Early warning, timely response: A guide to safe schools.* Washington, DC: U.S. Department of Education; Walker, H.M., Horner, R.H., Sugai, G., Bullis, M., Sprague, J.R., Bricker, D., & Kaufman, M.J. (1996). Integrated approaches to preventing antisocial behavior patterns among school-age children and youth. *Journal of Emotional and Behavioral Disorders, 4*(4), 194–209.

15. See e.g., Elliott, D., Hatot, N.J., Sirovatka, P., & Potter, B.B. (2001). *Youth violence: A report of the Surgeon General.* Washington, DC: U.S. Surgeon General; Mihalic, S., Irwin, K., Elliott, D., Fagan, A., & Hansen, D. (2001, July). *Blueprints for violence prevention (OJJDP Juvenile Justice Bulletin).* Washington, DC: U.S. Department of Justice, Office of Juvenile Justice and Delinquency Prevention. [online] . . .

16. Meyer, G.R., Mitchell, L.K., Clementi, T., & Clement-Robertson, E. (1993). A dropout prevention program for at-risk high school students: Emphasizing consulting to promote positive climates. *Education and Treatment of Children, 16,* 135–146.

17. Public Agenda. (2004).

POSTSCRIPT

Should School Discipline Policies Be Stricter and Include "Zero Tolerance" Provisions?

In the 2006 *Phi Delta Kappan/Gallup Poll of the Public's Attitudes Toward the Public Schools*, school discipline was ranked only behind lack of adequate finances as the biggest problem schools must face. All states through legal provisions have declared the rights of students and staff to attend and work in safe schools. In California, voters in 1982 added the following provision to that State's Constitution:

All students and staff of public primary, elementary, junior high and senior high schools have the inalienable right to attend campuses which are safe, secure, and peaceful.

It is somewhat ironic, given the public's concerns regarding safe schools and the general support of strict disciplinary measures, that oftentimes the actual implementation of such measures is met with resistance and even lawsuits by parents and/or other student advocacy groups. Such opposition to school disciplinary decisions was largely unheard of when school officials functioned "in loco parentis" (in place of parents). Operating under that guideline school officials were free to administer discipline as parents might, including corporal punishment. But the "in loco parentis" doctrine was struck down by the U.S. Supreme Court's decision in the 1969 *Tinker v. Des Moines* case. That decision established that "students do not lose their constitutional rights at the school house gates." The decision signaled that public school officials do not operate "in loco parentis," but rather as extensions of the state and thus they must respect student constitutional rights including "due process" considerations in policies and processes related to school suspension and/or expulsion.

The National Association of Secondary School Principals (NASSP) in a document entitled *Civil Rights Implications of Zero Tolerance Programs* (February 2000) makes the point that zero tolerance policies emerged out of concerns regarding "disparate treatment" in school disciplinary matters. Thus, pre-established, mandatory punishments for zero tolerance violations were conceived of as a means to avoid inconsistencies and/or preferential treatment in serious discipline matters. In the same document, NASSP expresses support for zero tolerance policies in this way:

As a nation, we must take a strong and unified position that weapons, drugs, violent acts, discrimination, and harassment cannot and will not be tolerated in our schools. Students who commit such acts must be prepared to face the consequences of their actions. To back away from a zero tolerance policy places students and staff in harm's way and enhances the probability of future acts of violence.

Because it is an advocacy organization for school principals, NASSP does argue to allow principals greater discretion in administering discipline in zero tolerance cases. Some might suggest that allowing "greater discretion" would lead back to "disparate treatment."

The American Psychological Association (APA) in reporting on its Task Force on Zero Tolerance (2006), which studied the effectiveness of zero tolerance policies, made the following criticisms:

> The zero tolerance policies also do not consider children's lapses in judgment or developmental immaturity as a normal aspect of development. . . . Zero tolerance policies ignore the concept of intent even though this is a central theme in American concepts and systems of justice.

Given the wide divergence of opinions on this vitally important issue, further study is certainly in order. Some additional commentary and perspectives on the topic can be found in the September 2004 issue of the *American School Board Journal*, the September 2005 issue of *NEA Today*, and a 2003 article from The *Rutherford Institute*.

ISSUE 9

Can Large High Schools Provide a Quality Education?

YES: Rick Allen, from "Big Schools: The Way We Are," *Educational Leadership* (February 2002)

NO: Tom Vander Ark, from "The Case for Small High Schools," *Educational Leadership* (February 2002)

ISSUE SUMMARY

YES: Rick Allen, a staff writer and editor for ASCD, notes that, "More than 70 percent of U.S. high school students attend schools of more than 1000 students."

NO: Tom Vander Ark, former executive director for education of the Bill and Melinda Gates Foundation and a senior fellow at the foundation, charges, "Large, comprehensive high schools short-change too many students."

In public education it often seems that "yesterday's solution becomes today's problem." That's how it is with large high schools. In the 1920s, in order to accommodate rapidly increasing high school enrollments, many large high schools were built. It was felt that economies of scale would result from housing large numbers of students in a single facility. Later in 1959, James B. Conant, then president of Harvard University in his study *The American High School Today*, argued for large, comprehensive high schools that could provide the breadth and depth of curricular offerings necessary to serve the academic, vocational, and general education needs of the "whole" child. Large high schools also seemed to offer a logical approach to promote racial integration by drawing students from a larger geographic area, thus avoiding the racial homogeneity of small neighborhoods and towns. (Note: Much of the above account comes from a *Washington Post* interview with Diane Ravitch, professor of education at New York University, 2005.) Ravitch concluded that interview by stating, "It is ironic that today's reformers now find themselves undoing the reforms of the 20th century."

The "small schools" movement is a by-product of long-standing concerns regarding the quality of high school education. Such concerns are not new. The 1983 publication of *A Nation at Risk* suggested that the poor quality of secondary education might jeopardize our ability to compete economically with other nations. International tests showing that our students did not compare favorably with students from other countries underscored such concerns. Today, a growing concern relates to statistics that indicate only 70 percent of students graduate from high school in the traditional four years; that figure is nearly 50 percent in some large inner-city schools (NCES, 2005). This statement from the Bill and Melinda Gates Foundation, a major supporter of the small school movement, captures those concerns: "A new commitment to serving *all* students well has highlighted the failure of most comprehensive high schools to bring about significant improvement in student accomplishment over the past two decades."

In many cases, it is simply not feasible to close large high schools. In such circumstances, many large high schools are creating special interest academies or "smaller learning communities" within the large school structure. In that manner the large school advantages of a broad curriculum and a wide array of student activities can be retained while providing students with a more personalized educational setting.

The initial rush toward small schools is disquieting to some educators who initially championed the concept. Deborah Meier, a noted education reformer, warns," [s]mall is not the answer" (*Christian Science Monitor*, 2007). She and other reformers do not believe that simply creating small schools is the panacea for what ails schooling. They worry that failed practices of large schools may simply be repackaged into smaller schools. The small school movement began as a way to change school cultures and approaches to education in order to facilitate more individualized attention to students. Some observers believe that the current trend of evaluating schools by way of standardized testing is not compatible with individualization and may eventually cause the small school movement to fail. Meier states such concerns thusly, "[e]very time we have a good idea that we don't do well, it increases the cynicism."

YES ⤶

Rick Allen

Big Schools: The Way We Are

Large schools are a fact of life in the United States. Although the issue of school size and its link to academic achievement and social and emotional well-being has been debated continually in the current wave of school reform, the arguments are taking place in an education landscape of big schools that is unlikely to change soon.

More than 70 percent of U.S. high school students attend schools of more than 1,000 students, according to the U.S. Department of Education (McNeil, 2000). Large middle schools also are on the increase. Between 1968 and 1996, middle schools of more than 800 students increased from 16 percent to 30 percent (McEwin, Dickinson, & Jenkins, 1996). Although such populous cities as Los Angeles and Miami have high schools with enrollments of 5,000 students, outsize schools are not an exclusive creation of the late 20th century—DeWitt Clinton High School in the Bronx, New York, boasted an enrollment of 12,000 students in 1934, which placed it in the *1963 Guinness Book of World Records* as the largest high school in the world.

Researchers say that large schools are a result of Americans' penchants for efficiency, economies of scale, and curricular choice and their belief that it's cheaper to educate more students in one building than in several. Studies by Walberg (1992) and Howley (1994) note that between 1940 and 1990, despite the U.S. population growing 70 percent, the number of elementary and secondary public schools declined from 200,000 to 62,037 (Cotton, 1996).

How Did We Get So Big?

Although James Conant's *The American High School* (1959) accelerated the push for school consolidation amid worries that small schools couldn't offer the scientific rigor needed to win the Russian-American space race, the roots of large U.S. schools go deeper. Especially after World War I, urban schools were becoming larger to meet the needs of growing populations swelled by successive waves of immigrants:

> A major thrust of the Progressive Movement was the establishment of a national network of large high schools, designed to conform to such typically American ideals as efficiency, differentiation, specialization, depersonalization, and standardization; in effect, this network was a . . . well-oiled

From *Educational Leadership*, February 2002, pp. 36–38. Copyright © 2002 by ASCD. Reprinted by permission. The Association for Supervision and Curriculum Development is a worldwide community of educators advocating sound policies and sharing best practices to achieve the success of each learner. To learn more, visit ASCD at www.ascd.org

machine whose goal was the production of human capital. Few educational reform efforts have 'succeeded' as well as the comprehensive high school. (Lee & Smith, 1995)

In many cases, large urban high schools became the capstone of the Americanization process—efficient factories for producing citizen-workers employable in the well-run engines of U.S. commerce. Although megaschools now are regularly derided as impersonal factories that decrease achievement and increase student alienation and crime, in the past, reformers believed that the large urban high school was the logical staging ground for launching civic-minded adults into the larger society.

Because societies change, however, the heyday of beneficial big urban high schools is long gone, suggests Craig Howley, director of the ERIC Clearing house on Rural Education and Small Schools.

"Consolidation has a long history and has surely provided some benefits. Benefits are temporary, however, because the organizational structures are a legacy that seemingly run—with few exceptions—in one direction only: bigger and bigger. [Schools] may be better for a while, but as neighborhoods change, the good they once harbored can and does turn bad. So the benefits don't get passed down," says Howley.

"City schools, once prosperous beyond measure, are widely believed to be 'ungovernable.' We made them difficult to govern through making them large—expanding their levels of governance, piling on expertise after expertise—all in the pursuit of efficiency," he argues.

Howley's research shows that smaller schools maximize achievement in impoverished communities, whereas larger schools maximize achievement among the affluent. He speculates that well-off students do better in large schools because they are prepared in middle-class homes to be competitive, objective, credential-seeking, and "footloose"—that is, they're expected to apply to out-of-state colleges "in search of brilliant careers."

Limitless and Limiting Choices

Evanston Township High School, big and high-achieving like many of its counterparts in Chicago's North Shore suburbs, is a springboard for those brilliant careers. With an enrollment of 3,100 students, Evanston is unusual because, as well as being big, it is diverse. Evanston's student population is 50 percent white, 39 percent black, and 11 percent other minorities, with 25 percent of students coming from low-income families. About 70 percent of the class of 2000 went to four-year colleges, with another 8.6 percent entering two-year colleges.

The course offerings at Evanston exemplify what a big suburban school with a budget of $67 million can provide students. For example, the foreign language department offers four years of Latin, German, Hebrew, and Japanese, and two years of American Sign Language, in addition to the more common languages. A popular Asian studies program combines Japanese with content courses. This year, Swahili, spoken in East and Central Africa, is being offered for the first time. More than 350 students are already studying African history as part of a global studies requirement at the school.

As a result of offering Swahili, "we expect that interest in African studies will also grow," says Laura Cooper, assistant superintendent for curriculum and instruction. She notes that the Asian studies program has provided many Evanston students solid grounding for serious career choices "at an unusually young age."

Built in 1928, Evanston's three-story school building with 30 acres of floor space and 3.5 miles of corridors is currently undergoing a $12.5 million renovation to carve 28 new classrooms and 4 new science labs out of existing space. And there's no shortage of space at Evanston—the school was enlarged in 1966 to make room for 5,500 students. Still, with a current full-time staff of 529, including 294 teachers, how does Evanston prevent its 3,100 students from getting lost amid all the curricular choices and fellow students?

One answer is "limiting choice," says Cooper. "In the past five years, we've been ambitious to delete courses that were seen as escape courses because they lacked rigor. In some cases, it means taking away choice to ensure that in the freshman and sophomore year, they have core courses."

Karen Seashore, professor of educational policy and administration at the University of Minnesota, agrees that limiting choice is a good idea. The comprehensive curriculum is "one of the toughest issues in education in America" because with so much choice, students don't necessarily put together the best combinations of courses to promote achievement, says Seashore. Especially in urban schools, students say that they don't get enough information to make sensible choices.

"Schools with fewer choices have higher academic results because the curriculum is more coherent," says Seashore. An added problem of poor course selection is how it articulates with a career track, and with an average ratio of one high school guidance counselor to 700 students, counseling everybody about career preparation is difficult.

Seeking the Ties That Bind—To Excel

Making a school feel personal is a challenge for schools with thousands of students. Evanston has experimented with 201 "home bases" where a teacher meets with the same group of 15 students, diversified by race, each morning for the four years of high school. It's only 18 minutes at the beginning of the day, but teachers use it to discuss grades, attendance, or personal issues with students.

"If you don't have a personal relationship with students, you can't ask questions. We know an awful lot about them by the time they're seniors," says Cooper, who, because of her duties as assistant superintendent, shares a home base with another teacher.

One of Cooper's home base students had a hard time making the transition from the bilingual program to the mainstream classes because he worked after school to support his family. Cooper and another teacher worked with the student to carve out time during his school day to do homework. Happily, this particular student went on to join the honor roll during his senior year.

But ties to caring teachers are not the only way to personalize learning, Evanston's students recently told teachers. At an inservice day for the teachers, academically successful African American and Latino students talked about the barriers that still exist to higher achievement for minorities. To fight the clique mentality of high school life, minority students urged teachers to "assign partners for group work so that we don't just work with our current friends."

"It's not about friendships but about building working relationships," says Cooper. "Teachers need to take greater responsibility for creating a positive classroom culture where each student feels known and accepted."

Personalized Learning through Projects

Teachers, too, need help in forging working relationships in a large high school. Principal Donald Hoecherl likes to tell the story of two teachers who only discovered that they taught at the same huge high school during a chance encounter at a local grocery store. At G. Holmes Braddock Senior High School in Miami, Florida, Hoecherl instituted a monthly faculty meeting to bring together all 252 members of the instructional staff once a month "to make all people feel like they belong to one school."

Two years ago, Braddock billed itself as the "largest high school in the United States" at 5,300 students. Although its current enrollment of 4,730 doesn't exactly make it a slip of its former self, teachers no longer "float" without a classroom. Thirty-nine portable classrooms help house the overflow of students, although teachers still complain about an average class size of 30, says Hoecherl.

Hoecherl describes the school as "middle class," although 40 percent of its students qualify for free or reduced-price lunches. Nine out of 10 Braddock students are Hispanic, coming from a community that strongly supports education.

"I do not find school size a deterrent. I find it a great strength," says Hoecherl, who points to the school's range of sports and classes, including a top Advanced Placement program that offers 39 subjects. "Being big doesn't mean we expect less." At the same time, he admits that the first challenge of running a large school is "letting parents and the community know that size is not a problem."

To eliminate the perception that school is "a large place where students don't learn," Hoecherl last year brought in the Co-nect school reform model to train teachers to collaborate in project-based learning and the use of technology.

In the fall, Joy Hellard, who teaches English to gifted students, worked with the world history teacher, the design teacher, the media specialist, and a Co-nect consultant on an interdisciplinary project that involved students making models of buildings from ancient civilizations. Groups of students built large models of Aztec and Mayan temples, Chinese pagodas, and an interactive Egyptian pyramid large enough to walk through. Other students and parents toured the models, while student "curators" explained the details of these ancient cultures.

"At Braddock, if a better way is introduced to do something, everybody jumps on. I don't see so much compartmentalizing of subjects and hoarding of information. Teachers are open to showing kids the interconnectedness of information and how it relates to life," says Hellard.

Nevertheless, teaching in a school the size of Braddock is challenging. "It's a huge school. The bell rings and nearly 5,000 kids move to the next class in five minutes. It's a mall. A large two-story mall. But the kids are friendly, and the teachers are friendly and open. There's a feeling of safety despite the size. Most kids do the right thing," says Hellard.

Communicating the Vision

Down county from Braddock, American Senior High School has an enrollment of 2,900. Principal Alberto Rodriguez considers American one of the "smaller schools" in the area. But often school size is an issue of perception. Recently, Rodriguez was a member of an accreditation group evaluating three northern Florida high schools of 1,000 students each. His reaction as he entered the first building: "It's such a small high school!"

The smooth running of a high school as large and diverse as American—it's 54 percent Hispanic, 38 percent African American, and 6 percent white—depends on how the principal communicates his vision to staff and students, contends Rodriguez.

In 1997, when he became principal, Rodriguez urged teachers at American to "change the paradigm" in the school. He encouraged staff to "teach students with the same high expectations that they would want from their own children's teachers." He also makes sure teachers compare their students' passing rates on Florida's accountability tests to district and state figures so that teachers can decide where to improve their instruction.

Recently, Rodriguez's school was selected as a state model school that serves a high percentage of disadvantaged students because its test scores were comparable to schools with higher socioeconomic indicators. In 1998, roughly 63 percent of American's students tested at the bottom level in math on the Florida Comprehensive Assessment Tests (FCAT). By 2001, that figure had decreased to 23 percent. The number of students whose FCAT tests in reading placed them in the lowest level decreased from 49 percent to 38 percent during the same period.

"If you have nearly 65 percent of your kids scoring at the lowest level in math, that's a huge concern. That says that these students don't have reasoning skills—that they're just drifting through high school," says Rodriguez.

To prevent students from dropping out, American mandates that freshmen with a "dropout profile" in 8th grade—truancy, high absenteeism, and a disciplinary history—be enrolled in a Junior ROTC program. "The program is successful because students are taught discipline, good citizenship, and the value of a good education. It has been something of a boot camp, but it has also taken the shock away for students going from middle school into high school," says Rodriguez. After 9th grade, students may leave the program if their teachers agree that they have made sufficient progress.

Even in a school of thousands, Rodriguez believes "you can treat each child with nurturing and caring." Early in the school year, he meets with groups of 30 students in the school's media center. Within three weeks, Rodriguez meets with the entire student body. Students learn from Rodriguez that the school's "intense curriculum will prepare them for life" and that after-school tutoring and technology are available to help them. They in turn must "meet us halfway," says Rodriguez.

The principal shares his vision with staff, students, and parents, but stresses that "you've got to empower your staff" with decision-making responsibility. "You've got to delegate. You can't oversee everything. But you spot-check and snoop around," adds Rodriguez. "When you have a large school, you cannot micromanage."

Large School, Small Academies

Teachers were given an important role in shaping Newburgh Free Academy in Newburgh, New York, after the community mobilized against creating a mega-school in 1996. Now with 2,505 students, the 10th–12th grade public high school has turned to theme-based academies housed in one building.

Students at Newburgh can choose to attend one of eight academies that include performing arts, international studies, business, engineering and technology, communications, and health, or they can remain in the school's core liberal arts program. To receive funding from federal Smaller Learning Communities grants, teachers submitted a plan based on research and expert advice. They determined that the academies would be inter-disciplinary, involve parents and community resources, and have a cap of 125 students per grade. A third of the school's 10th–12th graders are in academies, but transfers into the specialized programs are growing.

Teachers integrate the academy theme into the content areas to provide meaning for students, who have chosen an academy on the basis of personal interests, explains Annette Saturnelli, executive director for funded programs for the Newburgh school district. "Students have to be intrinsically motivated to come to school," she says. The academies, combined with attendance tracking strategies, have resulted in a lower dropout rate, say school officials.

"Students have told me if it weren't for teachers being constantly in their lives, mentoring them, and letting them bring us their problems, they probably would not have graduated from high school," says Grace Bowles, a vocal music teacher who oversees the Academic, Arts, and Related Technologies Academy of 300 students.

Although state funding has been uncertain for academy activities that include hands-on experiences in the performing arts industry in New York City,

Bowles proudly points to the fact that the academy's first graduating class saw 80 of 110 students enter college studies in the performing arts.

Positive changes in school climate also have come to Newburgh as a result of the academies, says Saturnelli. Two years ago, an average of 12 teachers were out sick each day, a figure that dropped to five teacher absences per day in the last school year. Student violence, mainly fighting, decreased 62 percent in the same period, from 437 to 168 incidents. More students are taking the SAT, and the students' average score rose eight points to 960, inching toward the New York state average of 997. But the current SAT average still falls short of the 11-point annual rise sought by school officials.

To make the physical learning environment more intimate, Newburgh is undergoing a $21 million renovation that will restructure the school's existing space into three clusters, each of which will house three academies. Plans call for each cluster to have its own administrator, guidance counselor, computer lab, and science labs, but funding is making this uncertain. Liberal arts students—those not in an academy—will also be designated as their own smaller learning environment.

One of the challenges in sustaining the academies is recruiting students to enter them, says Newburgh principal Peter Copeletti. Although school officials are promoting the academies in the district's three junior high schools, Copeletti supports adding the 9th grade to the high school so students can explore the academies firsthand and make informed choices. Ironically, this would increase the schools' enrollment, a move the community rejected five years ago. But school administrators believe the academy system changes the nature of how large schools operate.

"We actually can get bigger and grow smaller," says Copeletti.

DeWitt Clinton: Up, Down, and Up Again

One historically large school, DeWitt Clinton High School in New York City's Bronx borough, also attributes a turnaround in academics and school climate to the creation of smaller learning environments. From its world record enrollment in the 1930s, the school declined in numbers and academic prestige in later years, so that by 1990, it had the highest dropout rate of any school in the Bronx. Long known for its academics, athletic prowess, and famous graduates (including poet Countee Cullen, actor Burt Lancaster, and a host of New York judges), by 1986, Clinton's star had fallen so much that it graduated fewer than 12 percent of its students.

When Clinton's enrollment was at its highest in the 1930s, the Bronx population was 50 percent Jewish, with Irish Catholics and other immigrant groups making up the difference in a fairly prosperous borough, says Bronx borough historian Lloyd Ultan, history professor at Fairleigh Dickinson University in New Jersey.

"Certain cultures had a tremendous educational tradition. That may have given a cast to the school. Also, in the 1930s, jobs were scarce, so you better darn well stay in school to get a job," explains Ultan.

Economic and social changes in the 1970s and 1980s contributed to Clinton's decline, says former assistant principal William Dougherty, now an education professor at Manhattan College. The opening of nearby John F. Kennedy High School in the early 1970s "bled off all the better students and the most involved parents," budget slashes closed down Clinton's gifted program and made it difficult to offer teachers competitive salaries, and the size of the school itself fractured faculty and students into four shifts, creating a school day that ran from 7 A.M. to 5:30 P.M., says Dougherty.

The leadership of current Superintendent of Bronx High Schools Norman Wechsler is often credited with the turnaround of Clinton during his six years as principal there in the 1990s.

"We needed to create the 'gang' or the 'church' or whatever you call it that was going to hold youngsters to high standards. That means you're in students' faces. If you don't love kids it doesn't work," says Wechsler. This "tough love" approach is the responsibility of teacher coordinators in each house who monitor students' attendance, lateness, behavior, effort, grades, and test scores, in addition to being alert to emotional downs on any particular day.

Clinton's current enrollment of 3,864 students is 56 percent Hispanic, 35 percent African American, 5 percent Asian, and 3 percent white, with 8 in 10 of its students eligible for free lunches. Students can enroll in one of 10 houses, organized by grade level—with student-picked names like "Rave" or "Trailblazers"—or by special interest. Each house has its own office, assistant principal, teacher coordinators, guidance counselors, and family assistants who reinforce the school-home link.

Assistant principal Marlene Diaz, who heads Clinton's International House, which includes 350 English language learners, says Wechsler's call for weekly house team meetings, which he would visit, made his leadership "crucial" for success.

"He was there to know what the problems were and what support we needed, whether it was equipment, staff, or new ideas," Diaz recalls.

Wechsler encouraged Diaz and other teachers to pay attention to how their students were progressing. In 1994, only 6.5 percent of Diaz's students tested out of entitlements. In 2000, 34 percent of her students did so, with a number of them transferring to the Macy/Excel program that caters to the school's most gifted students. By 2000, Clinton's graduation rate had risen to 60 percent, and graduates garnered $25 million in college scholarships and financial aid.

Because of Clinton's progress with smaller learning environments, Wechsler's vision for making big high schools into smaller learning communities will be carried out throughout the Bronx. With funding from a New Century High Schools consortium that includes the Bill & Melinda Gates Foundation, the Carnegie Foundation, and other private groups, Wechsler will lead a district-wide effort to create 15 smaller schools in the Bronx's five large high schools.

But a more intimate learning environment will be only one attribute of these schools, says Wechsler. "Small" will succeed only if other changes take place as well, he insists, including a constructivist approach to teaching and learning, project-based learning, interdisciplinary teaching and collaboration, and student performance monitoring—many of the reforms that other U.S. schools are using to increase achievement. To further develop what Wechsler calls Clinton's "golden age," the school will have to make progress in these areas as well, he says.

References

1. Cotton, K. (1996). *School size, school climate, and student performance.* Arlington, VA: American Association of School Administrators. Available. . . .

2. Lee, V. E., & Smith, J. B. (1995). Effects of high school restructuring and size on early gains in achievement and engagement. *Sociology of Education, 68*(4), 241–270.

3. Howley, C. (1994, June). *The academic effectiveness of small-scale schooling (an update).* ERIC Digest. Charleston, WV: Clearinghouse on Rural Education and Small Schools. (Eric Document Reproduction Service No. ED 372 897)

4. McEwin, C. K., Dickinson, T. S., & Jenkins, D. M. (1996). *America's middle schools: Practices and progress—A 25-year perspective.* Columbus, OH: National Middle School Association.

5. McNeil, P. (2000, April 14). *Smaller schools and learning communities: The wave of the future?* Presentation at the American Youth Policy Forum, Washington, DC. Available. . . .

6. Walberg, H. J. (1992). On local control: Is bigger better? In *Source book on school and district size, cost, and quality* (pp. 118–134). Minneapolis, MN: Minnesota University, Hubert H. Humphrey Institute of Public Affairs; and Oak Brook, IL: North Central Regional Educational Laboratory. (Eric Document Reproduction Service No. ED 361 164)

Tom Vander Ark

NO

The Case for Small High Schools

Large, comprehensive high schools shortchange too many students. The Bill & Melinda Gates Foundation believes that, with the right elements in place, small schools offer a promising alternative.

Although elementary and middle schools have been the focus of numerous reform efforts, high schools have largely been ignored—and many of them are struggling to keep up. Even in the mid-1990s, when high schools began receiving better-prepared students, achievement remained flat (Campbell, Voelkl, & Donahue, 2000). One of the main problems is size: Many of today's high schools have enrollments of 2,000, 3,000, even 4,000 students.

Now educators, policymakers, and parents are joining the chorus of researchers who have long trumpeted the benefits of small schools. Studies show that small schools have higher attendance rates and lower dropout rates, their students have higher grade point averages, and students and teachers report greater satisfaction with the school experience.

That's why the Bill & Melinda Gates Foundation is supporting efforts to create smaller, more personalized learning environments. The Foundation has invested more than $250 million in grants nationwide for creating new small schools and transforming large high schools through the schools-within-a-school model.

Large Schools: Missing the Grade

Compared with schools a generation ago, most schools today serve students who are more diverse, come from more varied life circumstances, and are less motivated by traditional means. In addition, technology has created a new world of opportunities and challenges, and the economy is increasingly rewarding those with a college education. But our high schools continue to operate as they did decades ago, and as a result they display serious shortcomings.

For example, many seniors lack basic reading and mathematics skills. Nearly one in five cannot identify the main idea in what they have read, and nearly two in five haven't mastered the use and computation of fractions, percents, and averages (National Center for Education Statistics, 2001a). Dropout rates are another indicator. Each year, 1 in 20 high school students drops out (Kaufman, Kwon, Klein, & Chapman, 2000), and dropout rates exceed 50 percent in many urban and poor rural school districts. Even many

From *Educational Leadership*, February 2002, pp. 55–61. Copyright © 2002 by ASCD. Reprinted by permission. The Association for Supervision and Curriculum Development is a worldwide community of educators advocating sound policies and sharing best practices to achieve the success of each learner. To learn more, visit ASCD at www.ascd.org

students who finish high school are not prepared for college. Although nearly 80 percent of all high school graduates go on to college, more than half must take remedial courses once they get there (National Educational Longitudinal Study: 1988–1994; Adelman, 1999).

Students of color are especially hurt by the failures of the education system. Latino students are the most likely to drop out of school, with only two-thirds earning diplomas or GEDs. In reading and mathematics, many African American and Latino students graduate from high school with skills at the middle school level (National Center for Education Statistics, 2001b). After two decades of progress, the achievement gap between white children and children of color and between low-income students and more affluent students widened or remained static during the 1990s (Campbell, Hombo, & Mazzeo, 2000). The much-discussed achievement gap is only part of the problem, however. The more daunting challenge is the wide gap between what all students should know and be able to do and the level at which most students are achieving.

Our schools are not failing—they are obsolete. They foster anonymity and stifle learning by systematically inhibiting those things that are most important: powerful sustained relationships; students' ability to address complex problems individually and as members of a team and to communicate in various ways; and the ability of teachers and administrators to take on increasing responsibility. The Challenge Designing systems of schools that work for all students is one of America's most important challenges, but the barriers to change—especially for secondary schools—are numerous and daunting. District policy, state law, and higher education all articulate their expectations in the form of credits, making it difficult for a high school to structure learning in segments other than blocks of 50 minutes each. Most high school teachers face 125 to 150 students every day and work in virtual isolation from other adults. Most school boards (and a few states) select textbooks, making it difficult for a group of teachers to develop an integrated, thematic curriculum. Principals seldom have staffing, budget, or curriculum autonomy. Archaic state and district funding models control the, resources a school receives, inhibiting new ideas and methods. High school faculties are so large that conversation and democratic decision making are very difficult.

Among other things, we must rethink our preconceptions about the 50-minute, discipline-based blocks of learning. High school must be a place where young people can grapple with such complex issues as globalization, environmental degradation, and terrorism, as well as the implications of new technologies and advances in science. Students need extended periods of time to study multidisciplinary topics, opportunities to work in teams on complex projects, and the expectation that they will communicate a reasoned perspective in a variety of ways.

Small Schools: Making the Grade

Although too many high schools are not providing students with the education they deserve, a growing number of public, charter, and private schools are defying this trend—and they are all small. Buoyed by research and increased momentum around the issue of small schools, more school leaders are considering redesigning their existing facilities with size as the guiding force. And though size is only one component of what makes a good school, it is a necessary one and one with tremendous ripple effects.

Researchers vary in how they define small schools, but from what we've seen, high schools with no more than 100 students per grade level create the kind of rich learning environment that leads to success. Research points to significant differences between large and small schools in a number of areas.

Cotton (1996) found no study that showed superior achievement in large schools compared with small schools. In other words, small schools have achievement that is at least equal to if not greater than achievement in large schools. One of the most powerful findings on small schools relates to their impact on low-income students. A study of schools in four states found that students in less-affluent areas achieve at higher levels when they attend small schools, and in lower-income communities the benefit of smaller schools is even greater. Phrased differently,

> The well-documented correlation between poverty and low achievement is much stronger—as much as 10 times stronger—in the larger schools than in smaller ones in all four states. (Howley & Bickel, 2000)

The Met High School in Providence, Rhode Island, serves a diverse population of 200 students, more than half of whom qualify for free or reduced-price lunch. In its first graduating class, every Met student was accepted to college. The school also boasts a dropout rate one-third lower than other Providence high schools. Studies of small schools in Chicago, New York, and Philadelphia have also found higher GPAs and lower dropout rates (Wasley et al., 2000; Raywid, 1996). Students in these schools are more motivated, feel more connected to their school, and are thus more likely to remain.

Small schools have fewer incidents of violence and report fewer discipline problems than large schools (Wasley et al., 2000). Small schools also tend to have less-invasive security measures, shunning such methods as drug sweeps and metal detectors. The Julia Richman Education Complex in midtown Manhattan once housed a large, failing urban high school. After closing and redesigning itself in the early 1990s, the facility is now home to a consortium of small schools, each with no more than 300 students. Metal detectors have been replaced with teachers who know every student's name, and incidents of violence have plummeted.

As far back as 1964, researchers reported that students in small schools were more likely to be involved in extracurricular activities and to hold important positions in school groups (Cotton, 1996). In fact, "the greater and more varied participation in extracurricular activities by students in small schools is the single best-supported finding in the school size research" (Cotton, 1996). For some small schools, such as Chicago's Best Practices High School, having after-school activities is less important than involving students during the regular school day. As the founders of the school write,

> Between 8:30 a.m. and 3:00 p.m., we're going to do our damnedest to
> know you, to care for you, to challenge you—and not to waste your time.
> At our school, involvement is not an after-school activity. (Daniels, Bizar, &
> Zemelman, 2001, p. 37)

Research shows that small schools don't necessarily cost more to operate
than large schools. And with the savings in remediation (as a result of having
fewer failing students), many consider small schools to be more cost-effective
than their larger counterparts (Gregory, 1992).

Small schools encourage collegial professional relationships and the
kind of ongoing learning that is vital, given the challenges that teachers face
today. In *The Power of Their Ideas*, Meier (1995) notes that "schools must be so
small that governance does not become the topic of discussion but issues of
education do" (p. 108).

The Need for Strong Leaders

Although the research on school size is compelling, size alone does not make
a good school. Good small schools share a common set of characteristics,
including strong leadership.

Leaders of small schools maintain a clear vision, facilitating the design
of a curriculum that is aligned with this vision, as well as appropriate organization and use of technology and facilities. They are instructional leaders
and teacher coaches, providing job-related learning experiences and time
for teachers to work together. They are marketing executives, communicating
the school's vision and the benefits of attending the school. They are col-
laborators, developing learning partnerships with businesses, community
groups, and institutions of higher education. They are competent administrators, distributing leadership and management tasks across the staff. At the
district level, school board members and superintendents play an important
role in ensuring that small schools have the autonomy and flexibility to
succeed.

The Importance of Autonomy

Autonomy is important in a number of areas, including curriculum, budget,
and staffing. Good small schools are created around a vision for teaching and
learning, a few important goals, and a coherent design that reflects both.
Small schools need curriculum autonomy to develop integrated learning
experiences that support their focus.

Small schools operate successfully around the country with the same
per-pupil funding as large schools. Like charter schools, however, they need
lump-sum funding to allow for flexibility and creativity. District funding formulas, staffing models, and programmatic funding frequently are barriers to
developing a personalized education program for all children.

Small schools need the opportunity to hire staff members who understand the mission of the school and have complementary skills. Central-office

placement and seniority schemes inhibit the ability of small schools to retain their focus.

In addition to providing autonomy for schools, districts need to develop a clearly articulated system of accountability for students, staff members, and schools. Performance contracts may be needed to help delineate goals, parameters, funding, and steps of intervention for underperformance. Oakland Unified School District recently adopted a New Small Autonomous Schools policy that clearly articulates these issues.

Moving toward Success

The research is clear: Today's large high schools are not working for most students, and smaller schools are reaching those who have floundered in big schools. Fundamental to the success of small schools are the relationships they foster. Students succeed in school when they connect with an adult or a subject. Small schools create spaces where young people have the opportunity to be known, to ask and to answer life's most important questions.

The Julia Richman Education Complex in Manhattan and the Met High School in Providence are among the best examples of what is possible if we reconsider the organization and architecture of our secondary schools. If we replace anonymity with community, sorting with support, and bureaucracy with autonomy, we can create systems of schools that truly help all students achieve.

References

Adelman, C. (1999, June). *Answers in the tool box: Academic intensity, attendance patterns, and bachelor's degree attainment.* Washington, DC: U.S. Department of Education. Available. . . .

Campbell, J. R., Hombo, C. M., & Mazzeo, J. (2000). *NAEP 1999 trends in academic progress: Three decades of student performance.* Washington, DC: U.S. Department of Education, Office of Educational Research and Improvement, National Center for Education Statistics. Available. . . .

Campbell, J. R., Voelkl, K. E., & Donahue, P. L. (2000). *NAEP 1996 trends in academic progress.* Washington, DC: U.S. Department of Education. Office of Educational Research and Improvement. National Center for Education Statistics. Available. . . .

Cotton, K. (1996). *School size, school climate, and student performance.* (School Improvement Research Series (SIRS), Close-up #20). Portland, OR: Northwestern Regional Educational Laboratory (NWREL). Available. . . .

Daniels, H., Bizar, M., & Zemelman, S. (2001). *Rethinking high school: Best practice in teaching, learning, and leadership.* Portsmouth, NH: Heinemann.

Gregory, T. (1992). Small is too big: Achieving a critical anti-mass in the high school. In *Source book on school and district size, cost, and quality* (pp. 1–31). Minneapolis: University of Minnesota and Hubert H. Humphrey Institute of Public Affairs; and Oak Brook, IL: North Central Regional Educational Laboratory.

Howley, C. B., & Bickel, R. (2000, February). *Results of four-state study: Smaller schools reduce harmful impact of poverty on student achievement* [Online]. The Rural School and Community Trust. Available. . . .

Kaufman, P., Kwon, J. Y., Klein, S., & Chapman, C. D. (2000). *Dropout rates in the United States: 1999.* Washington, DC: U.S. Department of Education, National Center for Education Statistics (NCES). Available. . . .

Meier, D. (1995). *The power of their ideas: Lessons for America from a small school in Harlem.* Boston: Beacon Press.

National Center for Education Statistics. (2001a). *NAEP summary data tables.* Washington, DC: U.S. Department of Education. Available. . . .

National Center for Education Statistics. (2001b). *NAEP 1999 long-term trend summary data tables.* Washington, DC: U.S. Department of Education. Available. . . .

National Educational Longitudinal Study: 1988–1994 (NELS:88), Data Analysis System. (1997, October). In L. Berkner, L. Chavez, & C. D. Carroll (Ed.), *Access to postsecondary education for the 1992 high school graduates.* Washington, DC: U.S. Department of Education, National Center for Education Statistics. Available. . . .

Raywid, M. A. (1996, April). *Taking stock: The movement to create mini-schools, schools-within-schools, and separate small schools.* New York: ERIC Clearinghouse on Urban Education. Available. . . .

Wasley, P., Fine, M., Gladden, M., Holland, N. E., King, S. P., Mosak, E., & Powell, L. C. (2000, June 20). *Small schools: Great strides: A study of new small schools in Chicago.*: New York: Bank Street College of Education. Available. . . .

POSTSCRIPT

Can Large High Schools Provide a Quality Education?

The education community's penchant for jumping onto bandwagons is well known and a case could be made that the rapid emergence of the small schools' movement is an example of that tendency. Fueled by $350 million from the Bill and Melinda Gates Foundation, the national school improvement project was launched five years ago. Since then, the foundation has provided gifts to schools totaling more than $2.4 billion with its focus increasingly on high schools. Such a focus is altogether appropriate given statistics showing high school noncompletion rates at 30 percent nationwide and approaching 50 percent in large urban high schools (noncompletion rates are defined as the percentage of ninth-grade students who do not graduate from high school in the normal four-year time-span). Given the fact that large urban high schools often serve a preponderance of minority students, related issues such as the increasing achievement gap between white and minority students add to the pressure to reduce school size. Proponents of reducing school size believe that it is far too easy for students to be lost in high schools with large enrollments. Tom Vander Ark ranked "anonymity of large schools and dehumanizing systems" as number one on his list of "the seven deadly sins of education."

Some suggest that high school size should be limited to 600 students.

But there is some evidence that the impetus toward creating smaller schools may be losing some of its momentum. Even Vander Ark admits that some mistakes were made in the initial priorities of the foundation's grants. In a 2005 interview with the *Seattle Times* he stated, "In too many places the difficult work of breaking up schools into smaller units monopolized the agenda and schools didn't get around to improving what happened in the classroom—which was the whole point to begin with." He continued, "It took our district grantees a couple of years to figure out that's [improving instruction] what the focus should be and to help us figure what the focus should be."

The foundation has now de-emphasized but not abandoned the movement toward smaller schools and instead is focusing grant priorities on improving instruction.

In many ways large, comprehensive high schools grew in popularity in the United States during the early to mid-twentieth century because of their compatibility with industrialization and the growth of large cities; their ability to school the massive number of immigrant children who were entering the country and needed to be "Americanized"; and their capability to provide a broad curriculum to educate the "whole" child. Many teachers and administrators who work in large high schools take issue with those who suggest that, by definition, large high schools are cold and contribute to the anonymity and isolation of students. Such teachers and administrators believe that, even in large high schools, caring educators can make students feel recognized and supported. Dan Meier, principal of Robinson Secondary School in Fairfax, Virginia, which enrolls over 4000 students in grades 7 to 12, reports that "many students praise their teachers for making the big school feel like home." He added, "You really work at trying to do as many things as you can to recognize the individual." Critics of large high schools point out that there are considerable differences between large high schools in affluent suburban settings and urban schools in impoverished areas.

For additional ideas on this topic, see James B. Conant, *The American High School Today* (1959); the entire issue of *Educational Leadership* (February 2002) is devoted to class size/school size; and *National Clearinghouse for Educational Facilities* (June 2007).

Internet References . . .

Phi Delta Kappan

One of the widest circulated educational journals, the *Kappan*'s monthly issues contain articles related to contemporary teaching practices.

http://pdkintl.org

Association for Supervision and Curriculum Development

The Association for Supervision and Curriculum Development publishes the popular monthly journal, *Educational Leadership*, which is similar to the *Kappan* in terms of content regarding teaching and classroom practices.

http://www.ascd.org

Sexuality Information and Education Council of the United States (SIECUS)

This site provides advocacy information regarding comprehensive sex education programs.

http://www.siecus.org

Abstinence Clearinghouse

This site contains advocacy information regarding abstinence-only sex education.

http://www.abstinence.net

American Association of University Women (AAUW)

This site contains the AAUW positions on various issues Title IX and single-sex classrooms.

http://www.aauw.org

Council for Exceptional Children

This is an international organization dedicated to improving educational outcomes for children with special needs.

http://www.cec.sped.org/

Teaching and Classroom Practices

*G*iven *the fact that on each school day millions of parents entrust their most precious possessions to the care and influence of teachers, it should come as no surprise that what teachers do and how they do it are subjects of great interest and potentially intense controversy. Beyond the concerns that individual parents have for the welfare of their children, our society is also deeply invested in what occurs in the nation's classrooms. Although there is little argument that student achievement is significantly influenced by the quality of teachers, there is no similar consensus regarding the content that teachers should be teaching and the practices that they should be employing in the classroom. To the contrary, controversy extends from curricular materials to computer use; from homework policies to student evaluation; from the appropriateness of sex education and athletic programs; and even to the instructional and learning dynamics caused by relationships among students. The questions addressed in this part of the book exemplify the types of debate and dialogue that emerge from differing values and viewpoints regarding teaching and classroom practices.*

- Should the Teaching of American History Focus on a Critique of Past Events and Individuals?
- Should Comprehensive Sexuality Education Be Taught in Public Schools?
- Do Single-Sex Classrooms and Schools Provide a Better Learning Environment?
- Is Grade Inflation a Problem?
- Does Homework Serve Useful Purposes?
- Does Participation in Sports Provide Positive Benefits to Youth?
- Will Increased Use of Computer Technology and Games Be Beneficial to Students?
- Is the Practice of Providing Accommodations to Children in Special Education a Good Idea?
- Are Character/Moral Education Programs Effective?

ISSUE 10

Should the Teaching of American History Focus on a Critique of Past Events and Individuals?

YES: Pedro Noguera and Robby Cohen, from "Patriotism and Accountability: The Role of Educators in the War on Terrorism," *Phi Delta Kappan* (April 2006)

NO: David McCullough, from "Knowing History and Knowing Who We Are," *Imprimis* (February 15, 2005)

ISSUE SUMMARY

YES: Pedro Noguera and Robby Cohen, professors in the Department of Education at New York University, assert that students need to be taught skills to critically analyze historical events in order to challenge "the patriotic assumptions and biases" of our country.

NO: Author, historian, and Pulitzer Prize–winner David McCullough suggests that it is easy to "second-guess" our past because we do not have to confront it as our present.

The question framing this issue speaks to the always volatile topic of curricular standards and subject matter content. When those standards and content are focused on the history of our nation, the ensuing arguments and disagreements can become quite vehement. Such was certainly the case in 1994 when controversy arose over the development and issuance of the National Standards for History by the National Center for History in the Schools led by Professor Gary Nash from UCLA. The furor basically involved what critics alleged was an overemphasis on a multicultural, "every person" theme, which in turn de-emphasized the more traditional "great man" approach to the study of history. Much of the debate and discussion involved the contents of the American history standards but similar concerns were expressed about the world history standards. The vehemence of that criticism is captured in this statement by Gilbert Sewall in "The Classroom Conquest of World History" (*Education Week,* June 13, 2001).

Academic revisionists, whose careers have moved forward, pulled by the intellectual troika of race, class, and gender, entertain radical ambitions for the world-history curriculum. Mr. Nash and other historians want to correct what they believe to be a "triumphal," "monocultural," and "ethnocentric" view of the West that is incomplete or false. Their buzzwords are inclusion, diversity, globalism, and empathy, concepts that classroom teachers embrace out of naiveté and workshop hectoring as conviction.

For his part, Gary Nash responded,

I reflect on a central paradox: that the emergence of a democratized historical practice in recent decades has brought forth a torrent of critics who have misled and confused much of the public about the nature of historical scholarship and the benefits of revising history. (The History Wars of the 1990s, *Lecture in History,* East Carolina University, 1996)

As noted above, much of the argument regarding what should be taught in American history classrooms emanates from the fact that if certain themes are to be emphasized, it will necessarily lead to a diminution of others. Nash captures the essence of a critique-based "every person" approach to the study of history with this statement, "[n]othing can serve patriotism worse than suppressing dark chapters of our past, smoothing over clearly documentable examples of shameful behavior in public places high and low, and gliding by disgraceful violations of our national credo" (1996). Chester E. Finn Jr., president of the Fordham Foundation, describes the more traditional "great man" approach:

The solemn duty of all educators is to make certain that all our children know who they are. Part of that can be accomplished by teaching them about America's founders, about their ideals, and about the character, courage, vision and tenacity with which they acted. From that inspiring history, true patriotism cannot help but grow. (*Phi Delta Kappan,* April 2006)

The controversy continues with authors Pedro Noguera and Robby Cohen stating, "[w]hat began as 13 states on the East Coast of North America expanded from sea to sea through a process of conquest and conflict." David McCullough asks, "[h]ow can we not want to know about the people who have made it possible for us to live, to have the freedoms we have, to be citizens of this greatest of countries in all time"?

YES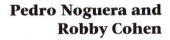

Pedro Noguera and
Robby Cohen

Patriotism and Accountability: The Role of Educators in the War on Terrorism

What are the responsibilities of educators while our nation is at war? This is not a question that comes up at most conferences or workshops on education, even though anyone familiar with our work as educators knows that it is nearly impossible to avoid taking a stance on the issue.

Should educators be expected to promote patriotism and support for the military effort in Iraq or Afghanistan? If our students seek our advice and counsel, should we encourage them to enlist? Or should we tell them that the decision is theirs to make? What about the Patriot Act? Should we urge our students to accept curtailments of our civil liberties as a necessary sacrifice in the "war on terrorism," a war against a stateless enemy that is not confined to a particular territory? Or should we warn them of the potential dangers that may arise when any government is allowed to invade the privacy of its citizens?

Ignoring these questions does not allow one to escape taking a stand. Even if you are uncomfortable speaking out for or against the war, it is important to understand that in times such as these we cannot pretend that education is apolitical work. Particularly now, when accountability has become a national mantra, we believe that educators must hold themselves accountable for ensuring that students acquire an intellectual grounding in history, civics, and culture that will enable them to develop informed opinions about the war, about U.S. foreign policy toward the Middle East, and about the implications of the war for civil liberties in American society.

Silence and inaction are nothing more than a form of complicity with the status quo. The war is raging now, and those who do not express opposition are in effect demonstrating complicity if not support. People— Iraqis, Afghanis, and Americans—are dying, and decisions are being made in Washington that will affect our future. Our schools are being used as recruiting grounds for the military because No Child Left Behind (NCLB) requires schools to provide military recruiters with access to schools and student records.[1] Our schools are not required to provide antiwar groups with equal access, so it seems clear that our education system is tilted toward war rather than peace.

From *Phi Delta Kappan*, by Pedro Noguera and Robby Cohen, April 2006, pp. 573–578. Copyright © 2006 by Phi Delta Kappan. Reprinted by permission of the publisher and Pedro Noguera and Robby Cohen.

During the 1960s, universities and colleges were the sites of demonstrations and sit-ins when campus administrators provided the federal government with access to student records for the military draft during the Vietnam War. Today, the use of student records for military recruitment provokes relatively little protest. Fear of terrorist attack, fear of being perceived as sympathizing with terrorists or enemies of the U.S., and the undocumented but enduring belief that the war in Iraq will prevent terrorists from attacking us here—all combine to make it increasingly difficult for individuals to take public positions against the war. Sensitivities are also heightened whenever American men and women (actually one-third of those serving in our armed forces in Iraq and Afghanistan are not U.S. citizens) are deployed to fight in a foreign land, and this too contributes to the chilling effect on domestic dissent. However, as educators, we have a special responsibility to encourage critical thinking among our students. Indeed, citizens who think critically are essential for the functioning of our democracy. We ought not to allow our nation's schools to remain cogs in a war machine, nor should we allow ourselves to become unwitting supporters.

Linking Accountability and Patriotism

Over the past decade there has been a new emphasis on accountability in our nation's schools. NCLB has required schools to produce evidence that students are learning (as measured by performance on standardized tests) and that when they graduate from school they possess basic competencies in math and literacy. While many educators (including both of us) applaud certain aspects of NCLB, federal education policy under President Bush has been increasingly linked to other Administration initiatives, including the war. Thus educators are being held accountable in new ways. As a result of this linkage, the stakes are increasingly high for teachers, administrators, and students.

Educators who support the war, the President, and the policies of the Administration may experience little difficulty doing what they can to embrace the military effort and NCLB with patriotic enthusiasm. They may do so either because they trust the President and his policies or because they believe that obedience and loyalty are essential when the nation is at war. They may have no qualms about promoting a similar brand of patriotism among their students and encouraging them to enlist in the military, even if they do not encourage their own children to do the same.

Others may secretly oppose the war and the policies of the Administration but fear making their opposition known. Perhaps they fear being accused of disloyalty or being seen as a troublemaker. Or perhaps they are concerned that if they speak out they will be censured, fired, or worse.

It is not surprising that many who oppose the war (and polls show that a majority of Americans no longer support it[2]), who question the rationale and logic used to justify the military occupation of Iraq and Afghanistan, and who regard NCLB as a threat to the integrity of public education may be reluctant to express their views openly. In some parts of the country, critics of the war,

including prominent politicians, journalists, and celebrities, have been casti-
gated for being "soft" on terrorism, and their patriotism has been questioned.
Just before launching the war in Afghanistan, the President declared, "You are
either with us or with the terrorists." When the lines of debate are drawn so
starkly, even passive neutrality may give rise to suspicion.

Yet educators who prefer to avoid controversy and who would rather
remain silent on these polarizing issues may find a stance of neutrality difficult to maintain during these tense times. When the National Education Association is called a terrorist organization by one secretary of education and
when the state superintendent of Connecticut is described as "un-American"
by another, simply because both have been critical of NCLB and other aspects
of federal education policy, it is clear that a link between war and education
has been forged. It may seem odd—and even unfair—for one's attitudes and
positions toward the war to be linked to one's position on NCLB and federal
education policy, but these are not ordinary times.

While no one wants to risk being questioned by the FBI, blacklisted, or
detained (or even deported if one is not a U.S. citizen) for taking public positions that are regarded as unpatriotic, it is important for us to remember that
the right to dissent is an essential part of our democracy. It is also important
to remember that, as educators, we have been given the great responsibility of
imparting knowledge that will prepare our students to become citizens in this
democracy. This is not a responsibility that can be taken lightly.

Accountability and Democratic Citizenship

As accountability has become the leading policy fixation in education, it
might be helpful for educators to think of patriotism and citizenship in terms
of accountability as well. Given that our nation is at war in at least two countries, shouldn't educators be accountable for ensuring that all students have
some understanding of why we are fighting, of whom we are at war with, and
of what is at stake?

Citizenship education is important in every society, but there is no place
where it is more vital than in the U.S., the world's preeminent military power.
Our government spends far more on the military than does any other nation.
We have military bases and troops deployed in more than 100 foreign countries and hundreds of nuclear warheads ready to be launched on the order of
the President. A nation with so strong a military and so vast a military presence must have an education system that is equally strong in teaching
its future citizens to think critically and independently about the uses of
American power and about the role of the American military in the world.

Unlike most military superpowers of the past, the U.S. is a democracy,
and the results of our elections can influence the global policies we pursue.
Since the rest of the world cannot vote in our elections, even though their
fate may be determined by the outcomes, it is up to us, as citizens and
as educators, to ensure that our teaching fosters the kind of informed debate
and discussion that is necessary for the functioning of a healthy democracy.

Such an approach to teaching must include a willingness to discuss controversial issues, such as the nature and implications of American imperialism, our role as a global power, and our ongoing desire to intervene in the affairs of other nations. Every student in our nation's secondary schools should be exposed to both sides of the debate about how the U.S. uses its power in the world. All students should be able to understand the rationale given for American troop deployments and military actions abroad, and before graduating, they should be able to write a coherent essay exploring the merits of various courses of action and putting forward their own perspective on the ethics of U.S. foreign policy.

To acquire this form of political literacy, our students must have an understanding of American and world history that goes far beyond regurgitating facts and dates or passing state history exams. They must also understand the complexity of politics in ways that exceed the typical offerings of the mainstream media. In short, they must learn, as Paulo Freire once admonished, to "read the world" so that they might have a clearer understanding of the forces shaping their lives.

Let us use the concept of imperialism to illustrate how these educational goals might be pursued. The American Heritage Dictionary defines imperialism, as "the policy of extending a nation's authority by territorial acquisition or by the establishment of economic and political hegemony over other nations." To determine whether it is appropriate to apply this term to the actions of the U.S., students would need to be exposed to a thematic approach to the history of America's territorial expansion, its ascendance to global power after the Spanish-Cuban-American War, and its emergence as the world's foremost superpower in the aftermath of World War II.

Such an approach to history would compel students to grapple with the meaning and significance of economic and political changes rather than merely to recall a chronology of isolated facts. It would also enable students to comprehend the significance of blatant contradictions in U.S. foreign policy. For example, many Americans do not realize that the United States once supported many of the groups that now are part of al Qaeda (including Osama bin Laden himself) when these individuals and groups were carrying out acts of terrorism in Afghanistan in opposition to the Soviet occupation of that country. They also may not know that Saddam Hussein was once a U.S. ally and that we supported him in his war against Iran, even when we knew he was using chemical weapons against the Kurds.[3]

We should teach history in ways that make it possible for students to make sense of contradictions such as these. Indeed, we must do so if our students are to appreciate the complex social processes that led to America's rise as an imperial power. This does not mean that we should engage in an unfair bashing of the United States. One way to avoid this is to provide readings that offer a variety of points of view on the same subject. However, even as we strive for balance and fairness, we should provide our students with the analytical skills to critique and evaluate the information they are exposed to so that they can develop a logical and historically grounded framework for comprehending present conflicts and foreign engagements.

To have a context for understanding the present war in Iraq, every student should know that war and violence were central to the founding and early development of the United States. What began as 13 states on the East Coast of North America eventually expanded from sea to sea through a process of conquest and conflict. Students should understand that, while some historians view this expansion in positive terms, as the growth of a liberty-loving republic, others see it as having been achieved by the near genocide of Native Americans and by the seizure of immense western territories from Mexico.[4]

Similarly, to appreciate the significance of President Bush's assertion that Saddam Hussein had weapons of mass destruction as a pretext for taking the nation to war, it would help students to know that similar tactics have been used in the past. The 1846 clash of U.S. and Mexican troops on lands that historically had belonged to Mexico; the sinking of the battleship Maine off the coast of Cuba in 1898, which Americans, without evidence, blamed on Spain; and the alleged but never confirmed second North Vietnamese attack on U.S. vessels in the Gulf of Tonkin in 1964 are examples of controversial rationales that were used to take the nation to war. Understanding the nature of these historical controversies—namely, who wanted the war, who opposed it, and why—would help students to appreciate the significance of the ongoing debate over how and why the U.S. entered the war with Iraq.

Accountability in teaching should also include ensuring that students have the ability to process the news and information they are exposed to each day so that they can understand how the war is being conducted and develop informed opinions about it. To be intelligent citizens today, students should be able to use the daily reporting from Iraq—from mainstream and alternative sources—to question and critique the claims of the Administration, such as Vice President Cheney's recent assertion that the insurgency in Iraq is in its "last throes." The parallels between such claims and the equally misleading claims made by the Johnson Administration during the Vietnam War are worth exploring, as they offer historical precedent as well as evidence that the Republicans have no monopoly on this kind of spin. As the saying goes, "In war, truth is the first casualty."

Students should understand both the risks involved if the U.S. leaves Iraq before peace and democracy are established and those involved in staying longer. Again, the parallels to Vietnam are haunting. Making sense of such issues and arriving at an intelligent, well-thought-out point of view requires an ability to critique arguments and opinions that are presented as facts and to recognize misleading statements.

In a recent essay titled "War and the American Constitutional Order," Mark Brandon asserts that, as of 2004, Americans had been involved in wars or military actions in 182 of the 228 years since the colonies declared independence in 1776.[5] He also points out that U.S. military actions became much more frequent in the 20th century. Remarkably, from 1900 to 2000 there were only six years in which the U.S. was not engaged in some form of military action. Today, we are pursuing an open-ended commitment to a global war on terrorism that knows no national or temporal boundaries.

Critics such as Andrew Bacevich write of a "new American militarism" whereby the nation's political elite, infatuated with the capabilities of high-tech weaponry and emboldened by the collapse of the Soviet Union and the lack of a countervailing superpower, has embraced military action as a first rather than a last resort to advance U.S. interests.[6] Our students need not accept Bacevich's arguments, but they do need to know enough about American history to be able to critique and debate them. Why has the U.S. been so reliant on military force for so much of its history? Do other nations have similar histories? What rationales have Americans used in the past to justify going to war? How do we reconcile this long history of U.S. warfare with the fact that U.S. territory has so rarely come under attack from foreign powers? Our students need to engage questions such as these with an understanding of history and with a critical frame of mind.

It is also well past time for U.S. schools to confront what is new about this latest U.S. war. This is the nation's first preemptive war. By conventional standards, the U.S. could well be seen as the aggressor in this war, since it invaded a far weaker state not in response to any immediate threat or attack on Americans but in response to a presumed threat (Iraq's alleged possession of weapons of mass destruction) that later proved to be nonexistent. Students need to grapple with the whole idea of preemptive war and its international implications. If the U.S. is entitled to wage such a war, attacking weaker nations whenever it construes a potential threat from them, then do we accord this same right to other major powers? Can China, for example, be given a green light to invade Taiwan if China's leaders believe that his smaller nation poses a threat to its security?

Our efforts to ensure that our students understand the war we are fighting should also include discussion of how our troops conduct themselves during the war. We must help our students to understand how it was possible for prisoners of war to be abused and tortured by American forces in Iraq and why it is that Amnesty International has referred to the prison at the Guantánamo military base in Cuba as the "Gulag of our times." Here the linkages between past and present can be made by simply asking why it is that the U.S. owns this naval base in Cuba.

We should encourage our students to debate who should be held accountable when atrocities such as these come to light. Those who torture, those who supervise and command them, both? They should know why the Geneva Conventions for the treatment of prisoners during war were adopted and why America's designation of certain prisoners as "unlawful combatants" represents a threat to Americans who may be captured. Likewise, similar kinds of questions must be asked of the Iraqi insurgents and of the terrorist groups whose suicide bombings and attacks on civilians have created the worst horrors of the war.

The extent to which our civil liberties should be curtailed as a result of the war on terrorism is yet another topic that should be fully explored. Is the Patriot Act fundamentally different from Sen. McCarthy's search for Communists during the Cold War years? Was President Roosevelt's decision to intern Japanese Americans during World War 11 similar to or different from the mass detentions of Muslims who are still being held without trial or legal representation throughout America today? With police searching bags at airports and security agencies possessing new powers to order wiretaps on Americans, students need to assess whether the national security rationales for these acts can stand up under critical scrutiny.

The Middle Eastern focus of much of the war on terrorism poses a serious challenge to our schools, because most students—indeed, most of our citizens—lack the kind of understanding of the history and culture of the region that would be needed to understand the complex issues. Not many public schools teach Arabic or have teachers with expertise in the history of Islam. With such educational deficiencies the norm in the U.S., it is little wonder that the American electorate was unable to sort out the secular tyranny of Saddam Hussein and the violent religious fanaticism of Osama bin Laden. Educators need to do better than politicians have in grappling with the complexities of the Middle East, and they need to make distinctions among those we regard as our enemies.

Perhaps the most provocative area of inquiry our students can explore as they reflect on their nation's international impact and posture is at the macro-historical level. What is it that motivates the U.S. to act as it does internationally? Is American foreign policy and war-making driven by democratic altruism? Or do economics and the search for markets, cheap labor, and raw materials shape the American agenda? Should the U.S. work with and support the United Nations, the international body we helped to create, or should we denounce the UN as an anti-American institution and reject the idea of allowing outsiders to debate questions pertinent to our defense and security?

While many of the topics we have highlighted are most easily dealt with in social studies and English classes, teachers in other subject areas should not shy away from participating in the process of citizenship education. American students need to understand how the rest of the world perceives us and why so many people who sympathized with the U.S. after September 11th no longer do. Teachers of all kinds should raise these issues with their students, not to dictate what they should think, but simply to encourage them to think. Too much is at stake for citizenship education to be treated as an isolated unit to be covered solely in a social studies class.

My Country Right or Wrong?

If we are honest in our approach to teaching history and getting our students to think critically about the war, we will point out that there is a tension between flag-waving nationalism and a willingness to confront the ugly side of American history. For example, American nationalism impels us to think of 9/11 not merely as a day of U.S. suffering or as an act of brutal violence, but as a rallying cry for a global war on terror. If we can put aside our nationalist lenses for a moment, we might seek to understand why many developing countries regard us as an international bully, a nation motivated more by power and greed than by altruism and a sincere commitment to human rights and democracy.

Chilean writer Ariel Dorfman reminds us that there is "more than one America and more than one September 11th."[7] Dorfman and millions of others remember another September 11, this one in 1973, as a day of mourning. That was the day that a U.S.-backed coup overthrew the democratically elected socialist president of Chile, Salvador Allende, and replaced his government with a military junta led by Gen. Augusto Pinochet. Dorfman asks Americans to recognize that their suffering is neither unique nor exclusive. He challenges us as educators to see that, when we push beyond the boundaries of a narrow patriotism, we see a world in which the U.S. plays a complex and contradictory role—sometimes as victim, sometimes as perpetrator, of antidemocratic violence.

Criticizing Islamic fundamentalists and rabid nationalists in other countries is easy. It is far more difficult to challenge the patriotic assumptions and biases of one's own country, especially during wartime.

The pioneers of the idea of public education—Thomas Jefferson, Horace Mann, and John Dewey—argued that schools were essential to the health and well-being of our republic. They understood that an uneducated citizenry would doom the republic because ignorant citizens would be incapable of electing good leaders or voting out of office those who abused their power. As educators, it is our democratic responsibility to foster critical thinking among our students.

Those who deem taking up such challenges as unpatriotic would do well to heed the warning of English writer G. K. Chesterton: "My country right or wrong is a thing that no patriot would think of saying except in a desperate case. It is like saying, 'My mother, drunk or sober.'"[8]

With NCLB seeing to it that our schools become sites of military recruitment, educators have an even stronger obligation to ensure that their students are able to make informed decisions about their future. They must be exposed to all sides of the debates over America's role as a superpower. They must be able to draw lessons from the past so that they will be more informed about the present. In short, they must be made to understand what they may be putting their young lives on the line for. To do anything less is irresponsible and a willful neglect of our professional duties as educators.

Notes

1. John Gehring, "Recruiting in Schools, a Priority for Military, Is Targeted by Critics," *Education Week*, 22 June 2005, p. 6.

2. See David Jackson, "Bush Continues to Stump for War Support," *USA Today*, 13 January 2006.

3. See Mahmood Mamdani, *Good Muslim, Bad Muslim: America, the Cold War, and the Roots of Terror* (New York: Doubleday, 2004).

4. James W. Loewen, *Lies My Teacher Told Me: Everything Your American History Textbook Got Wrong* (New York: New Press, 1995), pp. 67–129; and Walker LaFeber, *The American Age: U.S. Foreign Policy at Home and Abroad, 1750 to the Present* (New York: Norton, 1994), pp. 1–125.

5. Mark E. Brandon, "War and the American Constitutional Order," in Mark Tushnet, ed., *The Constitution in Wartime: Beyond Alarmism and Complacency* (Durham, N.C.: Duke University Press, 2005), p. 11.

6. Andrew J. Bacevich, *The New American Militarism: How Americans Are Seduced by War* (New York: Oxford University Press, 2005), passim.

7. Ariel Dorfman, *Other Septembers, Many Americas: Selected Provocations, 1980-2004* (New York: Seven Stories Press, 2004), p. 41.

8. Quoted in William B. Whitman, *The Quotable Politician* (Guilford, Conn.: Lyons Press, 2003), p. 242.

David McCullough

Knowing History and Knowing Who We Are

(Note: The following is an abridged transcript of remarks delivered on February 15, 2005, in Phoenix, Arizona, at a Hillsdale College National Leadership Seminar on the topic, "American History and America's Future.")

Harry Truman once said the only new thing in the world is the history you don't know. Lord Bolingbroke, who was an 18th century political philosopher, said that history is philosophy taught with examples. An old friend, the late Daniel Boorstin, who was a very good historian and Librarian of Congress, said that trying to plan for the future without a sense of the past is like trying to plant cut flowers. We're raising a lot of cut flowers and trying to plant them, and that's much of what I want to talk about tonight.

The task of teaching and writing history is infinitely complex and infinitely seductive and rewarding. And it seems to me that one of the truths about history that needs to be portrayed—needs to be made clear to a student or to a reader—is that nothing ever had to happen the way it happened. History could have gone off in any number of different directions in any number of different ways at any point along the way, just as your own life can. You never know. One thing leads to another. Nothing happens in a vacuum. Actions have consequences. These all sound self-evident. But they're not self-evident—particularly to a young person trying to understand life.

Nor was there ever anything like the past. Nobody lived in the past, if you stop to think about it. Jefferson, Adams, Washington—they didn't walk around saying, "Isn't this fascinating, living in the past?" They lived in the present just as we do. The difference was it was their present, not ours. And just as we don't know how things are going to turn out for us, they didn't either. It's very easy to stand on the mountaintop as an historian or biographer and find fault with people for why they did this or didn't do that, because we're not involved in it, we're not inside it, we're not confronting what we don't know—as everyone who preceded us always was.

Nor is there any such creature as a self-made man or woman. We love that expression, we Americans. But every one who's ever lived has been affected, changed, shaped, helped, hindered by other people. We all know, in our own lives, who those people are who've opened a window, given us an idea, given

From *Imprimis*, February 15, 2005, pp. 1–11. Copyright © 2005 by Hilldale College. Reprinted by permission.

us encouragement, given us a sense of direction, self-approval, self-worth, or who have straightened us out when we were on the wrong path. Most often they have been parents. Almost as often they have been teachers. Stop and think about those teachers who changed your life, maybe with one sentence, maybe with one lecture, maybe by just taking an interest in your struggle. Family, teachers, friends, rivals, competitors—they've all shaped us. And so too have people we've never met, never known, because they lived long before us. They have shaped us too—the people who composed the symphonies that move us, the painters, the poets, those who have written the great literature in our language. We walk around everyday, everyone of us, quoting Shakespeare, Cervantes, Pope. We don't know it, but we are, all the time. We think this is our way of speaking. It isn't our way of speaking—it's what we have been given. The laws we live by, the freedoms we enjoy, the institutions that we take for granted—as we should never take for granted—are all the work of other people who went before us. And to be indifferent to that isn't just to be ignorant, it's to be rude. And ingratitude is a shabby failing. How can we not want to know about the people who have made it possible for us to live as we live, to have the freedoms we have, to be citizens of this greatest of countries in all time? It's not just a birthright, it is something that others struggled for, strived for, often suffered for, often were defeated for and died for, for us, for the next generation.

Character and Destiny

Now those who wrote the Declaration of Independence in Philadelphia that fateful summer of 1776 were not superhuman by any means. Every single one had his flaws, his failings, his weaknesses. Some of them ardently disliked others of them. Every one of them did things in his life he regretted. But the fact that they could rise to the occasion as they did, these imperfect human beings, and do what they did is also, of course, a testimony to their humanity. We are not just known by our failings, by our weaknesses, by our sins. We are known by being capable of rising to the occasion and exhibiting not just a sense of direction, but strength.

The Greeks said that character is destiny, and the more I read and understand of history, the more convinced I am that they were right. You look at the great paintings by John Trumbull or Charles Willson Peale or Copley or Gilbert Stuart of those remarkable people who were present at the creation of our nation, the Founders as we call them. Those aren't just likenesses. They are delineations of character and were intended to be. And we need to understand them, and we need to understand that they knew that what they had created was no more perfect than they were. And that has been to our advantage. It has been good for us that it wasn't all just handed to us in perfect condition, all ready to run in perpetuity—that it needed to be worked at and improved and made to work better. There's a wonderful incident that took place at the Cambria Iron Company in Johnstown, Pennsylvania, in the 19th century, when they were building the first Bessemer steel machinery, adapted from what had been seen of the Bessemer process in Britain. There was a German engineer named John Fritz, and after working for months to get this machinery finished, he came into the plant one morning, and he said, "Alright boys, let's start her up and see why she doesn't work." That's very American. We will find out what's not working right and we will fix it, and then maybe it will work right. That's been our star, that's what we've guided on.

I have just returned from a cruise through the Panama Canal. I think often about why the French failed at Panama and why we succeeded. One of the reasons we succeeded is that we were gifted, we were attuned to adaptation, to doing what works, whereas they were trained to do everything in a certain way. We have a gift for improvisation. We improvise in jazz; we improvise in much of our architectural breakthroughs. Improvisation is one of our traits as a nation, as a people, because it was essential, it was necessary, because we were doing again and again and again what hadn't been done before.

Keep in mind that when we were founded by those people in the late 18th century, none of them had had any prior experience in either revolutions or nation-making. They were, as we would say, winging it. And they were idealistic and they were young. We see their faces in the old paintings done later in their lives or looking at us from the money in our wallets, and we see the awkward teeth and the powdered hair, and we think of them as elder statesmen. But George Washington, when he took command of the continental army at Cambridge in 1775, was 43 years old, and he was the oldest of them. Jefferson was 33 when he wrote the Declaration of Independence. John Adams was 40. Benjamin Rush—one of the most interesting of them all and one of the founders of the antislavery movement in Philadelphia—was 30 years old when he signed the Declaration. They were young people. They were feeling their way, improvising, trying to do what would work. They had no money, no navy, no real army. There wasn't a bank in the entire country. There wasn't but one bridge between New York and Boston. It was a little country of 2,500,000 people, 500,000 of whom were held in slavery, a little fringe of settlement along the east coast. What a story. What a noble beginning. And think of this: almost no nations in the world know when they were born. We know exactly when we began and why we began and who did it.

In the rotunda of the Capitol in Washington hangs John Trumbull's great painting, "The Declaration of Independence, Fourth of July, 1776." It's been seen by more people than any other American painting. It's our best known scene from our past. And almost nothing about it is accurate. The Declaration of Independence wasn't signed on July 4th. They didn't start to sign the Declaration until August 2nd, and only a part of the Congress was then present. They kept coming back in the months that followed from their distant states to take their turn signing the document. The chairs are wrong, the doors are in the wrong place, there were no heavy draperies at the windows, and the display of military flags and banners on the back wall is strictly a figment of Trumbull's imagination. But what is accurate about it are the faces. Every single one of the 47 men in that painting is an identifiable, and thus accountable, individual. We know what they look like. We know who they were. And that's what Trumbull wanted. He wanted us to know them and, by God, not to forget them. Because this momentous step wasn't a paper being handed down by a potentate or a king or a czar, it was the decision of a Congress acting freely.

Our Failure, Our Duty

We are raising a generation of young Americans who are by-and-large historically illiterate. And it's not their fault. There have been innumerable studies, and there's no denying it. I've experienced it myself again and again. I had a young woman come up to me after a talk one morning at the University of Missouri to tell me that she was glad she came to hear me speak, and I said I was pleased she had shown up. She said, "Yes, I'm very pleased, because until now I never understood that all of the 13 colonies—the original 13 colonies—were on the east coast." Now you hear that and you think: What in the world have we done? How could this young lady, this wonderful young American, become a student at a fine university and not know that? I taught a seminar at Dartmouth of seniors majoring in history, honor students, 25 of them. The first morning we sat down and I said, "How many of you know who George Marshall was?" Not one. There was a long silence and finally one young man asked, "Did he have, maybe, something to do with the Marshall Plan?" And I said yes, he certainly did, and that's a good place to begin talking about George Marshall.

We have to do several things. First of all we have to get across the idea that we have to know who we were if we're to know who we are and where we're headed. This is essential. We have to value what our forebears—and not just in the 18th century, but our own parents and grandparents—did for us, or we're not going to take it very seriously, and it can slip away. If you don't care about it—if you've inherited some great work of art that is worth a fortune and you don't know that it's worth a fortune, you don't even know that it's a great work of art and you're not interested in it—you're going to lose it. . . .

There was a wonderful professor of child psychology at the University of Pittsburgh named Margaret McFarland who was so wise that I wish her teachings and her ideas and her themes were much better known. She said that attitudes aren't taught, they're caught. If the teacher has an attitude of enthusiasm for the subject, the student catches that whether the student is in second grade or is in graduate school. She said that if you show them what you love, they'll get it and they'll want to get it. Also if the teachers know what they are teaching, they are much less dependent on textbooks. And I don't know when the last time you picked up a textbook in American history might have been. And there are, to be sure, some very good ones still in print. But most of them, it appears to me, have been published in order to kill any interest that anyone might have in history. I think that students would be better served by cutting out all the pages, clipping up all the page numbers, mixing them all up and then asking students to put the pages back together in the right order. The textbooks are dreary, they're done by committee, they're often hilariously politically correct and they're not doing any good. Students should not have to read anything that we, you and I, wouldn't want to read ourselves. And there are wonderful books, past and present. There is literature in history. Let's begin with Longfellow, for example. Let's begin with Lincoln's Second Inaugural Address, for example. These are literature. They can read that too.

History isn't just something that ought to be taught or ought to be read or ought to be encouraged because it's going to make us a better citizen. It will make us a better citizen; or because it will make us a more thoughtful and understanding human being, which it will; or because it will cause us to behave better, which it will. It should be taught for pleasure: The pleasure of history, like art or music or literature, consists of an expansion of the experience of being alive, which is what education is largely about.

And we need not leave the whole job of teaching history to the teachers. If I could have you come away from what I have to say tonight remembering one thing, it would be this: The teaching of history, the emphasis on the importance of history, the enjoyment of history, should begin at home. We who are parents or grandparents should be taking our children to historic sights. We should be talking about those books in biography or history that we have particularly enjoyed, or that character or those characters in history that have meant something to us. We should be talking about what it was like when we were growing up in the olden days. Children, particularly little children, love this. And in my view, the real focus should be at the grade school level. We all know that those little guys can learn languages so fast it takes your breath away. They can learn anything so fast it takes your breath away. And the other very important truth is that they want to learn. They can be taught to dissect a cow's eye. They can be taught anything. And there's no secret to teaching history or to making history interesting. Barbara Tuchman said it in two words, "Tell stories." That's what history is: a story. And what's a story? E.M. Forster gave a wonderful definition to it: If I say to you the king died and then the queen died, that's a sequence of events. If I say the king died and the queen died of grief, that's a story. That's human. That calls for empathy on the part of the teller of the story and of the reader or listener to the story. And we ought to be growing, encouraging, developing historians who have heart and empathy to put students in that place of those people before us who were just as human, just as real—and maybe in some ways more real than we are. We've got to teach history and nurture history and encourage history because it's an antidote to the hubris of the present—the idea that everything we have and everything we do and everything we think is the ultimate, the best. . . .

We should never look down on those people [from our past] and say that they should have known better. What do you think they're going to be saying about us in the future? They're going to be saying we should have known better. Why did we do that? What were we thinking of? All this second-guessing and the arrogance of it are unfortunate.

Listening to the Past

Samuel Eliot Morison said we ought to read history because it will help us to behave better. It does. And we ought to read history because it helps to break down the dividers between the disciplines of science, medicine, philosophy, art, music, whatever. It's all part of the human story and ought to be seen as such. You can't understand it unless you see it that way. You can't understand the 18th century, for example, unless you understand the vocabulary of the 18th century. What did they mean by those words? They didn't necessarily mean the same thing as we do. There's a line in one of the letters written by John Adams where he's telling his wife Abigail at home, "We can't guarantee success in this war, but we can do something better. We can deserve it." . . .

That line in the Adams letter is saying that how the war turns out is in the hands of God. We can't control that, but we can control how we behave. We can deserve success. When I read that line when I was doing the research on the book, it practically lifted me out of my chair. . . . It's a line from the play Cato. They were quoting something that was in the language of the time. They were quoting scripture of a kind, a kind of secular creed if you will. And you can't understand why they behaved as they did if you don't understand that. You can't understand why honor was so important to them and why they were truly ready to put their lives, their fortunes, their sacred honor on the line. Those weren't just words.

I want to read to you, in conclusion, a letter that John Quincy Adams received from his mother. Little John Adams was taken to Europe by his father when his father sailed out of Massachusetts in the midst of winter, in the midst of war, to serve our country in France. Nobody went to sea in the wintertime, on the North Atlantic, if it could possibly be avoided. And nobody did it trying to cut through the British barricade outside of Boston Harbor because the British ships were sitting out there waiting to capture somebody like John Adams and take him to London and to the Tower, where he would have been hanged as a traitor. But they sent this little ten-year-old boy with his father, risking his life, his mother knowing that she wouldn't see him for months, maybe years at best. Why? Because she and his father wanted John Quincy to be in association with Franklin and the great political philosophers of France, to learn to speak French, to travel in Europe, to be able to soak it all up. And they risked his life for that—for his education. We have no idea what people were willing to do for education in times past. It's the one sustaining theme through our whole country—that the next generation will be better educated than we are. John Adams himself is a living example of the transforming miracle of education. His father was able to write his name, we know. His mother was almost certainly illiterate. And because he had a scholarship to Harvard, everything changed for him. He said, "I discovered books and read forever," and he did. And they wanted this for their son. . . .

John Quincy Adams, in my view, was the most superbly educated and maybe the most brilliant human being who ever occupied the executive office. He was, in my view, the greatest Secretary of State we've ever had. He wrote the Monroe Doctrine, among other things. And he was a wonderful human being and a great writer. . . .

Citizenship isn't just voting. We all know that. Let's all pitch in. And let's not lose heart. They talk about what a difficult, dangerous time we live in. And it is very difficult, very dangerous and very uncertain. But so it has always been. And this nation of ours has been through darker times. And if you don't know that—as so many who broadcast the news and subject us to their opinions in the press don't seem to know—that's because we're failing in our understanding of history.

The Revolutionary War was as dark a time as we've ever been through. 1776, the year we so consistently and rightly celebrate every year, was one of the darkest times, if not the darkest time in the history of the country. Many of us here remember the first months of 1942 after Pearl Harbor when German submarines were sinking our oil tankers right off the coasts of Florida and New Jersey, in sight of the beaches, and there wasn't a thing we could do about it. Our recruits were drilling with wooden rifles, we had no air force, half of our navy had been destroyed at Pearl Harbor, and there was nothing to say or guarantee that the Nazi machine could be defeated—nothing. Who was to know? I like to think of what Churchill said when he crossed the Atlantic after Pearl Harbor and gave a magnificent speech. He said we haven't journeyed this far because we're made of sugar candy. It's as true today as it ever was.

POSTSCRIPT

Should the Teaching of American History Focus on a Critique of Past Events and Individuals?

Although this particular controversy involves content and emphases for the study of American history, similar scenarios are being played out in other subject matter areas such as mathematics in which debates over "new" math, "drill and kill," and the use of calculators go unresolved. The same is true in science in which the ongoing controversy over evolution versus creationism always seems to be present in any discussion of curriculum standards. Cutting across subject matter content areas are other curricular controversies related to too much or too little multiculturalism and/or ethnocentrism. And even at the most basic academic core of teaching children to read, the "war" between whole language and phonics continues to flare up.

It has been suggested that the very nature of these debates and the subsequent compromises that usually follow have resulted in a very irenic curriculum in the public schools—one that aims at not offending anyone or any group. But countering that point is the contention that the public schools are charged with educating "all of the children of all the people," and thus, the public school curriculum should not reflect a particular point of view or bias. Parents who want their beliefs emphasized in the school curriculum can send their children to a private or parochial school where those beliefs are operant. That is the point made by David Remes, a lawyer specializing in First Amendment matters, when he argued against allowing parents to "opt" their children out of curriculum they disagree with: "Public education is not 'public' just because it is free. It is 'public' because it is a kind of education—an education that instructs children as Justice William J. Brennan has put it, in 'a heritage common to all American groups and religions.' Public education is not and cannot be an education that instructs children in the orthodoxies of their parents."

As previously pointed out, decisions related to curriculum standards often lead to controversy. But, in fact, controversies that arise over curriculum content can be viewed as healthy in that they are evidence of public interest and awareness. Speaking to that point, the National Council for the Social Studies in the Executive Summary to their 1994 *Curriculum Standards for Social Studies,* stated: "The importance of social studies ensures that policymakers, educators, parents, and citizens of all kinds will want to know what students should be taught, how they will be taught, and how student achievement will be evaluated." The only thing wrong with that statement is that it seems to belie a professional inclination to assume that the named groups don't already have their own beliefs and biases regarding curriculum, teaching, and assessment. Perhaps that is why on this crucial topic the best decision making will result from a combination of professional input and public approval, which is the general process followed when a state formally adopts curriculum standards. It is also important that textbook publishers use state curriculum standards as guides in the development of their books.

The two articles comprising this issue certainly point out the glaring differences between the traditional approach to teaching American history as espoused by McCullough and the revisionist preferences of Noguera and Cohen.

Other articles dealing with this issue include: Elliott Self, *Social Studies Revived* (*Educational Leadership,* January 2004); Kim Marshall, *Standards Matter* (*Phi Delta Kappan,* October 2003); Paul R. Gross, *Politicizing Science Education* (The Thomas B. Fordham Foundation, 2000); also from The Thomas B. Fordham Foundation, a series on *The State of State Standards;* and from the Council for Basic Education, *Closing the Gap* (2000) and *Standards for Excellence in Education* (1998).

ISSUE 11

Should Comprehensive Sexuality Education Be Taught in Public Schools?

YES: SIECUS Report, from *Guidelines for Comprehensive Sexuality Education: Kindergarten through 12th Grade* (2004)

NO: Robert E. Rector, from "The Effectiveness of Abstinence Education Programs in Reducing Sexual Activity among Youth," Heritage Foundation (April 2002)

ISSUE SUMMARY

YES: The Sexuality Information and Education Council of the United States (SIECUS) believes that all students should receive instruction in "comprehensive school-based sexuality education" in all grade levels.

NO: Robert Rector, a senior research fellow at the Heritage Foundation, argues that abstinence-only education will help young people to develop the "foundations of healthy marital life" that will serve them well as adults.

Given the fact that the public schools are involved with educating "all of the children of all of the people," it should come as no surprise that there are very few topics and issues for which there is unanimity of opinion regarding the role of the school. Even where there is general agreement regarding a certain purpose, there can be profound and acrimonious disagreement about the specifics. For example, although there is general agreement that schools should promote and provide instruction on issues related to health and safety, there is much disagreement and contention over what the content of that instruction should actually be in practice. And obviously that particular content area, when it includes sex education, spills over into issues related to strongly held beliefs and concerns regarding morality, religion, and family values.

At one end of the spectrum there are those who do not believe that school is the appropriate place for students to have any instruction or information presented regarding human sexuality. They hold that presenting such material only causes children and adolescents to become more curious about sex and that in turn leads to experimentation. They point to alarming statistics regarding unwed teenage pregnancies, AIDs, and other sexually transmitted diseases and claim that such statistics are evidence of the general failure of sex education programs. Those very same statistics motivate others to support comprehensive sex education programs including the provision of information regarding birth control and disease prevention. Those favoring comprehensive sex education claim that by not providing such information to our children we are putting them in great danger and may be violating their constitutional rights.

With such diametrically opposed views existing about this topic it is not surprising that vast differences exist regarding the nature and quality of sex education programs. In an article in *WomensEnews* (March 11, 2002), Rebecca Veseley reports that:

> A 2000 study by the Kaiser Family Foundation found that 32 states do not even require sex education, leaving the decision up to school districts. One-third of public secondary schools in the United States teach an "abstinence only until marriage" curriculum, which discourages sex outside of heterosexual marriage, according to The Alan Guttmacher Institute. Other schools embrace so-called comprehensive education, teaching contraception methods and stressing abstinence. As a result, what adolescents learn differs not just from state to state, but often from school to school.

A number of states not requiring sex education do require that accurate information be supplied to students about AIDs, STDs, and the failure rate of various contraceptive methods. But student attendance at such informational presentations is usually subject to parental rights to "opt out" their child.

There are also strong political overtones to this issue. Veseley's report included reference to an Arizona bill that would require nonbiased, accurate information on the spectrum of human sexuality and its implications. The bill stated that the classes would be deemed "medically accurate" because the information would be drawn from the nonpartisan federal Centers for Disease Control and Prevention and peer-reviewed medical journals. Leslee Unruh, president and founder of the Abstinence Clearinghouse, which promotes chastity until marriage, responded, "We want to see medically accurate information in schools, but let's have an unbiased organization giving the information instead of these biased liberal groups." She describes the Centers for Disease Control and Prevention as an unacceptable source because it "promotes condom use" instead of emphasizing abstinence.

In the following selections, SIECUS and Robert Rector present their widely divergent views. SIECUS argues that young people need comprehensive sex education in order to become sexually healthy adults. Rector presents many statistics evidencing what he claims is the failure of comprehensive safe-sex programs.

YES ↵

Guidelines for Comprehensive Sexuality Education: Kindergarten through 12th Grade

Sexuality education is a lifelong process of acquiring information and forming attitudes, beliefs, and values about such important topics as identity, relationships, and intimacy. The Sexuality Information and Education Council of the United States (SIECUS) believes that all people have the right to comprehensive sexuality education that addresses the socio-cultural, biological, psychological, and spiritual dimensions of sexuality by providing information; exploring feelings, values, and attitudes; and developing communication, decision-making, and critical-thinking skills.

While parents are—and ought to be—their children's primary sexuality educators, they often need help and encouragement. Faith-based institutions, community-based organizations, and schools can play an important role.

SIECUS believes that comprehensive school-based sexuality education should be part of the education program at every grade. Such programs should be appropriate to the age, developmental level, and cultural background of students and respect the diversity of values and beliefs represented in the community. Comprehensive school-based sexuality education complements and augments the sexuality education children receive from their families, religious and community groups, and health care professionals.

SIECUS is not alone in the belief that school-based sexuality education is vitally important to the health and well-being of our nation's youth. National, state, and local polls have consistently found that a majority of parents want schools to provide comprehensive education about sexuality that includes such topics as abstinence, sexually transmitted diseases (STDs), HIV/AIDS, contraception, and disease prevention methods. In fact, many states mandate that some or all of these topics are covered in school curricula. Research also supports a comprehensive approach to sexuality education with numerous studies finding that such programs can help young people delay intercourse, reduce the frequency of intercourse, reduce the number of sexual partners they have, and increase their use of condoms and other contraceptive methods when they do become sexual active.

Educators and schools, however, are often left in the difficult position of trying to determine exactly what their sexuality education courses should look like with little or no guidance. For over a decade, SIECUS has published

Martha Kempner and Monica Rodriguez, *Guidelines for Comprehensive Sexuality Education Kindergarten-12th Grade, Third Edition* (New York: the Sexuality Information and Education Council of the United States, 2004), 11–19.

the *Guidelines for Comprehensive Sexuality Education: Kindergarten-12th Grade* to provide such guidance and help educators create new sexuality education programs and evaluate existing curricula. The *Guidelines*, created by a national task force of experts in the fields of adolescent development, health care, and education, provide a framework of the key concepts, topics, and messages that all sexuality education programs would ideally include.

History of the *Guidelines*

As the 1980s drew to a close, in part because of the rapidly growing AIDS pandemic, there was renewed interest in providing young people with the information and skills they needed to avoid unintended pregnancy and STDs. In fact, at that point, a number of states began to mandate that schools teach young people about STDs, HIV/AIDS, and other sexual health topics.

At the same time, however, debates were raging about whether young people should instead learn solely about abstinence, if certain controversial topics such as masturbation and abortion could be discussed in classrooms, and at what age other topics should be introduced.

This left many teachers confused and on their own. A 1989 study found that most sexuality education teachers created their own curricular material, often without guidance from the state or local school district. Other studies found that few of the teachers responsible for sexuality education had received formal training in the subject.

SIECUS realized that ultimately it would be the young people who suffered the most because they would not receive the high-quality education they needed to become sexually healthy adults.

In 1990, SIECUS undertook a major effort to change this by convening the National Guidelines Task Force, a group of leading educators, health professionals, and representatives from national organizations who focused on adolescent development, education, and sexuality. Task force members included representatives from the U.S. Centers for Disease Control and Prevention, the American Medical Association, the National School Boards Association, the National Education Association, the March of Dimes Birth Defects Foundation, and Planned Parenthood Federation of America, as well as school-based sexuality education teachers, national program developers, and experienced trainers.

These experts were charged with the difficult task of creating an ideal model of comprehensive sexuality education by developing a framework of the concepts, topics, skills, and messages young people should learn and determining the age-level at which each should be introduced.

In 1991, the task force released the *Guidelines for Comprehensive Sexuality Education: Kindergarten-12th Grade*. The *Guidelines* represented the first national model for comprehensive sexuality education and helped educators evaluate existing curricula and create new programs. Since they were first published, well over 100,000 copies have been distributed in both hard copy and electronic form. In addition, the *Guidelines* have been adapted and translated into Spanish for use in Latino communities in the U.S., and guidelines adaptation projects have produced national models in countries such as Brazil, India, Iceland, Nigeria, and Russia.

This Third Edition is based on the work of the original task force; the basic structure and content remain the same. Certain topics, messages, and age-levels, however, have been changed to reflect new information, ongoing community dialogue about the appropriate content of sexuality education, and the reality that today's young people are facing.

Structure of the *Guidelines*

The *Guidelines* are modeled after the landmark School Health Education Study (SHES) published in the late 1960s. SHES developed an innovative approach to structuring health knowledge by identifying broad concepts and related sub-concepts and then arranging these in a hierarchy for students in kindergarten through 12th grade.

Using this model, the task force sought to create an organizational framework of the important knowledge and skills related to sexuality and family living. To do this, the task force first determined the life behaviors of a sexually healthy adult which serve as outcome measures of successful sexuality education. They then compiled the information and determined the skills necessary to achieve these life behaviors and organized them into key concepts, topics, subconcepts, and age-appropriate developmental messages.

Key Concepts: Key concepts are broad categories of information about sexuality and family living. The *Guidelines* are organized into six key concepts, each of which encompasses one essential area of learning for young people. They are:

> **Key Concept 1:** *Human Development.* Human development is characterized by the interrelationship between physical, emotional, social, and intellectual growth.
>
> **Key Concept 2:** *Relationships.* Relationships play a central role throughout our lives.
>
> **Key Concept 3:** *Personal Skills.* Healthy sexuality requires the development and use of specific personal and interpersonal skills.
>
> **Key Concept 4:** *Sexual Behavior.* Sexuality is a central part of being human, and individuals express their sexuality in a variety of ways.
>
> **Key Concept 5:** *Sexual Health.* The promotion of sexual health requires specific information and attitudes to avoid unwanted consequences of sexual behavior.
>
> **Key Concept 6:** *Society and Culture.* Social and cultural environments shape the way individuals learn about and express their sexuality.

Life Behaviors: Life behaviors are essentially outcomes of instruction. For each of the broad categories identified as a key concept, the *Guidelines* note several life behaviors of a sexually healthy adult that reflect actions students will be able to take after having applied the information and skills.

For example, life behaviors under Key *Concept 3: Personal Skills*, include: "Identify and live according to one's values"; "Take responsibility for one's own behavior"; and "Practice effective decision-making." (A complete list of life behaviors appears [below].)

Topics: Topics are the individual subjects that need to be discussed in order to sufficiently address each key concept and help students achieve the desired outcomes or life behaviors. Each key concept is broken down into a number of component topics. . . .

Life Behaviors of a Sexually Healthy Adult

A sexually healthy adult will:

- Appreciate one's own body.
- Seek further information about reproduction as needed.
- Affirm that human development includes sexual development, which may or may not include reproduction or sexual experience.
- Interact with all genders in respectful and appropriate ways.
- Affirm one's own sexual orientation and respect the sexual orientations of others.
- Affirm one's own gender identities and respect the gender identities of others.
- Express love and intimacy in appropriate ways.
- Develop and maintain meaningful relationships.
- Avoid exploitative or manipulative relationships.
- Make informed choices about family options and relationships.
- Exhibit skills that enhance personal relationships.
- Identify and live according to one's own values.
- Take responsibility for one's own behavior.
- Practice effective decision-making.
- Develop critical-thinking skills.
- Communicate effectively with family, peers, and romantic partners.
- Enjoy and express one's sexuality throughout life.
- Express one's sexuality in ways that are congruent with one's values.
- Enjoy sexual feelings without necessarily acting on them.
- Discriminate between life-enhancing sexual behaviors and those that are harmful to self and/or others.
- Express one's sexuality while respecting the rights of others.
- Seek new information to enhance one's sexuality.
- Engage in sexual relationships that are consensual, non-exploitative, honest, pleasurable, and protected.
- Practice health-promoting behaviors, such as regular check-ups, breast and testicular self-exam, and early identification of potential problems.
- Use contraception effectively to avoid unintended pregnancy.

- Avoid contracting or transmitting a sexually transmitted disease, including HIV.
- Act consistently with one's own values when dealing with an unintended pregnancy.
- Seek early prenatal care.
- Help prevent sexual abuse.
- Demonstrate respect for people with different sexual values.
- Exercise democratic responsibility to influence legislation dealing with sexual issues.
- Assess the impact of family, cultural, media, and societal messages on one's thoughts, feelings, values, and behaviors related to sexuality.
- Critically examine the world around them for biases based on gender, sexual orientation, culture, ethnicity, and race.
- Promote the rights of all people to accurate sexuality information.
- Avoid behaviors that exhibit prejudice and bigotry.
- Reject stereotypes about the sexuality of different populations.
- Educate others about sexuality.

Developmental Messages: Developmental messages are brief statements that contain the specific information young people need to learn about each topic. For each topic, the *Guidelines* present developmental messages appropriate for four separate age levels which reflect stages of development. The levels are:

Level 1: middle childhood, ages 5 through 8; early elementary school

Level 2: preadolescence, ages 9 through 12; later elementary school

Level 3: early adolescence, ages 12 through 15; middle school/ junior high school

Level 4: adolescences, ages 15 through 18; high school . . .

It is also important to note that while the developmental messages contain the age-appropriate information that young people need to learn, they are not meant to simply be read or quoted verbatim in materials or activities. Instead, they are intended for educators and other adults who are in a better position to understand the best language and methods to use when sharing this information with young people.

Guidelines for Comprehensive Sexuality Education: Key Concepts and Topics

Key Concept 1: Human Development

Topic 1: Reproductive and Sexual Anatomy and Physiology

Topic 2: Puberty

Topic 3: Reproduction

Topic 4: Body Image

Topic 5: Sexual Orientation
Topic 6: Gender Identity

Key Concept 2: Relationships
Topic 1: Families
Topic 2: Friendship
Topic 3: Love
Topic 4: Romantic Relationships and Dating
Topic 5: Marriage and Lifetime Commitments
Topic 6: Raising Children

Key Concept 3: Personal Skills
Topic 1: Values
Topic 2: Decision-making
Topic 3: Communication
Topic 4: Assertiveness
Topic 5: Negotiation
Topic 6: Looking for Help

Key Concept 4: Sexual Behavior
Topic 1: Sexuality Throughout Life
Topic 2: Masturbation
Topic 3: Shared Sexual Behavior
Topic 4: Sexual Abstinence
Topic 5: Human Sexual Response
Topic 6: Sexual Fantasy
Topic 7: Sexual Dysfunction

Key Concept 5: Sexual Health
Topic 1: Reproductive Health
Topic 2: Contraception
Topic 3: Pregnancy and Prenatal Care
Topic 4: Abortion
Topic 5: Sexually Transmitted Diseases
Topic 6: HIV and AIDS
Topic 7: Sexual Abuse, Assault, Violence, and Harassment

Key Concept 6: Society and Culture
Topic 1: Sexuality and Society
Topic 2: Gender Roles
Topic 3: Sexuality and the Law
Topic 4: Sexuality and Religion
Topic 5: Diversity
Topic 6: Sexuality and the Media
Topic 7: Sexuality and the Arts

Goals, Values, and Fundamental Principles

Although the *Guidelines* are designed to be adaptable to the needs and beliefs of different communities, they are nonetheless based on certain specific values relating to sexuality and the nature of ideal sexuality education. Before developing the concepts and messages in the *Guidelines*, the National Guidelines Task Force agreed upon the goals of sexuality education, the values inherent in the *Guidelines*, and a number of fundamental principles about the implementation of sexuality education.

The Goals of Sexuality Education   The primary goal of sexuality education is to promote adult sexual health. It should assist young people in developing a positive view of sexuality, provide them with information they need to take care of their sexual health, and help them acquire skills to make decisions now and in the future. The *Guidelines* recognize that the goals of sexuality education fall into four areas:

> *Information:* Sexuality education seeks to provide accurate information about human sexuality, including growth and development, human reproduction, anatomy, physiology, masturbation, family life, pregnancy, childbirth, parenthood, sexual response, sexual orientation, gender identity, contraception, abortion, sexual abuse, HIV/AIDS, and other sexually transmitted diseases.

> *Attitudes, Values, and Insights:* Sexuality education seeks to provide an opportunity for young people to question, explore, and assess their own and their community's attitudes about society, gender, and sexuality. This can help young people understand their family's values, develop their own values, improve critical-thinking skills, increase self-esteem and self-efficacy, and develop insights concerning relationships with family members, individuals of all genders, sexual partners, and society at large. Sexuality education can help young people understand their obligations and responsibilities to their families and society.

> *Relationships and Interpersonal Skills:* Sexuality education seeks to help young people develop interpersonal skills, including communication, decision-making, assertiveness, and peer refusal skills, as well as the ability to create reciprocal and satisfying relationships. Sexuality education programs should prepare students to understand sexuality effectively and creatively in adult roles. This includes helping young people develop the capacity for caring, supportive, non-coercive, and mutually pleasurable intimate and sexual relationships.

> *Responsibility:* Sexuality education seeks to help young people exercise responsibility regarding sexual relationships by addressing such issues as abstinence, how to resist pressures to become involved in unwanted or early sexual intercourse, and the use of contraception and other sexual health measures.

Values Inherent in the *Guidelines*   The *Guidelines* are based on a number of values about sexuality, young people, and the role of families. While these values reflect those of many communities across the country, they are not universal. Parents, educators, and community members will need to review these values to be sure that the program that is implemented is consistent with their community's beliefs, culture, and social norms. The values inherent in the *Guidelines* are:

- Every person has dignity and self worth.
- All children should be loved and cared for.
- Young people should view themselves as unique and worthwhile individuals within the context of their cultural heritage.
- Sexuality is a natural and healthy part of living.
- All persons are sexual.
- Sexuality includes physical, ethical, social, spiritual, psychological, and emotional dimensions.
- Individuals can express their sexuality in varied ways.
- Parents should be the primary sexuality educators of their children.
- Families should provide children's first education about sexuality.
- Families should share their values about sexuality with their children.
- In a pluralistic society, people should respect and accept the diversity of values and beliefs about sexuality that exist in a community.
- Sexual relationships should be reciprocal, based on respect, and should never be coercive or exploitative.
- All persons have the right and obligation to make responsible sexual choices.
- Individuals, families, and society benefit when children are able to discuss sexuality with their parents and/or trusted adults.
- Young people develop their values about sexuality as part of becoming adults.
- Young people explore their sexuality as a natural process in achieving sexual maturity.
- Early involvement in sexual behaviors poses risks.
- Abstaining from sexual intercourse is the most effective method of preventing pregnancy and STD/HIV.
- Young people who are involved in sexual relationships need access to information about healthcare services.

Fundamental Principles   While the *Guidelines* were created to be adaptable to a wide variety of communities and settings, they are based on a number of fundamental principles about the nature of ideal sexuality education programs. The task force believed that sexuality education programs benefit from:

- *Being Part of a Comprehensive Health Education Program:* Sexuality education should be offered as part of an overall comprehensive health education program. Sexuality education can best address the broadest range of issues in the context of health promotion, social and gender equality, and disease prevention. Communities and schools should seek to integrate the concepts and messages in the *Guidelines* into their overall health education initiatives.

- *Well-Trained Teachers:* Sexuality education should be taught by specially trained teachers. Professionals responsible for sexuality education must receive training in human sexuality, including the philosophy and methodology of sexuality education. While ideally teachers should attend academic courses or programs in schools of higher education, in-service courses, continuing education classes, and intensive seminars can also help prepare sexuality educators.
- *Community Involvement:* The community must be involved in the development and implementation of sexuality education programs. School-based programs must be carefully developed to respect the diversity of values and beliefs represented in the community. Parents, family members, teachers, administrators, community and religious leaders, and students should all be involved.
- *A Focus on All Youth:* All children and youth will benefit from comprehensive sexuality education regardless of gender, sexual orientation, ethnicity, socio-economic status, or disability. Programs and materials should be adapted to reflect the specific issues and concerns of the community as well as any special needs of the learners. In addition, curricula and material should reflect the cultural diversity represented in the classroom.
- *A Variety of Teaching Methods:* Sexuality education is most effective when young people not only receive information but are also given the opportunity to explore their own and society's attitudes and values and to develop or strengthen social skills. A wide variety of teaching methods and activities can foster learning such as interactive discussions, role plays, demonstrations, individual and group research, group exercises, and homework assignments.

Robert E. Rector

The Effectiveness of Abstinence Education Programs in Reducing Sexual Activity among Youth

Teenage sexual activity is a major problem confronting the nation and has led to a rising incidence of sexually transmitted diseases (STDs), emotional and psychological injuries, and out-of-wedlock childbearing. Abstinence education programs for youth have been proven to be effective in reducing early sexual activity. Abstinence programs also can provide the foundation for personal responsibility and enduring marital commitment. Therefore, they are vitally important to efforts aimed at reducing out-of-wedlock childbearing among young adult women, improving child well-being, and increasing adult happiness over the long term.

Washington policymakers should be aware of the consequences of early sexual activity, the undesirable contents of conventional "safe sex" education programs, and the findings of the professional literature concerning the effectiveness of genuine abstinence programs. In particular, policymakers should understand that:

- **Sexually transmitted diseases (STDs), including incurable viral infections, have reached epidemic proportions.** Annually, 3 million teenagers contract STDs; STDs afflict roughly one in four teens who are sexually active.
- **Early sexual activity has multiple negative consequences for young people.** Research shows that young people who become sexually active are not only vulnerable to STDs, but also likely to experience emotional and psychological injuries, subsequent marital difficulties, and involvement in other high-risk behaviors.
- **Conventional "safe sex" programs (sometimes erroneously called "abstinence plus" programs) place little or no emphasis on encouraging young people to abstain from early sexual activity.** Instead, such programs strongly promote condom use and implicitly condone sexual activity among teens. Nearly all such programs contain material and messages that would be alarming and offensive to the overwhelming majority of parents.
- **Despite claims to the contrary, there are 10 scientific evaluations showing that real abstinence programs can be highly effective in**

reducing early sexual activity. Moreover, real abstinence education is a fairly young field; thus, the number of evaluations of abstinence programs at present is somewhat limited. In the near future, many additional evaluations that demonstrate the effectiveness of abstinence education will become available.

Consequences of Early Sexual Activity

Young people who become sexually active enter an arena of high-risk behavior that leads to physical and emotional damage. Each year, influenced by a combination of a youthful assumption of invincibility and a lack of guidance (or misguidance and misleading information), millions of teens ignore those risks and suffer the consequences.

Sexually Transmitted Diseases

The nation is experiencing an epidemic of sexually transmitted diseases that is steadily expanding. In the 1960s, the beginning of the "sexual revolution," the dominant diseases related to sexual activity were syphilis and gonorrhea. Today, there are more than 20 widespread STDs, infecting an average of more than 15 million individuals each year. Two-thirds of all STDs occur in people who are 25 years of age or younger. Each year, 3 million teens contract an STD; overall, one-fourth of sexually active teens have been afflicted.

There is no cure for sexually transmitted viral diseases such as the human immunodeficiency virus (HIV) and herpes, which take their toll on people throughout life. Other common viral STDs are the Human Papillomavirus (HPV)—the leading viral STD, with 5.5 million cases reported each year, and the cause of nearly all cases of cervical cancer that kill approximately 4,800 women per year—and Chlamydia trachomatis, which is associated with pelvic inflammatory disease that scars the fallopian tubes and is the fastest growing cause of infertility.

Significantly, research shows that condom use offers relatively little protection (from "zero" to "some") for herpes and no protection from the deadly HPV. A review of the scientific literature reveals that, on average, condoms failed to prevent the transmission of the HIV virus—which causes the immune deficiency syndrome known as AIDS—between 15 percent and 31 percent of the time. It should not be surprising, therefore, that while condom use has increased over the past 25 years, the spread of STDs has likewise continued to rise.

Emotional and Psychological Injury

Young people who become sexually active are vulnerable to emotional and psychological injury as well as to physical diseases. Many young girls report experiencing regret or guilt after their initial sexual experience. In the words of one psychiatrist who recalls the effects of her own sexual experimentation in her teens, "The longest-standing, deepest wound I gave myself was heartfelt; that sick, used feeling of having given a precious part of myself—my soul—to so many and for nothing, still aches. I never imagined I'd pay so dearly and for so long."

Sexually active youth often live with anxiety about the possibility of an unwanted pregnancy or contracting a devastating STD. Those who do become infected with a disease suffer emotional as well as physical effects. Fears regarding the course the disease are coupled with a loss of self-esteem and self-confidence. In a survey by the Medical Institute for Sexual Health, 80 percent of those who had herpes said that they felt "less confident" and "less desirable sexually."

In addition, early sexual activity can negatively affect the ability of young people to form stable and healthy relationships in a later marriage. Sexual relationships among teenagers are fleeting and unstable, and broken intimate relationships can have serious long-term developmental effects. A series of broken intimate relationships can undermine an individual's capacity to enter into a committed, loving marital relationship. In general, individuals who engage in premarital sexual activity are 50 percent more likely to divorce later in life than those who do not. Divorce, in turn, leads to sharp reductions in adult happiness and child well-being.

Marital relationships that follow early sexual activity can also suffer from the emotional impact of infertility resulting from an STD infection, ranging from a sense of guilt to depression. In the words of one gynecologist and fertility specialist, "Infertility is so devastating, it often disorients my patients to life itself. This is more than shock or even depression. It impacts every level of their lives, including their marriage."

Correlation between Sexual Activity and Other High-Risk Behaviors

Research from a variety of sources indicates a correlation between sexual activity among adolescents and teens and the likelihood of engaging in other high-risk behaviors, such as tobacco, alcohol, and illicit drug use.

A study reported in *Pediatrics* magazine found that sexually active boys aged 12 through 16 are four times more likely to smoke and six times more likely to use alcohol than are those who describe themselves as virgins. Among girls in this same age cohort, those who are sexually active are seven times more likely to smoke and 10 times more likely to use marijuana than are those who are virgins. The report describes sexual activity as a "significant associate of other health-endangering behaviors" and notes an increasing recognition of the interrelation of risk behaviors. Research by the Alan Guttmacher Institute likewise finds a correlation between risk behaviors among adolescents and sexual activity; for example, teenagers who use alcohol, tobacco, and/or marijuana regularly are more likely to be sexually active.

Out-of-Wedlock Childbearing

Today, one child in three is born out of wedlock. Only 14 percent of these births occur to women under the age of 18. Most occur to women in their early twenties. Thus, giving birth control to teens in high school through safe-sex programs will have little effect on out-of-wedlock childbearing.

Nearly half of the mothers who give birth outside marriage are cohabiting with the child's father at the time of birth. These fathers, like the mothers, are typically in their early twenties. Out-of-wedlock childbearing is, thus, not the result of teenagers' lack of knowledge about birth control or a lack of availability of birth control. Rather, it is part of a crisis in the relationships of young adult men and women. Out-of-wedlock childbearing, in most cases, occurs because young adult men and women are unable to develop committed, loving marital relationships. Abstinence programs, therefore, which focus on developing loving and enduring relationships and preparation for successful marriages, are an essential first step in reducing future levels of out-of-wedlock births.

The Silent Scandal: Promoting Teen Sex

With millions of dollars in sex-education programs at stake, it is not surprising that the groups that have previously dominated the arena have taken action to block the growing movement to abstinence-only education. Such organizations, including the Sexuality Information and Education Council of the United States (SEICUS), Planned Parenthood, and the National Abortion and Reproductive Rights Action League (NARAL), have been prime supporters of "safe-sex" programs for youth, which entail guidance on the use of condoms and other means of contraception while giving a condescending nod to abstinence. Clearly, the caveat that says "and if you do engage in sex, this is how you should do it" substantially weakens an admonition against early non-marital sexual activity.

Not only do such programs, by their very nature, minimize the abstinence component of sex education, but many of these programs also implicitly encourage sexual activity among the youths they teach. Guidelines developed by SEICUS, for example, include teaching children aged five through eight about masturbation and teaching youths aged 9 through 12 about alternative sexual activities such as mutual masturbation, "outercourse," and oral sex. In addition, the SEICUS guidelines suggest informing youths aged 16 through 18 that sexual activity can include bathing or showering together as well as oral, vaginal, or anal intercourse, and that they can use erotic photographs, movies, or literature to enhance their sexual fantasies when alone or with a partner. Not only do such activities carry their own risks for youth, but they are also likely to increase the incidence of sexual intercourse.

In recent years, parental support for real abstinence education has grown. Because of this, many traditional safe-sex programs now take to calling themselves "abstinence plus" or "abstinence-based" education. In reality, there is little abstinence training in "abstinence-based" education. Instead, these programs are thinly disguised efforts to promote condom use. The actual content of most "abstinence plus" curricula would be alarming to most parents. For example, such programs typically have condom use exercises in which middle school students practice unrolling condoms on cucumbers or dildoes.

Effective Abstinence Programs

Critics of abstinence education often assert that while abstinence education that exclusively promotes abstaining from premarital sex is a good idea in theory, there is no evidence that such education can actually reduce sexual activity among young people. Such criticism is erroneous. There are currently 10 scientific evaluations (described below) that demonstrate the effectiveness of abstinence programs in altering sexual behavior. Each of the programs evaluated is a real abstinence (or what is conventionally termed an "abstinence only") program; that is, the program does not provide contraceptives or encourage their use.

The abstinence programs and their evaluations are as follows:

1. **Virginity Pledge Programs.** An article in the *Journal of the American Medical Association* by Dr. Michael Resnick and others entitled "Protecting Adolescents From Harm: Findings from the National Longitudinal Study on Adolescent Health" shows that "abstinence pledge" programs are dramatically effective in reducing sexual activity among teenagers in grades 7 through 12. Based on a large national sample of adolescents, the study concludes that "Adolescents who reported having taken a pledge to remain a virgin were at significantly lower risk of early age of sexual debut." . . .

2. **Not Me, Not Now.** Not Me, Not Now is a community-wide abstinence intervention targeted to 9- to 14-year-olds in Monroe County, New York, which includes the city of Rochester. The Not Me, Not Now program devised a mass communications strategy to promote the abstinence message through paid TV and radio advertising, billboards, posters distributed in schools, educational materials for parents, an interactive Web site, and educational sessions in school and community settings. The program sought to communicate five themes: raising awareness of the problem of teen pregnancy, increasing an understanding of the negative consequences of teen pregnancy, developing resistance to peer pressure, promoting parent-child communication, and promoting abstinence among teens.

   Not Me, Not Now was effective in reaching early teen listeners, with some 95 percent of the target audience within the county reporting that they had seen a Not Me, Not Now ad. During the intervention period, the program achieved a statistically significant positive shift in attitudes among pre-teens and early teens in the county. The sexual activity rate of 15-year-olds across the county (as reported in the Youth Risk Behavior Survey) dropped by a statistically significant amount from 46.6 percent to 31.6 percent during the intervention period. Finally, the pregnancy rate for girls aged 15 through 17 in Monroe County fell by a statistically significant amount, from 63.4 pregnancies per 1,000 girls to 49.5 pregnancies per 1,000. The teen pregnancy rate fell more rapidly in Monroe County than in comparison counties and in upstate New York in general, and the difference in the rate of decrease was statistically significant.

3. **Operation Keepsake.** Operation Keepsake is an abstinence program for 12- and 13-year-old children in Cleveland, Ohio. Some 77 percent of the children in the program were black or Hispanic. An evaluation of the program in 2001, involving a sample of over 800 students, found that "Operation Keepsake had a clear and sustainable impact on . . . abstinence beliefs." The evaluation showed that the program reduced the rate of onset of sexual activity (loss of virginity) by roughly two-thirds relative to comparable students in control schools who did not participate in the program. In addition, the program reduced by about one-fifth the rate of current sexual activity among those with prior sexual experience.

4. **Abstinence by Choice.** Abstinence by Choice operates in 20 schools in the Little Rock area of Arkansas. The program targets 7th, 8th, and 9th grade students and reaches about 4,000 youths each year. A recent evaluation, involving a sample of nearly 1,000 students, shows that the program has been highly effective in changing the attitudes that are directly linked to early sexual activity. Moreover, the program reduced the sexual activity rates of girls by approximately 40 percent (from 10.2 percent to 5.9 percent) and the rate for boys by approximately 30 percent (from 22.8 percent to 15.8 percent) when compared with similar students who had not been exposed to the program. (The sexual activity rate of students in the program was compared with the rate of sexual activity among control students in the same grade in the same schools prior to the commencement of the program.)

5. **Virginity Pledge Movement.** A 2001 evaluation of the effectiveness of the virginity pledge movement using data from the National Longitudinal Study of Adolescent Health finds that virginity pledge programs are highly effective in helping adolescents to delay sexual activity. According to the authors of the study:

> Adolescents who pledge, controlling for all of the usual characteristics of adolescents and their social contexts that are associated with the transition to sex, are much less likely than adolescents who do not pledge, to have intercourse. The delay effect is substantial and robust. Pledging delays intercourse for a long time.

The study, based on a sample of more than 5,000 students, concludes that taking a virginity pledge reduces by one-third the probability that an adolescent will begin sexual activity compared with other adolescents of the same gender and age, after controlling for a host of other factors linked to sexual activity rates such as physical maturity, parental disapproval of sexual activity, school achievement, and race. When taking a virginity pledge is combined with strong parental disapproval of sexual activity, the probability of initiation of sexual activity is reduced by 75 percent or more.

6. **Teen Aid and Sex Respect.** An evaluation of the Teen Aid and Sex Respect abstinence programs in three school districts in Utah showed that both programs were effective among the students who were at the greatest risk of initiating sexual activity. Approximately

7,000 high school and middle school students participated in the evaluation. To determine the effects of the programs, students in schools with the abstinence programs were compared with students in similar control schools within the same school district. Statistical adjustments were applied to further control for any initial differences between program participants and control students. The programs together were shown to reduce the rate of initiation of sexual activity among at-risk high school students by over a third when compared with a control group of similar students who were not exposed to the program. Statistically significant changes in behavior were not found among junior high students. . . .

7. **Family Accountability Communicating Teen Sexuality (FACTS).** An evaluation performed for the national Title XX abstinence program examined the effectiveness of the Family Accountability Communicating Teen Sexuality abstinence program in reducing teen sexual activity. The evaluation assessed the FACTS program by comparing a sample of students who participated in the program with a group of comparable students in separate control schools who did not participate in the program. The experimental and control students together comprised a sample of 308 students. The evaluation found the FACTS program to be highly effective in delaying the onset of sexual activity. Students who participated in the program were 30 percent to 50 percent less likely to commence sexual activity than were those who did not participate.

8. **Postponing Sexual Involvement (PSI).** Postponing Sexual Involvement was an abstinence program developed by Grady Memorial Hospital in Atlanta, Georgia, and provided to low-income 8th grade students. A study published in Family Planning Perspectives, based on a sample of 536 low-income students, showed that the PSI program was effective in altering sexual behavior. A comparison of the program participants with a control population of comparable low-income minority students who did not participate showed that PSI reduced the rate of initiation of sexual activity during the 8th grade by some 60 percent for boys and over 95 percent for girls. As the study explained:

> The program had a pronounced effect on the behavior of both boys and girls who had not been sexually involved before the program. . . . By the end of eighth grade, boys who had not had the program were more than three times as likely to have begun having sex as were boys who had the program. . . . Girls who had not had the program were as much as 15 times more likely to have begun having sex as were girls who had had the program.

The effects of the program lasted into the next school year even though no additional sessions were provided. By the end of the 9th grade, boys and girls who had participated in PSI were still some 35 percent less likely to have commenced sexual activity than were those who had not participated in the abstinence program.

9. **Project Taking Charge.** Project Taking Charge is a six-week abstinence curriculum delivered in home economics classes during the
school year. It was designed for use in low-income communities
with high rates of teen pregnancy. The curriculum contains these
elements: self-development; basic information about sexual biology
(anatomy, physiology, and pregnancy); vocational goal-setting; family communication; and values instruction on the importance of
delaying sexual activity until marriage. The effect of the program
has been evaluated in two sites: Wilmington, Delaware, and West
Point, Mississippi. The evaluation was based on a small sample of 91
adolescents. Control and experimental groups were created by randomly assigning classrooms to either receive or not receive the program. The students were assessed immediately before and after the
program and through a six-month follow-up.

In the six-month follow-up, Project Taking Charge was shown
to have had a statistically significant effect in increasing adolescents' knowledge of the problems associated with teen pregnancy,
the problems of sexually transmitted diseases, and reproductive
biology. The program was also shown to reduce the rate of onset of
sexual activity by 50 percent relative to the students in the control
group, although the authors urge caution in the interpretation of
these numbers due to the small size of the evaluation sample.

10. **Teen Aid Family Life Education Project.** The Teen Aid Family Life
Education Project is a widely used abstinence education program for
high school and junior high students. An evaluation of the effectiveness of Teen Aid, involving a sample of over 1,300 students, was performed in 21 schools in California, Idaho, Oregon, Mississippi,
Utah, and Washington. The Teen Aid program was shown to have a
statistically significant effect in reducing the rate of initiation of
sexual activity (loss of virginity) among high-risk high school students, compared with similar students in control schools. Among at-
risk high school students who participated in the program, the rate
of initiation of sexual activity was cut by more than one-fourth,
from 37 percent to 27 percent. A similar pattern of reduction was
found among at-risk junior high school students, but the effects did
not achieve statistical significance. The program did not have statistically significant effects among lower-risk students.

Conclusion

Real abstinence education is essential to reducing out-of-wedlock childbearing, preventing sexually transmitted diseases, and improving emotional and
physical well-being among the nation's youth. True abstinence education programs help young people to develop an understanding of commitment, fidel-
ity, and intimacy that will serve them well as the foundations of healthy
marital life in the future.

Abstinence education programs have repeatedly been shown to be effective in reducing sexual activity among their participants. However, funding
for the evaluation of abstinence education programs until very recently has
ranged from meager to nonexistent. Currently, the number of adequately

funded evaluations of abstinence education is increasing. At present, there are several promising new evaluations nearing completion. As each year passes, it can be expected that the number of evaluations showing that abstinence education does significantly reduce sexual activity will grow steadily.

Abstinence education is a nascent and developing field. Substantial funding for abstinence education became available only within the past few years. As abstinence programs develop and become more broadly available, future evaluations will enable the programs to hone and increase their effectiveness.

POSTSCRIPT

Should Comprehensive Sexuality Education Be Taught in Public Schools?

For all of its emotion and rhetoric, the highly charged debate between those who advocate abstinence-only programs and those who favor comprehensive sex education is an argument over means rather than ends. There appears be a consensus that school is an appropriate place to provide instruction in topics related to human sexuality and reproduction. The conflict is over what should comprise that instruction.

A poll (2004) by NPR, the Kaiser Family Foundation, and Harvard's Kennedy School of Government found that only 7 percent of Americans say sex education should not be taught in schools. Other findings from the poll suggest that in spite of general agreement that there should be some form of sex education, this does not mean that the public agrees on what kind of sex education is best. The poll reports that, even though 15 percent of Americans believe that schools should teach only about abstinence and should not provide information on condoms and other forms contraception, 45 percent of the public believes that abstinence should be part of sex education instruction, but that other topics such as birth control should also be included.

With federal funds now being made available for abstinence-only programs, that type of approach to sex education will likely become more popular in schools and other community-based organizations. The provision of federal funding to support abstinence-only causes concern among opponents who are quick to point out linkages between abstinence-only programs and certain religious groups. Opponents such as the America Association of University Women (AAUW) argue that such linkages raise First Amendment questions related to the separation of church and state. AAUW claims that "federally funded abstinence-only sex education blurs the line separating church and state through its religiously slanted teachings" (January 2007).

As the NPR poll points out, abstinence-only education contrasts with the broad sex education curriculum that most Americans seem to want. The findings of the poll indicate that the public's awareness of sexual activity among teenagers and the implications and consequences of that activity has resulted in acceptance of the necessity to broach this subject in the classroom. With the dangers involved with AIDs and other sexually transmitted diseases the case could be made that schools, as part of their responsibility for student safety, have an obligation to address such issues. How that will be translated into actual classroom instruction will likely be a function of the attitudes and values of given communities, school boards, and school administrators.

Additional references on this issue include:

Advocates for Youth, "Comprehensive Sex Education," 2007.

National Coalition Against Censorship, "Paper Against Abstinence Only Education," June 2001.

Melissa G. Pardue, Robert E. Rector, and Shannan Martin, "Government Spends $12 on Safe Sex and Contraceptives for Every $1 Spent on Abstinence," Heritage Foundation Backgrounder No. 1718, January 14, 2004.

Robert E. Rector, Kirk A. Johnson, and Lauren R. Noyes, "Sexually Active Teenagers Are More Likely to Be Depressed and to Attempt Suicide," Heritage Foundation Center for Data Analysis Report No. 03-04, June 3, 2003.

ISSUE 12

Do Single-Sex Classrooms and Schools Provide a Better Learning Environment?

YES: Leonard Sax, from "What's the Evidence? What Have Researchers Found When They Compare Single-Sex Education with Coeducation?" *National Association for Single-Sex Public Education* (May 2007)

NO: American Association of University Women, from "AAUW Position on Single-Sex Education" (January 2007)

ISSUE SUMMARY

YES: Leonard Sax, founder and executive director of the National Association for the Advancement of Single-Sex Public Education, argues that students in single-sex schools not only do better academically, but they also have more positive attitudes about education.

NO: The American Association of University Women (AAUW) counters that gains in women's rights are endangered by recent political moves to allow more single-sex education.

In October of 2006 the following press release was issued by the U.S. Department of Education:

> U.S. Secretary of Education Margaret Spellings today announced the release of final Title IX single-sex regulations that give communities more flexibility in offering additional choices to parents in the education of their children. . . .

These new regulations amend existing regulations that implement Title IX of the Education Amendments of 1972, which prohibit sex discrimination in education programs or activities that receive federal funds.
According to Secretary Spellings:

> Research shows that some students may learn better in single-sex education environments. The Department of Education is committed to giving

communities more choices in how they go about offering varied learning environments to their students. These final regulations permit communities to establish single-sex schools and classes as another means of meeting the needs of students. They also establish that enrollment in a single-sex class should be a completely voluntary option for students and their families and they uphold the prohibitions against discrimination of Title IX.

Title IX regulations have always permitted school districts to provide public single-sex elementary and secondary schools under certain circumstances. The new regulations make it easier to offer single-sex classes, activities, or schools. The new regulations do not require single-sex education but make it easier for educators to offer, and for parents and students to choose, single-sex educational opportunities. Enrollment in a single-sex class must be completely voluntary and a substantially equal coeducational class in the same subject must be provided.

It is interesting to note that some individuals and/or groups who once were strong advocates for the desegregation of schools now find themselves in support of schools limited to a single sex and/or race. Conversely some who fought hard to provide females with the same educational opportunities and choices available to males now oppose the opportunity to choose single-sex schools or classrooms. These seemingly inconsistent positions actually are reflective of changes over the past 50 years in how we view the purposes of our schools. Beginning in the 1950s and up through the 70s schools were seen as a means to change society. Equity issues involving both race and gender were addressed by changing the organization and operation of schools and throwing out the old doctrine of "separate but equal" and ushering in desegregation and Title IX. But since the 80s the focus on the sociological aspects of schooling has faded and has been replaced by an emphasis on academic standards, accountability, and student achievement.

Proponents of single-sex education such as Leonard Sax argue that such an approach provides better academic opportunities for both sexes and improves student attitudes toward school. Opponents such as the AAUW are concerned that a relaxation of prohibitions against single-sex education may work against the continued pursuit of gender equity in education.

YES ↵

Leonard Sax

What's the Evidence? What Have Researchers Found When They Compare Single-Sex Education with Coeducation?

May 2007

Dr. Leonard Sax, executive director of NASSPE, led a two-day workshop at the campus of Stetson University in DeLand, Florida. Researchers at Stetson University have completed a three-year pilot project comparing single-sex classrooms with coed classrooms at Woodward Avenue Elementary School, a nearby neighborhood public school. For example, students in the 4th grade at Woodward were assigned either to single-sex or coed classrooms. All relevant parameters were matched: the class sizes were all the same, the demographics were the same, all teachers had the same training in what works and what doesn't work, etc. On the FCAT (Florida Comprehensive Assessment Test), here were the results:

Percentage of Students Scoring Proficient on the FCAT

> boys in coed classes: 37% scored proficient
> girls in coed classes: 59% scored proficient
> girls in single-sex classes: 75% scored proficient
> boys in single-sex classes: 86% scored proficient

Remember, these students were all learning the same curriculum in the same school. And, this school "mainstreams" students who are learning-disabled, or who have ADHD etc. Many of those boys who scored proficient in all-boys classes had previously been labeled "ADHD" or "ESE" in coed classes.

Our upcoming October 2007 conference will feature two presentations from Woodward Avenue Elementary School. First, the four researchers from Stetson University who organized the study will present their findings over the three years of the pilot project. Next, a team of teachers from the school itself will share their experiences regarding strategies which work, and strategies which don't work.

June 2005

In June 2005, researchers at Cambridge University released results of a four-year study of gender differences in education. The researchers investigated hundreds of different schools, representing a wide variety of socioeconomic and ethnic backgrounds, seeking to identify strategies which improved performance of both girls and boys while narrowing the gender gap between girls and boys. What makes this study really unique is that the researchers did not merely observe and document what they found; they then intervened, and attempted to graft those strategies onto other, less successful schools. A total of 50 schools were involved either as "originator schools" (schools which had successfully improved student performance while narrowing the gender gap) or "partner schools" (less successful schools onto which the "originator" strategies were grafted). One of those strategies was single-sex education. These researchers found that the single-sex classroom format was remarkably effective at boosting boy's performance particularly in English and foreign languages, as well as improving girls' performance in math and science. Here is how Dr. Sax (director of NASSPE) summarized the report in his newsletter to NASSPE e-subscribers (if you would like to be on our e-mailing list, please send us an e-mail):

I had the honor of sharing the podium last week with the lead authors of the study, Michael Younger and Molly Warrington. Together, we did six presentations in two days! It was a great privilege to be able to discuss the study with the lead investigators face-to-face. Michael Younger more than once referred to the improved performance of the boys in the single-sex foreign languages classes as "astonishing." Both researchers emphasized that it is not sufficient simply to put all the girls in one room and all the boys in another and say "let's give it a whirl." Teachers and administrators need to be committed to the program and must be determined to see it through.

The full report contains many fascinating insights from students and teachers. Consider this comment from one of the boys in the single-gender class: *"We don't just do war poems and Macbeth, we do Wordsworth too. It's a challenge, in a way, which Mr J sets us to show the girls we're capable of doing it, but I couldn't talk about these things if there were girls there!"* (p. 85)

The researchers conducted extensive interviews with individuals students, and thus were able to distinguish among students rather than lumping all the boys into one group and all the girls into another. The researchers were particularly interested in gender-atypical boys: boys who don't care for sports, for example. How do these pupils fare in the all-boys classroom? Here's another excerpt: *"Interviews with [these] 'non-macho' boys suggest that these boys did not feel exposed in single-sex classes. . . . Such boys told us—without exception—that they felt at ease and comfortable, that they did not experience bullying or aggressive behaviour from other boys, and that they were not intimidated by the atmosphere in all-boys' classes."* (p. 86)

Most of the studies comparing single-sex education with coeducation focus on **grades** and **test scores** as the parameters of interest. Before we look at those studies, we want you to consider another variable altogether: namely, *breadth of educational opportunity.* Girls in all-girls schools are more likely to study subjects such as advanced math, computer science, and physics. Boys in all-boys schools are more than twice as likely to study subjects such as foreign languages, art, music, and drama. Those boys might not get better *grades* in those subjects than comparable boys get in more gender-typical subjects. Studies which focus only on grades and test scores won't detect any difference in outcome. For more about benefits beyond grades and test scores, see the advantages for girls page and the advantage for boys page.

Returning to grades and test scores: These are three categories of evidence:

1. Major nationwide studies, involving tens or hundreds of thousands of students, in countries such as Australia or the United Kingdom where single-sex public education is widely available;
2. "Before and after" studies, examining a particular school or schools before and after the introduction of single-sex classrooms. Because these studies usually involve no change in resources—the facilities and student-teacher ratios are the same before and after the switch—the school serves as its own control;
3. Academic studies, in which investigators study coed and single-sex schools while attempting to control for extraneous variables

First category of evidence   Major nationwide studies: England, Australia, Jamaica

England, July 2002   The National Foundation for Educational Research was commissioned to study the effect of school size and school type (single-sex vs. coed) on academic performance. The Foundation studied 2,954 high schools throughout England, where single-sex public high schools are widely available. They released their report on July 8 2002. They found:

1. Even after controlling for students' academic ability and other background factors, both girls and boys did significantly better in single-sex schools than in coed schools. In this age group (senior high school), the benefits were larger and more consistent across the board for girls than for boys. Specifically, girls at all levels of academic ability did better in single-sex schools than in coed schools; whereas for boys, the beneficial effect of single-sex schools was significant only for boys at the lower end of the ability scale. For higher-achieving boys, there was no statistically significant effect of school type on performance, positive or negative. (Remember, though, that this study only examined students in grades 9 through 12; other evidence [see below] suggests that single-sex education is most effective for boys in kindergarten and elementary school.)
2. Girls at single-sex schools were more likely to take non-traditional courses—courses which run against gender stereotypes—such as advanced math and physics. The researchers concluded that girls'

schools are "helping to counter rather than reinforce the distinctions between 'girls' subjects' such as English and foreign languages and 'boys' subjects' such as physics and computer science" (p. 43). No such effect was seen for boys: for example, boys at single-sex schools were no more likely (actually somewhat less likely) to take courses in cooking than were boys at coed schools.

3. Schools of medium size (about 180 students per grade) seemed to do best. At smaller schools, there was a lack of course offerings especially at the advanced levels. At much larger schools, student performance appeared to suffer.

The Foundation concluded: "It would be possible to infer from the findings that, in order to maximise performance, [public] schools should [have] about 180 pupils per cohort, or year, and be single-sex." You can read the Foundation's summary of the report (with links to obtain the complete study) here.

A large Australian study, 2001   The Australian Council for Educational Research compared performance of students at single-sex and coeducational schools. Their analysis, based on six years of study of over 270,000 students, in 53 academic subjects, demonstrated that both boys and girls who were educated in single-sex classrooms scored on average 15 to 22 percentile ranks higher than did boys and girls in coeducational settings. The report also documented that "boys and girls in single-sex schools were more likely to be better behaved and to find learning more enjoyable and the curriculum more relevant." The report concludes: "Evidence suggests that coeducational settings are limited by their capacity to accommodate the large differences in cognitive, social and development growth rates of boys and girls aged between 12 and 16." The findings of the Australian commission were widely reported throughout the English-speaking world (including Australia, New Zealand, England, Scotland, Ireland etc.)—but have never been mentioned in any American newspaper.

You can read a summary of the ACER report at the ACER's own Web site.

Some critics used to argue that single-sex public schools attract children from more affluent families. These critics suggested that the superior performance of students in single-sex schools may be due to the higher socioeconomic class from which such students are purportedly recruited, rather than the single-sex character of the school itself. However, both the ACER study in Australia just mentioned, and the Foundation study mentioned at the top of the page, both found no evidence to support that hypothesis. In the United States, Cornelius Riordan has shown that girls who attend single-sex Catholic schools typically come from a lower socioeconomic background than girls who attend coed Catholic schools. Among boys, Professor Riordan found no difference in socioeconomic status. In 1998, the British Office for Standards in Education (OFSTED) tested whether socioeconomic variables might account for the superior performance of students in single-sex schools. They examined test results from 800 public schools, single-sex and coeducational. OFSTED found that the superior performance of students in single-sex schools cannot be accounted for by socioeconomic factors, but appears instead to be a direct result of single-sex education. They also found that students in single-sex schools have a significantly more positive attitude toward learning.

Source   Clare Dean, "Inspectors say girls' schools are the best," *Times Educational Supplement,* October 9, 1998.

The Foundation study, which suggests that single-sex education is more beneficial for girls than for boys, is somewhat at variance with an earlier study which suggested that single-sex education was more beneficial for boys than for girls. Educator Graham Able published a study of student performance in 30 coeducational and single-sex schools in England. Dr. Able's study documented superior academic performance of students in single-sex schools, after controlling for socioeconomic class and other variables. "The most significant finding was that the advantage of single-sex schooling is even greater for boys in terms of academic results than for girls," Able said. "The unsubstantiated mythology of the educational establishment has been that girls do better in single sex schools but that boys are 'brought on' by the more studious girls in a co-educational environment. This mythology has never been supported by any objective evidence, and any policy derived from it must presumably sacrifice the advantages to one sex in order to promote the cause of the other," he wrote. "[Our] results suggest that single sex schools give an even greater academic advantage to boys than for girls. This directly contradicts the popular educational myth that boys do better in the classroom if girls are present to set them a good example. One could reasonably conclude from this study that both boys and girls are academically disadvantaged in co-educational schools, but that the disadvantage is greater for the boys."

Source   Alison Gordon, "In a class of their own: boys benefit even more than girls from single-sex schools, A-level grades study reveals," in *The Mail on Sunday* (UK), June 11 2000, p. 42. If you would like to read Graham Able's complete study, you may send an e-mail to NASSPE, or call us at 301 972 7600, or send a fax to 301 972 8006.

A classic study from Jamaica   Marlene Hamilton, studying students in Jamaica, found that students attending single-sex schools outperformed students in coed schools in almost every subject tested. At the time of the study, public single-sex schools were still widely available in Jamaica, so that there were few if any socioeconomic or academic variables which distinguished students at single-sex schools from students at coed schools. Hamilton noted the same pattern of results which has been found in most studies worldwide: Girls at single-sex schools attain the highest achievement; boys at single-sex schools are next; boys at coed schools are next; and girls at coed schools do worst of all.

Source   Marlene Hamilton. Performance levels in science and other subjects for Jamaican adolescents attending single-sex and coeducational high schools, *International Science Education,* 69(4):535–547, 1985.

Second category of evidence   "Before and after" studies critics of single-sex education sometimes object that studies comparing students at single-sex schools with students at coed schools are intrinsically untrustworthy, because (they say) one can never control for all the confounding variables. "Before and after" studies are done at just one school, before and after its transformation to a single-sex school. Same students, same teachers, same facilities. These studies offer another compelling proof of the superiority of single-sex education.

In 2000, Benjamin Wright, principal of the Thurgood Marshall Elementary School in Seattle, Washington, led his school in a transformation from traditional coed classrooms to single-sex classrooms . . . with astonishing results. Mr. Wright was concerned about the high number of discipline referrals he was seeing: about 30 children every day were being sent to the principal's office because of discipline problems (about 80% were boys). He decided to make the switch to single-sex classrooms in hopes of decreasing the discipline problem.

The results exceeded his hopes. Discipline referrals dropped from about 30 per day to just one or two per day. "Overnight. The change in the atmosphere happened overnight." Same kids, same teachers. Switching to single-sex classrooms had a dramatic effect, instantly.

But improved discipline wasn't the only benefit of the change. "We were just doing it to make sure that the discipline was taken care of. But once we made the switch, the boys were able to focus on academics, and so were the girls. The boys, remarkably, shocked the state with what they did on the Washington Assessment of Student Learning. Our boys went from being in the 10 to 30 percent listing to 73 percent. They went from a reading average of about 20 percent to 66 percent. Our boys outperformed the entire state in writing. They went from being in a low percentile of 20-something to 53 percent in writing.

These results aren't confined to elementary schools. An inner-city high school in Montreal made the switch from coed classrooms to single-sex classrooms five year ago. Since making that switch, absenteeism has dropped from 20 percent before the switch to 7 percent now. About 80 percent of students pass their final exams, compared with 65 percent before the switch. And, the rate of students going on to college has nearly doubled. You can read more about this Montreal high school here.

> Numerous similar cases have been documented in the United Kingdom. For example: John Fairhurst, principal of the Fairhurst High School (in Essex, in southeastern England) decided to reinvent his school as two single-sex academies under one roof. The students would take the same courses from the same teachers, but boys and girls would attend separate classes. Three years after making the change, the proportion of Shenfield boys achieving high scores on standardized tests had risen by 26%. The girls performance improved only slightly less, by 22% and they still outperformed the boys.

Source   Judith O'Reilly, "Mixed school hits new heights with single-sex classes." *Sunday Times* (London), August 20, 2000.

A similar experiment in Mill Hill, also in England, achieved similar results. In Mill Hill, the county high school was divided up into a girls' wing and a boys' wing in 1994. Since that time, the number of pupils scoring high on the GCSE exam has risen from 40 percent to 79 percent. Dr. Alan Davison, the principal, comments that "Men and women's brains are different. It is crucial that we in education recognise that."

Source *Times Educational Supplement* (London, UK), "News & Opinion," August 25 2000, "London School Segregates . . . "

The "before and after" experience of schools undertaking this transformation has been so consistent, and so impressive, that the British Secretary of Education (then David Blunkett) asked the Office for Standards in Education (OFSTED) to investigate whether this model should be applied widely throughout Britain, in a wholesale conversion of coed schools to single-sex academies.

Source Nicholas Pyke, "Blunkett plans single-sex classrooms." *The Independent* (London), August 20, 2000, p. 8. Note: In June 2001, Mr. Blunkett was promoted to the post of Home Secretary.

Researchers at Manchester University in England tested this approach more formally. They assigned students at five public schools either to single-sex or to coed classrooms. 68 percent of boys who were assigned to single-sex classes subsequently passed a standardized test of language skills, vs. 33 percent of boys assigned to coed classes. Among the girls, 89 percent assigned to single-sex classes passed the test, vs. 48 percent of girls assigned to coed classes.

Source Julie Henry, "Help for the boys the girls," *Time Educational Supplement* (London, UK), June 1 2001.

Similar findings were reported by researchers at Cambridge University, who examined the effects of single-sex classrooms in schools in four different neighborhoods, including rural, suburban and inner-city schools. They found that "using single-sex groups was a significant factor in establishing a school culture that would raise educational achievement." For example, at Morley High School in Leeds, only one-third of boys had been earning passing grades in German and French prior to institution of the program. After the change to single-sex classes, 100% of boys earned passing grades. Click on the link to read the story which appeared in the Sunday *Telegraph* March 30, 2003.

Third Category of Evidence: Academic Studies Comparing Single-Sex Schools with Coed Schools

Cornelius Riordan, professor of sociology at Providence University in Rhode Island, published a series of studies in the 1980's and early 1990's comparing short- and long-term outcomes of graduates of single-sex Catholic schools in the United States with graduates of coed Catholic schools in the United States. On a variety of measures, Riordan found that girls in single-sex schools consistently outperformed girls at coed schools. In Riordan's studies, the beneficial effect for boys is smaller than it is for girls (contrast this finding with Graham Able's report [see above] that the benefits of single-sex schooling are greater for boys than for girls). Riordan believes that the beneficial effects of single-sex schooling are most impressive for children from underprivileged backgrounds. However, this belief sets him apart from many other researchers in the field, particularly outside the United States.

Source Cornelius Riordan. *Girls and Boys in School: together or separate?* New York: Teachers College Press, 1990.

Researchers at the University of Michigan compared graduates of Catholic single-sex high schools with graduates of Catholic coeducational private schools. Boys in the single-sex high schools scored better in reading, writing, and math than did boys at coed high schools. Girls at the single-sex schools did better in science and reading than girls in coed schools. In fact, these researchers found that students at single-sex schools had not only superior academic achievement, but also had higher educational aspirations, more confidence in their abilities, and a more positive attitude toward academics, than did students at coed high schools. And, girls at the single-sex schools had less stereotyped ideas about what women can and cannot do.

Source Valerie Lee and Anthony Bryk. Effects of single-sex secondary schools on student achievement and attitudes. *Journal of Educational Psychology,* 78:381–395, 1986.

The same University of Michigan team later reported that the beneficial effects of single-sex education don't end after students leave the school. They found that graduates of single-sex schools were more likely to go to a prestigious college, and more likely to aspire to graduate school or professional school, than were graduates of coed schools. That finding held for both girls and boys.

Source Valerie Lee and H. M. Marks. Sustained effects of the single-sex secondary school experience on attitudes, behaviors, and values in college. *Journal of Educational Psychology,* 82:578–592, 1990.

In one remarkable study of 2,777 English high school students, girls at coed schools were found to lose ground to boys in science and vocabulary as they progressed through high school. Exactly the opposite occurred at single-sex schools: the girls at single-sex schools outperformed both the boys at single-sex schools and the boys at coed schools. Again, this study reported the familiar pattern: girls at single-sex schools on top, followed by boys at single-sex schools, then boys at coed schools, with girls at coed schools doing the worst.

Source J. D. Finn. Sex differences in educational outcomes: a cross-national study. *Sex Roles,* 6:9–25, 1980.

Not Just Better Students; More Well-Rounded People

The benefits of single-sex schools are not only academic. Just as importantly, single-sex education has been shown to broaden students' horizons, to allow them to feel free to explore the own strengths and interests, not constrained by gender stereotypes. A British researcher compared the attitudes of 13 and 14 year-old pupils toward different subjects. Students at coed schools tended to have gender-typical subject preferences: boys at coed schools liked math and science and did NOT like drama or languages, whereas boys at single-sex schools were more interested in drama, biology and languages. Likewise, girls at girls-only schools were more interested in math and science than were girls at coed schools.

Source A. Stables. Differences between pupils from mixed and single-sex schools in their enjoyment of school subjects and in their attitudes to science and to school. *Educational Review,* 42(3):221–230, 1990.

A University of Virginia study published in 2003 found that boys who attended single-sex schools were more than twice as likely to pursue interests in subjects such as art, music, drama, and foreign languages, compared to boys of comparable ability who attended coed schools. **Single-sex schools break down gender stereotypes.** Coed schools reinforce gender stereotypes.

Source Abigail Norfleet James and Herbert Richards, "Escaping Stereotypes: educational attitudes of male alumni of single-sex and coed schools," *Psychology of Men and Masculinity,* 4:136–148, 2003.

Andrew Hunter, now the principal of Merchiston Castle School in Edinburgh (Scotland) agrees. Having taught in both coed schools and single-sex schools, Mr. Hunter observes that there is "a subtle and invidious pressure towards gender stereotyping in mixed [= coed] schools". Girls tend to be cautious about going into subjects or activities which are thought of as essentially boys' things, but in boys' schools boys feel free to be themselves and develop, to follow their interests and talents in what might be regarded as non-macho pursuits: music, arts, drama.

Quoted in Elizabeth Buie, "Today's sexual evolution," *The Herald (Glasgow),* November 21 2000, p. 16.

Brian Walsh, who has been a principal at both boys' schools and coed schools, made this observation: "Boys ordinarily do not even try to sing in a coed school, whereas they love choral singing in a boys' school; in the coed setting they make fun of French pronunciation, whereas in the single-sex setting they enjoy becoming fluent in French; in drama, they muck up or clown around to avoid seeming imperfect in a coed setting, whereas they excel at drama when by themselves".

Quoted in David Riesman. A margin of difference: the case for single-sex education. In J. R. Blau (editor), *Social roles and social institutions,* Boulder, Colorado: Westview Press, 1990, pp. 243–244.

> At many coed schools, it's not "cool" for kids to be excited about school. The game of who likes who, who's going out with who, who's cool and who's not, is what's really important at most coed schools. That's seldom the case at single-sex schools. Edison Trickett and Penelope Trickett, comparing students at private single-sex schools in the United States with students at private coed schools in the United States, found that students in the single-sex schools had a far more positive attitude toward academics than did students in coed schools. This finding held for both boys and girls. The students at the single-sex schools also developed better organizational skills, and were more involved in classroom activities.

Source Edison Trickett, Penelope Trickett, et al. The independent school experience: aspects of the normative environment of single-sex and coed secondary schools, *Journal of Educational Psychology,* 74(3):374–381, 1982.

American Association of
University Women

 **NO**

Separated by Sex: Title IX and Single-Sex Education

Title IX of the Education Amendments of 1972 prohibits sex discrimination in public and private institutions that receive federal financial assistance. The American Association of University Women strongly supports Title IX and opposes any efforts that would weaken its effectiveness. AAUW's 2005–2007 Public Policy Program commits AAUW to the ". . . vigorous enforcement of Title IX and all other civil rights laws pertaining to education."[1]

AAUW has long been a proponent of public education, and believes a strong, free public education system is the foundation of a democratic society. AAUW also believes that the principles of nondiscrimination and applicable civil rights laws should be strictly adhered to in the provisions of that education. Unfortunately, some policies that purport to improve student performance—such as private school vouchers and single-sex education in the public schools—skirt critical civil rights protections. Steps should be taken to improve student performance and educational outcomes, but the rights of students should not be trampled in the process.

Historically, public single-sex education has often harmed girls by depriving them of equal educational opportunities. Where programs are established separately for both boys and girls, they have tended to be distinctly unequal, with fewer resources allocated for girls programs and stereotypical notions limiting vocational options. As a result, the U.S. Supreme Court—relying on the U.S. Constitution and Title IX—struck a careful balance, placing strict limits on the availability of public single-sex education while at the same time explicitly allowing for such programs if they were carefully constructed to remedy existing or past discrimination. Recent Title IX regulatory changes have removed these previous restrictions on public single-sex education; whether these changes will stand up to constitutional muster is an open question. However, one point remains clear, and is underscored by the U.S Department of Education's own research: single-sex education is not a silver bullet to improving performance in our public schools.

When elements of a good education are present, girls and boys succeed. What does foster an improved educational environment? The following elements have been documented as successful practices and qualities, regardless of the gender make-up of the school:[2]

- a focused academic curriculum
- small class size
- qualified teachers
- sufficient funding
- parental involvement
- equitable teaching practices
- maintaining appropriate and consistent discipline

AAUW believes that discrimination in education can only be prevented by maintaining strong civil rights standards. While this country has taken great strides towards equity, there is still work to be done before we can say that males and females are treated equitably in education.[3] Furthermore, the progress women and girls have made depends on the constant and continued enforcement of anti-discrimination protections such as Title IX.

Boy Crisis Debunked

Despite the current hype over the "boy crisis," which is often given as a justification for allowing unrestricted, publicly funded single-sex education, women and girls still face inequities in educational opportunities. AAUW's groundbreaking 1992 report *How Schools Shortchange Girls*[4] revealed startling evidence of inequity in education, which continues in critical areas to this day. At the time, girls were not receiving the same quality or quantity of education as their male counterparts. By disaggregating such data, the report also showed disparities among girls, which exist today.

As women continue to make gains in education and the workplace, it is important to remember that these successes do not come at the expense of men. Unfortunately, that is the insidious implication underlying much of the recent assaults on Title IX that are in turn fueling erroneous notions of a "boy crisis" as well as calls that perhaps Title IX's work is done. AAUW maintains that education is not a zero sum game, and that the real issue is about girls doing better, not about boys doing worse. Recent independent research also debunks the "boy crisis" and supports AAUW's position.[5] AAUW is proud of women and girls' achievements, and believes policies and reforms that allow women **and** men to excel are beneficial for society as a whole.

Although many improvements have been made since the 1972 enactment of Title IX, much still remains to be accomplished before real equity is achieved. Women and girls still experience:

- the prevalence of sexual harassment and bullying[6]
- under representation in math, science, and technology programs[7]
- lower scores on standardized tests[8]
- sex-segregated vocational education programs, with females overwhelmingly directed into training programs for historically female— and traditionally low-wage— jobs[9]

- exclusion of female students from many athletic opportunities, including athletic scholarships worth hundreds of millions of dollars[10]
- wage disparities (for example, in 2004, a typical college-educated woman working fulltime earned $31,223 a year, compared to $40,798 for a college-educated man—a stark difference of $9,575).

AAUW believes that single-sex programs can in some instances perform a valuable role in combating these inequities. For example, to remedy the persistent effects of discrimination, federal, state, local, and private entities have developed a considerable network of gender-based scholarships and financial assistance aimed at supporting women seeking to enter historically male-dominated fields. Some institutions have also created outreach programs, such as summer residential math and science institutes for girls on college campuses aimed at encouraging female high school and junior high school students to consider engineering and other nontraditional career options. In light of the history of discrimination against women in education and the barriers that female students continue to face based on their gender, such programs have a legitimate place.

Single-Sex Education and No Child Left Behind

The No Child Left Behind Act,[11] the 2001 reauthorization of the Elementary and Secondary Education Act, allows for limited use of innovative programs education funding "to provide same-gender schools and classrooms (consistent with applicable law),"[12] which includes Title IX of the Education Amendments of 1972. However, the law gave no mandate to change Title IX regulations. Rather, NCLB only required the U.S. Department of Education to issue guidelines on applicable laws to schools seeking innovative programs funding. While the U.S. Department of Education Office for Civil Rights fulfilled this requirement, this May 2002 guidance was cursory and did not adequately address how schools can implement single-sex education consistent with applicable law—not only Title IX but also all relevant Supreme Court decisions and constitutional protections.

Despite the lack of a mandate and the prior Title IX regulations' allowance for limited exceptions to create single-sex schools and classes in public education, in May 2002—ironically on the same date they issued their inadequate NCLB-mandated guidance—the U.S. Department of Education issued a Notice of Intent to Regulate expressing the intent to amend the Title IX regulations "to provide more flexibility for educators to establish single-sex classes and schools at the elementary and secondary levels."[13] The proposed regulations were released in March 2004. At the time, single-sex education options were available in a number of public school systems, highlighting that the prior regulations offered the flexibility for situations where single-sex offerings address student needs. The U.S. Department of Education received public comments overwhelmingly opposed to any changes to these regulations, but issued final regulations not much different from those released for public comment in March 2004. The new regulations went into effect Nov. 24, 2006.

New Single-Sex Regulations Undermine Title IX

In October 2006, OCR announced its decision to issue final regulations to ease limits on single-sex education. The new regulations allow the exclusion of students from classes based on gender.[14] While OCR suggested that discrimination against women is not as prevalent as it was in 1972 when Title IX was passed, OCR also admitted that "there are still more gains to be made."[15] Despite this acknowledgement, OCR moved forward in its effort to weaken the very law that brought about the massive achievements women and girls have made in the last thirty years. While the environment for women in education has vastly improved, this does not justify easing discrimination protections. AAUW believes single-sex education without proper attention to civil rights protections can reinforce problematic gender stereotypes, increase discrimination, and restrict the educational opportunities open to both girls and boys. AAUW opposed the change in Title IX regulations for the following reasons:

- The regulations are tantamount to an executive fiat, undermining the principles upheld in **Brown v. Board of Education (1954)**. In the Brown decision, the U.S. Supreme Court said "separate but equal" is inherently unequal. Such separation sets up opportunities for discrimination and perpetuates stereotypes, whether intended or not. The U.S. Supreme Court also found in the Virginia Military Institute case, *United States v. Virginia*, that "sex classifications may be used to compensate women for particular economic disabilities they may have suffered, to promote equal employment opportunities, to advance full development of the talent and capabilities of our Nation's people."[16] The inherent difficulty in providing equal opportunity is that by separating the sexes schools become open to liability they don't currently face. Even though Title IX regulations were altered in the name of added flexibility in single-sex education, schools still have to comply with constitutional requirements—although AAUW is very concerned that there is now little oversight to see that they do so.
- The regulations pose no accountability or reporting requirements consistent with the No Child Left Behind Act. Although NCLB places a premium on implementing strategies that are based on sound science, the regulations break from this standard. Schools are not required to demonstrate that a significant education problem needed to be fixed, nor are they required to demonstrate that single-sex classes or schools will fix such a problem. Schools will have the authority to "tinker" with gender equity without having to prove that such actions are even necessary. Furthermore, while the regulations require schools to self-evaluate single-sex practices every two years, schools are not required to report these internal evaluations to the OCR, and evaluations are not required to be scientifically valid or reliable.
- The regulations divert attention away from more serious education problems. Rather than implementing sound strategies to improve achievement in core academic subjects, the administration persists in experimenting on our nation's children with unproven, controversial options. The president's FY 2005 budget proposed funding NCLB at $9.4 billion below authorized levels, in effect making NCLB an unfunded

mandate; over the course of its existence, NCLB has been underfunded to the tune of $40 billion.[17] Meaningful school reform—for boys and girls—begins with fulfilling our existing promises to children and their parents by fully funding programs authorized in NCLB.

- Prior to the regulatory change, Title IX already allowed flexibility for schools to segregate students by sex when there was **a legitimate reason to do so, while maintaining civil rights protections.** Prior to the issuance of the new regulations, Title IX prohibited single-sex classes or programs within coed public schools, with some limited exceptions. Single-sex was permitted for physical education activities involving contact sports, sex education at the elementary and secondary levels, and choral groups. Other than these exceptions, Title IX prohibited single-sex programs unless such programs were designed to overcome the effects of past discrimination to allow girls to overcome historical barriers to equal education. To meet this standard, a school district had to show that the sex-based exclusion was necessary to overcome sex-based barriers that have disadvantaged those who will benefit from the program. For example, an all-girl math class may have met this standard if the class was designed to compensate for girls' limited participation in math.

- The regulations require more resources than most schools can afford. State and local education agencies are deeply concerned about a lack of funding to implement existing NCLB requirements as well as the rising shortage of highly qualified teachers. These regulation changes could be costly for schools that choose to implement them because the schools would likely have to add new teachers for every subject area.

- The goals of single-sex education will not be uniform, and the most basic safeguards are thrown out. The regulations allow each school to identify the educational objective for sex segregation. Schools do not have to justify segregation and can identify any range of objectives for why segregation is necessary. The new regulations would even allow schools to create sex-segregated programs based on parent or student preferences—a practice that would never be allowed were the issue to be segregation on the basis of race.

- The regulations do not identify what is meant by "substantially equal." In fact, the regulations do not mandate equal treatment for students excluded from a single-sex program. Although the regulations require "substantially equal" opportunities for both sexes in the aggregate, they do not necessarily require equal opportunities school by school, class by class, or subject by subject. The regulations do not require that if, for example, a school chooses to create a single-sex math class for boys, that they offer a "substantially equal" single-sex math class for girls. The school in this example would only be required to offer only a "substantially equal" coeducational class for the excluded sex. AAUW does not believe substantially equal or "close enough" is good enough for our children; it is not an acceptable legal standard or educational policy.
  - The development of such classes and schools is usually rationalized by efforts to make the case that single-sex classes or schools are better in certain situations; if this were the case, in denying that opportunity to the excluded sex, schools would be necessarily creating an unequal learning environment.

- AAUW does not oppose the idea of single-sex education, so long as it is appropriate, necessary, and done in a manner consistent with constitutional requirements and existing anti discrimination laws. Within public education, single-sex classes and schools must comply with relevant civil rights law, be initiated in response to demonstrated need, and be designed to inform and improve the coeducational public school system. AAUW supports pilot and voluntary single-sex classes that meet the above criteria. AAUW would not necessarily oppose pilot single-sex public schools that expand the research and meet the above criteria. Unfortunately, the new regulations are not nearly rigorous enough to ensure adequate civil rights protections, and do not put safeguards in place to limit the problematic stereotypes that have historically limited girls' opportunities.
- Single-sex Education is Not the Solution. Because about 90 percent of elementary and secondary students attend public school,[18] AAUW believes legislators must develop strong, fair public schools—not single-sex education—to improve student achievement.
  - Apply qualities of a good education. While single-sex education experiments have produced positive results for some students in some cases, research indicates that the properties of a good education—not a sex-segregated environment—make the difference.
  - Foster an equitable learning environment. Schools striving to achieve an equitable learning environment must adopt reforms that will help all students learn better. Strategies include teacher development in gender-fair teaching methods; recruitment and visibility of female and minority administrators to provide role models; adoption and dissemination of school nondiscrimination policies, sexual harassment policies and prevention programs; and equitable athletic opportunities.
- **The regulations rely on unproven assumptions about the benefits of single-sex programs.** The research supporting the effect of single-sex education on improving educational outcomes is inconclusive at best, and some shows potentially harmful effects. In fact, in its most recent report, the U.S. Department of Education calls its own 2005 results on the benefit of single-sex education "equivocal."[19] Further, much of that research is of questionable value. A 2006 study completed at the College of Education at Arizona State University showed that the research into single-sex education is not of acceptable quality, let alone conclusive. According to the study, the "research . . . is mostly flawed by failure to control for important variables such as class, financial status, selective admissions, religious values, prior learning or ethnicity."[20] Less than 2 percent of the over 2,000 quantitative studies were of high enough methodological quality to be accepted by the National Center for Education Statistics, even with relaxed standards.[21]
  - Expand the research base. Research must be conducted with the goal of improving public education for all students. Pilot single-sex education experiments must have clear research questions in mind and an established process for data collection and evaluation. Pilot programs should continue for a sufficient time to ensure that their effectiveness can be adequately measured. The same course content and assessments should be used in single-sex and coed classes to

enable comparisons. Schools should also consider instituting "girl-friendly" pedagogy in one coed class to test whether segregation or teaching style makes the difference.

Conclusion

AAUW is particularly concerned that the new regulations may cross a constitutional line when it comes to Title IX. These civil rights protections have been hugely successful, and now is not the time to roll back the clock. AAUW opposed the change to the Title IX single-sex education regulations and believes that Title IX should serve as a crucial backstop to ensuring that all students have equal education opportunities.

The U.S. Constitution supports the prior Title IX regulations' treatment of single-sex education. The Constitution bars excluding one sex from public school programs unless the exclusion is supported by an exceedingly persuasive justification. To date, the U.S. Supreme Court has only recognized programs designed to remedy sex-based disadvantages.

AAUW is concerned about the future of education for our nation's girls and boys—both sexes must thrive for our country to compete in the global marketplace. But stripping girls of civil rights protections that provide them with opportunities to excel is not a solution to helping improve educational opportunities for all our children. While important advancements for women and girls have been made, inequity and the necessity to fight it still exist today.

Notes

1. 2005–07 AAUW Public Policy Program (approved June 2005).
2. AAUW Educational Foundation. *Separated by Sex: A Critical Look at Single-sex Education for Girls.* Pp. 30, 46–48, 56. 1998.
3. Brake, Deborah L. "A Legal Framework for Single-sex Education" p. 5. *WEEA Digest*; October 1999. Professor Brake listed the following ongoing problems and barriers that exist for women and girls in education: "1) discrimination against pregnant girls and young mothers, combined with wholly inadequate educational opportunities for these students that exacerbate high drop-out rates and foster economic dependence, with all of its attendant problems; 2) the rampant nature of sexual harassment; 3) substantial under representation of females in math, science, and other technology programs; 4) significantly lower test scores by female students on a wide variety of standardized tests; 5) prejudices against girls' participation in the classroom; 6) biased curricula; 7) predominantly sex-segregated vocational education programs, with females overwhelmingly directed into training programs for historically female—and traditionally low-wage—jobs; 8) the exclusion of female students from many athletic opportunities, including athletic scholarships worth hundreds of millions of dollars; and 9) the exclusion of women from consideration by entire classes of other scholarships, many for student infields in which men already have a participation advantage."

4. AAUW Educational Foundation. The AAUW Report: *How Schools Shortchange Girls.* 1992.
5. Mead, Sara. *The Truth About Boys and Girls.* Education Sector. June 2006.
6. AAUW Educational Foundation. *Drawing the Line: Sexual Harassment on Campus,* p. 2. 2005.
7. National Science Foundation. *Women, Minorities and Persons with Disabilities in Science and Engineering.* 2002.
8. National Coalition for Women and Girls in Education. *Title IX at 30,* p. 49. 2002.
9. National Women's Law Center. *Tools of the Trade: Using the Law to Address Sex Segregation in High School Career and Technical Education,* p. 6-7. 2005.
10. National Collegiate Athletic Association. *NCAA Gender Equity Report, 2003-2004.* Statistics available from Women's Sports Foundation. . . .
11. U.S. Census Bureau. Income, Poverty, and Health Insurance Coverage in the United States, 2005. U.S. Government Printing Office.
12. Public Law 107-110.
13. Public Law 107-110, section 5131(a)(23).
14. U.S. Department of Education. "Nondiscrimination on the Basis of Sex in Education Programs or Activities Receiving Federal Financial Assistance." May 2002. . . .
15. U.S. Department of Education, Office for Civil Rights. "Nondiscrimination on the Basis of Sex in Education Programs or Activities Receiving Federal Financial Assistance-Final Rule." *Federal Register:* Volume 71, Number 206, Page 62529-62543. October 25, 2006. . . . U.S. Department of Education, Office for Civil Rights. "Nondiscrimination on the Basis of Sex in Education Programs or Activities Receiving Federal Financial Assistance—Notice of Proposed Rulemaking." *Federal Register:* Volume 69, Number 46, Page 11275-11285, p. 11276. March 9, 2004. . . .
16. *United States v. Virginia,* et al., 518 U.S. 515 (1996).
17. National Education Association. "Schools Lack Funding to Comply With No Child Left Behind, According to New Report from Center on Education Policy." March 29, 2006. . . .
18. U.S. Department of Education, National Center for Education Statistics. *Digest of Education Statistics, 2005* (NCES 2006-030). 2006. . . .
19. U.S. Department of Education. *Single-sex versus Coeducational Scheduling: A Systematic Review.* 2005. . . .
20. Bracey, Gerald W. "Separate but Superior? A Review of Issues and Data Bearing on Single-Sex Education," p. ii. Education Policy Research Unit, Department of Education, Arizona State University. November 2006.
21. Bracey, Gerald W. "Separate but Superior? A Review of Issues and Data Bearing on Single-Sex Education," p. ii. Education Policy Research Unit, Department of Education, Arizona State University. November 2006.

POSTSCRIPT

Do Single-Sex Classrooms and Schools Provide a Better Learning Environment?

This particular issue provides an excellent example of how educational issues are often a part of a larger sociopolitical controversy. Certainly whether or not children's learning and academic progress are better served in single-sex classrooms would seem to be a very important question deserving serious research and reflection unencumbered by political and sociological considerations. That is not to be. Schools do not exist in a vacuum and in particular public schools as extensions of government are inextricably linked to public opinion and politics. And with this particular issue, involving as it does gender and racial equity, the public and politicians are deeply invested.

The following excerpts from a position paper of the National Coalition for Civil Rights provides a historical and legal framework for understanding the controversy generated by this issue:

> Title IX of the Education Amendments of 1972 prohibits sex discrimination in education programs that receive federal financial assistance. The law covers approximately 16,000 local school districts, 3,200 colleges and universities, 5,000 for-profit schools, state education and vocational rehabilitation agencies, and numerous libraries and museums. Since its enactment, Title IX has immeasurably improved educational opportunities for women and girls, and lifted glass ceilings that kept women from reaching the highest ranks of academia.
>
> The extent of blatant discrimination against female students prior to the enactment of this landmark law cannot be overstated. In many schools, girls were routinely required to take home economics and were excluded from classes that might lead to "non-traditional" career paths. Many colleges and universities—both public and private—either excluded female students altogether or enforced strict quotas for their admission. Athletic opportunities for girls and young women were scarce or non-existent.
>
> Thankfully, the days of *de jure* discrimination in education are over. As then-Education Secretary Richard Riley said in marking the 25th anniversary of Title IX in 1997, "America is a more equal, more educated, and more prosperous nation because of the far-reaching effects of this legislation."
>
> Vigorous enforcement of Title IX is an essential element of the ongoing campaign for gender equity in education. . . . [In passing Title IX] Congress was mindful of the record of single-sex education, a record permeated by harmful stereotypes that tended to limit opportunities for young women.

242

So-called "parallel programs" for girls have often been distinctly unequal in scope and resources. The regulations allow for the creation of single-sex classrooms in specific circumstances, such as physical education classes or activities involving contact sports, competitive athletics, human sexuality, and choirs. Single-sex classes and schools can also be created for compensatory purposes to allow girls and women to overcome barriers to equal education.

Senator Kay Hutchison (Texas), one of the sponsors of the No Child Left Behind legislation that contains provisions to expand single-sex education, states:

> Single-sex educational programs have been available in private schools for years. It's time our nation's public school children have the same options as their private school contemporaries. We want to give school districts the flexibility to respond to the particular needs of their students. Our goal is to give parents and school districts more choices.

Opponents of single-sex education point to the failure of California's experiment with the concept. In 1997 six school districts were funded by the State to open "academies" to experiment with single-gender classroom instruction. Within two years most of the academies had been abandoned and all six are now closed. A Ford Foundation study of the experiment basically labeled it a failure. However, some supporters of the idea criticize the Ford Foundation study and claim that its authors were biased and unscientific. One such critic Christina Sommers states, "The report repeatedly puts the aim of eliminating gender stereotypes ahead of the academic and moral needs of children."

Other materials on this topic include:

Ilana DeBare, *Where Girls Come First: The Rise, Fall and Surprising Revival of All Girls' Schools*, J. P. Tarcher, March 2004.

David Sadker and Karen Zittleman, "Single-sex Schools: A Good Idea Gone Wrong?" *Christian Science Monitor*, April 8, 2004.

National Association for Single Sex Public Education (NASSPE), *U.S. Department of Education Releases New Regulations for Single-sex Classrooms*, March 2004.

U.S. Department of Education, *Department to Provide More Educational Options for Parents*, March 2004.

ISSUE 13

Is Grade Inflation a Problem?

YES: Perry A. Zirkel, from "Grade Inflation: High Schools' Skeleton in the Closet," *Education Week* (March 2007)

NO: Alfie Kohn, from "The Dangerous Myth of Grade Inflation," *The Chronicle of Higher Education* (November 2002)

ISSUE SUMMARY

YES: Perry A. Zirkel, university professor of education and law at Lehigh University, writes that, "If a majority of students . . . are in the honor society, it is no longer an honor."

NO: Alfie Kohn, author and educational commentator, avers that there are no data to support the claims regarding the existence of grade inflation.

It is perhaps predictable in this era of standards, high-stakes tests, and accountability that attention is also being directed toward grading patterns with a particular focus on whether or not teachers and professors are too lenient in their grading practices. This issue transcends grade and school levels. Beginning in the primary grades the practice of "social promotion" is seen by some as an example of grade inflation. At the high school level many schools now award an additional grade point to students taking advanced placement or honors courses. Thus, top students can now earn a grade point average higher than a 4.0, which in the past represented straight A's. At the university some professors accuse others of awarding high marks in order to get better evaluations from students.

Some argue that grade inflation is part of a larger problem of "dumbing down" the curriculum by presenting less rigorous and less demanding course material, assignments, and examinations with the obvious results being that students are able to fulfill requirements and receive high marks with less effort and thought than in the past. Opponents of that reasoning will respond by noting that older generations always seem to believe that "standards were higher in the good old days."

Some of the questions generated by this issue include: Does the potential of hurting a child's self-esteem justify promoting that child from one grade level to the next even if the achievement required in the first level has not been attained? Have unrealistic expectations and pressures from students and parents caused teachers to give higher grades than are deserved? Is the issuance of failing marks discouraged by school and university administrators and policies? Do traditional letter grades still mean what they did in the past? Does the litigious nature of our society contribute to the problem by causing teachers to be wary about issuing low grades? Related to this latter question is a recent lawsuit in California involving a parent suing a high school baseball coach because the coach did not give the litigant's son an opportunity to pitch, thus depriving him of the opportunity for a college scholarship or a professional contract. The case was dismissed.

As noted above the controversy exists at all levels. Harvard professor Harvey C. Mansfield, in "Grade Inflation: It's Time to Face the Facts" (*Chronicle of Higher Education*, April 6, 2001), stated that grade inflation at his institution began in the late 1960s and early 1970s and coincided with the advent of affirmative action. He also suggests that the practice of using student course evaluations as part of the university's process of evaluating professors may cause those professors to avoid giving low marks. Others, however, do not believe that grade inflation is necessarily a wide-reaching problem. Laura Horn, one of the authors of a report from the U.S. Department of Education profiling undergraduates in postsecondary education in 1999–2000, notes, "The issue of grade inflation has mostly been at the more-selective four year institutions." According to the report 38 percent of community college students received C's or D's or lower (Catherine E. Shoichet, "Reports of Grade Inflation May Be Inflated, Study Finds," *Chronicle of Higher Education*, July 12, 2002).

In the articles that follow, Perry A. Zirkel wonders how grade point averages can go up when student test scores go down. Alfie Kohn states that the crusade against grade inflation is led by conservatives and that it is related to some of their favorite targets including the radicalism of universities, political correctness, and too much concern about students' self-esteem.

YES ↩

Perry A. Zirkel

Grade Inflation: High Schools' Skeleton in the Closet

Grade inflation is what happens when grades go up but the academic achievement they represent does not, at least not at the same pace. As with monetary inflation, the associated problems include the decreasing value and credibility of the currency, which, in the case of grades, counts for not just family pride and kudos, but also future educational and employment opportunities. Unlike monetary inflation, however, which is publicly monitored and controlled, grade inflation constitutes a hoax on the public, which continues to think that C represents a middling or average grade and that an A or, even more strongly, a 4.0 grade point average is exceptional.

Lately, most of the attention given to this phenomenon has been at the college level. Princeton University drew extensive media coverage in 2004 when it established a quota on the number of A's given out at the undergraduate level. It was an effort to reduce their proportion in the total number of grades from almost 50 percent to a cap of 35 percent. Earlier, Dartmouth University had begun to include the class average for a course along with a student's grade, to put the mark in context. The developments were further illustration of the upward trajectory uncovered in *Grade Inflation: A Crisis in College Education*, statistics professor Valen E. Johnson's 2003 book examining grading changes at Duke University over time. The American Academy of Arts and Sciences concluded in 2002 that the national evidence was undeniable and called for change. Grade inflation's "self-sustaining character," it said, eventually erases "meaningful distinctions."

But the cumulative evidence suggests that grade inflation is just as pronounced at the high school level—and corrective efforts to combat it even more negligible. In the 1990s, ACT researchers Robert Ziomek and Joseph Svec found that high school students' GPAs were notably outpacing their ACT assessment scores. A 2002 study of Arkansas students by Sean W. Mulvenon and Antoinette R. Thorn found strong evidence of grade inflation in that state, based on standardized-achievement-test scores and grades. In 2004, the U.S. Department of Education, correcting its previous study of transcripts concluding that "significant" grade inflation was "not as pervasive . . . as assumed," found that the average GPA of high school graduates had increased from 2.68 in 1990 to 2.94 in 2000. Later in 2004, the College Board, echoing its studies for

From *Education Week*, March 2007, pp. 1–3. Copyright © 2007 by Perry Zirkel. Reprinted by permission.

246

earlier periods, reported that the proportion of SAT test-takers who claimed a high school grade average of A had risen from 13 percent to 18 percent over the past 10 years, while the SAT scores of those students had dropped by 5 points in verbal and 1 point in math.

In late February of this year, the Education Department issued the latest "nation's report card" on 12th grade reading and math, which showed that the average GPA of high school graduates had increased even further, to 2.98 in 2005, which approximates a letter grade of B. Given the wider spread on the downside and the weight of an occasional F or D, this means that in all likelihood more than half the grades were B's or A's. The upward patterns were parallel, from the highest- to the lowest-graded core subject (which were, in order, social studies, English, science, and math). At the same time, however, these students' average reading scores on the National Assessment of Educational Progress had decreased by a statistically significant extent since 1992: The proportion of high school seniors performing at or above the proficient level on the NAEP reading test dropped from 40 percent to 35 percent. Although changes in the NAEP math test precluded such longitudinal comparisons, only 23 percent of the high school seniors performed at or above the proficient level.

Yet, rather than doing something to correct the problem, high schools in both the public and private sectors have developed cover-up strategies to game the system. These artifices include dropping class rank, quietly changing to a 5- or 6-point scale, and purportedly retaining a 4-point scale but providing for weighted grades, so that the top students have GPAs that well exceed 4.0. To illustrate, a friend of mine recently asked me to "put in a good word" to the admissions office of the university where I teach about his granddaughter, who was applying there. When I asked the girl for some information about her academic profile, she told me that she had a 3.89 average. Only after a conversation that escalated into a probing cross-examination did I find out that this grade point average was on a 6-point scale, and that her school did not use class rank.

Moreover, high school teachers and administrators, mimicking their higher education counterparts, have concocted various rationales to deflect attention away from the trend. The defenses include the need for student self-esteem; the competition for college; state policies for financial aid based on GPA, such as Georgia's HOPE Scholarships; and the denigration of competitive grades altogether. High schools in California have been experimenting with deleting D's, since this grade, like the penny, has arguably become valueless. Others have experimented with mastery learning while retaining the normative grades of A through F, rather than switching to a pass-fail or "mastery-nonmastery" scale. Euphemisms abound, such as the category "basic" for those who do not obtain the minimum passing level on NAEP and its No Child Left Behind law equivalents in each state.

If high schools seek to drop grades or substitute another approach to measuring learning, such as narratives, portfolios, criterion-based mastery, or a new series of numbering or letters, fine. Just let them be clear and open about it, so that the public is not duped with the false expectations that arise from the traditional, normative A-F or 0-4 grading system. The problem is that high schools want to eat their cake and have it too, which causes the public to eventually become fed up. Whether it's the Super Bowl, the Oscars, the Pulitzer Prize, or a 4.0 GPA, the distinction is only meaningful for the exceptional ones at the very top. If a majority of the students in a high school are in the honor society, it is no longer an honor.

Perhaps inadvertently, then, the federal the No Child Left Behind law aids and abets the diluting, deceptive effect of grade inflation. While insisting on objective tests of achievement, Congress has joined the deceit by using normative language for a standards-based approach: As in Garrison Keillor's fictional Lake Wobegon, no child is left behind and, thus, all the children are "above average."

Unless and until high schools, along with the levels of schooling above and below them, are willing to provide a more honest and publicly understandable system of grading, we will continue to pay the price in terms of national and state insistence on standardized high-stakes tests to measure students and schools. The long-standing and unmitigated pattern of grade inflation is a major contributor to the latest call for high school reform. Now the time has come for school boards, administrators, and teachers to make a coordinated, concerted, and courageous effort—something akin to an Alan Greenspan approach—to reverse this devaluing trend.

Alfie Kohn ➔ **NO**

The Dangerous Myth of Grade Inflation

Grade inflation got started . . . in the late '60s and early '70s. . . . The grades that faculty members now give . . . deserve to be a scandal.

—Professor Harvey Mansfield,
Harvard University, 2001

Grades A and B are sometimes given too readily—Grade A for work of not very high merit, and Grade B for work not far above mediocrity. . . . One of the chief obstacles to raising the standards of the degree is the readiness with which insincere students gain passable grades by sham work.

— Report of the Committee on Raising the Standard,
Harvard University, 1894

Complaints about grade inflation have been around for a very long time. Every so often a fresh flurry of publicity pushes the issue to the foreground again, the latest example being a series of articles in *The Boston Globe* last year that disclosed—in a tone normally reserved for the discovery of entrenched corruption in state government—that a lot of students at Harvard were receiving A's and being graduated with honors.

The fact that people were offering the same complaints more than a century ago puts the latest bout of harrumphing in perspective, not unlike those quotations about the disgraceful values of the younger generation that turn out to be hundreds of years old. The long history of indignation also pretty well derails any attempts to place the blame for higher grades on a residue of bleeding-heart liberal professors hired in the '60s. (Unless, of course, there was a similar countercultural phenomenon in the 1860s.)

Yet on campuses across America today, academe's usual requirements for supporting data and reasoned analysis have been suspended for some reason where this issue is concerned. It is largely accepted on faith that grade inflation—an upward shift in students' grade-point averages without a similar rise in achievement—exists, and that it is a bad thing. Meanwhile, the truly substantive issues surrounding grades and motivation have been obscured or ignored.

The fact is that it is hard to substantiate even the simple claim that grades have been rising. Depending on the time period we're talking about, that claim may well be false. In their book *When Hope and Fear Collide* (Jossey-Bass, 1998), Arthur Levine and Jeanette Cureton tell us that more undergraduates in 1993 reported receiving A's (and fewer reported receiving grades of C or below) compared with their counterparts in 1969 and 1976 surveys. Unfortunately, self-reports are notoriously unreliable, and the numbers become even more dubious when only a self-selected, and possibly unrepresentative, segment bothers to return the questionnaires. (One out of three failed to do so in 1993; no information is offered about the return rates in the earlier surveys.)

To get a more accurate picture of whether grades have changed over the years, one needs to look at official student transcripts. Clifford Adelman, a senior research analyst with the U.S. Department of Education, did just that, reviewing transcripts from more than 3,000 institutions and reporting his results in 1995. His finding: "Contrary to the widespread lamentations, grades actually declined slightly in the last two decades." Moreover, a report released just this year by the National Center for Education Statistics revealed that fully 33.5 percent of American undergraduates had a grade-point average of C or below in 1999–2000, a number that ought to quiet "all the furor over grade inflation," according to a spokesperson for the Association of American Colleges and Universities. (A review of other research suggests a comparable lack of support for claims of grade inflation at the high-school level.)

[Addendum 2004: A subsequent analysis by Adelman, which reviewed college transcripts from students who were graduated from high school in 1972, 1982, and 1992, confirmed that there was no significant or linear increase in average grades over that period. The average GPA for those three cohorts was 2.70, 2.66, and 2.74, respectively. The proportion of A's and B's received by students: 58.5 percent in the '70s, 58.9 percent in the '80s, and 58.0 percent in the '90s. Even when Adelman looked at "highly selective" institutions, he again found very little change in average GPA over the decades.]

However, even where grades *are* higher now as compared with then, that does not constitute proof that they are inflated. The burden rests with critics to demonstrate that those higher grades are undeserved, and one can cite any number of alternative explanations. Maybe students are turning in better assignments. Maybe instructors used to be too stingy with their marks and have become more reasonable. Maybe the concept of assessment itself has evolved, so that today it is more a means for allowing students to demonstrate what they know rather than for sorting them or "catching them out." (The real question, then, is why we spent so many years trying to make good students look bad.) Maybe students aren't forced to take as many courses outside their primary areas of interest in which they didn't fare as well. Maybe struggling students are now able to withdraw from a course before a poor grade appears on their transcripts. (Say what you will about that practice, it challenges the hypothesis that the grades students receive in the courses they complete are inflated.)

The bottom line: No one has ever demonstrated that students today get A's for the same work that used to receive B's or C's. We simply do not have the data to support such a claim.

Consider the most recent, determined effort by a serious source to prove that grades are inflated: "Evaluation and the Academy: Are We Doing the Right Thing?" a report released this year by the American Academy of Arts and Sciences. Its senior author is Henry Rosovsky, formerly Harvard's dean of the faculty. The first argument offered in support of the proposition that students couldn't possibly deserve higher grades is that SAT scores have dropped during the same period that grades are supposed to have risen. But this is a patently inapt comparison, if only because the SAT is deeply flawed. It has never been much good even at predicting grades during the freshman year in college, to say nothing of more important academic outcomes. A four-year analysis of almost 78,000 University of Califo rnia students, published last year by the UC president's office, found that the test predicted only 13.3 percent of variation in freshman grades, a figure roughly consistent with hundreds of previous studies. . . .

Even if one believes that the SAT is a valid and valuable exam, however, the claim that scores are dropping is a poor basis for the assertion that grades are too high. First, it is difficult to argue that a standardized test taken in high school and grades for college course work are measuring the same thing. Second, changes in aggregate SAT scores mostly reflect the proportion of the eligible population that has chosen to take the test. The American Academy's report states that average SAT scores dropped slightly from 1969 to 1993. But over that period, the pool of test takers grew from about one-third to more than two-fifths of high-school graduates—an addition of more than 200,000 students.

Third, a decline in overall SAT scores is hardly the right benchmark against which to measure the grades earned at Harvard or other elite institutions. Every bit of evidence I could find—including a review of the SAT scores of entering students at Harvard over the past two decades, at the nation's most selective colleges over three and even four decades, and at all private colleges since 1985—uniformly confirms a virtually linear rise in both verbal and math scores, even after correcting for the renorming of the test in the mid-1990s. To cite just one example, the latest edition of "Trends in College Admissions" reports that the average verbal-SAT score of students enrolled in all private colleges rose from 543 in 1985 to 558 in 1999. Thus, those who regard SAT results as a basis for comparison should *expect* to see higher grades now rather than assume that they are inflated.

The other two arguments made by the authors of the American Academy's report rely on a similar sleight of hand. They note that more college students are now forced to take remedial courses, but offer no reason to think that this is especially true of the relevant student population—namely, those at the most selective colleges who are now receiving A's instead of B's. [Addendum: Adelman's newer data challenge the premise that there has been *any* increase. In fact, "the proportion of all students who took at least one remedial course [in college] dropped from 51 percent in the [high school] class of 1982 to 42 percent in the class of 1992."]

Finally, they report that more states are adding high-school graduation tests and even standardized exams for admission to public universities. Yet that trend can be explained by political factors and offers no evidence of an objective decline in students' proficiency. For instance, scores on the National Assessment of Educational Progress, known as "the nation's report card" on elementary and secondary schooling, have shown very little change over the past couple of decades, and most of the change that has occurred has been for the better. As David Berliner and Bruce Biddle put it in their tellingly titled book *The Manufactured Crisis* (Addison-Wesley, 1995), the data demonstrate that "today's students are at least as well informed as students in previous generations." The latest round of public-school bashing—and concomitant reliance on high-stakes testing—began with the Reagan administration's "Nation at Risk" report, featuring claims now widely viewed by researchers as exaggerated and misleading.

⋅◈⋅

Beyond the absence of good evidence, the debate over grade inflation brings up knotty epistemological problems. To say that grades are not merely rising but inflated—and that they are consequently "less accurate" now, as the American Academy's report puts it—is to postulate the existence of an objectively correct evaluation of what a student (or an essay) deserves, the true grade that ought to be uncovered and honestly reported. It would be an understatement to say that this reflects a simplistic and outdated view of knowledge and of learning.

In fact, what is most remarkable is how rarely learning even figures into the discussion. The dominant disciplinary sensibility in commentaries on this topic is not that of education—an exploration of pedagogy or assessment—but rather of economics. That is clear from the very term "grade inflation," which is, of course, just a metaphor. Our understanding is necessarily limited if we confine ourselves to the vocabulary of inputs and outputs, incentives, resource distribution, and compensation.

Suppose, for the sake of the argument, we assumed the very worst—not only that students are getting better grades than did their counterparts of an earlier generation, but that the grades are too high. What does that mean, and why does it upset some people so?

To understand grade inflation in its proper context, we must acknowledge a truth that is rarely named: The crusade against it is led by conservative individuals and organizations who regard it as analogous—or even related—to such favorite whipping boys as multicultural education, the alleged radicalism of academe, "political correctness" (a label that permits the denigration of anything one doesn't like without having to offer a reasoned objection), and too much concern about students' self-esteem. Mainstream media outlets and college administrators have allowed themselves to be put on the defensive by accusations about grade inflation, as can be witnessed when deans at Harvard plead nolo contendere and dutifully tighten their grading policies.

What are the critics assuming about the nature of students' motivation to learn, about the purpose of evaluation and of education itself? (It is surely revealing when someone reserves time and energy to complain bitterly about how many students are getting A's—as opposed to expressing concern about, say, how many students have been trained to think that the point of going to school is to get A's.)

"In a healthy university, it would not be necessary to say what is wrong with grade inflation," Harvey Mansfield asserted in an opinion article last year (*The Chronicle,* April 6, 2001). That, to put it gently, is a novel view of health. It seems reasonable to expect those making an argument to be prepared to defend it, and also valuable to bring their hidden premises to light. Here are the assumptions that seem to underlie the grave warnings about grade inflation:

The professor's job is to sort students for employers or graduate schools   Some are disturbed by grade inflation—or, more accurately, grade compression—because it then becomes harder to spread out students on a continuum, ranking them against one another for the benefit of postcollege constituencies. One professor asks, by way of analogy, "Why would anyone subscribe to *Consumers Digest* if every blender were rated a 'best buy'?"

But how appropriate is such a marketplace analogy? Is the professor's job to rate students like blenders for the convenience of corporations, or to offer feedback that will help students learn more skillfully and enthusiastically? (Notice, moreover, that even consumer magazines don't grade on a curve. They report the happy news if it turns out that every blender meets a reasonable set of performance criteria.)

Furthermore, the student-as-appliance approach assumes that grades provide useful information to those postcollege constituencies. Yet growing evidence—most recently in the fields of medicine and law, as cited in publications like *The Journal of the American Medical Association* and the *American Educational Research Journal*—suggests that grades and test scores do not in fact predict career success, or much of anything beyond subsequent grades and test scores.

Students should be set against one another in a race for artificially scarce rewards   The essence of grading is exclusiveness," Mansfield said in one interview. Students "should have to compete with each other," he said in another.

In other words, even when no graduate-school admissions committee pushes for students to be sorted, they ought to be sorted anyway, with grades reflecting relative standing rather than absolute accomplishment. In effect, this means that the game should be rigged so that no matter how well students do, only a few can get A's. The question guiding evaluation in such a classroom is not "How well are they learning?" but "Who's beating whom?" The ultimate purpose of good colleges, this view holds, is not to maximize success, but to ensure that there will always be losers.

A bell curve may sometimes—but only sometimes—describe the range of knowledge in a roomful of students at the beginning of a course. When it's over, though, any responsible educator hopes that the results would skew drastically to the right, meaning that most students learned what they hadn't known before. Thus, in their important study, *Making Sense of College Grades* (Jossey-Bass, 1986), Ohmer Milton, Howard Pollio, and James Eison write, "It is not a symbol of rigor to have grades fall into a 'normal' distribution; rather, it is a symbol of failure—failure to teach well, failure to test well, and failure to have any influence at all on the intellectual lives of students." Making sure that students are continually re-sorted, with excellence turned into an artificially scarce commodity, is almost perverse.

What does relative success signal about student performance in any case? The number of peers that a student has bested tells us little about how much she knows and is able to do. Moreover, such grading policies may create a competitive climate that is counterproductive for winners and losers alike, to the extent that it discourages a free exchange of ideas and a sense of community that's conducive to exploration.

Harder is better (or higher grades mean lower standards)   Compounding the tendency to confuse excellence with victory is a tendency to confuse quality with difficulty—as evidenced in the accountability fad that has elementary and secondary education in its grip just now, with relentless talk of "rigor" and "raising the bar." The same confusion shows up in higher education when professors pride themselves not on the intellectual depth and value of their classes but merely on how much reading they assign, how hard their tests are, how rarely they award good grades, and so on. "You're going to have to *work* in here!" they announce, with more than a hint of machismo and self-congratulation.

Some people might defend that posture on the grounds that students will perform better if A's are harder to come by. In fact, the evidence on this question is decidedly mixed. Stringent grading sometimes has been shown to boost short-term retention as measured by multiple-choice exams—never to improve understanding or promote interest in learning. The most recent analysis, released in 2000 by Julian R. Betts and Jeff Grogger, professors of economics at the University of California at San Diego and at Los Angeles, respectively, found that tougher grading was initially correlated with higher test scores. But the long-term effects were negligible—with the exception of minority students, for whom the effects were negative.

It appears that something more than an empirical hypothesis is behind the "harder is better" credo, particularly when it is set up as a painfully false dichotomy: Those easy-grading professors are too lazy to care, or too worried about how students will evaluate them, or overly concerned about their students' self-esteem, whereas *we* are the last defenders of what used to matter in the good old days. High standards! Intellectual honesty! No free lunch!

The American Academy's report laments an absence of "candor" about this issue. Let us be candid, then. Those who grumble about undeserved grades sometimes exude a cranky impatience with—or even contempt for—the late adolescents and young adults who sit in their classrooms. Many people teaching in higher education, after all, see themselves primarily as researchers and regard teaching as an occupational hazard, something they're not very good at, were never trained for, and would rather avoid. It would be interesting to examine the correlation between one's view of teaching (or of students) and the intensity of one's feelings about grade inflation. Someone also might want to examine the personality profiles of those who become infuriated over the possibility that someone, somewhere, got an A without having earned it.

Grades motivate   With the exception of orthodox behaviorists, psychologists have come to realize that people can exhibit qualitatively different kinds of motivation: intrinsic, in which the task itself is seen as valuable, and extrinsic, in which the task is just a means to the end of gaining a reward or escaping a punishment. The two are not only distinct but often inversely related. Scores of studies have demonstrated, for example, that the more people are rewarded, the more they come to lose interest in whatever had to be done in order to get the reward. . . .

Those unfamiliar with that basic distinction, let alone the supporting research, may be forgiven for pondering how to "motivate" students, then concluding that grades are often a good way of doing so, and consequently worrying about the impact of inflated grades. But the reality is that it doesn't matter how motivated students are; what matters is *how* students are motivated. A focus on grades creates, or at least perpetuates, an extrinsic orientation that is likely to undermine the love of learning we are presumably seeking to promote.

Three robust findings emerge from the empirical literature on the subject: Students who are given grades, or for whom grades are made particularly salient, tend to display less interest in what they are doing, fare worse on meaningful measures of learning, and avoid more challenging tasks when given the opportunity—as compared with those in a nongraded comparison group. College instructors cannot help noticing, and presumably being disturbed by, such consequences, but they may lapse into blaming students ("grade grubbers") rather than understanding the systemic sources of the problem. A focus on whether too many students are getting A's suggests a tacit endorsement of grades that predictably produces just such a mind-set in students.

These fundamental questions are almost completely absent from discussions of grade inflation. The American Academy's report takes exactly one sentence—with no citations—to dismiss the argument that "lowering the anxiety over grades leads to better learning," ignoring the fact that much more is involved than anxiety. It is a matter of why a student learns, not only how much stress he feels. Nor is the point just that low grades hurt some students' feelings, but that grades, per se, hurt all students' engagement with learning. The meaningful contrast is not between an A and a B or C, but between an extrinsic and an intrinsic focus.

Precisely because that is true, a reconsideration of grade inflation leads us to explore alternatives to our (often unreflective) use of grades. Narrative comments and other ways by which faculty members can communicate their evaluations can be far more informative than letter or number grades, and much less destructive. Indeed, some colleges—for example, Hampshire, Evergreen State, Alverno, and New College of Florida—have eliminated grades entirely, as a critical step toward *raising* intellectual standards. Even the American Academy's report acknowledges that "relatively undifferentiated course grading has been a traditional practice in many graduate schools for a very long time." Has that policy produced lower quality teaching and learning? Quite the contrary: Many people say they didn't begin to explore ideas deeply and passionately until graduate school began and the importance of grades diminished significantly.

If the continued use of grades rests on nothing more than tradition ("We've always done it that way"), a faulty understanding of motivation, or excessive deference to graduate-school admissions committees, then it may be time to balance those factors against the demonstrated harms of getting students to chase A's. Ohmer Milton and his colleagues discovered—and others have confirmed—that a "grade orientation" and a "learning orientation" on the part of students tend to be inversely related. That raises the disturbing possibility that some colleges are institutions of higher learning in name only, because the paramount question for students is not "What does this mean?" but "Do we have to know this?"

A grade-oriented student body is an invitation for the administration and faculty to ask hard questions: What unexamined assumptions keep traditional grading in place? What forms of assessment might be less destructive? How can professors minimize the salience of grades in their classrooms, so long as grades must still be given? And: If the artificial inducement of grades disappeared, what sort of teaching strategies might elicit authentic interest in a course?

To engage in this sort of inquiry, to observe real classrooms, and to review the relevant research is to arrive at one overriding conclusion: The real threat to excellence isn't grade inflation at all; it's grades.

POSTSCRIPT

Is Grade Inflation a Problem?

The issue of grade inflation can be seen as part of a broader concern shared by many that the nation's schools do not adhere to the type of rigorous academic standards necessary to adequately educate our future citizens, leaders, and workforce. As Alfie Kohn points out in his article, this concern is certainly not new. The current focus on standards and accountability flows from the 1950s when the launching of the Russian space satellite "Sputnik" shook our collective confidence in the schools and generated much criticism of them. In a similar fashion, the publication of *A Nation At Risk* in 1983 rekindled concerns that we would lose our preeminence on the world scene if our schools did not adopt and implement more rigorous academic standards.

Although most discussions on grade inflation focus on secondary schools and universities, a case can be made that the practice at the elementary school level of social promotion is itself a form of grade inflation. The U.S. Department of Education has issued a position paper on social promotion and the equally controversial issue of grade retention. The introduction to that position paper states:

> Working to give students the opportunity to reach high standards of learning demands that educators and state and local leaders take responsibility for ending the practice of social promotion—where students are allowed to continue to pass through school with their peers without satisfying academic requirements or meeting performance indicators at key grades.
>
> Research indicates, and common sense confirms, that passing students on to the next grade when they are unprepared neither increases student achievement nor properly prepares students for college and future employment. At the same time, research also shows that holding students back to repeat a grade (retention) without changing instructional strategies is ineffective. Much evidence suggests that the achievement of retained students still lags behind that of their peers after repeating a grade, making it an ineffective strategy for enabling students to catch up. Retention in grade also greatly increases the likelihood that a student will drop out of school—and being held back twice makes dropping out a virtual certainty.
>
> Students who are promoted without regard to their achievement or are retained often fall even further behind their classmates, and those who do not drop out usually finish school without the knowledge and skills expected of a high school graduate. Both being promoted without regard to effort or achievement or retained without extra assistance sends a message to students that little is expected from them, that they have little worth, and that they do not warrant the time and effort it would take to help them be successful in school.

Neither social promotion nor the diametrically opposite practice of grade retention appear to be particularly effective measures and an emerging consensus seems to be that promotion plus additional scaffolding and support for lagging students may be a better idea. Others argue that the real problem is in the grade level structure that uses the child's age as the only placement criterion.

Those who believe that grade inflation is a problem would likely contend that many of the same considerations that drive social promotion also influence teachers to give higher grades to students than their actual achievement should merit. Some of those considerations include a concern for the student's self-esteem, a belief in positive reinforcement, and/or a reward for student effort or improvement. And there are many educators who would suggest that those types of consideration are more important than sorting and classifying students by grades.

Another argument often proffered regarding this issue is that the school curriculum has been "dumbed down" to the point that not much effort is needed on the part of students to fulfill class requirements and pass examinations based on less-than-rigorous material.

Other references on this topic include: S. Rosh, *Grade Inflation at American Colleges and Universities* (Gradeinflation.com, March 2003); H. Rosovosky and M. Hartley, *Evaluation and the Academy: Are We Doing the Right Thing?* (American Academy of Arts and Sciences, 2002); M. Donald Thomas and William L. Bainbridge, *Grade Inflation: The Current Fraud* (Effective School Research, January 1997); R. Milzoff, A. Paley, and B. Reed, Grade *Inflation Is Real* (Harvard Crimson, March 2001); B. Bartlett, *The Truth About Grade Inflation* (National Center for Policy Analysis, February 2003).

ISSUE 14

Does Homework Serve Useful Purposes?

YES: Robert J. Marzano and Debra J. Pickering, from "The Case for and against Homework," *Educational Leadership* (March 2007)

NO: Diane W. Dunne, from "Homework Takes a Hit!" *Education World* (2005)

ISSUE SUMMARY

YES: Robert J. Marzano, president of the Marzano and Associates educational consulting firm, and Debra J. Pickering, director of staff development in Littleton Pubic Schools, believe that homework is a "powerful instructional tool."

NO: Diane W. Dunne, a writer for *Education World*, interviews author and freelance journalist John Buell, who believes that homework places inordinate burdens on children and families, especially those who are poor.

Schooling in the United States contains many sacrosanct traditions that seem to successfully resist challenges regarding their efficacy in contributing to student learning. Certainly the practice of assigning and requiring the completion of *homework* can be listed as one of those traditions. Homework has long been employed as an instructional tool with various rationales supporting its use. Such rationales include training to enhance academic discipline, practice and drill to exercise the intellect, providing an advanced organizer for upcoming classroom work, assessing student knowledge, and engaging parents in the student's schooling. Periodically some of those rationales are challenged or debunked, but the tradition itself lives on.

Teachers often use homework not only as a learning tool but also as a means to provide students with an additional opportunity to improve their grade and thus increase the probability that they will pass the course. This can be of particular value to those students who do not do well on examinations and other types of evaluation.

But as many teachers report, a growing number of students, especially at the secondary level, simply refuse to do the required homework, thus not only losing any learning advantages that might have accrued to them, but also losing ground in terms of the credit ascribed to completing the homework. The net result is that something designed to help students becomes instead a factor in their lack of success in school.

Some might argue that a student's failure to complete or even attempt homework is symptomatic of a lack of motivation or self-discipline on the student's part and/or a lack of involvment/supervison by parents and, for a given student, that may indeed be the case. Also the notion of having students use non-school time to support and expand their learning seems logical and reasonable.

But such arguments, as pointed out by Buell in the Dunne article, may be overly simplistic when applied to all students. Factors related to family structure and responsibilities, family income and student employment, and access to instructional support and materials such as libraries and computers can either enhance or impede a student's opportunity and/or ability to do homework. Another concern relates to the availability of time and whether or not the time devoted to homework may detract from a student's opportunities to pursue other worthy, non-school activities.

The tremendous range of diversity related to demographic factors and family circumstances makes the homework issue more complex than it may appear at first glance. Additionally, curriculum development and new requirements in areas such as community service learning, which involve non-school time, will also have implications for secondary school students vis-à-vis homework. Some teachers are also beginning to voice concerns that the increased emphasis on accountability and high-stakes standardized testing may cause schools to use class time for review and test preparation purposes, thus forcing greater reliance on homework as a means to cover the regular curriculum.

Another complicating aspect of this homework issue is the availability (or lack thereof) of access to computers. Not only does this contribute to greater disparity of opportunity among students, but it also complicates the teacher's role in evaluating the "originality and ownership" of the submitted homework.

Assuming that the assignment of homework is going to continue to be an accepted part of schooling, teachers and school administrators would do well to address several questions raised by the following articles:

- How can the school impress on parents the importance of their involvement in all aspects of their child's education including homework?
- Are there resources available to support parents in their efforts to be involved in their child's education?
- Does the school have a homework policy that addresses how much and how often homework is assigned to students?
- Does the school have a "homework assistance" program?

YES ↵

Robert J. Marzano and
Debra J. Pickering

The Case for and against Homework

Homework has been a perennial topic of debate in education, and attitudes toward it have been cyclical (Gill & Schlossman, 2000). Throughout the first few decades of the 20th century, educators commonly believed that homework helped create disciplined minds. By 1940, growing concern that homework interfered with other home activities sparked a reaction against it. This trend was reversed in the late 1950s when the Soviets' launch of *Sputnik* led to concern that U.S. education lacked rigor; schools viewed more rigorous homework as a partial solution to the problem. By 1980, the trend had reversed again, with some learning theorists claiming that homework could be detrimental to students' mental health. Since then, impassioned arguments for and against homework have continued to proliferate.

We now stand at an interesting intersection in the evolution of the homework debate. Arguments against homework are becoming louder and more popular, as evidenced by several recent books as well as an editorial in *Time* magazine (Wallis, 2006) that presented these arguments as truth without much discussion of alternative perspectives. At the same time, a number of studies have provided growing evidence of the usefulness of homework when employed effectively.

The Case for Homework

Homework is typically defined as any tasks "assigned to students by school teachers that are meant to be carried out during nonschool hours" (Cooper, 1989a, p. 7). A number of synthesis studies have been conducted on homework, spanning a broad range of methodologies and levels of specificity. Some are quite general and mix the results from experimental studies with correlational studies.

Two meta-analyses by Cooper and colleagues (Cooper, 1989a; Cooper, Robinson, & Patall, 2006) are the most comprehensive and rigorous. The 1989 meta-analysis reviewed research dating as far back as the 1930s; the 2006 study reviewed research from 1987 to 2003. Commenting on studies that attempted to examine the causal relationship between homework and student achievement by comparing experimental (homework) and control (no homework) groups, Cooper, Robinson, and Patall (2006) noted,

> With only rare exceptions, the relationship between the amount of homework students do and their achievement outcomes was found to be

From *Educational Leadership*, March 2007, pp. 74–79. Copyright © 2007 by ASCD. Reprinted by permission. The Association for Supervision and Curriculum Development is a worldwide community of educators advocating sound policies and sharing best practices to achieve the success of each learner. To learn more, visit ASCD at www.ascd.org

positive and statistically significant. Therefore, we think it would not be imprudent, based on the evidence in hand, to conclude that doing homework causes improved academic achievement. (p. 48)

The Case against Homework

Although the research support for homework is compelling, the case against homework is popular. *The End of Homework: How Homework Disrupts Families, Overburdens Children, and Limits Learning* by Kralovec and Buell (2000), considered by many to be the first high-profile attack on homework, asserted that homework contributes to a corporate-style, competitive U.S. culture that overvalues work to the detriment of personal and familial well-being. The authors focused particularly on the harm to economically disadvantaged students, who are unintentionally penalized because their environments often make it almost impossible to complete assignments at home. The authors called for people to unite against homework and to lobby for an extended school day instead.

A similar call for action came from Bennett and Kalish (2006) in *The Case Against Homework: How Homework Is Hurting Our Children and What We Can Do About It*. These authors criticized both the quantity and quality of homework. They provided evidence that too much homework harms students' health and family time, and they asserted that teachers are not well trained in how to assign homework. The authors suggested that individuals and parent groups should insist that teachers reduce the amount of homework, design more valuable assignments, and avoid homework altogether over breaks and holidays.

In a third book, *The Homework Myth: Why Our Kids Get Too Much of a Bad Thing* (2006a), Kohn took direct aim at the research on homework. In this book and in a recent article in *Phi Delta Kappan* (2006b), he became quite personal in his condemnation of researchers. For example, referring to Harris Cooper, the lead author of the two leading meta-analyses on homework, Kohn noted,

> A careful reading of Cooper's own studies . . . reveals further examples of his determination to massage the numbers until they yield something—anything—on which to construct a defense of homework for younger children. (2006a, p. 84)

He also attacked a section on homework in our book *Classroom Instruction that Works* (Marzano, Pickering, & Pollock, 2001).

Kohn concluded that research fails to demonstrate homework's effectiveness as an instructional tool and recommended changing the "default state" from an expectation that homework *will* be assigned to an expectation that homework *will not* be assigned. According to Kohn, teachers should only assign homework when they can justify that the assignments are "beneficial" (2006a, p. 166)—ideally involving students in activities appropriate for the home, such as performing an experiment in the kitchen, cooking, doing crossword puzzles with the family, watching good TV shows, or reading. Finally, Kohn urged teachers to involve students in deciding what homework, and how much, they should do.

Some of Kohn's recommendations have merit. For example, it makes good sense to only assign homework that is beneficial to student learning instead of assigning homework as a matter of policy. Many of those who conduct research on homework explicitly or implicitly recommend this practice. However, his misunderstanding or misrepresentation of the research sends the inaccurate message that research does not support homework. . . . Homework has decades of research supporting its effective use. Kohn's allegations that researchers are trying to mislead practitioners and the general public are unfounded and detract from a useful debate on effective practice.

The Dangers of Ignoring the Research

Certainly, inappropriate homework may produce little or no benefit—it may even decrease student achievement. All three of the books criticizing homework provide compelling anecdotes to this effect. Schools should strengthen their policies to ensure that teachers use homework properly.

If a district or school discards homework altogether, however, it will be throwing away a powerful instructional tool. Cooper and colleagues' (2006) comparison of homework with no homework indicates that the average student in a class in which appropriate homework was assigned would score 23 percentile points higher on tests of the knowledge addressed in that class than the average student in a class in which homework was not assigned.

Perhaps the most important advantage of homework is that it can enhance achievement by extending learning beyond the school day. This characteristic is important because U.S. students spend much less time studying academic content than students in other countries do. A 1994 report examined the amount of time U.S. students spend studying core academic subjects compared with students in other countries that typically outperform the United States academically, such as Japan, Germany, and France. The study found that "students abroad are required to work on demanding subject matter at least twice as long" as are U.S. students (National Education Commission on Time and Learning, 1994, p. 25).

To drop the use of homework, then, a school or district would be obliged to identify a practice that produces a similar effect within the confines of the school day without taking away or diminishing the benefits of other academic activities—no easy accomplishment. A better approach is to ensure that teachers use homework effectively. To enact effective homework policies, however, schools and districts must address the following issues.

Grade Level

Although teachers across the K–12 spectrum commonly assign homework, research has produced no clear-cut consensus on the benefits of homework at the early elementary grade levels. In his early meta-analysis, Cooper (1989a) reported the following effect sizes (p. 71):

- Grades 4–6: ES = .15 (Percentile gain = 6)
- Grades 7–9: ES = .31 (Percentile gain = 12)
- Grades 10–12: ES = .64 (Percentile gain = 24)

The pattern clearly indicates that homework has smaller effects at lower grade levels. Even so, Cooper (1989b) still recommended homework for elementary students because

> homework for young children should help them develop good study habits, foster positive attitudes toward school, and communicate to students the idea that learning takes work at home as well as at school. (p. 90)

The Cooper, Robinson, and Patall (2006) meta-analysis found the same pattern of stronger relationships at the secondary level but also identified a number of studies at grades 2, 3, and 4 demonstrating positive effects for homework. In *The Battle over Homework* (2007), Cooper noted that homework should have different purposes at different grade levels:

- For students in *the earliest grades*, it should foster positive attitudes, habits, and character traits; permit appropriate parent involvement; and reinforce learning of simple skills introduced in class.
- For students in *upper elementary grades*, it should play a more direct role in fostering improved school achievement.
- In *6th grade and beyond*, it should play an important role in improving standardized test scores and grades.

Time Spent on Homework

One of the more contentious issues in the homework debate is the amount of time students should spend on homework. The Cooper synthesis (1989a) reported that for junior high school students, the benefits increased as time increased, up to 1 to 2 hours of homework a night, and then decreased. The Cooper, Robinson, and Patall (2006) study reported similar findings: 7 to 12 hours of homework per week produced the largest effect size for 12th grade students. The researchers suggested that for 12th graders the optimum amount of homework might lie between 1.5 and 2.5 hours per night, but they cautioned that no hard-and-fast rules are warranted. Still, researchers have offered various recommendations. For example, Good and Brophy (2003) cautioned that teachers must take care not to assign too much homework. They suggested that

> homework must be realistic in length and difficulty given the students' abilities to work independently. Thus, 5 to 10 minutes per subject might be appropriate for 4th graders, whereas 30 to 60 minutes might be appropriate for college-bound high school students. (p. 394)

Cooper, Robinson, and Patall (2006) also issued a strong warning about too much homework:

> Even for these oldest students, too much homework may diminish its effectiveness or even become counterproductive. (p. 53)

Cooper (2007) suggested that research findings support the common "10-minute rule" (p. 92), which states that all daily homework assignments combined should take about as long to complete as 10 minutes multiplied by the student's grade level. He added that when required reading is included as a type of homework, the 10-minute rule might be increased to 15 minutes.

Focusing on the amount of time students spend on homework, however, may miss the point. A significant proportion of the research on homework indicates that the positive effects of homework relate to the amount of homework that the student *completes* rather than the amount of time spent on homework or the amount of homework actually assigned. Thus, simply assigning homework may not produce the desired effect—in fact, ill-structured homework might even have a negative effect on student achievement. Teachers must carefully plan and assign homework in a way that maximizes the potential for student success (see Research-Based Homework Guidelines).

Parent Involvement

Another question regarding homework is the extent to which schools should involve parents. Some studies have reported minimal positive effects or even negative effects for parental involvement. In addition, many parents report that they feel unprepared to help their children with homework and that their efforts to help frequently cause stress (see Balli, 1998; Corno, 1996; Hoover-Dempsey, Bassler, & Burow, 1995; Perkins & Milgram, 1996).

Epstein and colleagues conducted a series of studies to identify the conditions under which parental involvement enhances homework (Epstein, 2001; Epstein & Becket, 1982; Van Voorhis, 2003). They recommended *interactive* homework in which

- Parents receive clear guidelines spelling out their role.
- Teachers do not expect parents to act as experts regarding content or to attempt to teach the content.
- Parents ask questions that help students clarify and summarize what they have learned.

Good and Brophy (2003) provided the following recommendations regarding parent involvement:

> Especially useful for parent-child relations purposes are assignments calling for students to show or explain their written work or other products completed at school to their parents and get their reactions (Epstein, 2001; Epstein, Simon, & Salinas, 1997) or to interview their parents to develop information

about parental experiences or opinions relating to topics studied in social studies (Alleman & Brophy, 1998). Such assignments cause students and their parents or other family members to become engaged in conversations that relate to the academic curriculum and thus extend the students' learning. Furthermore, because these are likely to be genuine conversations rather than more formally structured teaching/learning tasks, both parents and children are likely to experience them as enjoyable rather than threatening. (p. 395)

Going beyond the Research

Although research has established the overall viability of homework as a tool to enhance student achievement, for the most part the research does not provide recommendations that are specific enough to help busy practitioners. This is the nature of research—it errs on the side of assuming that something does not work until substantial evidence establishes that it does. The research community takes a long time to formulate firm conclusions on the basis of research. . . .

In addition, research in a specific area, such as homework, sometimes contradicts research in related areas. For example, Cooper (2007) recommended on the basis of 60-plus years of homework research that teachers should not comment on or grade every homework assignment. But practitioners might draw a different conclusion from the research on providing feedback to students, which has found that providing "feedback coupled with remediation" (Hattie, 1992) or feedback on "testlike events" in the form of explanations to students (Bangert-Drowns, Kulik, Kulik, & Morgan, 1991) positively affects achievement.

Riehl (2006) pointed out the similarity between education research and medical research. She commented,

> When reported in the popular media, medical research often appears as a blunt instrument, able to obliterate skeptics or opponents by the force of its evidence and arguments. . . . Yet repeated visits to the medical journals themselves can leave a much different impression. The serious medical journals convey the sense that medical research is an ongoing conversation and quest, punctuated occasionally by important findings that can and should alter practice, but more often characterized by continuing investigations. These investigations, taken cumulatively, can inform the work of practitioners who are building their own local knowledge bases on medical care. (pp. 27–28)

If relying solely on research is problematic, what are busy practitioners to do? The answer is certainly not to wait until research "proves" that a practice is effective. Instead, educators should combine research-based generalizations, research from related areas, and their own professional judgment based on firsthand experience to develop specific practices and make adjustments as necessary. Like medical practitioners, education practitioners must develop their own "local knowledge base" on homework and all other aspects of teaching. Educators can develop the most effective practices by observing changes in the achievement of the students with whom they work every day.

Research-Based Homework Guidelines

Research provides strong evidence that, when used appropriately, homework benefits student achievement. To make sure that homework is appropriate, teachers should follow these guidelines:

- Assign purposeful homework. Legitimate purposes for homework include introducing new content, practicing a skill or process that students can do independently but not fluently, elaborating on information that has been addressed in class to deepen students' knowledge, and providing opportunities for students to explore topics of their own interest.
- Design homework to maximize the chances that students will complete it. For example, ensure that homework is at the appropriate level of difficulty. Students should be able to complete homework assignments independently with relatively high success rates, but they should still find the assignments challenging enough to be interesting.
- Involve parents in appropriate ways (for example, as a sounding board to help students summarize what they learned from the homework) without requiring parents to act as teachers or to police students' homework completion.
- Carefully monitor the amount of homework assigned so that it is appropriate to students' age levels and does not take too much time away from other home activities.

References

Balli, S. J. (1998). When mom and dad help: Student reflections on parent involvement with homework. *Journal of Research and Development in Education, 31*(3), 142–148.

Bangert-Drowns, R. L., Kulik, C. C., Kulik, J. A., & Morgan, M. (1991). The instructional effects of feedback in test-like events. *Review of Educational Research, 61*(2), 213–238.

Bennett, S., & Kalish, N. (2006). *The case against homework: How homework is hurting our children and what we can do about it.* New York: Crown.

Bloom, B. S. (1984). The search for methods of group instruction as effective as one-to-one tutoring. *Educational Leadership, 41*(8), 4–18.

Cooper, H. (1989a). *Homework.* White Plains, NY: Longman.

Cooper, H. (1989b). Synthesis of research on homework. *Educational Leadership, 47*(3), 85–91.

Cooper, H. (2007). *The battle over homework* (3rd ed.). Thousand Oaks, CA: Corwin Press.

Cooper, H., Robinson, J. C., & Patall, E. A. (2006). Does homework improve academic achievement? A synthesis of research, 1987–2003. *Review of Educational Research, 76*(1), 1–62.

Corno, L. (1996). Homework is a complicated thing. *Educational Researcher, 25*(8), 27–30.

Epstein, J. (2001). *School, family, and community partnerships: Preparing educators and improving schools.* Boulder, CO: Westview.

Epstein, J. L., & Becker, H. J. (1982). Teachers' reported practices of parent involvement: Problems and possibilities. *Elementary School Journal, 83,* 103–113.

Fraser, B. J., Walberg, H. J., Welch, W. W., & Hattie, J. A. (1987). Synthesis of educational productivity research [Special issue]. *International Journal of Educational Research, 11*(2), 145–252.

Gill, B. P., & Schlossman, S. L. (2000). The lost cause of homework reform. *American Journal of Education, 109,* 27–62.

Good, T. L., & Brophy, J. E. (2003). *Looking in classrooms* (9th ed.). Boston: Allyn & Bacon.

Graue, M. E., Weinstein, T., & Walberg, H. J. (1983). School-based home instruction and learning: A quantitative synthesis. *Journal of Educational Research, 76,* 351–360.

Hattie, J. A. (1992). Measuring the effects of schooling. *Australian Journal of Education, 36*(1), 5–13.

Hoover-Dempsey, K. V., Bassler, O. C., & Burow, R. (1995). Parents' reported involvement in students' homework: Strategies and practices. *The Elementary School Journal, 95*(5), 435–450.

Kavale, K. A. (1988). Using meta-analyses to answer the question: What are the important influences on school learning? School *Psychology Review, 17*(4), 644–650.

Kohn, A. (2006a). *The homework myth: Why our kids get too much of a bad thing.* Cambridge, MA: Da Capo Press.

Kohn, A. (2006b). Abusing research: The study of homework and other examples. *Phi Delta Kappan. 88*(1), 9–22.

Kralovec, E., & Buell, J. (2000). *The end of homework: How homework disrupts families, overburdens children, and limits learning.* Boston: Beacon.

Marzano, R. J., & Pickering, D. J. (2007). *Response to Kohn's allegations.* Centennial, CO: Marzano & Associates. Available. . . .

Marzano, R. J., & Pickering, D. J. (in press). Errors and allegations about research on homework. *Phi Delta Kappan.*

Marzano, R. J., Pickering, D. J., & Pollock, J. E. (2001). *Classroom instruction that works: Research-based strategies for increasing student achievement.* Alexandria, VA: ASCD.

National Education Commission on Time and Learning (1994). *Prisoners of time.* Washington, DC: U.S. Department of Education.

Paschal, R. A., Weinstein, T., & Walberg, H. J. (1984). The effects of homework on learning: A quantitative synthesis. *Journal of Educational Research, 78,* 97–104.

Perkins, P. G., & Milgram, R. B. (1996). Parental involvement in homework: A double-edge sword. *International Journal of Adolescence and Youth, 6*(3), 195–203.

Riehl, C. (2006). Feeling better: A comparison of medical research and education research. *Educational Researcher, 35*(5), 24–29.

Van Voorhis, F. (2003). Interactive homework in middle school: Effects on family involvement and science achievement. *Journal of Educational Research, 96,* 323–338.

Walberg, H. J. (1999). Productive teaching. In H. C. Waxman & H. J. Walberg (Eds.), *New directions for teaching practice research* (pp. 75–104). Berkeley, CA: McCutchen.

Wallis, C. (2006). Viewpoint: The myth about homework. *Time, 168*(10), 57.

 **NO**

Homework Takes a Hit!

Homework, an entrenched tradition in education, is taking a hit from the authors of a controversial book that proposes ending the practice. In an Education World e-interview, John Buell, co-author of *The End of Homework: How Homework Disrupts Families, Overburdens Children, and Limits Learning,* states that there is no solid evidence to support the current intensification of homework as a way of improving academic achievement.

During the early part of the 20th century, society banned homework. Too much homework was considered unhealthful; it deprived kids of outdoor play and sunshine.

Then, during the early 1960s, the emphasis on homework intensified as the United States raced to put a man on the moon ahead of the Russians.

The trend continued and today, policy makers emphasize homework as a way of helping students achieve academic success. That trend should end, according to John Buell and Etta Kralovec, co-authors of *The End of Homework: How Homework Disrupts Families, Overburdens Children, and Limits Learning* (Beacon Press, 2000).

Kids have too much homework, the authors say. Homework reflects the trend in the American workplace toward 12-hour workdays. Buell and Kralovec suggest in their book that the current emphasis on homework is unfair to poor children because they don't have the same opportunities at home to complete their assignments. The authors also say piling on homework is a way to prepare children for 12-hour workdays, which pleases business leaders. The real question: Does homework enhance a child's lifelong desire to learn?

In their book, Buell and Kralovec ask policy makers, educators, business leaders, and parents to examine the homework question with open minds. The tendency to pile on the homework is actually a twist on the American work ethic gone terribly astray, they say. Children's homework dominates nearly all aspects of American home life.

People need to achieve balance between work and play, the authors say. Adults need to cut back on the number of hours they spend on work—so do kids. The authors contend that excessive amounts of homework leave kids little time for recreation, civic service, and family relationships.

Kralovec and Buell offer suggestions for putting homework in its rightful place. High school students, they say, should do additional schoolwork *at school*. That way, teachers can give kids the help they need to complete their work. The student school week should never extend beyond 40 hours, which was deemed appropriate for an adult workweek back in 1938, the authors point out. They maintain there is no real evidence that homework contributes to academic success. Kralovec and Buell propose research to look into several questions that they raise about the homework issue. They also point out that there is no valid reason for young children to do homework.

John Buell answered Education World's questions about the issues Buell and Kralovec raised in their book.

Education World: You've appeared on national television programs, made the front pages of major newspapers, and given countless interviews. Does the attention and reaction to your book surprise you?

John Buell: I am pleasantly surprised, but I do think the attention to this book is partially a result of three intersecting and destructive trends in American life: increasing demands on schools, growing time pressures on adults, and the demands homework places on both children and adults. Something has to give in this equation.

EW: People have equated homework with educational success for decades. You say that teachers transfer their responsibilities to parents by sending kids home with lots of homework. How much flak are you getting from educators because of your book?

Buell: I am not suggesting that teachers are looking for ways to dodge their responsibilities. I believe that teachers themselves are under increased pressure today for two reasons. Political and business leaders look to education as the solution for all that ails us, whether it is working class economic stagnation or the problems with teenage pregnancy or AIDS. Because teachers are asked to cover more than they can be reasonably expected to accomplish in the classroom, they often have to send assignments home with the intent of introducing material slighted during the day. I think this is unfair to teachers.

We have received a range of reactions from teachers. Some have argued that their homework assignment practices have been essential to their teaching. Others have been very pleased by the book and have commented that the book should inaugurate a long overdue debate on the topic.

EW: Why did you write this book? What factors compelled you to devote your time to this issue?

Buell: About a decade ago, my co-author and I undertook a study of high school dropouts for the Maine Department of Education. The study involved intensive interviews with teenagers who had recently dropped out of school. We asked these students if there was a moment when it became clear to them that they could no longer continue in school. We found, much to our surprise, that every one of the students interviewed cited problems with homework. Homework was a major reason why they gave up on school. Their reactions couldn't simply be attributed to laziness. They cited stories of younger siblings for whom they were primary care givers and of lack of availability of resources, including even safe, secure, and quiet spaces in which to complete their assignments. In many instances, principals and teachers confirmed the stories they provided.

We certainly don't claim that this was the only factor that led to those students' dropping out, but it was clear that homework played a very negative role in the educational development of those students. We were especially surprised because homework was not a topic that we asked about explicitly nor was it a factor that we had anticipated as we began our research.

It became apparent to us that homework demands represented a disproportionate burden for children of the poor and became a real factor in their decision to leave school.

At that point, we began to reflect further on the topic, including talking with many working- and middle-class parents. We found that even for children from working- and middle-class families–for whom dropout rates are much lower–homework still constituted an immense problem. It became clear to us that homework is a contested issue not merely because its pedagogical rationale is questionable nor even because it constitutes a disproportionate burden for poor and working-class families but also because of very widespread time pressures on a large majority of our population.

EW: Suggesting an end to homework flies in the face of the American Dream, which is based on a strong work ethic. Working hard usually does result in reward. Why isn't that true in the case of homework?

Buell: We are not suggesting that students shouldn't work hard or that there shouldn't be rewards for hard work, but even work has its limits. Hard work is most effective when it is done in the context of appropriate support and assistance for that work. Furthermore, I would at least partially challenge what I take to be the thrust of your question. The quality of American life improved substantially in the post World War II period for many Americans not only because of hard work but also because unions and other progressive forces placed limits on the working day. Without those limits, even work itself would not have been adequately or fairly compensated.

EW: You write that corporate America talks about family-friendly policies, and policy makers promote family values, but in reality, corporate America expects its workers to work long hours of overtime and policy makers expect students to do lots of homework. You offer specific suggestions for making changes. Can you highlight some steps corporations, parents, and schools might take?

Buell: That is a very good question. Even if one believes in homework, the tasks are not likely to be well monitored nor will adequate assistance be provided if parents have little or no time to spend with their kids. From our perspective, the other kinds of support that children need from parents will also be inadequate. There is a progressive minority of businesses that recognize and have designed workplaces that both make the best use of their workers' talents and give workers a voice in such decisions as job-ladder construction and hours of labor.

Those businesses are family friendly businesses. In general, however, workers have had to fight for those rights. I believe the recent Verizon strike is significant in this regard. Ending forced overtime was a major demand of the union. The quality of family life and the future of our children will be far more enhanced by such struggles than by spending long hours at the kitchen table doing homework.

EW: Some teachers say that kids will waste their spare time watching TV and playing video games if teachers don't assign homework. What are your comments about that opinion?

Buell: This is one of the most frequent questions we get. Just because we assign more homework, there is no guarantee that students will do it *or* turn their television sets off *when* they do homework. One problem with just piling on homework is that we assume someone is at home to monitor and assist. I think in practice that students would watch less television if they and their parents had more time for other sorts of activities and interests.

I also find it curious that we worry so much about television watching and so little about the ways that the television all of us watch has become so completely commercialized. Nor do we pay as much attention as we should to the ways commercial television has entered many American classrooms. Some European nations have non-commercial television that does contribute significantly to the educational and cultural development of citizens of all ages.

EW: You write that homework is the great social class discriminator and that it hurts poor, disadvantaged kids and widens the achievement gap between the poor and the privileged. Please explain.

Buell: I believe we need to place the homework debate in a larger context than it usually receives. Homework is by definition work a young student does at home. Nearly one-fifth of American children grow up in poverty. That is discussed in the business or front-page section of our papers—if it is discussed at all—but is too seldom mentioned in connection with homework.

One minimal prerequisite for doing homework is having a quiet and secure space where the worker can concentrate. Poverty in practice means that most poor children lack even that rudimentary asset.

Our ethnographic studies showed that many children from poor backgrounds want to do their homework but simply cannot. Then they go to school and are often condemned for failure to complete assignments that other children in the class completed. That, in turn, often affects how school personnel treat them.

I hasten to add this is not an argument about reducing standards for poor children. We believe there are more effective and equitable strategies to enhance the performance of all children. I'll touch on some of these in my answer to the next question.

EW: I recently wrote an article about the KIPP School in Houston, a public charter middle school. Most of the students come from economically disadvantaged families. The students post significant academic achievement, however. Students there attend school from 7:30 a.m. until 5 p.m., five days a week, five hours on Saturday mornings, and most of the summer—longer than the 40-hour workweek you recommend for high school students. Parents are required to help their children with homework two hours every night. Teachers give out their pager and home phone numbers to help students with homework, and there is a homework hotline. Do you think that this school is hurting these students in the long run?

Buell: I would need to know much more about this school to give you a thoughtful answer, but I have some preliminary observations. Let's accept at face value the claim that scores and achievement are going up. From a research perspective, one does not know how much of the gain is to be attributed to homework per se and how much to the availability of teachers to provide assistance with that homework. Remember that the students and/or students and family alone do most homework in this society.

My larger reservation about this situation from what I know of it is that we are making extraordinary demands of children and parents to jump-start achievement levels for students who probably have long lived in educationally disadvantaged communities. Even if their scores are going up now, I would be inclined to argue all these intense remedial programs wouldn't have been necessary in the first place if public education were adequate and equitable.

Research does show us the unequivocal benefits of well-thought-out professional development programs for teachers, especially for teachers who teach in schools with students from traditions that are culturally and linguistically different from their own. Those conclusions were established once again in the recent Rand Corporation analysis of student test scores from the past ten years. They concluded that those states that had the greatest student achievement gains shared the following school reform policies: smaller class size, greater access to pre-K programs, and more spending on resources for teachers. Professional development programs are especially valuable for teachers in schools with students from cultural and linguistic traditions different from their own.

I would also like to point out that despite homework's long-entrenched role in our culture and the extensive research attention devoted to it, as far as I know, no one has attempted to assess the effects of homework on a lifelong interest in learning. In that context, I would like at least to pose a thought experiment: Let us suppose we could prove that an intensive educational experience in school plus homework outside of school (say ten hours a day and perhaps five on weekends) would yield students who could do calculus by the time they were 12 or 13. Would or should we pursue that strategy and what might we give up for that?

EW: You talk about after-school programs. Is that the answer not only to promoting more mastery of curriculum but also to supervising children after school before parents get home from work?

Buell: Children need good after-school programs, and for kids in high school, such programs may provide homework assistance. I am concerned that in practice, many after-school programs are not staffed by individuals who are qualified to assist with homework. I would still argue that homework, even for high school students, needs reasonable limits. I also believe in the long run that our children will achieve their full potential only when parents have more time to spend with them. This is not an argument for returning women to the household. I believe both parents need to assume parenting responsibilities, and business needs to make this possible.

POSTSCRIPT

Does Homework Serve Useful Purposes?

The enduring image of Abe Lincoln reading and studying by candlelight in the family log cabin makes a compelling case for the virtues and values of homework. Indeed, the acceptability of employing homework as an instructional tool not only has history and tradition on its side, but also has strong parent support for homework. As pointed out in a book by Harris Cooper (*The Battle Over Homework*: *Common Ground for Administrators, Teachers, and Parents*, Corwin Press, 2001), a recent national survey of 803 parents of public school students showed that 64 percent of parents believed that their child was getting "about the right amount of homework," 25 percent felt that there was "too little" homework, and only 10 percent believed that their child was getting "too much homework." Positive parental views regarding homework were also recorded in the annual Phi Delta Kappa/Gallup Poll of 2000, in which 68 percent of the respondents indicated that they believed that classroom work and homework provided the best way to measure student academic achievement, whereas only 26 percent felt that test scores provided the best measure. Further evidence of parental belief in the importance of homework was reported in the 1997 Phi Delta Kappan/Gallup Poll, in which only 13 percent of the respondents reported that they did not spend any time helping their child with homework. That is significantly down from the 34 percent in 1986 who provided no help.

But tradition and positive parental perceptions are not always the best guides to effective educational practices. At one time "caning or paddling" was considered an appropriate and acceptable disciplinary technique (and some may still view it that way). Denying school attendance to unwed expectant mothers until recently was a common and widely supported policy in most school systems. Thus, it is entirely appropriate and important that questions be asked and research conducted regarding the efficacy and other effects of homework on students in spite of the prevailing wisdom that supports it. Addressing the question of how much daily homework should be assigned, the National Education Association and the National Parent Teacher Association (2000) recommend "the ten minute rule," that is, 10 minutes times the grade level of the involved student.

A sidebar issue related to homework that teachers and school administrators are beginning to address is the proliferation of Web sites and Internet resources devoted to "homework assistance." By using that phrase for an Internet search students can be linked to 484,000 Web sites from which they can obtain book reports, essays, answers to math and science questions, and a seemingly infinite array of other information. Certainly this information can be used for legitimate educational purposes but it can also provide students with more than just "assistance." This type of electronic assistance may also eventually reduce the involvement of parents with their children's homework.

Other articles and viewpoints regarding this issue include: Harris Cooper, "Homework for All: In Moderation" (*Educational Leadership*, vol. 58, no. 7, April 2001); U.S. Department of Education, *Homework Tips for Parents* (May 2003); Nebraska State Education Association, *Homework; A Concern for the Whole Family* (publication date unknown); Doug Gavel, "Homework Wars Provoke Debate" (*Harvard Gazette*, September 2000); Tom Loveless, *Do Students Have Too Much Homework* (Brookings Institution Press, 2003); Brian P. Gill and Steven L. Schlossman, "Too Much Homework Isn't the Problem" (*Pittsburgh Post Gazette*, December 21, 2003); David Skinner, "The Homework Delusion" (*The Public Interest*, 2004); Alfie Kohn, "The Truth About Homework" (*Education Week*, September 6, 2006).

ISSUE 15

Does Participation in Sports Provide Positive Benefits to Youth?

YES: Jordan D. Metzl and Carol Shookhoff, from "The Benefits of Youth Sports," *The Young Athlete: A Sports Doctor's Complete Guide for Parents,* eNotAlone (2002)

NO: Josephson Institute of Ethics, from "What Are Your Children Learning? The Impact of High School Sports on the Values and Ethics of High School Athletes," *Survey of High School Athletes* (February 2007)

ISSUE SUMMARY

YES: Jordan D. Metzl, medical director of the Sport Medicine Institute for Young Athletes, and Carol Shookhoff, an educational writer, propose that youth sports "offer benefits and lessons that carry over into all aspects of life."

NO: The Josephson Institute of Ethics presents results from a national survey of over 5000 high school athletes including a finding that athletes "cheat in school at a higher rate than their non-sport classmates."

High school programs seemingly exist in the category of "apple pie, flag, and motherhood" with respect to their enthusiastic acceptance by the general public. The notion of school sponsorship of athletic programs is not new; indeed, football games between schools can be traced back to the late 1800s. A major boost for high school sports programs occurred in 1918 with the NEA's publication of the "Seven Cardinal Principles of Secondary Education," which included "health" and "worthy use of leisure time." Even though large, comprehensive high schools generally offer a wide range of co/extra-curricular activities, in most schools it is the athletic program that has the greatest number of student participants and receives the greatest level of publicity and public support. In many states high school sports programs culminate in state championships and national exposure for schools and student athletes. The following data from the National Federation of State High

School Associations (September 2006) provide evidence of the popularity of high school sports:

> Based on figures from the 50 state high school athletic/activity associations, plus the District of Columbia, that are members of the NFHS, participation for the 2005-06 school year rose by 141,195 students to 7,159,904, according to the 2005-06 High School Athletics Participation Survey conducted by the NFHS. Through the survey, it was also determined that 53.5 percent of students enrolled in high schools participate in athletics.
>
> In addition to the overall numbers, the girls participation total of 2,953,355 set an all-time record. The boys total also increased, reaching 4,206,549, the highest participation in the past 28 years. This year's boys participation figure is second only to the record 4,367,442 in 1977-78.
>
> Basketball remained the most popular sport for girls with 452,929 participants, followed by outdoor track and field (439,200), volleyball (390,034), fast pitch softball (369,094), soccer (321,555), cross country (175,954), tennis (173,753), swimming and diving (147,413), competitive spirit squads (98,570) and golf (64,195).
>
> In boys sports, 11-player football once again topped the list with 1,071,775 participants, followed by basketball (546,335), outdoor track and field (533,985), baseball (470,671), soccer (358,935), wrestling (251,534), cross country (208,303), golf (161,284), tennis (153,006) and swimming and diving (107,468).
>
> Texas held its title as having the most sports participants with 742,341, followed by California (678,019), New York (350,349), Illinois (323,703), Michigan (321,250), Ohio (316,529), Pennsylvania (267,147), New Jersey (243,260), Florida (214,023) and Minnesota (213,476).

It should be noted that the growth of girls participation is directly attributable to the 1972 Title IX legislation that mandated gender equity in high school and university sports programs. The opportunity for participation afforded to young women by that legislation is extremely important because the admission criteria of colleges and universities rate such participation as a key factor in acceptance and the awarding of scholarships.

Athletic competition, whether as a participant or a fan, is undeniably a part of American culture. Yet not everyone is convinced that competition is a good thing. Alfie Kohn, in "The Case Against Competition" (*Working Mother*, September 1987), wrote:

> In a competitive culture, a child is told that it isn't enough to be good—he must triumph over others. Success comes to be defined as victory, even though these are really two very different things. . . . The more he competes, the more he needs to compete to feel good about himself.

In their article, Metzl and Shookhoff stress the positive features of participation in sports, whereas the data from the Josephson Institute provide some support for the position expressed above by Kohn.

YES

Jordan D. Metzl and
Carol Shookhoff

The Benefits of Youth Sports

Mens Sana in Corpore Sano (A Sound Mind in a Sound Body)

Sports are for fun, but they also offer benefits and lessons that carry over into all aspects of life.

When kids are asked why they play sports, here's what they say:

- To have fun
- To improve their skills
- To learn new skills
- To be with their friends
- To make new friends
- To succeed or win
- To become physically fit

Kids usually get the benefits they seek from sports and more. Kids need attention and respect (in that order), but they have few ways to get them. What is unique about sports is that they offer kids an arena where they can earn attention and respect by exerting their natural abilities. Kids are good at sports because sports are essentially about speed, strength, coordination, vision, creativity, and responsiveness—the necessary physical attributes are the attributes of youth.

Given that athletics involves all aspects of the human being, it is not surprising that participants benefit in all of the areas they mention. According to researchers at the Institute for the Study of Youth Sports at Michigan State University, kids who participate in organized sports do better in school, have better interpersonal skills, are more team oriented, and are generally healthier.

Participation in sports provides opportunities for leadership and socialization, as well as the development of skills for handling success and failure.

Moreover, when playing games, children learn how rules work. They see how groups need rules to keep order, that the individual must accept the rules for the good of the group, that rules entail a consideration of the rights of others. They also learn about competition, but within a restricted and safe system where the consequences of losing are minimized.

Benefits for girls have been of particular interest to researchers. The President's Council on Physical Fitness and Sports reports many developmental benefits of participating in youth sports for girls, including increased self-esteem and self-confidence, healthier body image, significant experiences of competency and success, as well as reduced risk of chronic disease. Furthermore, female athletes "do better academically and have lower school dropout rates than their nonathletic counterparts."

The Women's Sports Foundation lists many ways that sports specifically benefit female athletes. These include their being less likely to become pregnant as teenagers, less likely to begin smoking, more likely to quit smoking, more likely to do well in science, and more likely to graduate from high school and college than female nonathletes. Female athletes also take greater pride in their physical and social selves than their sedentary peers; they are more active physically as they age; they suffer less depression. There is also some evidence that recreational physical activity decreases a woman's chances of developing breast cancer and helps prevent osteoporosis.

I am convinced that sports offer a unique arena in which children can successfully exert their talents. The arena is unique for two reasons. First, sports engage the child as a complete human being: all facets—not just physical, but also social, cognitive, and psychological—are engaged harmoniously in striving toward peak fulfillment. Second, sports involve youths working in an ongoing community composed of their peers as well as their peers' families. Sports, that is, offer children an exhilarating, satisfying, rewarding way to participate in a larger world not generally accessible to nonathletes.

Physical Benefits

- **Fitness.** Kids who play sports develop general physical fitness in a way that's fun, and they establish lifelong habits for good health. This is particularly important at a time when obesity in the United States has reached epidemic proportions: the incidence of obesity has increased by more than 50 percent among America's children and teens since 1976 and continues to grow at a staggering rate!
- **Stress relief.** Sports allow kids to clear their minds of academic and social pressures, to literally run off the tension that's accumulated in their muscles. In the words of one patient, "If you play really hard, you feel better because playing takes your mind off things that bother you, and afterwards you can concentrate better." Most doctors recognize the positive mental effect of physical exertion, even though we're not sure exactly why this is so. I know that my ability to study in college and medical school was greatly enhanced when I ran during the day, and I'm not the only athlete to find this true. Many athletes get better grades in-season (theories posit the discipline and the need to manage time, along with an increased ability to concentrate). During exams, Duke University opens its gyms twenty-four hours a day to provide stress relief for its students.
- **Mastery.** Sports give kids a satisfying, enjoyable way to develop their own talents: through personal effort they get good at something

they're interested in. Doing something well makes them feel good about themselves, but equally important, it teaches them about the process of how to improve and work more effectively. Learning a skill—to dribble left-handed, say, or to execute an effective second serve—entails a recognition that practice is essential and that improvement is incremental. The process of repetition teaches the athlete how to master a move and also how to experiment with different approaches to improve a skill. The feedback in sports is usually immediate and visible—does the ball go into the basket?—so that the athlete can change or repeat what she's doing and figure out how to get better. Not only that, the whole process of seeing practice lead to improvement gives kids a feeling of control, a feeling all too rare in their lives.

- **Healthy habits.** Because sports increase an awareness of one's body and how it responds to different stimuli and circumstances, sports help prevent drug and alcohol abuse. Most athletes value what their bodies can do and want to maintain those abilities. Being an athlete also gives kids an acceptable reason for telling their friends no to drugs, booze, and other high-risk, unhealthy behaviors. (Of course, not all athletes avoid drugs and alcohol.)

Personal Benefits

- **Valuing preparation.** Sports help kids learn to distinguish between effort and ability. Sports increase self-discipline and the awareness of the value of preparation because kids can see the difference in their performance.

    Competitive athletes learn the importance of effort, being prepared (mentally and physically), and enlightened risk-taking. They see that raw physical talent is not always sufficient to win the game, but that preparation is essential. This includes mental preparation (staying focused) and physical fitness as well as practicing the plays with their teammates in team sports. They learn to evaluate risk versus reward. Another invaluable lesson is discovering that mistakes are part of learning; they signal that a particular approach is unsuccessful and you must try another. Kids also learn to deal productively with criticism as part of improvement and preparation.

- **Resilience.** Sports provide an unparalleled model for dealing with disappointment and misfortune. Young athletes learn to handle adversity, whether it's picking themselves up after losing a big game or not getting as many minutes as they wanted. They find ways to deal with losing and go on, because there's another big game next week or next year. They figure out what to do to get what they want for themselves. They put in extra time on fitness or work on specific weaknesses in their game (long-ball trapping, hitting to the opposite field, looking the ball into their hands).

    Athletes also learn to deal with the physical and psychological effects of injury. I broke my jaw playing soccer and missed most of the season my junior year in high school. I went through the classic stages of grief, from "This can't be true" to ultimate acceptance. Two months of sitting out, waiting to heal, and dealing with physical and emotional pain was devastating. There were times early on when I sat in my bed whimpering from pain. But as time went on and my jaw began to heal, I somehow began to realize what almost all athletes in pain realize: the only person who is going to help you is yourself. You find the limits of what you can ask of yourself and know that you will deliver. This learning to get the best out of yourself carries over into all aspects of life. People can find their internal drive through training and hard work, but adversity really brings it out. In my case, I came back with stronger resolve. In my senior year I became an all-district soccer player and was propelled toward a college soccer career.

- **Attitude control.** Older teens learn that a confident attitude improves their performance, and that they have some control over their attitude. They learn to disregard comparative stats in preparing for an opponent and instead to adopt "attitude enhancers" such as visualization exercises, team or individual rituals, singing specific songs together, or having dinner as a team the night before the game. Some might call these superstitions, others, self-fulfilling prophecies, but they work.

- **Leadership opportunities.** Team sports offer kids a rare opportunity to serve as leaders. Kids can be in a position to assess the strengths and weaknesses of their various teammates and help to exploit their strengths and compensate for their weaknesses. They can minimize conflicts among players. They can reinforce values—such as fair play, teamsmanship, hard work, mental preparation—by speaking up when appropriate and setting a good example. They can also take the initiative in arranging for team dress on game days (football players wear their jerseys to class, female basketball players wear their warm-up pants), organizing team dinners or team movie nights, and inviting teachers and administrators to their games.

- **Identity and balance.** Being part of a group is inordinately important to kids, and sports make kids feel like they belong, whether it's to the group of athletes in general or their team in particular. Sports also contribute to a teenager's sense of a stable identity with particular values. "I'm a football player" is a very different statement than "I play football." People are complicated, however; no individual is just one thing. It's better to encourage children—and adults—not to assume a single identity to the exclusion of all else.

- **Time management.** Young athletes learn to manage their time productively. They know they have to get their homework done, so they learn not to waste time (some of them even quit watching television and hanging out at the mall). They plan ahead, so that big school projects don't catch them by surprise. They even figure out they have to eat well and get a good night's sleep. Countless athletes, in school and the workplace, say that being an athlete taught them discipline that is invaluable in their lives on and off the field.

- **Long-term thinking.** Athletes learn the fundamental lesson of sacrificing immediate gratification for long-term gain. This is the basis for personal success as well as for civilization in general, and no lesson can be more valuable.

Social Benefits

Sports are a social activity. Team sports are obviously done with other people, but even individual sports are often done as a team (tennis, golf, track). All sports, however, are intended to be performed in front of others, and the social ramifications are many. Here are some of them.

- **Relationships with other kids.** Athletes develop relationships with their teammates. For boys, sports are a primary, and unfortunately sometimes the sole, way of socializing with others. In many schools and communities, nonathletic males find it difficult to develop a social network at all. For girls, who according to the feminist theorist Carol Gilligan tend to define themselves through their relationships rather than their achievements, sports offer yet another way to make friends and create an alternate peer group. According to Mike Nerney, a consultant in substance abuse prevention and education, multiple peer groups are always a good idea for teens, who have an intense need for inclusion and belonging, but who can also be volatile, cruel to each other, and foment destructive behavior as a group. Having a refuge when relations go wrong with one group can alleviate a great deal of stress and offer an alternative for kids who feel uncomfortable or frightened by peers who engage in high-risk activities.

- **Teamwork.** On a team, kids learn about cooperation, camaraderie, give-and-take. They learn that while their natural position might be wide receiver, the team needs a cornerback, so they sacrifice their personal desires and play defense. They learn that you don't have to like someone in order to work together toward a common goal. They also discover that you can work for people you don't respect and still be productive, improve your skills, and have fun. A team is a natural environment in which to learn responsibility to others: you can't stay out carousing the night before a game; sometimes you need to pass up a party in order to show up and play well.

    Kids learn these lessons from their teammates and, most important, a coach who encourages the good of the team over the needs of an individual player. This attitude is sometimes rare in today's sports climate, where what's glorified is to "be the man." I think the earlier the message is instilled about the good of the larger whole, the better for kids in the long run.

- **Diversity.** Organized sports sponsored by clubs or youth leagues not affiliated with schools offer players an opportunity to meet a variety of kids from different backgrounds. Students from public, private, and parochial schools come together in a common enterprise, crossing socioeconomic and ethnic lines, so that over time all players broaden their sense of how other people live. The genuinely multicultural environment is of tremendous importance in our polarized society. Kids play on the same team, wear the same uniform, share the same objectives and experiences. Sports are a great equalizer: rich or poor, black, brown, or white, are irrelevant. What counts is talent and heart.

- **Relationships with adults.** When coaches, parents, and kids see each other at practice and games week after week, year after year, the adults learn to admire and praise the kids' prowess and progress, even when kids are as young as third graders. This kind of attention helps youngsters learn to balance their own evaluation of their improving skills with the appraisal of others who are not blood relatives; they also begin the lifelong process of figuring out whom to listen to when they hear conflicting advice or assessments. In addition, for young athletes of all ages, attention from interested adults is not only flattering but also helps them overcome shyness and develop poise when talking to relative strangers in social situations. The ability to feel comfortable in a variety of social circumstances will be progressively more valuable in a world of multiple cultures and decreasing numbers of supportive communities.

  Sports give kids an opportunity to spend ongoing periods of time with an adult in a shared endeavor. Indeed, kids may spend more time with their coach than with any other adult in their lives, especially if they're on a school team or a club team that practices two or more times a week. Ideally this coach cares about them as whole beings rather than particular talents who can run for touchdowns or block opponents' shots. To thrive, kids need to be with adults who want them to do well in a variety of endeavors, who notice their improvements and hard work, who manifest sound values, and who don't pay attention to them solely because of their contributions to the win column.

  The coach-player relationship can be very strong, and even parentlike. Coaches of young athletes take on a tremendous responsibility to set a good example and treat their players respectfully. Thankfully, most coaches take this responsibility very seriously.

  Sometimes, the coach-player relationship can even be life-saving. A female coach of a varsity boys' team reported that one of her players came to her saying, "I need to talk to you. I found blood in my urine."

  "Let me ask you something," the coach replied. "Have you been having unprotected sex?"

  "No, of course not. I can't believe you asked me that," he said. "Well, I need to know what direction to take you in. No matter what happened, you need to see a doctor."

  The coach recalled, "This boy was very good looking and very popular. I knew what was going on. The doctor found he had picked up a venereal disease which could have made him infertile. The boy called me from the doctor's office to say thank you."

- **Participating in a community.** Sports foster a sense of community: they give both participants and spectators the experience of belonging to something larger than themselves, the need for which seems to be hard-wired into the human brain. This is why kids love playing for their schools, why high school football games in small cities can draw tens of thousands of spectators week after week, and why adults identify with their college teams years after they have graduated. Playing for an institution or a community gives kids a chance to feel that they are making a genuine contribution to a larger group.

Highs and Lows

Sports can actually change the physiology of athletes and fans. Physical exertion can raise the level of pheronemes and endorphins, brain chemicals that cause exhilaration. Exercise can also elevate the serum testosterone level, which makes the heart beat faster. Spectators can feel depressed when their team loses and elated when their team wins. They, too, undergo physiological changes when watching their team: fans of the winning team experience an increase in testosterone, whereas supporters of the losers undergo a decrease in testosterone.

When playing for school or club teams, young athletes are afforded the opportunity to see how grownups and children treat one another and how this treatment has long-term consequences. They can see which adults care about kids, are willing to do their fair share and more, and take a stand for what they believe in. They see which parents are cooperative—pitching in to help with snacks, driving their kids' teammates to games, serving as team treasurer, volunteering to line the fields on cold, rainy mornings. They hear parents screaming at the officials and recognize which ones know the rules and which don't. They see who supports their own children and others, who bullies their children or the officials. They see parents who teach their children to assume they are always right, are better than the other players, and that someone else, anyone else, is always at fault if things go wrong. They also see how the kids in these families emulate or reject their parents' behavior. They think about how they will treat their own children and how they will behave with their friends as members of groups.

One hockey father says, "Part of the benefit of sports is that children observe its complex social dynamic among coaches, parents, players, and officials. There's a wide range of ethics, such as the attitude toward authority. Do you try to abide by the spirit of the rules, get away with what you can, accept what an official says, or do you argue and yell at him, or complain about it? Another major element they encounter is the difference between teammates who are good at communicating and sharing versus those who are out to get what they can for themselves. This is a dichotomy adults face throughout life. Kids involved in sports have to consciously or subconsciously figure out where they fit into those various spectrums."

Participating for years on the same team not only improves the play, because the players learn each other's strengths and weaknesses and where they'll be on the field or court, but it gives kids a wider view of the world and the people in it.

Similarities of Sports and the Arts

Are the benefits of sports unique? Many have noted that the arts produce many of the same benefits as sports, for both participant and spectator.

Sports entail all elements of human life—physical, emotional, cognitive, social—but in a simplified, orderly form. Sports boil life down to competition governed by agreed-upon rules. The opponents are known, the goals clear and quantifiable. Athletes practice the skills necessary to excel and gain a sense of control and mastery. Sports are a public performance, which fosters a sense of community among people—participants as well as spectators—who would otherwise be strangers. At their best, they produce a sense of exhilaration.

The arts are the other significant leisure activity that distills life down to simpler forms. The arts simplify life by selecting and arranging certain elements to create a unified, expressive whole. They too are intended for an audience. The performing arts, dance in particular, have much in common with sports: they take place outside of everyday life, the activities are physical and demand practice, and performance can produce exhilaration and a sense of community.

What makes sports different from the arts is that they demand a spontaneous response to surprise. A dance is choreographed; the dancers know what they are to do at every moment. A game has set plays, but the athletes must respond to what their opponents do, or to the unexpected bounce of the ball. The denouement of the game is uncertain, often until its final seconds. This combination of total human exertion with an environment that balances control, spontaneity, and uncertainty leads to the unique excitement and satisfaction of sports, for both athletes and spectators.

 **NO**

What Are Your Children Learning?
The Impact of High School Sports
on the Values and Ethics of
High School Athletes

Report Reveals High School Sports can Dramatically Affect Students' Ethics On and Off the Field

National Survey Reveals Good and Bad News for Parents and School Administrators

Are Coaches Teaching Our Young Athletes the Right Way to Play?

According to a report released this week by the Josephson Institute of Ethics, the values of young athletes are dramatically impacted by their sports experience.

The report, "What Are Your Children Learning? The Impact of High School Sports on the Values and Ethics of High School Athletes," summarizes the responses of 5,275 high school athletes to a written survey administered in 2005 and 2006.

Michael Josephson, president of the nonprofit Josephson Institute and founder of the national program, CHARACTER COUNTS!, said the report contains both good and bad news for parents and school administrators. "The good news is that the majority of high school athletes trust and admire their coaches and are learning positive life skills and good values from them. They are less cynical about ethical issues and less likely to steal than their classmates.

"The bad news," Josephson added, "is that many coaches—particularly in the high profile sports of boys' basketball, baseball and football—are teaching kids how to cheat and cut corners. In addition, far too many boys and girls engage in other dishonest, deceptive and dangerous practices without regard for the rules or traditional notions of fair play and sportsmanship."

Among the most prominent findings:

- **Major Gender Differences.** There are dramatic differences in the attitudes and behavior of male and female athletes. On virtually every question girl athletes expressed a deeper commitment to honesty and fair play and were much less likely to endorse cheating or other questionable practices in the pursuit of victory.

- **Some Sports Are Worse than Others.** Boys engaged in baseball, football and basketball are considerably more likely to cheat on the field and in school and to engage in conduct involving deliberate injury, intimidation and conscious rule-breaking than boys involved in other sports. Generally, boys participating in swimming, track, cross country, gymnastics and tennis were markedly less likely to cheat or to engage in bad sportsmanship than their male counterparts in other sports. Girls involved in basketball and softball were more likely to engage in illegal or unsportsmanlike conduct than girls involved in other sports.
- **Theft.** Athletes are less likely than non-sports students to engage in theft—still, more than one in four male athletes (27%) admitted stealing from a store in the past 12 months compared with 32% of boys not involved in sports. The highest rate of theft reported was from male gymnasts (36%), football players (33%) and male basketball players (32%). One in five girl athletes (20%) engaged in theft compared to 23% for all high school girls.
- **Cheating in School.** High school students involved in sports cheat in school at a higher rate than their non-sport classmates. Nearly two-thirds (65%) of the boys and girls participating in sports cheated on an exam in the past year in comparison to 60% of the total high school population (based on a 2006 Josephson Institute survey of 35,000 students). Whether this enhanced propensity to cheat is due to values that put winning over honesty, or a reflection of pressures to stay eligible, or simply difficulties managing their time given the high demands of sports, the fact remains that for most kids, sports promotes rather than discourages cheating.
  - Varsity athletes of both genders cheat at a higher rate than non varsity athletes (67% to 63%).
  - The highest cheating rates were for those involved in football (72%), girls' softball (72%), girls' basketball (71%), cheerleading (71%), hockey (70%), and baseball (69%). Female cross country athletes (39%), male cross country (53%), male swimmers (53%) and female swimmers (57%) were the least likely to cheat in school.
- **Use of Performance Enhancing Drugs.** Given the common view that steroids and other performance enhancing drugs (PEDs) are unhealthy as well as illegal, a disturbing number of male athletes (6.4%) admit to having used them in the past year (2% of females admitted using PEDs).
- **Athletes Think Highly of Coaches.** The vast majority of high school athletes say their coaches "consistently set a good example of ethics and character" (90%) and that their current coach "wants them to do the ethically right thing, no matter what the cost" (91%).
- **Many Coaches Teach Negative Lessons.** Despite the athletes' positive views of the character and intentions of their coaches, athletes revealed attitudes and conduct suggesting that many coaches are teaching negative lessons about cheating and bad sportsmanship.
  - **Illegal holding**—43% of the boys and 22% of girls think it is proper for a coach to teach basketball players how to illegally hold and

push in ways that are difficult to detect (51% of football, 49% of baseball and 47% of boys basketball players agreed).

- **Using the other team's playbook**—Two-fifths (41%) of the boys and one-fourth of the girls (25%) saw nothing wrong with using a stolen playbook sent by an anonymous supporter before a big game. Baseball (48%) and football (48%) players were the most likely to approve of the use of the other team's playbook.
- **Faking an injury**—More than one in three (37%) of the boys and one in five (20%) of girls think it is proper for a coach to instruct a player in football to fake an injury in order to get a needed time-out (44% of baseball and 43% of football players endorsed this strategy).
- **Illegally altering hockey stick**—23% of boys (28% in hockey) and 11% of girls said it was a proper part of the game for a hockey player to illegally alter a hockey stick.
- **Illegal start**—More than one-fourth (28%) of boys and 14% of girls approved of a soccer goalie deliberately violating the rules by moving forward three steps past the line on a penalty kick. The baseball and soccer players were much more likely to endorse this practice— 37% of baseball players, 38% of boy soccer players and 18% of girl soccer players.
- **Wrong player shooting free throws**—One in four (25%) of the boys and just 13% of girls thought it is proper to try to trick a basketball referee by sending the wrong person to the line to shoot a free throw.
- **Altering the field of play—building up the foul line**—one-quarter of the males (26%) (including 36% of the baseball players and 32% of the boy volleyball players) said it was proper for a baseball coach to instruct a groundskeeper to build up the third base foul line to help keep bunts fair.
- **Soaking the field to slow down the other team**—More than one-fourth (27%) of the boys (including 36% of the baseball players and 31% of the football players) and 13% of the girls thought it was a proper gamesmanship strategy for a football coach to instruct a groundskeeper to soak the field to slow down the opposing team.
- **Throwing at a batter**—
  - 25% of the boys (48% of baseball players) and 9% of the girls (10% of girl softball players) agreed it was a proper part of the game for a baseball coach to order his pitcher to throw at an opposing hitter in retaliation.
  - 30% of the boys (40% of baseball players) and 16% of the girls (20% of softball players) said it was acceptable for a softball pitcher to deliberately throw at a batter who homered the last time up.
- **Mistake in score**—More than two in five (41%) of boys and less than one-quarter (23%) of girls think it is acceptable for a volleyball coach to say nothing when an official makes a mistake in the score that favors his team. Football and baseball players were considerably more likely to endorse this practice (50% and 49% respectively).
- **Trash talk**—42% of boys (54% in football and 49% in boys basketball) and 18% of the girls approve of trash talk consisting of demeaning the defender's skill after every score.

- **Showboating**—43% of boys (48% of football players) and 33% of girls said it was acceptable for a player to do an elaborate showboat dance in front of the opponent's bench after scoring.
- **Motivation through insults**—More than one-third of the boys (37%) but only 13% of the girls said it was okay for a coach to use profanity and personal insults to motivate players.
- **Swearing at official to motivate team**—34% of the boys (40% in baseball and 39% in football) and 12% of girls approved of a high school coach trying to pump up his team by swearing at the officials to get himself thrown out of a game.
- **Holding back an athlete in school**—29% of the boys (34% in football) and 16% of girls think it is acceptable for a coach to urge parents to have an academically successful athlete repeat a grade in middle school so that the athlete will be older and bigger for his high school sports career.
- **Kids Would Rather Play Than Win.** The overwhelming majority of high school athletes value winning but would much rather play for a losing team than sit on the bench for a winning team and believe winning is not essential for the enjoyment of the sport.
- **Hazing Widespread.** Nearly one-third of the boys (30%) and 21% of the girls said that degrading hazing or initiation rituals are common at their school.

Personal Behavior off the Field

- **Theft.** Athletes are less likely than non-sports students to engage in theft—still, more than one in four boys (27%) and one in five girls (20%) engaged in high school athletics admitted stealing from a store in the past 12 months.
  - Theft by male athletes was 27% compared to 32% from the complete high school sample; 20% of female athletes cheated compared to 23% of all high school girls.
  - The highest rate of theft reported was from male gymnasts (36%), football players (33%) and male basketball players (32%).
- **Cheating in School.** High school students involved in sports cheat in school at a higher rate than their non-sport classmates.
  - Nearly two-thirds (65%) of the boys and girls participating in sports cheated on an exam in the past year in comparison to 60% of the total high school population (based on a 2006 Josephson Institute survey of 35,000 students).
  - Varsity athletes of both genders cheat at a higher rate than non varsity athletes (67% to 63%).
  - Whether this enhanced propensity to cheat is due to values that put winning over honesty or a reflection of pressures to stay eligible or simply manage their time given the high demands of sports, the fact remains that for most kids, sports promotes rather than discourages cheating.
  - The cheating rate for those involved in football (72%), girls' softball (72%), girls' basketball (71%), cheerleading (71%), hockey (70%), and baseball (69%) was the highest.

- Female cross country athletes (39%), male cross country (53%), male swimmers (53%) and female swimmers (57%) were the least likely to cheat in school.
- **Use of Performance Enhancing Drugs.** Given the common view that steroids and other performance enhancing drugs (PEDs) are unhealthy as well as illegal a disturbing number of male athletes (6.4%) admit to having used them in the past year (2% of females admitted using PEDs).
  - **Use by sport.** Male gymnasts (13.3%) and baseball players (9.4%) admitted use of PEDs. Among the females, softball players were more likely to use PEDs than their counterparts in other sports (3% vs. 2%).
  - **Lowest use.** On the other hand, athletes in our survey from boys' volleyball and track and girls' gymnastics, cross country, and swimming reported no use of PEDs.
- **Use of Alcohol.** Despite strict rules in high school forbidding the use of alcohol, about half of athletes of both genders (49%) admitted to drinking alcohol in the past year. This is the same rate reported for non-athletes in the larger study of 35,000 students.

POSTSCRIPT

Does Participation in Sports Provide Positive Benefits to Youth?

In this era of standards and accountability it is understandable that most of the offerings within the high school curriculum are subject to scrutiny and even criticism. Over the past two decades we have seen academic areas comprising much of the core curriculum be challenged over standards, emphases, and efficacy. Academic "wars" have broken out over the content and teaching approaches in reading, mathematics, history, science, and approaches to learning English. In many cases, curricula and instructional materials have been modified or replaced. But there is one major area of high school offerings that has escaped such attention and evaluation. The high school athletic program continues to receive general acceptance and support. Advocates such as the National Federation of State High School Associations (NFHS) believe that interscholastic sports "promote citizen-ship and sportsmanship. They instill a sense of pride in [the school and] community, teach lifelong lessons of teamwork and self discipline and facilitate the physical and emotional development of our nation's youth" (2000). NFHS also suggests that high school sports can contribute to students' success in life; a survey of 75 Fortune 500 companies indicated that 95 percent of the corporate executives had participated in sports during high school.

There are others, albeit a minority, who caution against the uncritical acceptance of the value of sports programs. Jay Coakley, a former professor at the University of Colorado and author of the book *Sport in Society: Issues and Controversies* (McGraw-Hill, 1997), questions the validity of studies that show that involvement in sports programs contributes to participants outperforming nonparticipants on academic measures. He contends that participants are different to begin with and that their participation in sports is not the cause of their academic success, but rather that sports programs "attract students who already have characteristics associated with academic and social success in high school."

The Citizenship Through Sports Alliance, a coalition of professional and amateur sports organizations, convened an expert panel to evaluate youth sports programs throughout the nation. The expert panel was composed of authors, attorneys, researchers, youth sports organization leaders, youth coaches, and parents. Their common goal was to articulate where youth sports is succeeding and where it is failing. Although commending the many people who contribute time and support to make youth sports happen, the panel also presented the following critique:

> The panel is greatly concerned that, on the whole, youth sports has:
>
> - Lost its child-centered focus, meaning less emphasis on the child's experience and more emphasis on adult-centered motives, such as winning.
> - Suffered from the actions of over-invested sports parents, who maintain unrealistic expectations and fail to behave in a way that promotes the development of their own child and others.
> - Failed to provide sufficient background checks, training and evaluations for coaches, who are so instrumental in the youth sports experience.
> - Focused on early sports specialization, leading to burnout, overuse injuries and a hyper-competitive atmosphere focused on travel team participation at an ever-younger age.
> - Lost the voice of the child, who is participating in sports for his or her own goals, which experts say include fun, friends, fitness and skill development. The panel hopes that by increasing awareness of these challenges, it can stimulate dialogue about ways to improve youth sports, enabling more young people to benefit from all that youth sports has to offer. (2005)

In addition to the references noted above, additional commentary includes, John Roberts, *Why School Sports Are Worth Saving* (University of Toronto Colloquium, January 2000); Colin Dunlap, *"High School Sports"* (*Pittsburgh Gazette*, January 26, 2007); and Elizabeth Conant, *The Value of Sports: Does Venus Have Biceps?* (Spring 2005).

ISSUE 16

Will Increased Use of Computer Technology and Games Be Beneficial to Students?

YES: David Williamson Shaffer, Kurt R. Squire, Richard Halverson, and James P. Gee, from "Video Games and the Future of Learning," *Phi Delta Kappan* (October 2005)

NO: Lowell W. Monke, from "The Overdominance of Computers," *Educational Leadership* (December 2005/January 2006)

ISSUE SUMMARY

YES: Associate professor David W. Shaffer, assistant professors Kurt R. Squire and Richard Halverson, and professor James P. Gee of the school of education at the University of Wisconsin, Madison, suggest that schools need to catch up with other sectors of society in using technology and video games as tools for improvement.

NO: Lowell W. Monke, assistant professor of education at Wittenberg University, states "nearly everything children do today involves technologies that distance them from direct contact with the living world."

James Burke and Robert Ornstein, in *The Axe-Maker's Gift* (1995), describe the historical development of technology (from the axe to the computer) and detail both the benefits and the down-side that have accrued to humankind due to these "advancements." In describing the "double-edged" nature of technology, Burke and Ornstein suggest that technology has historically tended to concentrate power in the hands of those who master its use(s), but that modern computer technology has the potential to end this reductionism and help empower greater numbers of people.

Given the wide acceptance of the notion that we are in the midst of the "Information Age," it is understandable that schools are seen as being pivotal to whether or not our children will be beneficiaries or victims of this new age. The number of computers in our schools has grown dramatically. In 1994, 35 percent of schools and 3 percent of classrooms had Internet access; by 1999 those proportions were 95 percent and 63 percent, respectively.

Former President Clinton's goal of a computer in every classroom is rapidly being realized.

Given the momentum and rhetoric pushing for increased use of computer technology in our schools, there is considerable pressure on teachers and school administrators to increase such use. This pressure emanates from the belief that not only do all students need to be computer literate, but that the application of technology can improve all areas of schooling and learning. In spite of what seems to be an inevitable movement toward increased use of computers in schools, there are those who urge a more cautious if not resistive stance.

Social critic and communications professor Neil Postman in a 1990 speech delivered to the German Informatics Society made the following statement:

> I believe that you will have to concede that what ails us, what causes us the most misery and pain . . . has nothing to do with the sort of information made accessible by computers. The computer and its information cannot answer any of the fundamental questions we need to address to make our lives more meaningful and humane. . . . The computer is, in a sense, a magnificent toy that distracts us from facing what we most needed to confront. . . . Does one blame the computer for this? Of course not. It is, after all, only a machine. But it is presented to us, with trumpets blaring . . . as a technological messiah.

Whether or not technology is having much impact on classroom instruction is disputed by Larry Cuban, professor of education at Stanford University, who makes the point that the proliferation of computer equipment in the schools is not being matched with a corresponding increase in effective use. Cuban reports that only two teachers out of ten in this country are serious users of computers in their classrooms (several times a week), while four to five out of ten never use the machines at all (*Education Week,* August 4, 1999).

Henry Becker, professor of education at the University of California, Irvine in responding to Cuban, draws from a 1998 national survey of some 4000 teachers on Teaching, Learning, and Computing (TLC) and states the following:

> Thus, in a certain sense Cuban is correct—computers have not transformed the teaching practices of a majority of teachers, particularly teachers of secondary academic subjects. However, under the right conditions . . . where teachers' personal philosophies support a student-centered, constructivist pedagogy that incorporates collaborative projects defined partly by student interest—computers are clearly becoming a valuable and well-functioning instructional tool. (*Education Policy Analysis Archives,* vol. 8, no. 51, November 15, 2000)

The two selections that follow exemplify the widely divergent beliefs and values that accompany this controversy. In their article, Shaffer, Squire, Halverson, and Gee express their belief that increased use of technology and especially digital games holds much promise for enhancing student learning. Monke argues that the developmental needs of children may not be well served by an overemphasis on technology.

295

YES ⬋ David Williamson Shaffer, Kurt R. Squire, Richard Halverson, and James P. Gee

Video Games and the Future of Learning

Computers are changing our world: how we work, how we shop, how we entertain ourselves, how we communicate, how we engage in politics, how we care for our health. The list goes on and on. But will computers change the way we learn? The short answer is yes. Computers are already changing the way we learn—and if you want to understand how, just look at video games. Not because the games that are currently available are going to replace schools as we know them any time soon, but because they give a glimpse into how we might create new and more powerful ways to learn in schools, communities, and workplaces—new ways to learn for a new Information Age. Look at video games because, while they are wildly popular with adolescents and young adults, they are more than just toys. Look at video games because they create new social and cultural worlds—worlds that help us learn by integrating thinking, social interaction, and technology, all in service of doing things we care about.

We want to be clear from the start that video games are no panacea. Like books and movies, they can be used in antisocial ways. Games are inherently simplifications of reality, and today's games often incorporate—or are based on—violent and sometimes misogynistic themes. Critics suggest that the lessons people learn from playing video games as they currently exist are not always desirable. But even the harshest critics agree that we learn *something* from playing video games. The question is, How can we use the power of video games as a constructive force in schools, homes, and workplaces?

In answer to that question, we argue here for a particular view of games—and of learning—as activities that are most powerful when they are personally meaningful, experiential, social, and epistemological all at the same time. From this perspective, we describe an approach to the design of learning environments that builds on the educational properties of games but grounds them deeply within a theory of learning appropriate to an age marked by the power of new technologies.

Virtual Worlds for Learning

The first step toward understanding how video games can—and, we argue, will—transform education is changing the widely shared perspective that games are "mere entertainment." More than a multibillion–dollar industry, more than a compelling toy for both children and adults, more than a route to computer literacy, video games are important because they let people participate in new worlds. They let players think, talk, and act in new ways. Indeed, players come to *inhabit* roles that are otherwise inaccessible to them. A 16-year-old in Korea playing Lineage can become an international financier, trading raw materials, buying and selling goods in different parts of the virtual world, and speculating on currencies.[1] A Deus Ex player can experience life as a government special agent, operating in a world where the lines between terrorism and state-sponsored violence are called into question.

These rich virtual worlds are what make video games such powerful contexts for learning. In game worlds, learning no longer means confronting words and symbols that are separated from the things those words and symbols refer to. The inverse square law of gravitational attraction is no longer something to be understood solely through an equation. Instead, students can gain virtual experience walking in a world with a mass smaller than that of Earth, or they can plan manned space flights—a task that requires understanding the changing effects of gravitational forces in different parts of the solar system. In virtual worlds, learners experience the concrete realities that words and symbols describe. Through these and similar experiences in multiple contexts, learners can understand complex concepts without losing the connection between abstract ideas and the real problems they can be used to solve. In other words, the virtual worlds of games are powerful because they make it possible to develop *situated understanding*.

Although the stereotypical gamer is a lone teenager seated in front of a computer, game playing can also be a thoroughly social phenomenon. The clearest examples are the "massively multiplayer" online games, in which thousands of players are simultaneously online at any given time, participating in virtual worlds with their own economies, political systems, and cultures. Moreover, careful study shows that most games—from console action games to PC strategy games—have robust game-playing communities. Whereas schools largely sequester students from one another and from the outside world, games bring players together—competitively and cooperatively—in the virtual world of the game and in the social community of its players. In schools, students largely work alone, with school-sanctioned materials; avid gamers seek out news sites, read and write FAQs, participate in discussion forums, and become critical consumers of information.[2] Classroom work rarely has an impact outside the classroom; its only real audience is the teacher. Game players, in contrast, develop reputations in online communities, cultivate audiences by contributing to discussion forums, and occasionally even take up careers as professional gamers, traders of online commodities,[3] or game designers and modders (players who use programming tools to modify games). The virtual worlds of games are powerful, in other words, because playing games means developing a set of *effective social practices*.

By participating in these social practices, game players have an opportunity to explore new identities. In one well-publicized case, a heated political contest erupted for the presidency of Alphaville, one of the towns in The Sims Online.

Arthur Baynes, the 21-year-old incumbent, was running against Laura McKnight, a 14-year-old. The muckraking, accusations of voter fraud, and political jockeying taught young Laura about the realities of politics. The election also gained national attention on National Public Radio, as pundits debated the significance of games that allowed teens not only to argue and debate politics but also to run a political system in which the virtual lives of thousands of real players were at stake. The complexity of Laura's campaign, political alliances, and platform—a platform that called for a stronger police force and a significant restructuring of the judicial system—shows how deep the disconnect has become between the kinds of experiences made available in schools and those available in online worlds. The virtual worlds of games are rich contexts for learning because they make it possible for players to experiment with new and *powerful identities.*[4]

The communities that game players form similarly organize meaningful learning experiences outside of school contexts. In the various websites devoted to the game Civilization, for example, players organize themselves around the shared goal of developing the skills, habits, and understandings that are necessary to become experts in the game. At Apolyton.net, one such site, players post news feeds, participate in discussion forums, and trade screenshots of the game. But they also run a radio station, exchange saved game files in order to collaborate and compete, create custom modifications, and, perhaps most unusually, run their own university to teach other players to play the game at deeper levels. Apolyton University shows us how part of expert gaming is developing a set of values—values that highlight enlightened risk taking, entrepreneurship, and expertise rather than the formal accreditation emphasized by institutional education.[5]

If we look at the development of game communities, we see that part of the power of games for learning is the way they *develop shared values.* In other words, by creating virtual worlds, games integrate knowing and doing. But not just knowing and doing. Games bring together ways of knowing, ways of doing, ways of being, and ways of caring: the situated understandings, effective social practices, powerful identities, and shared values that make someone an expert. The expertise might be that of a modern soldier in Full Spectrum Warrior, a zoo operator in Zoo Tycoon, or a world leader in Civilization III. Or it might be expertise in the sophisticated practices of gaming communities, such as those built around Age of Mythology or Civilization III.

There is a lot being learned in these games. But for some educators, it is hard to see the educational potential of the games because these virtual worlds aren't about memorizing words or definitions or facts. But video games are about a whole lot more.

From Fact Fetish to Ways of Thinking

A century ago, John Dewey argued that schools were built on a fact fetish, and the argument is still valid today. The fact fetish views any area of learning—whether physics, mathematics, or history—as a body of facts or information.

The measure of good teaching and learning is the extent to which students can answer questions about these facts on tests.

But *to know* is a verb before it becomes a noun in *knowledge*. We learn by doing—not just by doing any old thing, but by doing something as part of a larger community of people who share common goals and ways of achieving those goals. We learn by becoming part of a community of practice and thus developing that community's ways of knowing, acting, being, and caring—the community's situated understandings, effective social practices, powerful identities, and shared values.[6]

Of course, different communities of practice have different ways of thinking and acting. Take, for example, lawyers. Lawyers act like lawyers. They identify themselves as lawyers. They are interested in legal issues. And they know about the law. These skills, habits, and understandings are made possible by looking at the world in a particular way—by thinking like a lawyer. Doctors think and act in their own ways, as do architects, plumbers, steel-workers, and waiters or physicists, historians, and mathematicians.

The way of thinking—the epistemology—of a practice determines how someone in the community decides what questions are worth answering, how to go about answering them, and how to decide when an answer is sufficient. The epistemology of a practice thus organizes (and is organized by) the situated understandings, effective social practices, powerful identities, and shared values of the community. In communities of practice, knowledge, skills, identities, and values are shaped by a particular way of thinking into a coherent *epistemic frame*.[7] If a community of practice is a group with a local culture, then the epistemic frame is the grammar of the culture: the ways of thinking and acting that individuals learn when they become part of that culture.

Let's look at an example of how this might play out in the virtual world of a video game. Full Spectrum Warrior (Pandemic Studios, for PC and Xbox) is a video game based on a U.S. Army training simulation.[8] But Full Spectrum Warrior is not a mere first-person shooter in which the player blows up everything on the screen. To survive and win the game, the player has to learn to think and act like a modern professional soldier.

In Full Spectrum Warrior, the player uses the buttons on the controller to give orders to two squads of soldiers, as well as to consult a GPS device, radio for support, and communicate with commanders in the rear. The instruction manual that comes with the game makes it clear from the outset that players must take on the values, identities, and ways of thinking of a professional soldier if they are to play the game successfully. "Everything about your squad," the manual explains, "is the result of careful planning and years of experience on the battlefield. Respect that experience, soldier, since it's what will keep your soldiers alive."[9]

In the game, that experience—the skills and knowledge of professional military expertise—is distributed between the virtual soldiers and the real-world player. The soldiers in a player's squads have been trained in movement formations; the role of the player is to select the best position for them on the field. The virtual characters (the soldiers) know part of the task (various movement formations), and the player knows another part (when and where to engage in such formations). This kind of distribution holds for every aspect of military knowledge in the game. However, the knowledge that is distributed between virtual soldiers and real-world player is not a set of inert facts; what is distributed are the values, skills, practices, and (yes) facts that constitute authentic military professional practice. This simulation of the social context of knowing allows players to act as if in concert with (artificially intelligent) others, even within the single-player context of the game.

In so doing, Full Spectrum Warrior shows how games take advantage of situated learning environments. In games as in real life, people must be able to build meanings on the spot as they navigate their contexts. In Full Spectrum Warrior, players learn about suppression fire through the concrete experiences they have while playing. These experiences give a working definition of suppression fire, to be sure. But they also let a player come to understand how the idea applies in different contexts, what it has to do with solving particular kinds of problems, and how it relates to other practices in the domain, such as the injunction against shooting while moving.

Video games thus make it possible to "learn by doing" on a grand scale—but not just by wandering around in a rich computer environment to learn without any guidance. Asking learners to act without explicit guidance—a form of learning often associated with a loose interpretation of progressive pedagogy—reflects a bad theory of learning. Learners are novices. Leaving them to float in rich experiences with no support triggers the very real human penchant for finding creative but spurious patterns and generalizations. The fruitful patterns or generalizations in any domain are the ones that are evident to those who already know how to look at the domain and know how complex variables in the domain interrelate. And this is precisely what the learner does not yet know. In Full Spectrum Warrior, the player is immersed in activity, values, and ways of seeing but is guided and supported by the knowledge built into the virtual soldiers and the weapons, equipment, and environments in the game. Players are not free to invent everything for themselves. To succeed in the game, they must live by—and ultimately come to master—the epistemic frame of military doctrine. Full Spectrum Warrior is an example of what we suggest is the promise of video games and the future of learning: the development of epistemic games.[10]

Epistemic Games for Initiation and Transformation

We have argued that video games are powerful contexts for learning because they make it possible to create virtual worlds and because acting in such worlds makes it possible to develop the situated understandings, effective social practices, powerful identities, shared values, and ways of thinking of important communities of practice. To build such worlds, one has to understand how the epistemic frames of those communities are developed, sustained, and changed. Some parts of practice are more central to the creation and development of an epistemic frame than others, so analyzing the epistemic frame tells you, in effect, what might be safe to leave out in a re-creation of the practice. The result is a video game that preserves the connections between knowing and doing that are central to an epistemic frame and so becomes an epistemic game. Such epistemic games let players participate in valued communities of practice to develop a new epistemic frame or to develop a better and more richly elaborated version of an already mastered epistemic frame.

Initiation. Developing games such as Full Spectrum Warrior that simultaneously build situated understandings, effective social practices, powerful identities, shared values, and ways of thinking is clearly no small task. But the good news is that in many cases existing communities of practice have already done a lot of that work. Doctors know how to create more doctors; lawyers know how to create more lawyers; the same is true for a host of other socially valued communities of practice. Thus we can imagine epistemic games in which players learn biology by working as a surgeon, history by writing as a journalist, mathematics by designing buildings as an architect or engineer, geography by fighting as a soldier, or French by opening a restaurant. More precisely, these players learn by inhabiting virtual worlds based on the way surgeons, journalists, architects, soldiers, and restaurateurs develop their epistemic frames.

To build such games requires understanding how practitioners develop their ways of thinking and acting. Such understanding is uncovered through *epistemographies* of practice: detailed ethnographic studies of how the epistemic frame of a community of practice is developed by new members. Gathering this information requires more work than is currently invested in most "educational" video games. But the payoff is that such work can become the basis for an alternative educational model. Video games based on the training of socially valued practitioners let us begin to build an education system in which students learn to work (and thus to think) as doctors, lawyers, architects, engineers, journalists, and other important members of the community. The purpose of building such education systems is not to train students for these pursuits in the traditional sense of vocational education. Rather, we develop such epistemic frames because they can provide students with an opportunity to see the world in a variety of ways that are fundamentally grounded in meaningful activity and well aligned with the core skills, habits, and understandings of a post-industrial society.[11]

One early example of such a game is Madison 2200, an epistemic game based on the practices of urban planning.[12] In Madison 2200, players learn about urban ecology by working as urban planners who are redesigning a downtown pedestrian mall popular with local teenagers. Players get a project directive from the mayor, addressed to them as city planners, including a city budget plan and letters from concerned citizens about crime, revenue, jobs, waste, traffic, and affordable housing. A video features interviews about these issues with local residents, business-people, and community leaders. Players conduct a site assessment of the street and work in teams to develop a land use plan, which they present at the end of the game to a representative of the city planning office.

Not surprisingly, along the way players learn a good deal about urban planning and its practices. But something very interesting happens in an epistemic game like Madison 2200. When knowledge is first and foremost a form of activity and experience—of doing something in the world within a community of practice—the facts and information eventually come for free. A large body of facts that resists out-of-context memorization and rote learning comes easily if learners are immersed in activities and experiences that use these facts for plans, goals, and purposes within a coherent domain of knowledge. Data show that, in Madison 2200, players start to form an epistemic frame of urban planning. But they also develop their understanding of ecology and are able to apply it to urban issues. As one player commented, "I really noticed how urban planners have to think about building things. Urban planners also have to think about how the crime rate might go up or the pollution or waste, depending on choices." Another said about walking on the same streets she had traversed before the workshop, "You notice things, like that's why they build a house there, or that's why they build a park there."

The players in Madison 2200 do enjoy their work. But more important is that the experience lets them inhabit an imaginary world in which they are urban planners. The world of Madison 2200 recruits these players to new ways of thinking and acting as part of a new way of seeing the world. Urban planners have a particular way of addressing urban issues. By participating in an epistemic game based on urban planning, players begin to take on that way of seeing the world. As a result, it is fun, too. . . .

Epistemic Games and the Future of Schooling

Epistemic games give players freedom to act within the norms of a valued community of practice—norms that are embedded in nonplayer characters like the virtual soldiers in Full Spectrum Warrior or the real urban planners and planning board members in Madison 2200. To work successfully within the norms of a community, players necessarily learn to think as members of the community. Think for a moment about the student who, after playing Madison 2200, walked down the same streets she had been on the day before and noticed things she had never seen. This is situated learning at its most profound—a transfer of ideas from one context to another that is elusive, rare, and powerful. It happened not because the student learned more information but because she learned it in the context of a new way of thinking—an epistemic frame—that let her see the world in a new way.

Although there are not yet any complete epistemic games in wide circulation, there already exist many games that provide similar opportunities for deeply situated learning. Rise of Nations and Civilization III offer rich, interactive environments in which to explore counterfactual historical claims and help players understand the operation of complex historical modeling. Railroad Tycoon lets players engage in design activities that draw on the same economic and geographic issues faced by railroad engineers in the 1800s. Madison 2200, of course, shows the pedagogical potential of bringing students the experience of being city planners, and we are in the process of developing projects that similarly let players work as biomechanical engineers,[18] journalists,[19] professional mediators,[20] and graphic designers.[21] Other epistemic games might allow a player to experience the world as an evolutionary biologist or as a tailor in colonial Williamsburg.[22]

But even if we had the world's best educational games produced and ready for parents, teachers, and students to buy and play, it's not clear that most educators or schools would know what to do with them. Although the majority of students play video games, the majority of teachers do not. Games, with their anti-authoritarian aesthetics and inherently anti-Puritanical values, can be seen as challenging institutional education. Even if we strip away the blood and guts that characterize some video games, the reality is that, as a form, games encourage exploration, personalized meaning-making, individual expression, and playful experimentation with social boundaries— all of which cut against the grain of the social mores valued in school. In other words, even if we sanitize games, the theories of learning embedded in them run counter to the current social organization of schooling. The next challenges for game and school designers alike is to understand how to shape learning and learning environments to take advantage of the power and potential of games and how to integrate games and game-based learning environments into the predominant arena for learning: schools.

How might school leaders and teachers bring more extended experiments with epistemic games into the culture of the school? The first step will be for superintendents and spokespersons for schools to move beyond the rhetoric of games as violent-serial-killer-inspiring time-wasters and address the range of learning opportunities that games present. Understanding how games can provide powerful learning environments might go a long way toward shifting the current anti-gaming rhetoric. Although epistemic games of the kind we describe here are not yet on the radar of most educators, they are already being used by corporations, the government, the military, and even by political groups to express ideas and teach facts, principles, and world views. Schools and school systems must soon follow suit or risk being swept aside.

A New Model of Learning

The past century has seen an increasing identification of learning with schooling. But new information technologies challenge this union in fundamental ways. Today's technologies make the world's libraries accessible to anyone with a wireless PDA. A vast social network is literally at the fingertips of anyone with a cell phone. As a result, people have unprecedented freedom to bring resources together to create their own learning trajectories.

But classrooms have not adapted. Theories of learning and instruction embodied in school systems designed to teach large numbers of students a standardized curriculum are dinosaurs in this new world. Good teachers and good school leaders fight for new technologies and new practices. But mavericks grow frustrated by the fundamental mismatch between the social organization of schooling and the realities of life in a postindustrial, global, high-tech society. In the push for standardized instruction, the general public and some policy makers may not have recognized this mismatch, but our students have. School is increasingly seen as irrelevant by many students who are past the primary grades.

Thus we argue that, to understand the future of learning, we should be looking beyond schools to the emerging arena of video games. We suggest that video games matter because they present players with simulated worlds—worlds that, if well constructed, are not just about facts or isolated skills but embody particular social practices. And we argue that video games thus make it possible for players to participate in valued communities of practice and so develop the ways of thinking that organize those practices.

Our students will learn from video games. The questions we must ask and answer are: Who will create these games, and will they be based on sound theories of learning and socially conscious educational practices? The U.S. Army, a longtime leader in simulations, is building games like Full Spectrum Warrior and America's Army—games that introduce civilians to a military world view. Several homeland security games are under development, as are a range of games for health education, from games to help kids with cancer take better care of themselves to simulations to help doctors perform surgery more effectively. Companies are developing games for learning history (Making History), engineering (Time Engineers), and the mathematics of design (Homes of Our Own).[23]

This interest in games is encouraging, but most educational games to date have been produced in the absence of any coherent theory of learning or underlying body of research. We need to ask and answer important questions about this relatively new medium. We need to understand how the conventions of good commercial games create compelling virtual worlds. We need to understand how inhabiting a virtual world develops situated knowledge—how playing a game like Civilization III, for example, mediates players' conceptions of world history. We need to understand how spending thousands of hours participating in the social, political, and economic systems of a virtual world develops powerful identities and shared values.[24] We need to understand how game players develop effective social practices and skills in navigating complex systems and how those skills can support learning in other complex domains. And most of all, we need to leverage these understandings to build games that develop for players the epistemic frames of scientists, engineers, lawyers, political activists, and members of other valued communities of practice—as well as games that can help transform those ways of thinking for experienced professionals.

Video games have the potential to change the landscape of education as we know it. The answers to the fundamental questions raised here will make it possible to use video games to move our system of education beyond the traditional academic disciplines—derived from medieval scholarship and constituted within schools developed in the Industrial Revolution—and toward a new model of learning through meaningful activity in virtual worlds. And that learning experience will serve as preparation for meaningful activity in our postindustrial, technology-rich, real world.

Notes

1. Constance A. Steinkuehler, "Emergent Play," paper presented at the State of Play Conference, New York University Law School, New York City, October 2004.

2. Kurt R. Squire, "Game Cultures, School Cultures," *Innovate*, in press.

3. As Julian Dibbell, a journalist for *Wired* and *Rolling Stone*, has shown, it is possible to make a better living by trading online currencies than by working as a freelance journalist!

4. Constance A. Steinkuehler, "Learning in Massively Multiplayer Online Games," in Yasmin Kafai et al., eds., *Proceedings of the Sixth International Conference of the Learning Sciences* (Mahwah, N.J.: Erlbaum, 2004), pp. 521-28.

5. Kurt R. Squire and Levi Giovanetto, "The Higher Education of Gaming," eLearning, in press.

6. Jean Lave and Etienne Wenger, *Situated Learning: Legitimate Peripheral Participation* (Cambridge: Cambridge University Press, 1991).

7. David Williamson Shaffer, "Epistemic Frames and Islands of Expertise: Learning from Infusion Experiences," in Kafai et al., pp. 473-80.

8. The commercial game retains about 15% of what was in the Army's original simulation. For more on this game as a learning environment, see James P. Gee, "What Will a State of the Art Video Game Look Like?," *Innovate*, in press.

9. *Manual for Full Spectrum Warrior* (Los Angeles: Pandemic Studios, 2004), p. 2.

10. David Williamson Shaffer, "Epistemic Games," *Innovate*, in press.

11. David Williamson Shaffer, "Pedagogical Praxis: The Professions as Models for Postindustrial Education," *Teachers College Record*, July 2004, pp. 1401-21.

12. Kelly L. Beckett and David Williamson Shaffer, "Augmented by Reality: The Pedagogical Praxis of Urban Planning as a Pathway to Ecological Thinking," *Journal of Educational Computing Research*, in press; and Shaffer, "Epistemic Games."

13. Roger C. Schank, *Virtual Learning: A Revolutionary Approach to Building a Highly Skilled Work Force* (New York: McGraw-Hill, 1997).

14. Roger C. Schank et al., "The Design of Goal-Based Scenarios," *Journal of the Learning Sciences*, vol. 3, 1994, pp. 305-45; and A. S. Gordon, "Authoring Branching Storylines for Training Applications," in Kafai et al., pp. 230-38.

15. Kurt R. Squire, "Game-Based Learning: Present and Future State of the Field," e-Learning Consortium, an X-Learn Perspective Paper, Masie Center, February 2005, available at . . . 2005.

16. Richard Halverson, "Systems of Practice: How Leaders Use Artifacts to Create Professional Community in Schools," *Education Policy Analysis Archives*, vol. 11, 2003, p. 37; and idem, "Accessing, Documenting and Communicating Practical Wisdom: The Phronesis of School Leadership Practice," *American Journal of Education*, vol. 111, 2004, pp. 90-121.

17. Richard Halverson and Yeonjai Rah, "Representing Leadership for Social Justice: The Case of Franklin School," *Journal of Cases in Educational Leadership*, Spring 2005.

18. Gina Svarovsky and David Williamson Shaffer, "SodaConstructing Knowledge Through Exploratoids," *Journal of Research in Science Teaching*, in press.

19. Shaffer, "Pedagogical Praxis."

20. David Williamson Shaffer, "When Computer-Supported Collaboration Means Computer-Supported Competition: Professional Mediation as a Model for

Collaborative Learning," *Journal of Interactive Learning Research,* vol. 15, 2004, pp. 101–15.

21. David Williamson Shaffer, "Learning Mathematics Through Design: The Anatomy of Escher's World," *Journal of Mathematical Behavior,* vol. 16, 1997, pp. 95–112.

22. Kurt R. Squire and Henry Jenkins, "Harnessing the Power of Games in Education," *Insight,* vol. 3, 2004, pp. 5–33.

23. Ibid.

24. Kurt R. Squire, "Sid Meier's Civilization III," *Simulations and Gaming,* vol. 35, 2004, pp. 135–40.

Lowell W. Monke

NO

The Overdominance of Computers

The debate chums on over the effectiveness of computers as learning tools. Although there is a growing disillusionment with the promise of computers to revolutionize education, their position in schools is protected by the fear that without them students will not be prepared for the demands of a high-tech 21st century. This fallback argument ultimately trumps every criticism of educational computing, but it is rarely examined closely.

Let's start by accepting the premise of the argument: Schools need to prepare young people for a high-tech society. Does it automatically follow that children of all ages should use high-tech tools? Most people assume that it does, and that's the end of the argument. But we don't prepare children for an automobile-dependent society by finding ways for 10-year-olds to drive cars, or prepare people to use alcohol responsibly by teaching them how to drink when they are 6. My point is that preparation does not necessarily warrant early participation. Indeed, preparing young people quite often involves strengthening their inner resources—like self-discipline, moral judgment, and empathy—before giving them the opportunity to participate.

Great Power and Poor Preparation

The more powerful the tools—and computers are powerful—the more life experience and inner strength students must have to handle that power wisely. On the day my Advanced Computer Technology classroom got wired to the Internet, it struck me that I was about to give my high school students great power to harm a lot of people, and all at a safe distance. They could inflict emotional pain with a few keystrokes and never have to witness the tears shed. They could destroy hours of work accomplished by others who were not their enemies—just poorly protected network users whose files provided convenient bull's-eyes for youth flexing newfound technical muscles.

I also realized that it would take years to instill the ethical discipline needed to say *no* to flexing that technical power. Young people entering my course needed more firsthand experiences guided by adults. They needed more chances to directly connect their own actions with the consequences of those actions, and to reflect on the outcomes, before they started using tools that could trigger serious consequences on the other side of the world.

From *Educational Leadership*, December 2005/January 2006, pp. 20–23. Copyright © 2006 by ASCD. Reprinted by permission. The Association for Supervision and Curriculum Development is a worldwide community of educators advocating sound policies and sharing best practices to achieve the success of each learner. To learn more, visit ASCD at www.ascd.org

Students need more than just moral preparation. They also need authentic experiences. As more students grow up spending much of their time in environments dominated by computers, TV and video games, their diminished experience with real, concrete things prevents them from developing a rich understanding of what they study on computers. The computer is a purely symbolic environment; users are always working with abstract representations of things, never with the things themselves. In a few months my students could learn to build complex relational databases and slick multimedia presentations. But unless they also had a deep knowledge of the physical world and community relationships, they would be unable to infuse depth and meaning into the information they were depicting and discussing.

Do Computers Help Achievement?

Educational technology researchers, who tend to suffer from a severe inability to see the forest for the trees, typically ignore the impact that saturating society with computers and other screen environments is having on children. University of Munich economists Thomas Fuchs and Ludger Woessmann recently examined data from a study of 174,000 15-year-olds in 31 nations who took the Programme for International Student Assessment tests. They found, after controlling for other possible influences, that the more access students had to computers in school and at home, the *lower* their overall test scores were (2004). The authors suggest that rather than inherently motivating young people or helping them learn, computers more likely distract them from their studies. But there may be other problems behind this phenomenon that point to inherent contradictions in the use of educational technology.

For example, although we know that computer programs can help small children learn to read, we also know that face-to-face interaction is one of the most important ingredients in reading readiness (Dodici, Draper, & Peterson, 2003). As a result of increased time spent with computers, video games, and TV, the current generation of elementary students will experience an estimated 30 percent fewer face-to-face encounters than the previous generation (Hammel, 1999). Thus, teachers may be employing the very devices for remediating reading problems that helped cause the problems in the first place.

The issue is not just balancing computer time with other activities in schools. Both inside and outside school, children' lives are dominated by technology. Nearly everything a child does today—from chatting with friends to listening to music to playing games—tends to involve the use of technologies that distance children from direct contact with the living world. If the task of schools is to produce men and women who live responsible, fulfilling lives—not just human cogs for the high-tech machinery of commerce—then we should not be intensifying childrens high-tech existence but compensating for it. Indeed, as advanced technology increasingly draws us toward a mechanical way of thinking and acting, it becomes crucial that schools help students develop their distinctly human capacities. What we need from schools is not balance in using high technology, but an effort to balance childrens machine-dominated lives.

To prepare children to challenge the cold logic of the spreadsheet-generated bottom line, we need to teach them to value what that spreadsheet cannot factor in: commitment, loyalty, and tradition. To prepare them to find meaning in the abstract text and images encountered through screens, we need to first engage them in physical realities that screen images can only symbolize. To fit students to live in an environment filled with human-made products, we need to first help them know and respect what cannot be manufactured: the natural, the living, the wild. To prepare students to live well-grounded lives in a world of constant technological change, we need to concentrate their early education on things that endure.

The Cost of Failing to Compensate

Anyone who has spent time in schools knows that what is keeping today's youth from succeeding academically has nothing to do with a lack of technical skills or access to computers. Rather, it is the lack of qualities like hope, compassion, trust, respect, a sense of belonging, moral judgment, stability, community support, parental care, and teacher competence and enthusiasm that keeps so many students imprisoned in ignorance.

Ironically, what students will most need to meet the serious demands of the 21st century is the wisdom that grows out of these inner human capacities and that is developed by community involvement. If the 20th century taught us anything at all, it should have been that technology can be a very mixed blessing. Children entering elementary schools today will eventually have to wrestle with the mess that their elders have left them because of our own lack of wisdom about technology's downside: global warming, increasingly lethal weapons, nuclear waste, overdependence on automobiles, overuse of pesticides and antibiotics, and the general despoiling of our planet. They will also have to take on ethical conundrums posed by advanced technology, such as what to do about cloning, which decisions are off-limits to artificial intelligence devices, and whether or not parents should be allowed to "enhance" the genetic makeup of their offspring (only the wealthy need apply).

Those decisions should not be left to technicians in labs, CEOs in boardrooms, or politicians in debt to those who stand to profit from the technology. Our children should be at the decision tables as adults, and we want them to be able to stand apart from high technology and soberly judge its benefits and detriments to the entire human race.

How can young people develop the wisdom to judge high technology if they are told from the moment they enter school, implicitly if not explicitly, that they need high-tech tools to learn, to communicate, to think? Having been indoctrinated early with the message that their capacity to deal with the world depends not on their own internal resources but on their use of powerful external machines, how can students even imagine a world in which human beings impose limits on technological development or use?

Where to Go from Here

Keep to Essentials in the Early Years

So how, specifically, should educators make decisions and policies about the appropriateness of digital technologies for students of different ages?

One approach to tackling this dilemma comes from the Alliance for Childhood. During the last eight years, the Alliance (whose board of directors I serve on) has engaged educators, children's health professionals, researchers, and technology experts in developing guidelines for structuring a healthy learning environment for children, and has developed a list of essential conditions. Educators should ask themselves to what extent heavy use of computers and the Internet provides children in the lower grades with these essential school experiences:

- Close, loving relationships with responsible adults.
- Outdoor activity, nature exploration, gardening, and other encounters with nature.
- Time for unstructured play as part of the core curriculum.
- Music, drama, puppetry, dance, painting, and the other arts, both as separate classes and as a catalyst to bring other academic subjects to life.
- Hands-on lessons, handicrafts, and other physically engaging activities that provide effective first lessons for young children in the sciences, mathematics, and technology.
- Conversation with important adults, as well as poetry, storytelling, and hearing books read aloud.

This vision places a high priority on a child's direct encounters with the world and with other living beings, but it does not reject technology. On the contrary, tools are an important part of the vision. But at the elementary level, the tools should be simple, putting less distance between the student and the world and calling forth the student's own internal resources.

Schools must also be patient with children' development. It would strike anyone as silly to give the smallest student in a 2nd grade class a scooter so that the child could get around the track as fast as the other kids his or her age. But our society shows decreasing willingness to wait for the natural emergence of students' varying mental and emotional capacities. We label students quickly and display an almost pathological eagerness to apply external technical fixes (including medications) to students who often simply aren't ready for the abstract, academic, and sedentary environment of today's early elementary classrooms. Our tendency to turn to external tools to help children cope with demands that are out of line with their tactile and physically energetic nature reflects the impact that decades of placing faith in technical solutions has had on how we treat children.

Study Technology in Depth after Elementary School

After children have had years to engage in direct, firsthand experiences, and as their abstract thinking capacities emerge more fully, it makes sense to gradually introduce computers and other complex, symbolic environments.

Techno-Byte

Percentage of U.S. students who used computers in school in 2003:

- 97 percent of high school students.
- 95 percent of middle school students.
- 91 percent of students in grades 1–5.
- 80 percent of kindergarten students.
- 67 percent of nursery school students.

—National Center for Education Statistics, 2005

Computer hardware and software should also become the focus of classroom investigation. A student in a technological society surrounded by black boxes whose fundamental principles he or she does not understand is as functionally illiterate as a student in a world filled with books that he or she can't read. The only thing worse would be to make technology "invisible," preventing children from even being aware of their ignorance.

By high school, digital technologies should take a prominent place in students' studies, both as tools of learning and as tools to learn about. During the last two years of high school, teachers should spend considerable time outfitting students with the high-tech skills they will need when they graduate. This "just-in-time" approach to teaching technical skills is far more efficient—instructionally and financially—than continually retraining younger students in technical skills soon to be obsolete. In addition, students at all education levels should consciously examine technology's role in human affairs.

I am not suggesting that we indiscriminately throw computers out of classrooms. But I do believe it's time to rethink the past decision to indiscriminately throw them in. The result of that rethinking would be, I hope, some much-needed technological modesty, both in school and eventually in society in general. By compensating for the dominance of technology in students' everyday lives, schools might help restore the balance we need to create a more humane society.

The irony of postmodern education is that preparing children for a high-tech future requires us to focus our attention more than ever before on the task of understanding what it means to be human, to be alive, to be part of both social and biological communities—a quest for which technology is increasingly becoming not the solution but the problem.

References

Dodici, B. J., Draper, D. C., & Peterson, C. A. (2003). Early parent-child interactions and early literacy development. *Topics in Early Childhood Special Education, 23*(3), 124–136.

Fuchs, T., & Woessmann, L. (2004, November). *Computers and student learning: Bivariate and multivariate evidence on the availability and use of computers at home and at school.* CESifo Working Paper Series (#1321). Available. . . .

Hammel, S. (1999, Nov. 29). Generation of loners? Living their lives online. *U.S. News and World Report*, p. 79.

POSTSCRIPT

Will Increased Use of Computer Technology and Games Be Beneficial to Students?

The phrase "boon or bane" is an apt description of the widely divergent views regarding the potentiality of technology, especially computer technology, to impact education. Schools, as is often their wont, are caught up in this controversy, and because we are, by definition, dealing with our children, the controversy is often emotional and contentious.

Peter Stokes, in an article entitled "How E-Learning Will Transform Education" (*Education Week*, September 13, 2000), made the following statement:

> Because e-learning represents a powerful convergence of technological opportunity and economic necessity, its emergence presents a unique occasion to undertake a considered re-evaluation of the role and function of education. . . . The work accomplished so far suggests that e-learning can play a substantive role in developing a new breed of literate citizens for the global economy of the 21st century.

Expressing an entirely different view, Stephen Leonard in an article "Confessions of a Cyber Teacher" (*edtechnot,* February 2004) wrote:

> But if the hypesters start suggesting that you are a "Luddite" because you oppose dropping huge sums of money into "ramping up" your local school, ask them for evidence to support the investments. That isn't the request of someone who fears technology, it is just common sense—something that has been altogether lacking in the headlong, bumbling rush into the techno-education future.

Mary Burns in her article "From Compliance to Commitment" (*Phi Delta Kappan*, December 2002) spoke to some interesting findings derived from a project to help teachers in poor schools create learner-centered environments through the use of technology. Burns reported that three major assumptions that generally drive professional development activities in technology were not borne out in her project. Those assumptions are: (1) teacher proficiency with technology results in greater use of technology by students and increased learner-centered instruction; (2) the best way to learn technology is to engage meaningfully with content; and (3) more is better. Burns's counterintuitive approach to professional development focused not on teacher proficiency but rather on teacher comfort with technology along with stressing the cultivation of a minimum set of skills; she did not focus on academic content but rather on the cultivation of certain learning concepts; and finally, because the schools involved in the project lacked resources, it was necessary to use a grouping model with several students on one computer. According to Burns each of those approaches contributed to a sense of sharing and caused teachers to create more learner-centered approaches. She also reported that computer labs had a lesser effect on increasing learner-centered activities.

There is an abundance of pro and con literature and information on this issue. Seminal works include Marshall McLuhan's, *Understanding Media* (1964) and *The Medium Is the Massage: An Inventory of Effects* (with Quentin Fiore, 1967). Neil Postman's cautionary works include *Amusing Ourselves to Death* (1985) and *Technopoly* (1992). In a similar vein is Todd Oppenheimer's *The Flickering Mind* (2003). Books that speak to the promise and value of educational technology include *Technology and Education Reform* by Barbara Means (1994); *Brave New Schools: Challenging Cultural Illiteracy Through Global Learning Networks* by Jim Cummins and Dennis Sayer (1995); and Don Tapscott, *Growing Up Digital* (1998). The entire December 2005//January 2006 of *Educational Leadership* is devoted to learning in the digital age.

ISSUE 17

Is the Practice of Providing Accommodations to Children in Special Education a Good Idea?

YES: MaryAnn Byrnes, from "Accommodations for Students with Disabilities: Removing Barriers to Learning," *National Association of Secondary School Principals Bulletin* (February 2000; updated 2007)

NO: James M. Kauffman, Kathleen McGee, and Michele Brigham, from "Enabling or Disabling? Observations on Changes in Special Education," *Phi Delta Kappan* (April 2004)

ISSUE SUMMARY

YES: MaryAnn Byrnes, associate professor in the Graduate School of Education at the University of Massachusetts and president of the Massachusetts Federation of the Council for Exceptional Children, argues that fairness and equal educational opportunities mandate that students with special needs be provided appropriate support.

NO: James M. Kauffman, professor of education at the University of Virginia, and special education teachers Kathleen McGee and Michele Brigham believe that the inappropriate use of accommodations denies special needs students the opportunity to achieve greater independence.

Certainly there is little argument with the goal that no child should be left behind in terms of his/her education and the concomitant opportunity to live a full and productive life. One of the more daunting challenges related to the attainment of that noble goal is the nurturing and schooling of children with special needs. Legislation and court decisions at state and federal levels leave no doubt that special needs children have protected rights to a "free and appropriate" education and that our public education system has a legal, if not a moral, obligation to provide that education. Despite the consensus regarding the requirement and worthiness of providing quality education to special needs youngsters, special education is not immune from controversy. Like so many issues in education, the phrase "the devil is in the details" most assuredly applies to special education programs. Educators, as well as parents of special needs children, are well aware of the lexicon of special education with its phrases, such as "the least restrictive environment," "mainstreaming," "full inclusion," "Individualized Education Program or IEP," and "accommodations."

One of the most controversial aspects of special education is the often confusing regulations related to school discipline. Federal law basically proscribes schools from applying traditional disciplinary measures (detention, suspension, or expulsion), if a special education student's misbehavior in school is a manifestation of the particular disability of that student. Thus, if a student identified as "emotionally handicapped"(EH) acts out in class against the teacher or another student, it is likely that the EH student could not be suspended from school because the misbehavior was triggered by the identified disability. The school could modify the student's IEP related to treatment, counseling, and/or other accommodations, but not of a disciplinary nature. On the other hand, if the IEP team determined the behavior was not a manifestation of the disability, then the special education student should be treated in the same manner as children without disabilities. Obviously the nuances and subjectivity inherent in making such judgments can lead to confusion and/or disagreements.

The issue of accommodations for students with special needs is another topic in which, even though there is little argument regarding the appropriateness of certain accommodations (e.g., access to educational facilities; assistance with speech, vision, hearing and other physical impairments; and provision of services for mental retardation), there is often disagreement regarding accommodations that provide special needs students with extra time on examinations, reduced academic requirements, and adult assistance such as reading test questions and scribing students' responses.

Some such as Byrnes argue that relevant accommodations are needed to provide special needs students with a fair opportunity for success. Others such as Kauffman, McGee, and Brigham believe that overusage of special accommodations will keep special needs students from developing a sense of personal responsibility and growth toward independence.

Certainly this issue is made even more complex by the push toward the least restrictive environment for special needs students as manifested in full inclusion of them into regular education classrooms. Although this particular movement itself is not without controversy, it has, at the very least, brought special education into the mainstream of educational policy as evidenced by its inclusion in the provisions of the No Child Left Behind Act.

MaryAnn Byrnes

Accommodations for Students with Disabilities: Removing Barriers to Learning

Accommodations can be confusing. Sometimes they seem like sensible actions that help students. At other times, accommodations seem to give an unfair advantage or make work too easy. This article explains the purpose of accommodations, demonstrating how they can be used to create equal access, not excuses.

Think about taking your driver's test without wearing glasses (if you do, that is). Not fair, you say; you need the glasses to see. You have just identified an accommodation that you need. Wearing glasses does not make a bad driver better or make driving easier; wearing glasses makes driving accessible. Glasses are so much a part of our lives that we rarely consider how they remove a barrier caused by a disability.

Every day, teachers encounter students on an Individualized Education Program (IEP) or 504 Plan, both of which address programs for students with disabilities. Most likely, the person charged with monitoring either plan has indicated that individual students need specific changes to instructional practices, assignments, or testing conditions.

It is usually easy to understand the need for glasses or wheelchairs or hearing aids. These sound like changes the student must make. Other accommodations, such as extended time, may not be as clear.

What Is an Accommodation?

An accommodation is an adjustment to an activity or setting that removes a barrier presented by a disability so a person can have access equal to that of a person without a disability. An accommodation does not guarantee success or a specific level of performance. Appropriate accommodations provide the opportunity for a person with a disability to participate equitably in a situation or activity.

Remember that pair of glasses you needed as your sight changed, or the time you broke your leg and could not drive. These conditions affected your life, even though your competence did not change. Your ability to interact with (have access to) reading material was reduced without your glasses. Your

From *NASSP Bulletin*, 2000 (revised 2007), pp. 21–27. Copyright © 2000 by National Association of Secondary School Principals. www.principals.org. Reprinted by permission.

ability to get to (have access to) work, or the grocery store, was limited without someone to transport you. The support provided by the glasses—or the driver—made it possible for you to use your abilities without the barrier presented by less than perfect vision or limited mobility.

Appropriate accommodations in IEPs or 504 Plans are intended to serve the same purpose. They identify ways to remove a barrier presented by a person's disability. Educators should focus on this relationship as they choose, and implement, accommodations.

Why Do We Need to Provide Accommodations?

Accommodations are required under Section 504 of the Federal Rehabilitation Act of 1974 as well as the Americans with Disabilities Act (ADA). Both of these federal laws prohibit discrimination against individuals who have a disability. Situations that limit access have been determined to be discriminatory.

Accommodations must be provided not just by teachers for students, but by employers for workers and governments for citizens. Curbs have been cut to provide access for people who use wheelchairs or crutches. Doors have been widened, and door handles altered, because some people with disabilities encountered barriers with the old designs. Employers provide computer adaptations or adjustments in work schedules and circumstances.

Individuals with disabilities may have a document called a 504 Plan which specifies required accommodations. Students who have a 504 Plan will not require special education services, just changes to the environment or instructional situation.

Students who have a disability and require special education services will have information about accommodations contained in their IEP. This legal document also details the direct services which will be provided and the goals of these services.

The Individuals with Disabilities Education Improvement Act (IDEA 2004), the federal law governing special education, mandates that teams identify accommodations necessary to provide equal access to instruction and the daily life of schools. Accommodations have become even more important as they specify how a student with a disability will participate in large-scale districtwide or statewide assessment systems.

Who Needs Accommodations?

According to Section 504, an individual with a disability is any person who has "a physical or mental impairment that substantially limits one or more major life activities." IDEA, the federal special education law, lists the following disabilities: autism, deaf-blindness, deafness, hearing impairment, mental retardation, multiple disabilities, orthopedic impairment, other health impairment, serious emotional disturbance, specific learning disability, speech or language impairment, traumatic brain injury and visual impairment.

Some conditions require accommodations under Section 504, but rarely require special education services. These can include medical conditions (such as cancer, asthma, or epilepsy); communicable diseases; some temporary medical conditions; physical impairments; and disorders of emotion or behavior. If medication controls focus, a student with attention deficit disorder (ADD) or attention deficit hyperactivity disorder (ADHD) might have a 504 Plan. To qualify, a substantial limitation of a major life activity must be demonstrated.

Students (or adults) who have disabilities may require accommodations to have equal access to education. Not every student with a disability will require accommodations, and not every student with a disability requires the same accommodation in every situation.

Think of Jim, a student who has limited mobility in his hands, affecting his ability to write. This disability will present a barrier in a class which requires him to take notes quickly or write essays in class. Jim might know the course material, but earn a poor grade on a written test, because his slow writing speed prevented him from finishing in the time allotted.

In a class that does not require rapid note-taking, essays, or written tests, no barrier may be present; equal access exists without accommodation. In this situation, Jim can learn, and demonstrate what he knows and can do, unaffected by his disability.

What Kind of Accommodations Are There?

Disabilities differ in individuals. Accommodations must be considered for each individual, not by disability category. The point is to understand the disability and the learning situation and then determine if these interact to pose a barrier to equal access. If so, decide whether an accommodation can be identified to remove the barrier. Next, be sure to implement the accommodation.

Remember the student described above. The limited mobility in Jim's hands presents a barrier in a class that requires note taking or other in-class writing. There are several accommodations that can result in equal access. Jim might tape the class and take notes later. These notes could be written or dictated into a computer. Essays could be composed using voice-recognition software or dictated using a tape recorder or a scribe. A computer might be adapted so that typing becomes an effective way to record information on paper. In still another type of accommodation, written tests could be replaced by oral exams. The appropriate accommodation is the one that best matches Jim and his classes.

Are There Some Accommodations That Should Not Be Used?

The answer to this question depends on context. An accommodation should not alter the essential purpose of an assignment or assessment. If the skill you want to measure is the ability to make multiple rapid hand movements, there is probably no accommodation that is appropriate for Jim; he will not do well because of his disability.

Similarly, if the purpose of a task is to determine whether someone has perfect vision without glasses, using those glasses is not an appropriate accommodation. If the purpose is to see how well a person reads text, the glasses become a reasonable accommodation. They remove a barrier so that the individual has access to print.

Who Decides about Accommodations?

The team that writes IEPs and 504 Plans reviews the disability and the curriculum and determines what accommodations, if any, are necessary. These are then written into the IEP or 504 Plan.

Return to Jim once more. As you review the requirements of your class, think of the most appropriate way to remove the barrier that is presented by the limited mobility Jim has in his hands.

If We Use Accommodations, How Will the Student Be Prepared for Independent Life in College or the World of Work?

Some people are concerned that the supports provided in school will result in the student being unable to work productively when he or she leaves school. Remember that Section 504 applies to colleges and employers as well. Colleges offer support centers and provide accommodations upon documentation that a disability exists. Employers are required to provide reasonable accommodations to any person who is otherwise qualified to fulfill the elements of the job.

If companies remove barriers at the workplace, educators should be willing and able to take barriers out of the school activities that prepare a student for the workplace. Teachers can help a student identify the type of accommodation that will be the least cumbersome for everyone, and will help the student to be most independent.

Don't Accommodations Just Make School Easier?

That depends on how you view the world. Does wearing glasses make driving easier? Not really—for a person with limited vision, wearing glasses makes driving accessible. With or without glasses, you need to be able to drive to pass the test. The same is true of an appropriate academic accommodation. Whether or not the accommodation is provided, the students still need to be able to demonstrate that they know required material.

Think about the important elements of your class. Often when you identify the main purpose of your assignments, and consider the skills and abilities of a student, you will see that an accommodation lets you determine more clearly what a student knows, understands, and can do. Is it more important that Jim write notes in class or master the material? Is it more important that Jim demonstrate good handwriting or the ability to communicate thoughts in print?

Does a Student Need to Follow the IEP Accommodations in All Classes?

The IEP or 504 Plan needs to address any area in which the student's disability affects life in school. Barriers might be present in every class, but not always. For example, a student who was blind would need to use Braille in all classes dealing with written material. Jim, our student with limited mobility in his hands, might not require accommodations in world languages or physical education.

Can We Make Accommodations without Having Students on an IEP?

Sometimes people confuse a teaching strategy with an accommodation. Teachers use an array of strategies that define their unique teaching style. Accommodations are specific actions designed to remove a barrier related to a disability. In some cases, a particular teacher's style includes practices that provide multiple options for all students. For example, if one of Jim's teachers permits students to choose oral or written assignments, the teaching strategy matches the kind of access Jim needs.

Teachers usually have the latitude to use a variety of strategies at their discretion. However, if you notice specific barriers connected to a student's disability, these should be discussed by the IEP team to ensure that access issues are formally addressed.

Can Teachers Give Different Assignments on the Same Content as a Way to Meet the Needs of Different Learning Styles without Lowering Standards?

Absolutely. Appropriate accommodations do not lower expectations; they increase access. The goal is to remove the barrier presented by the disability; a range of options might be one way to accomplish that. Some teachers find they tap student knowledge best in active projects; others prefer written work. Many schools use portfolios or performance activities to document student learning.

These assessment activities can be compelling and they utilize different methods of expression. A student like Jim, for example, might communicate a depth of understanding and analysis in a debate that would be difficult to capture in an on-demand written test. In contrast, student with a disability in speech could experience barriers in performance activities that do not exist on a paper-and-pencil task.

What If Accommodations Are Not Implemented?

Since accommodations facilitate equal access, refusing to provide them can be viewed as discrimination. IEPs and 504 plans are legal documents. Individuals who knowingly refuse to implement legally required accommodations make themselves personally liable for legal suit.

This sounds serious, and it is serious. Once accommodations are found to be necessary, everyone must implement them in situations where the student's disability poses a barrier that prevents equal access.

No individual has the option, however, of deciding not to implement an accommodation that is necessary. Telling students they could not wear glasses, or use a hearing aid, is unthinkable. Just as inappropriate is a decision not to allow Jim to use accommodations to remove the barrier posed by his disability, even though it means making some changes to your own work.

Specific Accommodations Questions

Now that the issues underlying accommodations have been addressed, it is time to talk about frequently-encountered accommodations that raise questions and concern. All these questions have come from secondary school faculty in a variety of school systems.

Why Is It Fair to Read Material Aloud to Some Students?

Some students have a learning disability that makes it difficult for them to decode print. They can understand the concepts; they can comprehend the material when they hear it; they can reason through the content. They just can't turn print into meaning. If the task is to determine if the student can read, you already know he/she will have difficulty. If the task is to determine if the student has content knowledge, reading material aloud removes the barrier of the learning disability. Reading to a student who does not understand the material will not result in a higher grade.

Why Is It Fair to Give Some Students Extra Time on Tests?

Some students have motor difficulties which make writing an enormous challenge. They may not be able to form the letters correctly. They may not be able to focus on their ideas while they work on the physical act of writing. They understand the material; and they know what they want to respond; it just takes longer to write the answer. If the task is to determine how quickly the student can respond, you already know he/she will have difficulty. If the task is to determine if the student has the knowledge, providing extra time removes the barrier of the motor disability. Providing extra time to a student who does not understand the material will not result in a higher grade.

Why Is It Fair to Permit Some Students to Respond Orally to Tests?

Think about the example above. For some students, responding orally would be a comparable accommodation. Here, too, allowing an oral response will not result in a higher grade if the student does not know the material.

If We Keep Using Accommodations, How Will Students Ever Learn to Be Independent?

Some accommodations will always be needed; for example, rarely does vision improve enough to make glasses unnecessary. Jim's hand mobility may never change.

Other accommodations may become unnecessary as students learn. A fourth grader with a significant reading disability might need a note-taker; three years later, that same student might have increased reading skills to the point where this accommodation is no longer necessary. Special education services seek to help students gain skill, and work independently, as much as possible. It is important to review accommodations every year to be sure they are needed.

Why Do Some IEPs Have Long Lists of Accommodations?

Some teams like to include a multitude of accommodations that *might help* the student. Unfortunately, long lists often create more problems than they solve. Teachers cannot remember the list. Accommodations might not be related to the student's disability. Teams should be sure accommodations are chosen only to address barriers. Accommodations included "just in case," are usually unrelated to the disability. If you had perfect vision, would you need glasses, "just in case?"

The Bottom Line

Researchers say accommodations create a level playing field for students with a disability. A well-chosen accommodation allows students with disabilities to have fair, equal access to educational activities.

It all comes down to deciding what is important. Think about your assignment and expectations. Think about the student's disability. If the combination creates a barrier, the accommodation removes it. The accommodation does not release a student from participating or demonstrating knowledge. It allows the student to participate equitably and demonstrate knowledge. And isn't that what school is all about?

References

Americans with Disabilities Act of 1990, P.L. 101-336, Section 2, 104 Stat. 328.1991.

Byrnes, M. (2000). Accommodations for students with disabilities: Removing barriers to learning. *National Association of Secondary School Principals' Bulletin. 84*, 21–27.

Fuchs, L. S. & Fuchs, D. (2001). Helping teachers formulate sound test accommodation decisions for students with learning disabilities. *Learning Disabilities Research & Practice, 16*(3), 174–181.

Individuals With Disabilities Education Improvement Act of 2004. 20 U.S.C.A. § 1400 *et seq.*(2005).

Livovich, Michael P. (1996). *Section 504 of the Rehabilitation Act of 1973 and the Americans with Disabilities Act. Providing access to a free appropriate public education: A public school manual.* Indianapolis, Indiana.

Vocational Rehabilitation Act of 1973, 29 U.S.C. Section 794.

James M. Kauffman, Kathleen McGee, and Michele Brigham

→ **NO**

Enabling or Disabling? Observations on Changes in Special Education

Schools need demanding and distinctive special education that is clearly focused on instruction and habilitation. Abandoning such a conception of special education is a prescription for disaster. But special education has increasingly been losing its way in the single-minded pursuit of full inclusion.

Once, special education's purpose was to bring the performance of students with disabilities closer to that of their nondisabled peers in regular classrooms, to move as many students as possible into the mainstream with appropriate support. For students not in regular education, the goal was to move them toward a more typical setting in a cascade of placement options. But as any good thing can be overdone and ruined by the pursuit of extremes, we see special education suffering from the extremes of inclusion and accommodation.

Aiming for as much normalization as possible gave special education a clear purpose. Some disabilities were seen as easier to remediate than others. Most speech and language disorders, for example, were considered eminently remediable. Other disabilities, such as mental retardation and many physical disabilities, were assumed to be permanent or long-term and so less remediable, but movement *toward* the mainstream and increasing independence from special educators were clear goals.

The emphasis in special education has shifted away from normalization, independence, and competence. The result has been students' dependence on whatever special programs, modifications, and accommodations are possible, particularly in general education settings. The goal seems to have become the *appearance* of normalization without the *expectation* of competence.

Many parents and students seem to want more services as they learn what is available. Some have lost sight of the goal of limiting accommodations in order to challenge students to achieve more independence. At the same time, many special education advocates want all services to be available in mainstream settings, with little or no acknowledgment that the services are atypical. Although teachers, administrators, and guidance counselors are often willing and able to make accommodations, doing so is not always in students' best long-term interests. It gives students with disabilities what anthropologist Robert Edgerton called a cloak—a pretense, a cover, which actually fools no one—rather than actual competence.

From *Kappa Delta Pi Record* by James M. Kauffman and Kathleen McGee, pp. 613-620. Copyright © 2004 by Phi Delta Kappan. Reprinted by permission.

In this article, we discuss how changes in attitudes toward disability and special education, placement, and accommodations can perpetuate disability. We also explore the problems of ignoring or perpetuating disability rather than helping students lead fuller, more independent lives. Two examples illustrate how we believe good intentions can go awry—how attempts to accommodate students with disabilities can undermine achievement.

"But he needs resource. . . . " Thomas, a high school sophomore identified as emotionally disturbed, was assigned to a resource class created to help students who had problems with organization or needed extra help with academic skills. One of the requirements in the class was for students to keep a daily planner in which they entered all assignments; they shared their planner with the resource teacher at the beginning of class and discussed what academic subjects would be worked on during that period.

Thomas consistently refused to keep a planner or do any work in resource (he slept instead). So a meeting was set up with the assistant principal, the guidance counselor, Thomas, and the resource teacher. As the meeting was about to begin, the principal announced that he would not stay because Thomas felt intimidated by so many adults. After listening to Thomas' complaints, the guidance counselor decided that Thomas would not have to keep a planner or show it to the resource teacher and that the resource teacher should not talk to him unless Thomas addressed her first. In short, Thomas would not be required to do any work in the class! When the resource teacher suggested that, under those circumstances, Thomas should perhaps be placed in a study hall, because telling the parents that he was in a resource class would be a misrepresentation, the counselor replied, "But he *needs* the resource class."

"He's too bright. . . ." Bob, a high school freshman with Asperger's Syndrome, was scheduled for three honors classes and two Advanced Placement classes. Bob's IEP included a two-page list of accommodations. In spite of his having achieved A's and B's, with just a single C in math, his mother did not feel that his teachers were accommodating him appropriately. Almost every evening, she emailed his teachers and his case manager to request more information or more help for Bob, and she angrily phoned his guidance counselor if she didn't receive a reply by the end of the first hour of the next school day.

A meeting was scheduled with the IEP team. When the accommodations were reviewed, Bob's mother agreed that all of them were being made. However, she explained that Bob had been removed from all outside social activities because he spent all night, every night, working on homework. The accommodation she demanded was that Bob have *no* homework assignments. The autism specialist agreed that this was a reasonable accommodation for a child with Asperger's Syndrome.

The teachers of the honors classes explained that the homework in their classes, which involved elaboration and extension of concepts, was even more essential than the homework assigned in AP classes. In AP classes, by contrast, homework consisted primarily of practice of concepts learned in class. The honors teachers explained that they had carefully broken their long assignments into segments, each having a separate due date before the final project, and they gave illustrations of their expectations. The director of special education explained the legal definition of accommodations (the mother said she'd never before heard that accommodations could not change the nature of the curriculum). The director also suggested that, instead of Bob's sacrificing his social life, perhaps it would be more appropriate for him to take standard classes. What Bob's mother was asking, he concluded, was not legal. She grew angry, but she did agree to give the team a "little more time" to serve Bob appropriately. She said she would "be back with her claws and broomstick" if anyone ever suggested that he be moved from honors classes without being given the no homework accommodation. "He's too bright to take anything less than honors classes, and if you people would provide this simple accommodation, he would do just fine," she argued. In the end, she got her way.

Attitudes toward Disability and Special Education

Not that many decades ago, a disability was considered a misfortune—not something to be ashamed of but a generally undesirable, unwelcome condition to be overcome to the greatest extent possible. Ability was considered more desirable than disability, and anything—whether a device or a service—that helped people with disabilities to do what those without disabilities could do was considered generally valuable, desirable, and worth the effort, cost, and possible stigma associated with using it.

The disability rights movement arose in response to the widespread negative attitudes toward disabilities, and it had a number of desirable outcomes. It helped overcome some of the discrimination against people with disabilities. And overcoming such bias and unfairness in everyday life is a great accomplishment. But the movement has also had some unintended negative consequences. One of these is the outright denial of disability in some cases, illustrated by the contention that disability exists only in attitudes or as a function of the social power to coerce.

The argument that disability is merely a "social construction" is particularly vicious in its effects on social justice. Even if we assume that disabilities are socially constructed, what should that mean? Should we assume that socially constructed phenomena are not "real," are not important, or should be discredited? If so, then consider that dignity, civil rights, childhood, social justice, and nearly every other phenomenon that we hold dear are social constructions. Many social constructions are not merely near and dear to us, they are real and useful in benevolent societies. The important question is whether the idea of disability is useful in helping people attain dignity or whether it is more useful to assume that disabilities are not real (i.e., that, like social justice, civil rights, and other social constructions, they are fabrications that can be ignored when convenient). The denial of disability is sometimes expressed as an aversion to labels, so that we are cautioned not to communicate openly and clearly about disabilities but to rely on euphemisms. But this approach is counterproductive. When we are able only to whisper or mime the undesirable difference called disability, then we inadvertently increase its stigma and thwart prevention efforts.

The specious argument that "normal" does not exist—because abilities of every kind are varied and because the point at which normal becomes abnormal is arbitrary—leads to the conclusion that no one actually has a disability or, alternatively, that everyone has a disability. Then, some argue, either no one or everyone is due an accommodation so that no one or everyone is identified as disabled. This unwillingness to draw a line defining something (such as disability, poverty, or childhood) is based either on ignorance regarding the nature of continuous distributions or on a rejection of the unavoidably arbitrary decisions necessary to provide special services to those who need them and, in so doing, to foster social justice.

Another unintended negative consequence of the disability rights movement is that, for some people, disability has become either something that does not matter or something to love, to take pride in, to flaunt, to adopt as a positive aspect of one's identity, or to cherish as something desirable or as a badge of honor. When disability makes no difference to us one way or the other, then we are not going to work to attenuate it, much less prevent it. At best, we will try to accommodate it. When we view disability as a desirable difference, then we are very likely to try to make it more pronounced, not to ameliorate it.

Several decades ago, special education was seen as a good thing—a helpful way of responding to disability, not something everyone needed or should have, but a useful and necessary response to the atypical needs of students with disabilities. This is why the Education for All Handicapped Children Act (now the Individuals with Disabilities Education Act) was written. But in the minds of many people, special education has been transformed from something helpful to something awful.

The full-inclusion movement did have some desirable outcomes. It helped overcome some of the unnecessary removal of students with disabilities from general education. However, the movement also has had some unintended negative consequences. One of these is that special education has come to be viewed in very negative terms, to be seen as a second-class and discriminatory system that does more harm than good. Rather than being seen as helpful, as a way of creating opportunity, special education is often portrayed as a means of shunting students into dead-end programs and killing opportunity.

Another unintended negative consequence of full inclusion is that general education is now seen by many as the *only* place where fair and equitable treatment is possible and where the opportunity to learn is extended to all equally. The argument has become that special education is good only as long as it is invisible (or nearly so), an indistinguishable part of a general education system that accommodates all students, regardless of their abilities or disabilities. Usually, this is described as a "unified" (as opposed to "separate") system of education. Special education is thus something to be avoided altogether or attenuated to the greatest extent possible, regardless of a student's inability to perform in a general setting. When special education is seen as discriminatory, unfair, an opportunity-killing system, or, as one writer put it, "the gold-plated garbage can of American schooling," then it is understandable that people will loathe it. But this way of looking at special education is like seeing the recognition and treatment of cancer as the cause of the problem.

The reversal in attitudes toward disability and special education—disability from undesirable to inconsequential, special education from desirable to awful—has clouded the picture of what special education is and what it should do for students with disabilities. Little wonder that special education stands accused of failure, that calls for its demise have become vociferous, and that contemporary practices are often more disabling than enabling. An unfortunate outcome of the changing attitudes toward disability and special education is that the benefit of special education is now sometimes seen as freedom from expectations of performance. It is as if we believed that, if a student has to endure the stigma of special education, then the compensation should include an exemption from work.

Placement Issues

Placing all students, regardless of their abilities, in regular classes has exacerbated the tendency to see disability as something existing only in people's minds. It fosters the impression that students are fitting in when they are not able to perform at anywhere near the normal level. It perpetuates disabilities; it does not compensate for them.

Administrators and guidance counselors sometimes place students in programs for which they do not qualify, even as graduation requirements are increasing and tests are mandated. Often, these students' *testing* is modified although their *curriculum* is not. The students may then feel that they have beaten the system. They are taught that the system is unfair and that the only way to win is by gaming it. Hard work and individual responsibility for one's education are often overlooked—or at least undervalued.

Students who consistently fail in a particular curriculum must be given the opportunity to deal with the natural consequences of that fact as a means of learning individual responsibility. For example, social promotion in elementary and middle school teaches students that they really don't have to be able to do the work to pass. Students who have been conditioned to rely on social promotion do not believe that the cycle will end until it does so—usually very abruptly in high school. Suddenly, no one passes them on, and no one gives them undeserved credit. Many of these students do not graduate in four years. Some never recover, while others find themselves forced to deal with a very distasteful situation.

No one wants to see a student fail, but to alter any standard without good reason is to set that same student up for failure later in life. Passing along a student with disabilities in regular classes, pretending that he or she is performing at the same level as most of the class or that it doesn't really matter (arguing that the student has a legal "right" to be in the class) is another prescription for disappointment and failure in later life. Indeed, this failure often comes in college or on the job.

Some people with disabilities do need assistance. Others do not. Consider Deborah Groeber, who struggled through degenerative deafness and blindness. The Office of Affirmative Action at the University of Pennsylvania offered to intercede at the Wharton School, but Groeber knew that she had more influence if she spoke for herself. Today, she is a lawyer with three Ivy League degrees. But not every student with disabilities can do or should be expected to do what Groeber did. Our concern is that too many students with disabilities are given encouragement based on pretense when they could do much more with appropriate special education.

Types of Accommodations

Two popular modifications in IEPs are allowing for the use of calculators and granting extended time on tests and assignments. Calculators can be a great asset, but they should be used when calculating complex problems or when doing word problems. Indiscriminate use of a calculator renders many math tests invalid, as they become a contest to see if buttons can be pushed successfully and in the correct order, rather than an evaluation of ability to do arithmetic or use mathematical knowledge.

Extended time on assignments and tests can also be a useful modification, but it can easily be misused or abused. Extended time on tests should mean *continuous* time so that a test is not studied for first and taken later. Sometimes a test must be broken into smaller segments that can be completed independently. However, this could put students with disabilities at a disadvantage, as one part of a test might help with remembering another part. Extensions on assignments need to be evaluated each time they are given, not simply handed out automatically because they are written into an IEP. If a student is clearly working hard, then extensions may be appropriate. If a student has not even been attempting assignments, then more time might be an avoidance tactic. Sometimes extended time means that assignments pile up and the student gets further and further behind. The result can then be overwhelming stress and the inability to comprehend discussions because many concepts must be acquired in sequence (e.g., in math, science, history, and foreign languages).

Reading tests and quizzes aloud to students can be beneficial for many, but great caution is required. Some students and teachers want to do more than simply read a test. Reading a test aloud means simply reading the printed words on the page *without* inflections that can reveal correct answers and without explaining vocabulary. Changing a test to open-notes or open-book, without the knowledge and consent of the classroom teacher, breaches good-faith test proctoring. It also teaches students dependence rather than independence and accomplishment. Similarly, scribing for a student can be beneficial for those who truly need it, but the teacher must be careful not to add details and to write only what the student dictates, including any run-on sentences or fragments. After scribing, if the assignment is not a test, the teacher should edit and correct the paper with the student, as she might do with any written work. But this must take place *after* the scribing.

How Misguided Accommodations Can Be Disabling

"Saving" a child from his or her own negative behavior reinforces that behavior and makes it a self-fulfilling prophecy. Well-intentioned guidance counselors often feel more responsibility for their students' success or failure than the students themselves feel. Sometimes students are not held accountable for their effort or work. They seem not to understand that true independence comes from *what* you know, not *whom* you know. Students who are consistently enabled and not challenged are never given the opportunity to become independent. Ann Bancroft, the polar explorer and dyslexic, claims that, although school was a torment, it was disability that forged her iron will. Stephen Cannell's fear for other dyslexics is that they will quit trying rather than struggle and learn to compensate for their disability.

Most parents want to help their children. However, some parents confuse making life *easier* with making life *better* for their children. Too often, parents feel that protecting their child from the rigors of academic demands is in his or her best interest. They may protect their child by insisting on curricular modifications and accommodations in assignments, time, and testing. But children learn by doing, and not allowing them to do something because they might fail is denying them the opportunity to succeed. These students eventually believe that they are not capable of doing what typical students can do, even if they are. Sometimes it is difficult for teachers to discern what a student actually can do and what a parent has done until an in-class assignment is given or a test is taken. At that point, it is often too late for the teacher to do much remediation. The teacher may erroneously conclude that the student is simply a poor test-taker.

In reality, the student may have been "protected" from learning, which will eventually catch up with him or her. Unfortunately, students may not face reality until they take a college entrance exam, go away to college, or apply for a job. Students who "get through" high school in programs of this type often go on to flunk out of college. Unfortunately, the parents of these students frequently blame the college for the student's failure, criticizing the postsecondary institution for not doing enough to help. Instead, they should be upset both with the secondary institution for not preparing the child adequately for the tasks to come and with themselves for their own overprotection.

The Benefits of Demands

Many successful adults with disabilities sound common themes when asked about their ability to succeed in the face of a disability. Tom Gray, a Rhodes Scholar who has a severe learning disability, claims that having to deal with the hardest experiences gave him the greatest strength. Stephen Cannell believes that, if he had known there was a reason beyond his control to explain his low achievement, he might not have worked as hard as he did. Today, he knows he has a learning disability, but he is also an Emmy Award-winning television writer and producer. Paul Orlalea, the dyslexic founder of Kinko's, believes God gave him an advantage in the challenge presented by his disability and that others should work with their strengths. Charles Schwab, the learning-disabled founder of Charles Schwab, Inc., cites his ability to think differently and to make creative leaps that more sequential thinkers don't make as chief reasons for his success. Fannie Flagg, the learning-disabled author, concurs and insists that learning disabilities become a blessing *only if you can overcome them.* Not every student with a disability can be a star performer, of course, but all should be expected to achieve all that they can.

Two decades ago, special educators thought it was their job to assess a student's achievement, to understand what the student wanted to do and what an average peer could do, and then to develop plans to bridge the gap, if possible. Most special educators wanted to see that each student had the tools and knowledge to succeed as independently as possible. Helping students enter the typical world was the mark of success for special educators.

The full-inclusion movement now insists that *every* student will benefit from placement in the mainstream. However, some of the modifications and accommodations now being demanded are so radical that we are doing an injustice to the entire education system. Special education must not be associated in any way with "dumbing down" the curriculum for students presumed to be at a given grade level, whether disabled or not.

Counselors and administrators who want to enable students must focus the discussion on realistic goals and plans for each student. An objective, in-depth discussion and evaluation must take place to determine how far along the continuum of successfully completing these goals the student has moved. If the student is making adequate progress independently, or with minimal help, special education services might not be necessary. If assistance is required to make adequate progress on realistic goals, then special education may be needed. Every modification and every accommodation should be held to the same standard: whether it will help the student attain these goals—*not* whether it will make life easier for the student. Knowing where a student is aiming can help a team guide that student toward success.

And the student must be part of this planning. A student who claims to want to be a brain surgeon but refuses to take science courses needs a reality check. If a student is unwilling to attempt to reach intermediate goals or does not succeed in meeting them, then special education cannot "save" that student. At that point, the team must help the student revisit his or her goals. Goals should be explained in terms of the amount of work required to complete them, not whether or not the teacher or parent feels they are attainable. When goals are presented in this way, students can often make informed decisions regarding their attainability and desirability. Troy Brown, a university dean and politician who has both a doctorate and a learning disability, studied at home with his mother. He estimates that it took him more than twice as long as the average person to complete assignments. Every night, he would go to bed with stacks of books and read until he fell asleep, because he had a dream of attending college.

General educators and special educators need to encourage all students to be responsible and independent and to set realistic expectations for themselves. Then teachers must help students to meet these expectations in a more and more independent manner. Special educators do not serve students well when they enable students with disabilities to become increasingly dependent on their parents, counselors, administrators, or teachers—or even when they fail to increase students' independence and competence.

Where We Stand

We want to make it clear that we think disabilities are real and that they make doing certain things either impossible or very difficult for the people who have them. We cannot expect people with disabilities to be "just like everyone else" in what they can do. . . .

In our view, students with disabilities *do* have specific shortcomings and *do* need the services of specially trained professionals to achieve their potential. They *do* sometimes need altered curricula or adaptations to make their learning possible. If students with disabilities were just like "regular" students, then there would be no need whatever for special education. But the school experiences of students with disabilities obviously will not be—*cannot* be—just like those of students without disabilities. We sell students with disabilities short when we pretend that they are no different from typical students. We make the same error when we pretend that they must *not* be expected to put forth extra effort if they are to learn to do some things—or learn to do something in a different way. We sell them short when we pretend that they have competencies that they do not have or pretend that the competencies we expect of most students are not important for them.

Like general education, special education must push students to become all they can be. Special education must countenance neither the pretense of learning nor the avoidance of reasonable demands.

POSTSCRIPT

Is the Practice of Providing Accommodations to Children in Special Education a Good Idea?

The following description of special education accommodations is taken from Price, Mayfield, McFadden, and Marsh, *Special Education for Inclusive Classrooms* (2001):

> The term "accommodation" has long been associated with compensatory education and modifications in the student's environment, instruction, and performance expectations. Today it has a quasi-legal meaning because of advances in legislation and litigation. In most cases a "reasonable accommodation" is a modification or adjustment that makes it possible for a student with a disability to have an equal opportunity. Reasonable accommodations may be made in the arrangement of the classroom, types of activities, or the facility to improve equal opportunity. Common accommodations are:
>
> Accessible classroom/location/furniture
> Advance notice of assignments
> Alternative ways of completing assignments (e.g., oral presentation versus written paper)
> Assistive computer technology
> Assistive listening devices
> Auxiliary aids and services (note takers, lab or library assistants, readers, interpreters)
> Captions for film and video material
> Course or program modifications
> Document conversion (alternative print formats: Braille, large print, tape, electronic, raised lettering)
> Test modifications
> Study skills and strategies training
> Time extensions
> Taped lectures
>
> There are many accommodations, but some of them are described in more detail in relationship to specific activities at the elementary and secondary levels. Curriculum modification must be functional, age-appropriate, and reflect transitions. Functional assessments measure the student's repertoire of skills needed to participate in a wide variety of settings. Functional curricula are those curricula that facilitate skill development essential to participate in a variety of settings. Chronological age-appropriate curricula

refer to curricula that include activities that are performed by nondisabled peers, which facilitate interactions with those peers. Student instruction must prepare them to function in future environments and environments outside of school or classroom.

With such a wide-ranging menu of possibilities, it is easy to see how difficult it might be to match the special education child's particular needs with the appropriate accommodation(s). It is the special needs student's Individualized Education Program (IEP) team that must determine what accommodations are appropriate and make them part of the written IEP. IEP team members include the parent(s), the child's general education and special education teachers, a district representative involved with special education, a school site counselor and/or administrator, an advisor for the parent(s) if needed, and in special circumstances the involved child.

There are some accommodations that the general education teacher may resist because of the extra workload involved, disruption of the normal class routine, or perceptions of other students. Examples of such modifications include marking correct answers rather than mistakes, limiting homework, allowing open-book tests, varying test formats, allowing notes to be used on tests, allowing retakes of tests or assignments, or providing extra-credit opportunities. Depending on the grade level involved, those types of accommodations may be misinterpreted by other students in the classroom and/or draw undesired attention to the special needs child. Usually such potential problems can be eliminated or at least ameliorated if the involved general education and special education teachers communicate and work cooperatively. Jane Baumel, a licensed educational psychologist, in an article entitled "General Education Accommodations" (*Schwab Learning,* 2003) made the following point, "Accommodations aren't intended to take the pale of real learning or instruction in basic skills. Instead, they provide ways for kids with learning problems to take in information or help them express heir knowledge."

Other sources of information on this topic include IDEA at ED.Gov; the Council for Exceptional Children; and *Taking Sides: Clashing Views in Special Education,* MaryAnn Byrnes (ed.) (McGraw-Hill Contemporary Learning Series, 2007).

ISSUE 18

Are Character/Moral Education Programs Effective?

YES: Tom Lickona, Eric Schaps, and Catherine Lewis, from "CEP's Eleven Principles of Effective Character Education," Character Education Partnership (2003)

NO: Patriotism for All, from "The Problem with Character Education" (2004–2006) and "Responsibility? You've Got to Be Kidding" (2004–2007)

ISSUE SUMMARY

YES: Tom Lickona, professor of education at the State University of New York, Eric Schaps, president of the Developmental Studies Center, and Catherine Lewis, author and character educator, present a number of basic principles that undergird successful character education programs.

NO: The "Patriotism for All" organization states "character education is not a verifiable scientific concept."

$\mathbf{A}$t its core any disagreement regarding character or moral education is a disagreement over values. Trying to answer the question of "What value/morals will comprise the character education curriculum?" is surely to invoke controversy and debate. But most assuredly schoolteachers and administrators do have an impact on student character. Recognition of the role of the school in the development of character is not a new idea. In "On the Early Education of the Citizen-Orator," Book I of *The Institutes of Oratory* (circa 95 A.D.), Quintilian described the characteristics of a good teacher thusly:

> Let him neither have vices in himself, nor tolerate them in others. Let his austerity not be stern, nor his affability too easy, lest dislike arise from the one, or contempt from the other. Let him discourse frequently on what is honorable and good, for the oftener he admonishes, the more seldom will he have to chastise.

In 1918, the NEA's "Seven Cardinal Principles of Secondary Education" included "Ethical Character," which was described as "instilling in the student the notion of personal responsibility and initiative. . . ."

A more contemporary statement emphasizing that educators are engaged in the character development of their students comes from David Elkind and Freddy Sweet from "You Are a Character Educator" in *Today's School* (September/October 2004):

> Let's get one thing perfectly clear—you are a character educator. Whether you are teacher, administrator, custodian, or school bus driver, you are helping shape the character of the kids you come in contact with. It's in the way you talk, the behaviors you model, the conduct you tolerate, the deeds you encourage, the expectations you transmit. Yes, for better or worse, you are already doing character education. The real question is what kind? Are you doing it well or poorly? By design or by default? And what kinds of values are you actually teaching?

It is that last question that creates the conflicts and controversies with this topic. Upon what values or morals should character education be based? Other educational programs that are sometimes included in the character education milieu are civic/citizenship education and community service learning. Both of those programs engender the same type of controversy that is debated here. With civic/citizenship education the question becomes what are qualities of a good citizen? On one side, the answer might include a reference to being law-abiding, whereas the other might involve the image of Rosa Parks and civil disobedience. With community service learning, advocates suggest that it will help students develop qualities of responsibility and caring for others. Opponents charge that requiring students to do community service is a form of "mandatory volunteerism," which is an oxymoron and does a disservice to the altruism involved with true volunteerism.

In the articles that follow Lickona, Schaps, and Lewis assert that certain "core values . . . affirm our human dignity." The "Patriotism for All" articles claim that many in character education stress "compliance with authority and conformity with conservative values."

YES ⬅

Tom Likona, Eric Schaps,
and Catherine Lewis

CEP's Eleven Principles of Effective Character Education

Effective Character Education

Promotes Core Ethical Values as the Basis of Good Character

Character education holds that widely shared, pivotally important, core ethical values—such as caring, honesty, fairness, responsibility, and respect for self and others—form the basis of good character. A school committed to character development stands for these values (sometimes referred to as "virtues" or "character traits"), defines them in terms of behaviors that can be observed in the life of the school, models these values, studies and discusses them, uses them as the basis of human relations in the school, celebrates their manifestations in the school and community, and holds all school members accountable to standards of conduct consistent with the core values.

In a school committed to developing character, these core values are treated as a matter of obligation, as having a claim on the conscience of the individual and community. Character education asserts that the validity of these values, and our responsibility to uphold them, derive from the fact that such values affirm our human dignity, promote the development and welfare of the individual person, serve the common good, meet the classical tests of reversibility (i.e., Would you want to be treated this way?) and universality (i.e., Would you want all persons to act this way in a similar situation?), and inform our rights and responsibilities in a democratic society. The school makes clear that these basic human values transcend religious and cultural differences, and express our common humanity.

Defines "Character" Comprehensively to Include Thinking, Feeling, and Behavior

Good character involves understanding, caring about, and acting upon core ethical values. A holistic approach to character development therefore seeks to develop the cognitive, emotional, and behavioral aspects of moral life. Students grow to understand core values by studying and discussing them, observing behavioral models, and resolving problems involving the values. Students learn to care about core values by developing empathy skills, forming

From *Character Education Partnership*, pp. 1–4. Copyright © 2003 by Character Education Partnership. Reprinted by permission.

caring relationships, helping to create community, hearing illustrative and inspirational stories, and reflecting on life experiences. And they learn to act upon core values by developing prosocial behaviors (e.g., communicating feelings, active listening, helping skills) and by repeatedly practicing these behaviors, especially in the context of relationships (e.g., through cross-age tutoring, mediating conflicts, community service). As children grow in character, they develop an increasingly refined understanding of the core values, a deeper commitment to living according to those values, and a stronger capacity and tendency to behave in accordance with them.

Uses a Comprehensive, Intentional, Proactive, and Effective Approach to Character Development

Schools committed to character development look at themselves through a moral lens to assess how virtually everything that goes on in school affects the character of students. A **comprehensive** approach uses all aspects of schooling as opportunities for character development. This includes what is sometimes called *the hidden curriculum* (e.g., school ceremonies and procedures; the teachers' example; students' relationships with teachers, other school staff, and each other; the instructional process; how student diversity is addressed; the assessment of learning; the management of the school environment; the discipline policy); the *academic curriculum* (i.e., core subjects, including the health curriculum); and *extracurricular programs* (i.e., sports teams, clubs, service projects, after-school care). "Stand alone" character education programs can be useful first steps or helpful elements of an ongoing effort but are not an adequate substitute for a holistic approach that integrates character development into every aspect of school life. Finally, rather than simply waiting for opportunities to arise, with an **intentional** and **proactive** approach, the school staff takes deliberate steps for developing character, drawing wherever possible on practices shown by research to be effective.

Creates a Caring School Community

A school committed to character strives to become a microcosm of a civil, caring, and just society. It does this by creating a community that helps all its members form caring attachments to one another. This involves developing caring relationships among students (within and across grade levels), among staff, between students and staff, and between staff and families. These caring relationships foster both the desire to learn and the desire to be a good person. All children and adolescents have needs for safety, belonging, and the experience of contributing, and they are more likely to internalize the values and expectations of groups that meet these needs. Likewise, if staff members and parents experience mutual respect, fairness, and cooperation in their relationships with each other, they are more likely to develop the capacity to promote those values in students. In a caring school community, the daily life of classrooms and all other parts of the school environment (e.g., the corridors, cafeteria, playground, school bus, front office, and teachers' lounge) are imbued with a climate of concern and respect for others.

Provides Students with Opportunities for Moral Action

In the ethical as in the intellectual domain, students are constructive learners; they learn best by doing. To develop good character, they need many and varied opportunities to apply values such as compassion, responsibility, and fairness in everyday interactions and discussions as well as through community service. By grappling with real-life challenges (e.g., how to divide the labor in a cooperative learning group, how to reach consensus in a class meeting, how to reduce fights on the playground, how to carry out a service learning project) and reflecting on these experiences, students develop practical understanding of the requirements of cooperating with others and giving of oneself. Through repeated moral experiences, students develop and practice the skills and behavioral habits that make up the action side of character.

Includes a Meaningful and Challenging Academic Curriculum That Respects All Learners, Develops Their Character, and Helps Them to Succeed

When students succeed at the work of school and feel a sense of competence and autonomy, they are more likely to feel valued and cared about as persons. Because students come to school with diverse skills, interests and needs, an academic program that helps all students succeed will be one in which the content and pedagogy are sophisticated enough to engage all learners. This means providing a curriculum that is inherently interesting and meaningful to students. A meaningful curriculum includes active teaching and learning methods such as cooperative learning, problem-solving approaches, and experience-based projects. These approaches increase student autonomy by appealing to students' interests, providing them with opportunities to think creatively and test their ideas, and fostering a sense of "voice and choice"—having a say in decisions and plans that affect them.

In addition, effective character educators look for the natural intersections between the academic content they wish to teach and the character qualities they wish to develop. These "character connections" can take many forms, such as addressing current ethical issues in science, debating historical practices and decisions, and discussing character traits and ethical dilemmas in literature. When teachers bring to the fore the character dimension of the curriculum, they enhance the relevance of subject matter to students' natural interests and questions, and in the process, increase student engagement and achievement.

Strives to Foster Students' Self-motivation

Character is often defined as "doing the right thing when no one is looking." The best underlying ethical reason for following rules, for example, is respect for the rights and needs of others—not fear of punishment or desire for a reward.

Similarly, we want students to be kind to others because of an inner belief that kindness is good and a desire to be a kind person. Growing in self-motivation is a developmental process that schools of character are careful not to undermine by excessive emphasis on extrinsic incentives. When such schools give appropriate social recognition for students' prosocial actions (e.g., "Thank you for holding the door—that was a thoughtful thing to do.") or celebrate character through special awards (e.g., for outstanding school or community service), they keep the focus on character. Schools of character work with students to develop their understanding of rules, their awareness of how their behavior affects others, and the character strengths—such as self-control, perspective taking, and conflict resolution skills—needed to act responsibly in the future. Rather than settle for mere compliance, these schools seek to help students benefit from their mistakes by providing meaningful opportunities for reflection, problem solving, and restitution.

Engages the School Staff as a Learning and Moral Community That Shares Responsibility for Character Education and Attempts to Adhere to the Same Core Values That Guide the Education of Students

All school staff—teachers, administrators, counselors, school psychologists, coaches, secretaries, cafeteria workers, playground aides, bus drivers—need to be involved in learning about, discussing, and taking ownership of the character education effort. First and foremost, staff members assume this responsibility by modeling the core values in their own behavior and taking advantage of other opportunities to influence the students with whom they interact.

Second, the same values and norms that govern the life of students serve to govern the collective life of adult members in the school community. Like students, adults grow in character by working collaboratively with each other and participating in decision-making that improves classrooms and school. They also benefit from extended staff development and opportunities to observe colleagues and then apply character development strategies in their own work with students.

Third, a school that devotes time to staff reflection on moral matters helps to ensure that it operates with integrity. Through faculty meetings and smaller support groups, a reflective staff regularly asks questions such as: What character-building experiences is the school already providing for its students? What negative moral experiences (e.g., peer cruelty, student cheating, adult disrespect of students, littering of the grounds) is the school currently failing to address? And what important moral experiences (e.g., cooperative learning, school and community service, opportunities to learn about and interact with people from different racial, ethnic, and socioeconomic backgrounds) is the school now omitting? What school practices are at odds with its professed core values and desire to develop a caring school community? Reflection of this nature is an indispensable condition for developing the moral life of a school.

Fosters Shared Moral Leadership and Long-range Support of the Character Education Initiative

Schools that are engaged in effective character education have leaders (e.g., the principal, a lead teacher or counselor, a district administrator, or preferably a small group of such individuals) who champion the effort. At least initially, many schools and districts establish a character education committee—often composed of staff, students, parents, and possibly community members—that takes responsibility for planning, implementation, and support. Over time, the regular governing bodies of the school or district may take on the functions of this committee. The leadership also takes steps to provide for the long-range support (e.g., adequate staff development, time to plan) of the character education initiative, including, ideally, support at the district and state levels. In addition, within the school students assume developmentally appropriate roles in leading the character education effort through class meetings, student government, peer mediation, cross-age tutoring, service clubs, task forces, and student-led initiatives.

Engages Families and Community Members as Partners in the Character-building Effort

Schools that reach out to families and include them in character-building efforts greatly enhance their chances for success with students. They take pains at every stage to communicate with families—via newsletters, e-mails, family nights, and parent conferences—about goals and activities regarding character education. To build greater trust between home and school, parents are represented on the character education committee. These schools also make a special effort to reach out to subgroups of parents who may not feel part of the school community. Finally, schools and families enhance the effectiveness of their partnership by recruiting the help of the wider community (i.e., businesses, youth organizations, religious institutions, the government, and the media) in promoting character development.

Evaluates the Character of the School, the School Staff's Functioning as Character Educators, and the Extent to Which Students Manifest Good Character

Effective character education must include an effort to assess progress. Three broad kinds of outcomes merit attention:

   a. **The character of the school:** To what extent is the school becoming a more caring community? This can be assessed, for example, with surveys that ask students to indicate the extent to which they agree with statements such as, "Students in this school (classroom) respect and care about each other," and "This school (classroom) is like a family."
   b. **The school staff's growth as character educators:** To what extent have adult staff—teaching faculty, administrators, and support personnel—developed understandings of what they can do to foster character

      development? Personal commitment to doing so? Skills to carry it out? Consistent habits of acting upon their developing capacities as character educators?

  c. **Student character:** To what extent do students manifest understanding of, commitment to, and action upon the core ethical values? Schools can, for example, gather data on various character-related behaviors: Has student attendance gone up? Fights and suspensions gone down? Vandalism declined? Drug incidents diminished?

Schools can also assess the three domains of character (knowing, feeling, and behaving) through anonymous questionnaires that measure student moral judgment (for example, "Is it wrong to cheat on a test?"), moral commitment ("Would you cheat if you were sure you wouldn't get caught?") and self-reported moral behavior ("How many times have you cheated on a test or major assignment in the past year?"). Such questionnaires can be administered at the beginning of a school's character initiative to get a baseline and again at later points to assess progress.

 **NO**

The Problem with Character Education

Most social psychologists, would have us transform the structure of the classroom rather than try to remake the students themselves—precisely the opposite of the character education approach.

Related to allowing only students with the majority religious belief to participate in the Pledge of Allegiance are character education programs in schools that likewise seek to reinforce the social and cultural values of the majority. Promoted as researched and proven programs to correct "bad" behavior in students, the available literature on the subject indicates that, at its foundation, character education is part of an agenda to introduce conservative ideology, alone, into the minds of every student. Worse, the available evidence shows that these programs cannot accomplish even that purpose.

A Morality Tale

A father asked his young daughter, "Tell me, why do you clean your room?"
"I do it because Mama and Papa ask me to."
"Why do we ask you?"
She replied, "It has to be done."

Not believing that she had quite answered it, she then started guessing, "Because it's nice to have a clean room?" (More something she might have been told that is mostly meaningless to her.) Then she hesitated and said, "Because it's responsibility." The father shuddered. This is something she picked up at school. The kind of non-reasoning a soldier uses during an act of genocide! Or rationalizing participation in an illegal war! It is the opposite of education: an unreasoned *because*.

By contrast, recently the family read a book that explained how cleaning your room keeps it organized and hygienic, prevents toys or their pieces from being lost, and cuts down on once-a-week laboriousness. You know . . . real education, with real reasons for doing things. No abstractions, no "shoulds" about it. And if you ask the daughter now, she will give you a reasoned answer.

Another question the father had asked was: "What did you learn in the Character Counts! assembly, today?" She told him, "Respect is the Golden Rule." He followed with, "What's the Golden Rule?" She shrugged. Even if she knew and was older, would she be able to answer the why of it? "Why should you do unto others as you would have them do unto you?"

If there are reasons for the Golden Rule, instead of just reciting the platitude, why is the school not simply stating them explicitly? In fact this widely acclaimed moral homily is a wonderful example of the simplicity problem with Character Counts! and character education, in general.

Are there actually valid reasons for following the Golden Rule? For instance:

- What if the other person doesn't also follow it?
- What if how you like things done to you is offensive in manner and result to others when done to them?
- What if more than one other is involved and their goals are in conflict?
- What if you both want things that will hurt you?
- Does following this principle lead to success, self-esteem, less abuse, less poverty, greater rights for all, a better environment?
- Which of these goals does the Golden Rule achieve more effectively than say, straight reciprocity (tit for tat), or the communist rule— "From each according to his ability, to each according to his need", or plain old manipulation via marketing, selling, framing, half-truth and other widely regarded political and commercial means of manipulating others for one's own "benefit"?

Accountability of School Programs

This is not nuance. These are the fundamentals for mature decision-making. Character Counts! and similar character education programs deliver no such clarity or insight, no depth, no contrast. Instead what we get are arbitrarily chosen, ill-defined pillars and folksy slogans whose language seems to be an appeal to a nebulous, sentimental, touchy-feely sensibility—stuffed with culturally idiosyncratic assumptions. In other words, there is nothing offered relevant to the complexity of real choices in the real world—even from the viewpoint of a young child.

One is left with a lingering suspicion that the entire Character Counts! program is full of this kind of "reactionary, conforming robot as moral being" instruction: compliance with authority, implied defect, group intimidation, contracted behavior, external recognition and rewards for behavior . . . Really, aren't grades bad enough for showing a kid how to do the right things for the wrong reasons?

Shouldn't all school programs be held to a higher standard than this, showing a sound basis in theory, and demonstrating real-world results before being adopted? Particularly, that the program be able to ensure it is not doing harm to our children?

To return to the main point, accountability, there are really only three practical questions one needs to answer to assess the desirability of implementing any program in the school:

1. Can the need for it be demonstrated in individuals?
2. If one is able to concretely identify a need for "better" character in some qualifying number of students, will any given program A) improve the condition or B) make it worse.
3. Does the degree of improvement and the number of students benefited justify the time and expense?

Character Education Is Not a Verifiable Scientific Concept

As applied to character education, in terms of the first question, "character" is an archaic, quasi-metaphysical term, more related to horoscopes than any scientific concept. It is a term with no agreed upon definition, even among proponents of character education that, moreover, confusingly blends personality and behavioral components. This reveals the fundamental problem with character education: how can there be accountability for a program that seeks to address something (a quality, ability, aptitude?) with no clearly defined or quantifiable attributes and which, therefore, can demonstrate neither need nor success.

This absence of anything to gauge or measure makes the second and third questions impossible to answer. We cannot know if correcting the lack of whatever CE proposes to improve does the students any good, at all.

But, let's say we can define character, not as a personality trait of some kind, but in terms of quantifiable behavior that hypothetically might link with something localized within the child (lying, cheating, stealing, bullying, etc. although it is notable that the list of problem behaviors does not include: conformity, lack of innovation, uncritical thinking, self-righteousness, ostentation, gluttony, greed, etc.).

Still, how does one leap from the desire to address *corrective* action for an arbitrarily selected set of behaviors in a trifling small handful of identifiable students to deciding to implement *pre-emptive* measures in the entire cohort of uninvolved students? Are we talking original sin here? Enough of them will err unless indoctrinated? In that case, character education programs are no less than ideological tools in a religious campaign.

Possibly the most telling indicator that the character education movement builds its educational claims on flawed scientific method and unfounded psychological and social theory is the absence of any study published in peer reviewed journals that would support character education. To the contrary, the flaws in the "research" that is promoted on the Character Counts! web site *are* well documented. Such a dearth of validity makes it hard to just give it the benefit of the doubt. To the contrary, properly conducted, peer reviewed studies have shown character education programs to be not only ineffectual, but *negatively correlated* with results!

There doesn't seem to be any objective reason for these program to be in our schools. In that regard, Character Counts! would seem to fall right in line with a string of similarly flawed and failed school programs: *religious education, moral education, values education* . . . Not to be deterred by lack of results, CC! and other character education programs forge ahead—each trotting out an entirely different list of politically-entangled core values and ways to implement them! It is unfortunate for the entire field that there is no agreed upon definition of character or any reliable way to measure it, otherwise, one might be able to see the benefit of one over the other—or any at all.

Another School Program That Excludes Students

However, all strains of character education do find agreement that the desired goals for these programs are compliance with authority and conformity with conservative values. Perhaps those goals are desirable in some societies. But that is an ideological position, not in line with the greatness of American "character", of independence and innovation that many, if not most us want for our children. When reading between the lines of the marketing appeal to school boards and parents, it becomes quite clear that character education, and Character Counts!, in particular, are plain attempts to inculcate conservative social values in students and return religious moral instruction to the classroom.

The uncomfortably close alliance of Character Counts! and conservative political and religious groups should give anyone in a free society serious pause. In fact, the stealth part of the marketing approach behind *character education*" as code word for *"religious indoctrination"* is very similar to how *intelligent design* winks at *religious creationism* and *abstinence* at the religious idea of *chastity*.

In this way, parents and school board members in localities across the nation have been sold on two unfounded, unsupported conclusions regarding Character Counts!:

1. Something needs to be done to develop character in our students.
2. It is possible to do something to develop character in our students.

Because the flimsy evidence and weak theory offered are not sufficient to justify it, if asked why they are in favor of adopting Character Counts! these same parents and board members can only offer sentimental and anecdotal reasons, while citing the popular clamour.

A university professor of physics, with children in public schools, offered:

> "We adults may want to lead by example by showing that we base decisions on evidence rather than speculation, hearsay, or the like. We make a big fuss in public about the lack of decent science education, and then we ourselves don't care squat about reasoning."

Ideologically and politically, it's a fine idea to brandish about nostalgic, unscientific terms like *character, responsibility, respect, citizenship* . . . But such concerns belong in popular politics and churches, outside the school. A scientific approach would agree with the conclusions of psychologists, sociologists and educational theorists that the source of these high-lighted "problem behaviors" in children does not derive from built-in flaws in them, rather that they are the natural and desirable expressions of growth, discovery and testing limits children need to explore on their own in order to mature.

Generation Gap—Especially in liberal republics, there is added stress in older generations when each succeeding generation exhibits their own version of the freedoms such societies enjoy. Our own generation was certainly freer than proceeding ones and we would expect that living in a free country—which increasingly supports children's rights—this trend will continue, unabated. Will there be excesses? In all likelihood. Is it natural and even necessary? Of course.

Fix the Problem, Not the Person

There is something that we can do, however. We can limit the destructive behavior in children which arises from their own healthy coping mechanisms when confronted with flaws in endemic to the system (injustices, hypocrisies, confused messages). In fact, most social psychologists would have us *transform the structure of the classroom rather than try to remake the students* themselves—precisely the opposite of the character education approach. As an example, was it the poor character of Rosa Parks that motivated her to disrespect authority and violate the law when she refused to move to the back of the bus? Is it lack of citizenship or patriotism that motivates children to decline participation in the Pledge of Allegiance?

This difference in approach is a very big deal. We hear, anecdotally, about the increase in cheating, lying and covering up in today's students. That there is any such increase is dubious. Even so, it is telling that, few, if any of these perceived problems have their root in poor character. They arise, for the most part, as a natural and appropriate human response when confronted with a system that teaches people to do the right things for the wrong reasons. And it doesn't take long to "get" that if it is the wrong reasons that are important (i.e., prizes, grades, test scores, trophies, salaries, bonuses, funding), then there is a surer way of having them—and that is doing the wrong things.

It is perhaps an unavoidable truth when W.C. Fields says: "Anything worth winning is worth cheating for." Yes, indeed! We can predict that, as more and more emphasis is placed on winning, ranking and appearances, even the *earning* of character prizes, instead of on the inherent pleasures of social interaction and learning and focusing on the equitable social structures that are required for them to flourish—including exemplary behavior by leadership at the highest levels of not using means tot justify ends—then we should find that things will be rapidly be getting worse and worse. Scheming and lying to win a reality show, steroids in professional sports, corporate cheating of stockholders and consumers, elimination of employee benefits, spinning the message, looking for the answer in drugs (legal or otherwise), the glorification of greed, war and fear.

If parents and school districts are truly serious about supporting our students and our community, isn't it so much more important that we get serious about addressing the irreconcilable systemic problems that we and our children confront rather than trying to bend over backwards to blame or change them. Our children come into this world just fine, thank you and stay that way. *Children aren't the problem, folks!* They are easy victims of the impossible situations we put them in (like having to abstain from the Pledge of Allegiance), the no-win conditions built of the priorities from our own misguided education. It may seem easier to put the fault on kids, but a more honorable and surer path is to assume responsibility by changing ourselves: our own attitudes, our social institutions—starting with the schools.

Following in the tradition of the *true character* of American greatness, entitled to the free pursuit of happiness, we have always been a people of *independence, innovation, egalitarianism, empathy, fairness and moderation,* dedicated—not to changing individuals—but to progressive change in our social institutions so as to embrace all of the wonderful variations of individual character and colorful diversities of culture in our country and help them to flourish. . . .

⋯◉⋯

Responsibility? You've Got to Be Kidding

Patriotism for All

Recently, an elementary child brought home the school newsletter announcing the celebration of the Character Counts! pillar, "Responsibility." (*Celebration is an educational technique?*)

Slogans and Lists

What followed were a few ideas that were supposed to be related to responsibility for parents to discuss with the student at home:

- *Do what you are supposed to do*
- *Persevere: keep on trying*

- *Always do your best*
- *Use self-control*
- *Be self-disciplined*
- *Think before you act—consider the consequences*
- *Be accountable for your choices*

Overall, the ideas expressed in this list are so reliant on cliché and so devoid of context and reasoning as to be nearly incomprehensible. Of all the possibilities, why is this list proposed as concepts relevant to responsibility? Even then, without definition or qualification, the sort of person this list defines is not what many parents would wish on their children.

By way of contrast, a wonderful TV show is "The Magic School Bus." It has one consistent behavioral theme: "Ask questions, take risks, get messy." This is entirely antithetical to the notion of "responsibility" as characterized in the slogans of the school newsletter.

Reading through the list, one cannot help but ask: Why? Why? Why? What is the context? Where is the reasoning for any of these "ideas" that would recommend them for discussion in our homes? Nowhere is there the hint of a means of balance or moderation. No method for prioritizing competing goals. No acknowledgement of the complexities inherent in every choice.

Each item in the school's list of slogans is problematic, and many in the same way:

Do what you are supposed to do
- According to what manual for conduct? Is the goal here to create some kind of submissive employee, or unquestioning citizen, a person who supports traditional rules of behavior (e.g., religious or conservative values)?
- According to whom? Your boss who tells you to fudge the accounts or hide some test results? Your commanding officer who orders you to commit a war crime? The law that tells you it's OK to make children feel excluded by their school and nation because being able to participate in the official patriotic exercise requires belief in God?
- With what priorities? Who wins when there are competing priorities? Your boss who wants you to work late or your marriage that needs you to spend more time at home? Your religion that preaches pacifism or your nation that asks your support for war?
- What about independence and innovation in culture and science, the keynotes of greatness in American society? These qualities are almost always in conflict with business as usual.

Persevere: keep on trying
- How is this remotely connected to responsibility?
- What if you have got it all wrong? How, for example, does this apply to gambling?
- Isn't a central tenet of responsibility to understand when you should reverse course and cut your losses?

- Isn't the disaster in Iraq, or the stubborn drive to cut taxes at any and all cost, enough to caution anyone that staying the course, purely for it's own sake, regardless of changing conditions, can quickly devolve into driving oneself off a cliff?

Always *do your best*

- It is an impossible goal, one that is absolutely undesirable in the context of achieving a well-rounded life. No one can do their best in one area without sacrificing excellence elsewhere. Are we not all sorely conscious that we have limited time and resources to bring hardly any of our activities that compete for our time and resources to full-fruition? How many lives were ruined in single-minded pursuit of success?
- I don't know how many times I have heard people say, "Well, I did my best" to mean, "It was as good as I could do (considering that I put little, if any, research, extra training or effort into it)." When employed meaninglessly like this, it readily deteriorates into a less reproachable way to say, "Well, I tried."
- This is right up there with, "Of course, you're entitled to your opinion," another perfect example of the typical kind of paradox that results from institutionalizing principles that suffer when made static. Unquestioned sloganeering becomes an unassailable wall used to deflect criticism, shirk intellectual integrity by not having to respond to criticism, and discourages excellence by making mediocrity OK.

Use self-control

- Whose version of self-control? Yet another way to state the first message, "submit to and internalize authority", this one hits at the emotional level.
- Literally, the whole concept is preposterous. Since when don't people control themselves?
- How much self-control? At what times? Certainly, there are times when humans require impulse control. But that is not a simple matter of repression. Whether a person becomes joyfully alive or a neurotic shell hinges on appropriateness: reasons and context are everything when imposing social restraints on natural impulses.
- Why not teach self-awareness? Instruction in how to negotiate competing drives? Teaching a child to recognize symptoms of the stage of emotional growth they are in, so that they can insert some rationality into their emotional reactions, would be more to the point of helping them to find balance and avoid discomfort when up against conflicting inner drives. For instance, a 6 year-old's emotions become stronger due to brain growth in that area. Distraction or helping them become aware of their new feelings is the approved psychological approach to relieving their distress (not yours). There is a similar approach for teen-age hormonal years. Even then, youth is the age of great discovery and creativity for this very reason. In many cases, imposing social restraints on natural impulses is counter-productive to the inquisitive, creative, explorative phases of life.

Be self-disciplined
- Again, what model of education proposes that a child should "stay within the lines" and "think inside the box" as opposed to being explorative and experimental?
- If there were a logical, practical reason for a child to behave in some specific way, why would it require any kind of discipline, self or otherwise? Why not simply provide an easily understood explanation of detailing how it is in the child's self-interest?
- Missing caveat. On the other hand, if there is no good reason, discipline and punishment make perfect sense. Threats and abuse are how slaves are made to comply with unjust demands. Why are we asking citizens in a free society to arbitrarily discipline themselves? To do what? Recite their lessons, speak only if spoken to, don't dance?
- In reality, we all know that the underlying idea here is that if the authority isn't around to check on you (boss, parent, teacher, God or Santa Claus) then you must conduct yourself as if they were still there disciplining you (what a phrase!) Otherwise, lacking a good reason why would you comply?
- "Think before you act—consider the consequences." I like this one. It actually defines much of what real responsibility is all about.
- But there is a glaring omission. One can only understand consequences with a thorough understanding of factors and the mechanisms of cause and effect. This requires a robust education that provides logical and critical thinking skills and a perspective into the long-ranging effects of one's actions. (It's not hard; the Magic School Bus does it every day.)

Be accountable for your choices
Huh? What is this supposed to mean? Accountable? How? To whom?

The Real Agenda: Conservative, Coached, Constricted Social Units

There is a theme that runs through each of these ideas—call it the dark side of "responsibility". It is the attempt to play on banal truisms in order to convince children:

1. That there is a very narrow course of action for all eventualities, a course that comes with few contradictions or complexities.
2. That the past is the best model for the future.
3. That one's courses of action have already been set and are not one's own to best determine.
4. That one's primary motivation should be not joy, but guilt.

It should be no secret to anyone that the intended sense in of the word "responsibility" as promoted by the school and the Character Counts! program it is actually "duty." Subservience to authority, tradition and discipline. These are the principles of military organization, which suits the purposes of religious and political conservatives just fine. Yet, this kind of training has no place in the public schools of a free, groundbreaking nation. . . .

Another Way—Starting Points

It should go without saying that first we have to make sure that the system is fair. No amount of rhetoric or stories or role-playing is going to have any impact when it is not supported by reality. The first place to start with that is the school and classroom. After that, if lessons and examples are still needed, the following framework can replace the homilies, slogans and list.

Tell Them Why—Not What

There are sound theoretical reasons for keeping silent when it comes to "shoulds", "oughts" or "have-tos" both at school and home. And as a practical matter, when conditions change on us as adults, we can avoid contradicting ourselves and in the process behaving arbitrarily like tyrants: "Because I said so." On the other hand, "Why" is instinctual in every human over 4. It is really a simple concept. When encouraged and nurtured, it flowers in children of all ages. Even very young children can understand having permission to say, "That's not a good reason."

There really is no reason any child should take the school seriously, if good reasons for recommended behavior do not accompany every lesson. Reasons are unaccountably absent in character education lessons—which is absurd. No person does something just because they should—not unless they are slaves or otherwise under threat if they don't. In fact, it would seem that if you just tell children "why", there is no need for the "what"—the pillars and the slogans, or lists presented in the form of commandments! (Really! "Do what you are supposed to do"?) Relevant explanations with sound reasons are sufficient unto themselves.

Watch the Politics

In the public schools of a diverse and democratic society, conservative social ideals and moral principles are hardly appropriate for pillars. But if they cannot be avoided, they must at least be balanced with contrasting liberal concepts. Fundamentally, a balancing dose of liberal ideals would shift the focus away from placing the entire burden on the personal flaws in individuals (the conservative and religious viewpoint) to placing it on working to improve the flaws in the structure of society. Lessons on these principles would include demonstrating how improving social conditions eliminates the causes of inequities and injustices that produce social discontinuity and how equal opportunity and the common welfare promotes cooperation and sense of community. Under these social conditions the need to make personal choices less "strategic" is automatically reduced.

Indeed, without adding fundamental pillars of equality and mutuality (fraternity), the other pillars become altruistic, utopian and dangerous. Confronted with imbalances of power and opportunity, the effective defense—besides trying to work within the system to change them (as we are here)—is to respond with equally unfair behavior. Choices people make are really not about right and wrong; they are practical. A simple demonstration is that when the economy is good, crime goes down. On the other hand, if people are poor, marginalized and not integrated in society, you get riots. No moral instruction needed, one way or the other, thank you. Unfortunately, as things stand right now, practical is pretty ugly.

In order to bring students' attention to dysfunctional structures of society, they can be encouraged to research the roots of social dissonance, explore the basis of socio-economic conditions and contemplate how to correct and improve them. In today's America, where the system is still too obviously rigged, it will seem in many ways "fairer" to cheat, lie and pilfer; indulge greed and pride; use money, anabolic drugs, or cronyism to get ahead—instead of merit; avoid intellectual honesty like a plague; use marketing manipulation to make your point, and finally, decide who is right by who is the strongest . . . you know the hallmarks of American society as seen by the rest of the world in 2005.

It is perhaps telling that, in the most harmonious societies (those where the murder and imprisonment rates are not those of 3rd world dictatorships), the social contract offers assurances of social safety and health, equal opportunity, and, the population and government are overwhelmingly *not religious* (e.g., moralizing seems to have an inverse effect on a nation's character). Again, it would be much simpler just to chuck the whole thing and keep politics out of education, but if we can't, let us at least present a more balanced political perspective.

Balance and Moderation as Key

A fundamental principle of character missed by every character education program is the call to cautions for moderation and balance. Aristotle was one of the earliest philosophers to seriously think about character. Character education and Character Counts!, in particular, seems not to take him into account at all. When it comes to character, Aristotle's conclusion is: moderation is everything. For instance, courage is a good trait to be able to call on, for too little courage will keep one defenseless, preventing learning and progressing. But too much courage results in foolhardiness in the face of danger. Trustworthiness is also handy to pull out when you need it. Too little of it and you will not be able to gain the confidence of others, too much and you will surely be taken unfair advantage of. Likewise, caring may have long-range social benefits, but works against you if not moderated so that you become a slave to others' needs.

In this respect it is also important to caution that there must be balance in any relationship where ethical behavior is expected. If a person expresses any of these traits under conditions, which are less than reciprocal, any action other than immediate self-interest is immoderate and will only feed the imbalance.

Account for Individual Differences

In the actual practice of moderation, the fact that each individual is unique must be taken into account. People are not the same. The optimal degree to which a trait is moderately expressed in a given individual is relative to her abilities and experience. The same act of courage in one person becomes an act of suicide in another with less ability or experience. The same taking-on of responsibility in one person, in another, enables her manipulation by others.

✿❦✿

The real question underlying all this is not the good or bad character of students; it is about on what basis one should act. We would argue that making appropriate choices requires very little in the way of any specific character enhancements. Equally inert is the attempt to indoctrinate impossible to define behavioral axioms (i.e., "Use self-control."). Appropriate choices require no more and no less than well-informed critical thinking with an eye to long-range consequences.

Rather than spend time and money investing in fixing children—character education—we can offer them real decision support by investing in academics—NOT the 3 R's—but science, history, government and through teachers and administrators providing model behavior and egalitarian conditions at school. Our children are the ones who are growing up to benefit or suffer from the long-range consequences of our actions. And yet, they are the ones, given the education and the opportunity, who are charged to preserve or change, not themselves, but their world in their own time.

Students are exposed to an unacceptable risk of getting it wrong when ideal behavior is presented in the form of unfounded, unreasoned rules and clichés, in simple absolutes to be exercised without caveats for individual circumstances or without consideration for unfair or arbitrary conditions. In a word, presented via character education, as we know it today.

On the other hand, the risk in personal and social choices is minimized when character education invokes the breadth and depth of reason by explaining "why", takes into consideration an even social playing field, and calls for moderation according to individual differences.

But that isn't character education at all. It is just education.

✿❦✿

Links to Sites and Articles for a More Inclusive Pledge

The fundamental problem with the Pledge of Allegiance is that it is not patriotic enough!

Encyclopedia—History of the Pledge and its controversies. . . .
Education World—Patriotism and Prayer: Can You Have One Without the Other? . . .

Restore the Pledge (Michael Newdow's own site). . . .
A Federated Republic or One Nation? . . .
Online Journal—Left Wing Conspiracy. . . .
Pledge of Allegiance statutes, state by state. . . .

POSTSCRIPT

Are Character/Moral Education Programs Effective?

In the overview of an informational handbook developed in 2006 by the North Carolina Department of Public Education to guide school districts in the implementation of mandated character education programs, the following quote from Martin Luther King Jr. is featured, "Intelligence plus character—that is the goal of true education." The overview continues with the following statement:

> The state of North Carolina has affirmed the development of character in our children is the cornerstone of education. In fact, throughout history, the very foundation of American education has been the preparation of students for life and full participation in a democratic society. Benjamin Franklin said, "Nothing is more important to the public weal [well-being] than to form and train up youth in wisdom and virtue." Today, more than ever, societal needs call for a renewed emphasis on traits such as respect, responsibility, integrity, and citizenship in the public schools.

On the surface, it would appear to be very difficult to disagree with the above statement, yet there are those who do. Jack Weinstein, professor of philosophy at the University of North Dakota, wrote in "What Is Moral Education?" (*The Undercurrent*, June 2006):

> Any model of moral [character] education that prescribes teaching specific moral rules is problematic, and not just because the rules are bound to be controversial. As a learning tool, teaching specific moral rules fails because this type of curriculum confuses knowledge and wisdom, and substitutes regurgitation for judgment. It presumes, for example, that if we repeat the Ten Commandments, we will obey them, and if we can recite the Golden Rule, we will treat people by its precepts.

Weinstein continued:

> For example, it may be the case that children should respect their elders, but what does respect mean? Are there not such instances when a child should ignore this command, particularly when an adult does not reciprocate respect? A child who understands respect as obedience—as many households suggest—combined with an adult who steps over his or her moral limits is a recipe for sexual abuse. . . .

We therefore have to develop curricula that motivate students to both want to do the right thing and be able to determine what that thing is, particularly in circumstances they neither expected nor experienced before.

Similar to Weinstein, John Covaleskie, an associate professor of education at Northern Michigan University in "Discipline and Morality: Beyond Rules and Consequences" (*The Educational Forum,* Winter 1992), argued that we need to help young people develop their own moral compass or conscience and that an important aspect of that is the capability "of feeling shame." He defined shame as "this voice of conscience that creates in me the desire, not to obey rules, but to do the right thing, and the awareness of what that means."

Another source of controversy regarding character education in the schools is the linkage of such programs with religious precepts and organizations. Beyond the arguments over whose values and whose morals are represented in character education curricula is the potential constitutional issue of separation of church and state if such programs and curricula are tied too closely to religious dogma.

Other positions regarding this issue include John Holt, *How Children Fail* (1964); Alfie Kohn, "How Not to Teach Values; A Critical Look at Character Education" (*Phi Delta Kappan,* February 1997); and Character Counts!, a character education advocacy organization.

Contributors to This Volume

EDITOR

DENNIS L. EVANS is director of the Administrative Credential program and faculty graduate advisor in the Ed.D. program in Educational Leadership in the Department of Education at the University of California, Irvine. He teaches Academic Writing in the Ed.D. program as well as courses in the department's undergraduate minor program and the secondary education and administrative services credential programs. Prior to coming to the university in 1992, he served as a high school principal for 21 years with his school receiving the U.S. Department of Education's Exemplary Secondary School Recognition award in 1985. He received a B.A. in political science from Whittier College, an M.Ed. from Whittier College, and his Ed.D. from the University of Southern California. His articles and essays have appeared in numerous educational journals and books. He has served as an expert witness in several court cases dealing with issues such as administrative supervision, teacher dismissal, and school uniforms. He serves as a member of the Board of Institutional Reviewers for the California Commission on Teacher Credentialing and has chaired several accreditation review teams for that body.

AUTHORS

RICK ALLEN is a staff writer and editor for the Association for Supervision and Curriculum Development.

THE AMERICAN ASSOCIATION OF UNIVERSITY WOMEN is an advocacy organization that promotes equity for all women and girls, lifelong education, and positive societal change.

MICHELE BRIGHAM is a special education resource teacher at Freedom High School in South Riding, Virginia. She is an adjunct professor of special education at the University of Virginia and George Mason University.

MARYANN BYRNES is an associate professor in curriculum and instruction at the University of Massachusetts. She has served as the president of the Massachusetts Federation of the Council for Exceptional Children. Her writing and research interests focus on special education.

THE CENTER FOR EDUCATION REFORM is an advocacy group supporting school choice and charter schools.

ROBERT (ROBBY) COHEN is a professor in the Steinhardt School of Education at New York University. He currently serves as chair of the Department of Teaching and Learning. His research interests include history education and the Berkeley free speech movement of 1964.

DIANE W. DUNNE is deputy editor of the *Hartford Business Journal.* Previously she was a news editor for *Education World.*

CHESTER E. FINN Jr. is the president of the Thomas B. Fordham Foundation. He is senior editor of *Education Next.* He is also a distinguished visiting fellow at Stanford's Hoover Institution. Author of 14 books, his most recent, is *Leaving No Child Behind: Options for Kids in Failing Schools,* coedited with Frederick M. Hess. His primary focus is the reform of primary and secondary education.

ANNIE LAURIE GAYLOR is the editor of *Women Without Superstition: No God, No Master,* an anthology of women freethinkers, and *Freethought Today,* a newspaper published by the Freedom from Religion Foundation in Madison, Wisconsin.

JAMES P. GEE is a professor of curriculum and instruction at the University of Wisconsin–Madison. His area of research interests includes literacy studies, educational linguistics, and social and critical theory.

RUTH BADER GINSBERG is an associate justice on the Supreme Court of the United States. She assumed that position in 1993.

RICHARD HALVERSON is an assistant professor of educational administration at the University of Wisconsin–Madison. His research interests include the use of data to influence instruction and successful leadership practices.

THE JOSEPHSON INSTITUTE OF ETHICS states that its mission is to improve the ethical quality of society. It offers consulting services in business ethics, character education, and sportsmanship.

LIAM JULIAN is associate writer and editor for the Thomas B. Fordham Foundation. He is an adjunct scholar of the James Madison Institute and a research fellow at the Hoover Institution.

JAMES M. KAUFFMAN is professor emeritus at the University of Virginia where he served as chair of the Department of Special Education. His research interests are in special education. Among his many books and publications is a new edition of *Characteristics of Emotional and Behavioral Disorders of Children and Youth.*

ALFIE KOHN is a writer and lecturer who comments on human behavior, education, and social theory. His 12 books include, *Unconditional Parenting; Punished by Rewards: The Trouble with Gold Stars, Incentive Plans, A's, Praise, and Other Bribes; No Contest: The Case Against Competition; The Schools Our Children Deserve: Moving Beyond Traditional Classrooms and "Tougher Standards"; The Case Against Standardized Testing: Raising the Scores, Ruining the Schools;* and his most recent *The Homework Myth.*

CATHERINE LEWIS is an author and character educator. She is affiliated with the Developmental Studies Center in Oakland, California.

TOM LICKONA is professor of education at the State University of New York. He has also been a visiting professor at Boston and Harvard Universities. His research area is developmental psychology with a focus on character education. He serves on the board of directors for the Character Education Partnership.

JAMES H. LYTLE is the former superintendent of Trenton, N.J., public schools and is a practice professor of education at the University of Pennsylvania's Graduate School of Education.

ROBERT J. MARZANO is president and founder of Marzano and Associates, an educational consulting firm specializing in school reform. He is also a senior scholar at Mid-continent Research for Education and Learning (McREL). He has authored numerous books; his most recent is *The Art and Science of Teaching: A Comprehensive Framework for Effective Instruction.*

ANN McCOLL is an associate professor in educational leadership/school law at the University of North Carolina, Charlotte.

MICHAEL W. McCONNELL is a judge on the 10th U.S. Circuit Court of Appeals and also serves as a professor in the School of Law at the University of Utah. He previously taught at the University of Chicago. His specialty is constitutional law and theory, with a focus on the religion clauses of the First Amendment. He is widely published in the field of church-state relations.

DAVID McCULLOUGH is a historian and author whose works focus on American history. He is twice winner of the National Book Award and the Francis Parkman Prize. He received the Pulitzer Prize for both *John Adams* and *Truman.* Among his other books are *The Johnstown Flood* and *The Great Bridge.*

KATHLEEN McGEE is a special education teacher.

JORDAN D. METZL is a sports medicine doctor and medical director of the Sports Medicine Institute for Special Surgery in New York City. He has been featured as a medical correspondent on CBS's *Saturday Early Show.*

LOWELL W. MONKE is an assistant professor of education at Wittenberg University. His research and writing interests revolve around alternative education, diversity, and the social and psychological impact of technology on children's development.

NATIONAL MIDDLE SCHOOL ASSOCIATION is an advocate for young adolescents and middle level education. It focuses on quality learning and academic achievement that are developmentally appropriate.

PEDRO NOGUERA is a professor in the Steinhardt School of Education at New York University. He is also the executive director of the Metropolitan Center for Urban Education. From 2000 to 2003 he was a professor at the Harvard graduate School of Education. His research interests include schools, race, and the urban environment.

PATRIOTISM FOR ALL is a Web site affiliated with Cox Network.

MICHAEL J. PETRILLI is vice president for national programs and policy at the Thomas B. Fordham Foundation. He is also a research fellow at Stanford University's Hoover Institution and executive editor of *Education Next.*

DEBRA J. PICKERING is a private consultant with 30 years of experience in K–12 schooling. She has coauthored several books with Robert Marzano.

PUBLIC AGENDA is a research organization dedicated to providing information to citizens on complex policy issues and polling the public to provide American leaders with data regarding public opinion and attitudes.

ROBERT RECTOR is a senior research fellow in domestic policy at the Heritage Foundation. He is the author of *America's Failed $5.4 Trillion War on Poverty,* a comprehensive examination of U.S. welfare programs, and co-editor of *Steering the Elephant: How Washington Works.*

ROB REICH is a professor of political science at Stanford University. His scholarly interests include philosophy and ethics and his most recent book is *Bridging Liberalism and Multiculturalism in American Education.*

BELLA ROSENBERG is the assistant to the president of the American Federation of Teachers.

LEONARD SAX is the founder and executive director of the National Association for the Advancement of Single-Sex Public education. He is a medical doctor with publications including *Why Gender Matters* and *Boys Adrift: The Five Factors Driving the Growing Epidemic of Unmotivated Boys.*

ERIC SCHAPS is president of the Developmental Studies Center in Oakland, California, a research organization. His interest area is the creation of caring classroom communities that emphasize prosocial values.

THE SEXUALITY INFORMATION AND EDUCATION COUNCIL is an advocacy organization promoting accurate information and comprehensive education about sexuality.

DAVID WILLIAMSON SHAFFER is an associate professor in the department of educational psychology at the University of Wisconsin–Madison. His research interests include how technologies change the way people think and learn. His most recent publication is *How Computer Games Help Children Learn.*

CAROL SHOOKHOFF is a freelance education writer and served as a contributing editor of *Founders Green,* a newsletter of Haverford College.

RUSSELL SKIBA is professor of counseling and educational psychology at Indiana University. He has served as director of the Equity Project with a focus on school discipline.

MARGARET SPELLINGS is the U.S. Secretary of Education. She was appointed to the post in 2005.

KURT SQUIRE is an assistant professor in the department of curriculum and instruction at the University of Wisconsin–Madison. His research interests are in educational communications, technology, and the design of games and simulations.

SUE SWAIM served from 1993 to 2007 as the executive director of the National Middle School Association.

CLARENCE THOMAS is an associate justice on the Supreme Court of the United States. He assumed that position in 1991.

THE UNITED STATES DEPARTMENT OF EDUCATION is the federal cabinet-level office dealing with educational matters.

LAWRENCE A. UZZELL is an independent researcher and former staff member of the U.S. Department of Education and U.S. House and Senate committees on education.

TOM VANDER ARK is the former executive director of the Bill and Melinda Gates Foundation and serves there as a senior research fellow. Prior to joining the foundation he served as superintendent of the Federal Way school district in Washington state.

THOMAS W. WASHBURNE is an attorney and director of labor policy for the Mackinac Center for Public Policy. He is the former director of the Home School Legal Defense Association's National Center for Home Education. In that capacity he oversaw HSLDA's policy staff and legislative activities.

CHERI PIERSON YECKE is K–12 Public Schools chancellor for the Florida Department of Education. She also previously served as Minnesota's commissioner of education.

PERRY A. ZIRKEL is university professor of education and law, where he formerly was dean of the College of Education. He writes regular columns for *Phi Delta Kappan* and *Principal.* He serves as cochair of the special education hearing appeals panel for Pennsylvania.